Princeton–Cambridge Studies in Chinese Linguistics II

Sino-Tibetan: A Conspectus

To the memory of

A. L. Kroeber

Sino-Tibetan
A Conspectus

PAUL K. BENEDICT
Visiting Scholar, Columbia University

Contributing Editor:
PROFESSOR JAMES A. MATISOFF
Department of Linguistics
University of California, Berkeley

CAMBRIDGE
at the University Press 1972

Published by the Syndics of the Cambridge University Press
Bentley House, 200 Euston Road, London NW1 2DB
American Branch: 32 East 57th Street, New York, N.Y. 10022

Library of Congress Catalogue Card Number: 78–154511

ISBN: 0 521 08175 0

Printed in Great Britain
at the University Printing House, Cambridge
(Brooke Crutchley, University Printer)

Foreword

The manuscript of this book was originally drafted over a quarter of a century ago. It was a distillation of a far more extensive compilation, 'Sino-Tibetan Linguistics', on which Paul Benedict and Robert Shafer had been working for many years and which still exists as an unpublished manuscript, some twelve volumes of it, in the files of the University of California and of the authors.

The fact that the book is published now, as well as the form it takes, is in large measure due to Professor James A. Matisoff of Columbia University. Naturally enough, books which lie unpublished for years gather some dust. They age, even if the facts they contain are relatively unchanging. Other books and articles appear, the documentation comes to seem dated; and the task of bringing the whole up to date becomes an almost superhuman one. Yet Professor Matisoff, discovering that this manuscript existed, perceived that its voluminous data and its almost Copernican vision, viewing the 'Sino-centric' linguistic area from a standpoint peripheral to it, had neither been duplicated nor superseded in the years since Dr Benedict completed his work and laid it aside to turn to other things.

The problem was how to produce a book which would preserve the sweep and incorporate the information of the original, but would yet allow acknowledgement of germane work accomplished since it was drafted. To pick the original apart and reweave it, as the men of ancient Syria rewove Chinese silk for the Roman market, would have been a daunting task, one that would almost certainly have prohibited the entire enterprise; and it is questionable that such an effort would have added significantly to the value of the book, considering that its audience is composed of linguistic specialists.

In consequence, Dr Benedict undertook to update the manuscript in certain regards, where he could add information or new perspectives specifically relevant to the linguistic problems under discussion. Thus such minor bits of quaintness as the rough figure for Chinese population in Note 1 have been left untouched. We have larger figures these days, but not necessarily dependable ones; and the question of just how many hundreds of millions speak some form of Chinese hardly affects the basic issue that a great many do – so many that we can hardly close our eyes to the study of that language and of its linguistic setting.

In addition to Dr Benedict's redrafting of text and notes, Professor Matisoff supplied a number of supplementary notes derived from his own studies centered upon Lahu and related languages of that stem. There are thus two series of notes, though they have been amalgamated into a single sequence for the readers' convenience. The old notes are indicated by roman numbers, the new ones by italic. Thus Note 12 is an old note, Note *13* new. Notes from Professor Matisoff are signed with his initials in parenthesis (JAM).

FRANK A. KIERMAN JR

Chinese Linguistics Project
Princeton University

Contents

Preface

The manuscript of this work, completed *ca.* 1942–3, was put aside until such time as further analysis could be attempted. It lay buried in the clutter of the author's library until unearthed in 1968 by Professor James Matisoff of Columbia University, who had it mimeographed to serve as a text for his pioneering course in Tibeto-Burman offered at that university. Its appearance in published form at this time is entirely the product of the enthusiasm of Professor Matisoff, who generously consented to edit this work, bringing the bibliographic data up to date and supplying modern material from his researches in the Burmese-Lolo branch of the stock.

The author prepared a new version of the original manuscript, rearranging some of the material and adding the minor emendations noted on the manuscript, then extensively annotated the whole, with emphasis on the Karen and Chinese sections. These annotations represent in part previously published findings (especially in Benedict, 1948bis), in part an intensive re-analysis of all the Sino-Tibetan materials, aided by the more recent publications in the field, notably those of Haudricourt (Karen reconstructions), Forrest (Lepcha analysis), Jones (Karen), Burling (Karen, Burmese-Lolo, Bodo-Garo and Kuki-Naga), Matisoff (Burmese-Lolo), Henderson (Tiddim Chin), Stern (Siyin), Kun Chang (Gyarung and Ch'iang) and Lo Ch'ang-p'ei (Trung).

In venturing once again into the mazes of Archaic and Ancient Chinese, the author came full circle in his scholarly peregrinations since he entered the Oriental field at Harvard University in 1935 under the critical preceptorship of Professor James R. Ware. On this return trip, however, he came much better prepared, especially with some knowledge of the early Chinese in relation to the Austro-Thai peoples, who so profoundly influenced their culture and their language. The last paragraph of the book, which has been left without emendation or annotation, adumbrates these later findings in some sense; it also illustrates the improved status of our present knowledge of Chinese (and of Sino-Tibetan generally), since the gloomy picture presented at that time is no longer applicable. We *do* now have a viable system of reconstruction for Sino-Tibetan, we *have* been able to reconstruct much of the earlier (lost) Chinese morphology (especially through tonal analysis) and we *do* now appear to have a reconstruction of the Sino-Tibetan tonal system (n. 494). We also now have a substantial body of Sino-Tibetan roots shared by Tibeto-Burman and/or Karen and Chinese, and this corpus promises to be extended rapidly as investigations in this field continue.

Preface

The author is deeply indebted to Professor Matisoff for having brought this work to fruition, and to Professor Frank Kierman of Princeton University for having made possible this publication. He also wishes to express his gratitude to the staff of the Sino-Tibetan Philology Project at the University of California, Berkeley, in the late 1930s and early 1940s, who labored so heroically in preparing the basic materials from which the bulk of the illustrations for this work have been drawn; to Mr Donald Walters of that staff, who did such yeoman service when pressed into duty as a linguist; to Marcia Benedict, who prepared many of the basic research tools involved in the project; to Dr LaRaw Maran, who contributed the modern Kachin forms cited here; to Professor Nicholas Bodman of Cornell University, who contributed material on northern Tibeto-Burman languages; to Professor Marvin Herzog, Department of Linguistics, Columbia University, and to the staff of the Columbia University Library, who made available Sino-Tibetan source material. Finally, the author's indebtedness to the late Professor A. L. Kroeber, polymath extraordinary, who had the wisdom and courage to initiate Sino-Tibetan studies at Berkeley, is recorded in the dedication of this work.

P. K. B.

Briarcliff Manor, New York
13 December 1969

Abbreviations

AD	*Analytic Dictionary* (Karlgren)	IN	Indonesian
Anc.	Ancient	K	Kachin
Ar.	Archaic	K-N	Kuki-Naga
AT	Austro-Thai	L	Lushei
B	Burmese	PN	Polynesian
B-G	Bodo-Garo	ST	Sino-Tibetan
B-L	Burmese-Lolo	STL	'Sino-Tibetan Linguistics' (Shafer and Benedict)
Bod.	Bodish	T	Tibetan
Ch.	Chinese	TB	Tibeto-Burman
G	Garo		
GS	*Grammata Serica* (Karlgren)		
GSR	*Grammata Serica Recensa* (Karlgren)		

Phonetic symbols/tone marks

BURMESE

level tone (unmarked)
falling tone (`)
'creaky voice' (´)

LAHU

all forms by JAM unless otherwise indicated; tones and other phonetic symbols as in JAM's publications on Lahu.

KAREN

as explained on p. 150.

CHINESE

as in Karlgren's publications; Ar. and Anc. forms separated by /, e.g. *səm/sâm* = Ar. *səm*, Anc. *sâm*.
Tones as described in note 494:

p'ing shêng	A
shang shêng	B
ch'ü shêng	C

Tibeto-Burman roots are numbered consecutively as they appear in the text.

§1. Introduction

The Sino-Tibetan linguistic stock, as delineated in the present work, comprises Chinese, Karen, and the various Tibeto-Burman languages, spoken over a wide area in China, Indochina, Siam, Burma, South and Southeast Asia.[1,2] A number of problems relating to this stock have been studied in some detail, yet no comprehensive review of the whole field has hitherto been attempted. The best known sketches, by Grube, Lacouperie, Trombetti, Przyluski, Schmidt and Li,[3] are superficial and, in some respects, altogether misleading. It is hoped that the present survey will help fill this gap in Far Eastern studies.[4]

1 The number of speakers, including over four hundred million Chinese, must be placed at approximately half a billion. In this respect, therefore, Sino-Tibetan ranks second to Indo-European among the language-stocks of the world.

2 The astronomical growth of the Chinese population since 1940 (1969 est. eight hundred million) still does not displace Indo-European from its number one position (JAM).

3 W. Grube, *Die sprachgeschichtliche Stellung des Chinesischen*, Leipzig, 1881; Terrien de Lacouperie, *Languages of China Before the Chinese*, London, 1887; A. Trombetti, *Elementi di Glottologia*, Bologna, 1923, pp. 153–67; J. Przyluski, 'Le Sino-Tibétain', in A. Meillet and M. Cohen, *Les Langues du Monde*, Paris, 1924, pp. 361–84; W. Schmidt, *Die Sprachfamilien und Sprachkreise der Erde*, Heidelberg, 1926, Chap. 3, 'Die Sprache Ost- und Südasiens'; Fang-kuei Li, 'Languages and Dialects', in *The Chinese Year Book*, 1936–7, pp. 121–8.

4 Although much has been written on one or another aspect of Sino-Tibetan comparative linguistics since 1940, nothing in my opinion has surpassed this *Conspectus* as the best general overview of the entire subject. For an exhaustive catalogue of materials on ST languages through 1957, see R. Shafer, *Bibliography of Sino-Tibetan Languages*, Wiesbaden, 1957. A more recent summary of ongoing research is T. Nisida's *Short History of Comparative Research into the Sino-Tibetan Languages* (*Sina-Tibetto syogo hikaku kenkyuu ryaku-si*), Azia Ahurika Bunken Tyoosa I-inkai, 1964. Where germane to a particular point, references to post-1940 works are found in the notes below, applied to the topics as they arise in the text (tones, vowels, Bodo-Garo, Karen, etc.); others are listed in the supplementary bibliography at the end of the work. General reference works on Sino-Tibetan since 1940 include, first of all, Shafer and Benedict's monumental 13-volume unpublished typescript (in the Library of the University of California, Berkeley), 'Sino-Tibetan Linguistics (STL)', *ca.* 1939–41, a distillation of material from all older sources and the prime source of information for the *Conspectus* itself (see n. 38); and Shafer's *Introduction to Sino-Tibetan*, Wiesbaden, 1966 (part I), 1967 (part II) (JAM).

Shafer's general classificatory scheme has now received some lexicostatistical support; see W. Glover, 'Cognate Counts via the Swadesh List in some Tibeto-Burman Languages of Nepal', *Occasional Papers of the Wolfenden Society on Tibeto-Burman Linguistics*, Vol. III (Ed. F. K. Lehman), Dept. of Linguistics, Univ.

§2. Taxonomy (general)

Two great taxonomic problems must be considered in connection with Sino-Tibetan, viz. the nature of the affiliations of the three primary groups, and the classification of the multitudinous divisions within Tibeto-Burman itself.[5] The former of these problems has been resolved in the following manner. Tibeto-Burman and Karen are regarded as constituting a superfamily (Tibeto-Karen) standing in opposition to Chinese. The relationship between Tibeto-Karen and Chinese is a distant one, comparable with that between Semitic and Hamitic, or between Altaic and Uralic. Karen, on the other hand, stands in relation to Tibeto-Burman much as Hittite stands in relation to Indo-European, i.e. Tibeto-Karen is on the same taxonomic level as Indo-Hittite.[6] On the negative side, Sino-Tibetan must be kept distinct from all other linguistic stocks.

The writer has recently attempted to show that Thai is related to Indonesian rather than to Chinese, and that the traditional view of a Chinese-Thai relationship must be abandoned.[7,8] A number of students, including Ramstedt, Donner, Lewy, Bouda, and Findeisen,[9] have sought to connect Yenisei-Ostyak (Ket) with Sino-

of Illinois, Urbana, 1970. This recent publication contains extensive word-lists on these languages, the material on Chepang confirming the author's original impression of this language as a key link between northern and southern groups within TB, e.g. the rare TB root **hus* 'moisture; wet' is represented in Chepang (*hus* 'dew') as are both TB roots for 'leech' (*pyaat* 'land leech', *lit* 'water leech'); even the seemingly isolated B *krwak* 'rat' has an apparent Chepang cognate in *rok-yu* 'rat', indicating an analysis **k-rwak* (with **k-* 'animal prefix') for the former (Chepang *-yu* apparently from TB **b-yəw*).

5 On the problems of subgrouping, see R. Shafer, 'Classification of the Sino-Tibetan languages', *Word* **11** (1955) (JAM).

6 For the Indo-Hittite hypothesis, see E. H. Sturtevant, *A Comparative Grammar of the Hittite Language*, Philadelphia, 1933, pp. 29–33.

7 'Thai, Kadai, and Indonesian: A New Alignment in Southeastern Asia', *American Anthropologist* n.s. **44** (1942), 576–601.

8 Recent studies, aided greatly by F. K. Li's uncovering of the Kam-Sui languages of south-central China, have led to the setting up of an Austro-Thai language stock comprising Thai, Kam-Sui, Ong-Be, the Kadai languages and Austronesian; see Benedict, 'Austro-Thai', *Behavior Science Notes* **1** (1966), 227–61; 'Austro-Thai Studies: Material Culture and Kinship Terms', *ibid.* **2** (1967), 203–44; 'Austro-Thai Studies: Austro-Thai and Chinese', *ibid.* **2** (1967), 275–336. All three articles plus a glossary of Austro-Thai (AT) roots will appear in book form under the title *Austro-Thai* (New Haven: HRAF Press, scheduled for 1972).

9 G. J. Ramstedt, 'Über den Ursprung der sog. Jenisej-ostjaken', *Journal de la Société Finno-Ougrienne*, **24** (1907), 1–6; K. Donner, 'Beiträge zur Frage nach dem Ursprung der Jenissei-ostjaken', *ibid.* **37** (1930), 1–21; E. Lewy, 'Zum Jenissei-

Tibetan, and this view has gained some favor (Schmidt, Trombetti), yet a critical examination of the evidence strongly indicates that the two stocks have nothing in common. Sporadic attempts to connect Sino-Tibetan with Caucasic (Hodgson, Bouda),[10] Mon-Khmer (Conrady),[11,12] or other linguistic families have been equally unsuccessful.[13,14]

§3. Taxonomy (Sino-Tibetan)

The Sino-Tibetan stock outlined above has been set up on the basis of a series of monosyllabic roots shared by Tibeto-Karen and Chinese. As shown below, certain

Ostyakischen', *Ungarische Jahrbücher* **13** (1933), 291–309; K. Bouda, 'Jenisseisch-tibetischen Wortgleichungen', *ZDMG* **90** (1936), 149–59; H. Findeisen, 'Die Keto', *Forke Festschrift*, Frankfurt a. M., 1937, pp. 52–68.

10 B. H. Hodgson, 'On the Mongolian Affinities of the Caucasians', *JASB* **22** (1853), 26–76; K. Bouda, 'Die Beziehungen des sumerischen zum baskischen, westkaukasischen und tibetischen', *Mitt. der Altorient. Gesell.*, Bd **12**, Hft 3, Leipzig, 1938.

11 A. Conrady, 'Eine merkwürdige Beziehung zwischen den austrischen und den indochinesischen Sprachen', *Kuhn Festschrift*, München, 1916, pp. 475–504; 'Neue austrisch-indochinesische Parallel', *AM* **1** (1922), 23–66. The direct comparisons suggested by R. Shafer, 'Annamese and Tibeto-Burmic', *HJAS* **6** (1942), 399–402, are not convincing.

12 See also K. Wulff, 'Über das Verhältnis des Malay-Polynesischen zum Indochinesischen', *Det Kunglige Danske Videnskabernes Selskab, Historisk-filologiske Meddelelser*, **27** (1942), ii (JAM).

13 Shafer himself has made extremely far-flung (and far-fetched) connections of ST with other language families: 'Eurasial', *Orbis* **12** (1963); 'Athapaskan and Sino-Tibetan', *IJAL* **18** (1952); 'Note on Athapaskan and Sino-Tibetan', *IJAL* **35** (1969) (JAM).

14 The Miao-Yao (MY) languages have also at times been linked with Sino-Tibetan. J. Greenberg ('Historical Linguistics and Unwritten Languages', in *Anthropology Today*, ed. A. L. Kroeber, Chicago: Univ. of Chicago Press, 1953) has categorically affirmed the reality of this relationship; also R. Shafer, an extravagantly ST-centric advocate, has presented some correspondences ('Miao-Yao', *Monumenta Serica* **22** (1964), 398–411) but these appear to involve loans from ST or TB, e.g. the numerals above '5' (see Benedict, 1967 bis) and 'look-alikes', notably the MY roots for '4' (this also led Benedict astray – see Benedict, 1967 bis), 'tongue' and 'moon'. The evidence from comparative AT studies now makes it clear that MY is simply another major branch of the huge AT stock; see Benedict, 'Austro-Thai and Sino-Tibetan' (mimeographed), read at *First Conference on Sino-Tibetan*, Yale University, October 1968. As noted in the same paper, Minchia[a] (Yünnan, China) is probably (originally) also an AT language, but it has been

a 民家

phonetic generalizations regarding these roots can be laid down, and we have no reason to distrust the genetic implications of this material. Both branches of Sino-Tibetan are characterized by the use of monosyllabic roots and the development of tonal systems, yet neither of these features is of 'critical' value, since each is shared by other stocks (Thai, Miao-Yao). As for syntax, Chinese and Karen place the object after the verb, while all Tibeto-Burman languages, without exception, place the object before the verb. In view of the generally archaic nature of Tibeto-Burman morphology, it is suggested that the Tibeto-Burman arrangement is the original one, whereas the Chinese and Karen word-order has been influenced by that of contiguous stocks (Thai, Miao-Yao, Mon-Khmer), all of verb + object type. The agreement in syntax between Karen and Chinese thus appears to be of secondary origin, and in any event is quite overshadowed by the preponderant lexical agreement between Karen and Tibeto-Burman. In general, lexical considerations are here of primary importance, morphological and syntactical considerations of secondary importance.[15]

§4. Tibeto-Burman classification

The Tibeto-Burman languages, over one hundred of which have been recorded, make up the linguistic 'center of gravity' of the Sino-Tibetan stock. This family, with a diversification roughly comparable with that of Indo-European, presents numerous problems of classification. Several large divisions or 'nuclei' can be distinguished, but a number of smaller units resist all efforts at taxonomic reduction. Some of these residual languages have been poorly or fragmentarily recorded, and it is not unlikely that fuller data in the future will enable us to fit many of them into a broader scheme of classification. For the present, however, the writer prefers simply to list them as distinct units, with a note as to their most probable affiliations.

The seven primary divisions or nuclei of Tibeto-Burman are listed below.

'overwhelmed' or 'invaded' by Chinese at an early (Ancient Chinese) period (Greenberg, *op. cit.*, simply relates it to Chinese).

15 It was precisely undue emphasis on general features such as monosyllabicism and tonalism that led to the all-inclusive 'Indo-Chinese' classifications of the past, in which Thai, Miao-Yao, and sometimes even Mon-Khmer, were lumped together with Tibeto-Burman, Karen and Chinese. It should be noted, however, that the lexical evidence itself must be critically gauged, e.g. the traditional Chinese-Thai hypothesis rested for the most part on comparisons drawn from a superficial level (see the writer's paper cited above).

Immediate genetic relationship must be inferred for the several languages within each nucleus, and somewhat less immediate relationship for other languages mentioned in connection therewith.

1. Tibetan-Kanauri (Bodish-Himalayish); perhaps also Dzorgai, Lepcha, and Magari.
2. Bahing-Vayu (Kiranti); perhaps also Newari.
3. Abor-Miri-Dafla (Mirish); perhaps also Aka, Digaro, Miju, and Dhimal.
4. Kachin; perhaps also Kadu-Andro-Sengmai (Luish) and Taman.
5. Burmese-Lolo (Burmish); perhaps also Nung.
6. Bodo-Garo (Barish); perhaps also Konyak and Chairel.
7. Kuki-Naga (Kukish); perhaps also Mikir, Meithei, and Mru.

The seven divisions above range in diversity from the complex Tibetan-Kanauri, Burmese-Lolo, and Kuki-Naga supergroups, each with a multitude of languages and dialects, through the fairly compact Bahing-Vayu, Abor-Miri-Dafla, and Bodo-Garo groups, down to Kachin, which consists only of the modern dialects of the language and one aberrant extinct dialect, Jili, recorded over a century ago by N. Brown (1837). Kachin, however, stands at the linguistic 'crossroads' of Tibeto-Burman, thus occupying a linguistic position comparable with its geographical setting (Northern Burma). Both lexically and morphologically, Kachin ties in with Tibetan, Bahing, and other northern languages as well as with Burmese, Bodo, Lushei, and other southern languages. From Kachin at this linguistic center of diversification, transitions are afforded by Nung to Burmese-Lolo on the east, and by the Konyak or 'Naked Naga' languages to Bodo-Garo on the west. The Kadu-Andro-Sengmai or Luish group, first recognized by Grierson,[16,17] shows special affinity for Kachin, as does Taman (R. G. Brown, 1911), but none of these languages is sufficiently well known to justify further classification.

Bahing-Vayu, Abor-Miri-Dafla, and Bodo-Garo are relatively compact units. Bahing is the best known of a number of little differentiated languages and dialects of Nepal – the Kiranti languages of Hodgson (1857–8). Two subtypes can be recognized, viz. Bahing (including Sunwari, Dumi, Khaling, Rai) and Khambu (including Sangpang, Nachereng, Rodong, Waling, Rungchengbung, Lambichong, Chingtang, Limbu, Yakha). Vayu and Chepang (Hodgson, 1848) stand fairly close to this Kiranti nucleus, whereas Newari, the old state language of Nepal, shows many points of divergence and cannot be directly grouped with

16 G. A. Grierson, 'Kadu and its Relatives', *BSOS* **2** (1921), 39–42.

17 The scanty material on the Luish group has now been supplemented by Bernot (1967), which includes a vocabulary of some 500 words of Cak as well as comparisons with other languages of the group.

Bahing and Vayu. Abor-Miri and Dafla make up the nucleus of the (so-called) 'North Assam' group of Konow[18] and the *Linguistic Survey of India* (*LSI*). Aka (or Hrusso) has the most points of contact with this nucleus, and Dhimal (in Sikkim) the fewest.[19] The Mishmi tribes of North Assam show a fundamental linguistic cleavage, not recognized in the *LSI*, into Digaro and Miju (Needham,

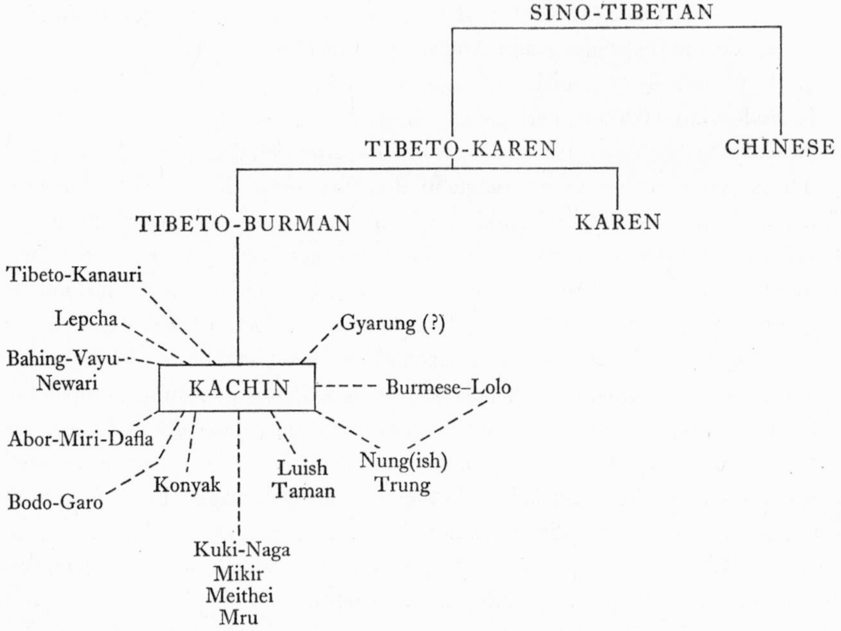

Schematic chart of ST groups

s.a., Robinson, 1855), both with rather vaguely defined resemblances to Abor-Miri-Dafla and Aka. Bodo (including Dimasa) and Garo are subtypes of a well-differentiated nucleus which includes also the moribund and phonetically aberrant Deori Chutiya language of North Assam (W. B. Brown, 1895).[20,21] The 'Naked Naga' (Konyak) languages of the northern Assam–Burma frontier region (Banpara, Namsang, Tableng, Tamlu, Moshang, Chang) are most profitably compared with Bodo-Garo, though some of the easternmost members of the

18 S. Konow, 'Note on the Languages spoken between the Assam Valley and Tibet', *JRAS* (1902), 127–37.

19 Note that Toto, listed as 'Non-Pronominalized Himalayan' in the *LSI* (Grierson, 1909), is hardly more than an aberrant dialect of Dhimal (Hodgson, 1847*a*).

20 Garo shows an interesting division into two subtypes, which we have named

group (Moshang and Shangge, in Needham, 1897) show points of contact with Kachin. Chairel, an extinct speech of Manipuri preserved only in a word-list by McCulloch (1859), is best grouped with Bodo-Garo and Konyak. Especially striking is the Kachin-Konyak-Bodo-Garo-Chairel distribution of distinctive roots for 'sun' and 'fire' (contrast general TB **niy* and **mey*):

	Kachin	Namsang	Moshang	Garo	Chairel
sun	*dźan*	*san*	*śar*	*sal*	*sal*
fire	*ʔwan*	*van*	*var*	*waʔl*	*phal*

Tibeto-Kanauri includes two subnuclear groups, viz. Bodish and Himalayish. Tibetan has been combined with a number of 'Tibetanoid' languages on the eastern and southern borders of Tibet (Gyarung, Takpa, Tsangla, Murmi, Gurung) to form the Bodish group, which in itself is considerably diversified. The Bodish group thus constituted shows intimate ties with the Himalayish languages of the western Tibet–India frontier area, yet the two groups are distinct and no transitional types occur. A major subtype of Himalayish, typified by Kanauri, includes also Chitkhuli, Thebor, Kanashi, Rangloi (or Tinan), Bunan, Manchati, and Chamba Lahuli, while a minor subtype is made up of four little-known languages of the state of Almora (Rangkas, Darmiya, Chaudangsi, Byangsi). Zhang-zhung, an extinct language known only from a Tun-huang manuscript,[22] appears to have been an early representative of the Kanauri subtype. Konow has suggested, largely on the basis of the complex pronominal system of Kanauri and other Himalayish languages, that a Munda substratum must be postulated for this area, but the argument is not convincing.[23] Dzorgai (western Szuchuan), Lepcha (Sikkim), and Magari (Nepal) all appear to be closer to Tibetan-Kanauri than to any other nucleus. Lepcha (or Rong),[24] which exhibits many of the transitional

'Garo A' (Rabha, Ruga, Atong) and 'Garo B' (Abeng, Achik, Awe), the latter spoken by the dominant political divisions of the tribe. This distinction is partially recognized in A. Playfair, *The Garos*, London, 1909.

21 See R. Burling, 'Proto-Bodo', *Language* **39**, 3 (1959) (JAM).

22 See F. W. Thomas, 'The Żaṅ-žuṅ Language', *JRAS* (1933), 405–10.

23 See S. Konow, 'On some facts connected with the Tibeto-Burman dialect spoken in Kanawar', *ZDMG* **59** (1905), 117–25. The vigesimal system of numeration, attributed by Konow to Munda influence, appears in several other Tibeto-Burman areas, e.g. among the Nung (see C. H. Desgodins, *La Mission du Thibet*, Paris, 1872, p. 260) and in the Assam–Burma area (Mikir *iŋ-kol*>*iŋ-koi*, Garo *kol*, Meithei *kul*, Kachin *khun*<*khul* 'score').

24 R. A. D. Forrest ('Lepcha and Mon-Khmer', *JAOS* **82**, 1962) has marshalled impressive evidence for the view that there is a Mon-Khmer substratum in this language, as shown especially by lexical correspondences for key items such as 'dog', 'water' and 'excrement'. The same paper includes an attempt to demonstrate a relationship between Lepcha infixed *-y-* and a hypothetical equivalent in

qualities of Kachin, might equally well be regarded as a separate nucleus linking Tibetan-Kanauri with Bahing-Vayu and groups on the south. Magari (Beames), which, like Newari, has been extensively influenced by Indic, shows interesting lexical agreements with Bahing-Vayu (especially Vayu and Chepang), and might be regarded as a Bodish-Bahing link. Dzorgai, the 'Outside Man-tze' of Lacouperie (*Languages of China*), is not sufficiently well known for more detailed classification.

Burmese-Lolo takes the form of a vast net of languages and dialects spread over a wide area in China (Szuchuan and Yünnan), Burma, Thailand, Laos and Vietnam. Three main subtypes can be distinguished, viz. Burmese-Maru (including Phön, Lashi, Atsi, Achang), Southern Lolo (including Phunoi,[25] Akha, Lahu, Black Lolo, White Lolo, Müng), and Northern Lolo (including Lisu, Ahi, Nyi, Lolopho, Chöko, Phupha, Ulu, Independent Lolo). Distinct residual subtypes are represented by Kanburi Lawa of northern Siam (Kerr), Moso (or Nakhi) of western Yünnan (Bacot),[26] and the so-called Hsi-fan[a] languages of western Szuchuan, including Manyak and Horpa (Hodgson, 1853 bis), Menia (Davies), and Muli (Johnston). Nung (or Nu-tzŭ[b]),[27] spoken in the upper reaches of the Nmai Kha valley (northern Irrawaddy drainage), stands fairly close to the Burmese-Lolo nucleus, yet has numerous points of contact with Kachin.

Three extinct languages of Burmese-Lolo type are known. Hsi-hsia,[c] spoken in northwestern China during the eleventh and twelfth centuries, is related not simply to Moso and Lolo, as recognized by Laufer,[28] but to Burmese-Lolo as a nucleus.

Chinese, but Forrest has now (personal communication, 1969) abandoned that theory in favor of the simpler explanation offered by Benedict (1943) which had escaped his attention (see §**22**).

25 T. Nisida has recently discovered a 'new' Loloish language (spoken in Chiengrai Province, Thailand), called Bisu, with a conservative final consonantism which seems to place it in the Phunoi-Pyen branch of the family; see his 'Bisu-go no kenkyuu', *TAK* **4**, 1; 'Bisu-go no keitoo (zoku)', *TAK* **4**, 5, 1966–7 (JAM).

26 See J. Rock, 'Studies in Na-khi literature', *BEFEO* **37** (1937); *A Na-Khi–English Encyclopedic Dictionary*, Serie Orientale Roma XXVII, Part I, Rome, 1963 (JAM).

27 See Lo Ch'ang-p'ei, *A Preliminary Report of the Trung Language of Kung-Shan* (Kunming, Yünnan, 1942) (in Chinese), and the briefer version, 'A preliminary study of the Trung language of Kung Shan', *HJAS* **8**, 3–4 (1945) (JAM). The Nung forms cited in the text are from Răwang (Barnard). The Mutwang dialect of Răwang has been described in two studies by R. H. Morse: 'Phonology of Răwang', *Anthrop. Ling.* **5**, No. 5, May 1963; 'Syntactic Frames of the Ruwàng (Rawang) Verb', *Lingua* **15** (1965), 338–69. Răwang and Trung are separate languages in a Nungish group which includes still other (poorly known) members.

28 B. Laufer, 'The Si-Hia Language: A Study in Indo-Chinese Philology', *TP* **17** (1916), 1–126. This study is based on the material assembled by A. I. Ivanov,

a 西番 b 猤子 c 西夏

The Hsi-hsia material, despite the not inconsiderable body of recent research,[29,30] has not yet received definitive treatment and the Burmese-Lolo affinities of the language have not been properly evaluated. It is not unlikely that Hsi-hsia is ancestral to at least some of the Hsi-fan languages, as suggested by the geographical factors involved. Pai-lang,[a] which appears in the form of short texts in the *Hou Han Shu* (third century A.D.), must take precedence over Tibetan and Burmese as the earliest recorded Tibeto-Burman language. Pai-lang presents formidable problems of interpretation, which have been only partially solved.[31] The Burmese-Lolo characteristics of the language, noted by Wang, are sufficiently clear, but the numerous and striking phonetic peculiarities demand further attention. The resemblances between Hsi-hsia and Pai-lang are of a generalized rather than specific nature. The third of this group of extinct languages is Pyu, the speech of a pre-Burmese people of Burma, probably to be identified with the P‘iao[b] of the Chinese annals. The extremely fragmentary nature of the Pyu inscriptions, which have been studied by C. O. Blagden,[32,33] discourages any attempt at precise

'Zur Kenntnis der Hsi-hsia Sprache', *Bull. de l'Acad. Imp. des Sciences de St Pétersbourg* **3** (1909), 1221–33. As pointed out independently by P. Pelliot in *TP* **24** (1926), 399–403, and E. von Zach in *OLZ* **30** (1927), 4–5, Laufer's failure to note that Ivanov had reversed the order of the Chinese characters used in transcription led to a number of serious errors.

29 N. Nevsky, 'A Brief Manual of the Si-Hia Characters with Tibetan Transcriptions', *Research Review of the Osaka Asiatic Society*, No. **4**, Osaka, 1926; A. Dragunov, 'Binoms of the type[c] in the Tangut–Chinese Dictionary', *Akademiĭa Nauk*, Doklady, Series B (1929), 145–8; S. N. Wolfenden, 'On the Tibetan Transcriptions of Si-Hia Words', *JRAS* (1931), 47–52; 'On the Prefixes and Consonantal Finals of Si-Hia as evidenced by their Chinese and Tibetan Transcriptions', *JRAS* (1934), 745–70; Wang Ching-ju,[d] 'Hsi-hsia wên han tsang i yin shih lüeh'[e] ('Notes on the Chinese and Tibetan Transcriptions of Hsi-hsia'), *CYYY* **2** (1930), 171–84; 'Hsi-hsia yen-chiu'[f] ('Hsi-hsia Studies'), *CYYY Monographs*, A-8 (1932), A-11 (1933).

30 See also T. Nisida, *Sei-ka-go no kenkyuu*, 2 vols., Zauhoo Press, 1964 (JAM).

31 See Wang, *art. cit.* (1932), pp. 15–55.

32 'A Preliminary Study of the Fourth Text of the Myazedi Inscriptions', *JRAS* (1911), 365–88; 'The "Pyu" Inscriptions', *JBRS* **7** (1917), 37–44 (reprinted from *Epigraphia Indica* **12**).

33 A comparative sketch of Pyu (by Benedict) is included in STL, Appendix VI to Vol. 12. R. Shafer ('Further Analysis of the Pyu Inscriptions', *HJAS* **7**, 1943, 313–66) attempted a direct comparison of the limited Pyu lexical material with Karen, but the evidence as a whole would appear specifically to exclude any special Pyu-Karen relationship, although one interesting correspondence of 'loan-word' type does exist: Pyu *tha* 'iron' (we should expect **thaʔ*), Karen *thaʔ*, *id.* (probably ultimately of AT origin); note also Ch. *t‘iet*,[g] *id.*

[a] 白狼 [b] 驃 [c] 尼卒 [d] 王靜如 [e] 西夏文漢藏譯音釋略
[f] 西夏研究 [g] 鐵

classification. The material brought to light thus far suggests a rapprochement with Nung rather than with Burmese-Lolo proper.

Kuki-Naga, the last of our seven primary nuclei to be considered, is of the same taxonomic order as Burmese-Lolo, i.e. it is made up of a long series of closely related languages and dialects with numerous cross-ties in all directions. A core of Kuki languages proper, in the southern Assam–Burma frontier region, must be recognized, as well as four subtypes within this core, viz. Central Kuki (incl. Lushei, Lai or Haka, Lakher), Northern Kuki (incl. Thado and Siyin), Old Kuki (incl. Bete, Rangkhol, Anal, Lamgang, Purum, Aimol, Kyaw), and Southern Kuki (incl. Sho, Yawdwin, Chinbok, Khami). The Old Kuki languages are spoken by 'marginal' tribes which have been driven out of the Chin and Lushei Hills by the more vigorous Kuki peoples, notably the Lushei. They represent a somewhat archaic variety of a fundamental Kuki type which has given rise to the Central and Northern Kuki languages. The Southern Kuki group, especially Khami, stands somewhat apart from this basic type.

The above classification of the Kuki languages agrees essentially with that of Konow[34] and the *LSI*. The *LSI* further sets up a distinct Naga family and a transitional Naga-Kuki group. Actually, however, no sharp (linguistic) distinction between Kuki and Naga can be maintained, and the two must be placed together under a single rubric (Kuki-Naga). The languages of the Naga tribes proper fall into two main subtypes, viz. Northern Naga (incl. Ao and Lhota) and Southern Naga (incl. Angami, Sema, and Rengma). Sopvoma (or Mao), in the latter group, exhibits some Kuki features, but the real transition here is afforded by the Western Kuki languages of Cachar and western Manipur (Empeo, Kabui, Kwoireng, Maram, Khoirao). The Tangkhul (or Luhupa) language of northern Manipur, several dialects of which have been recorded, stands somewhat closer to the basic Kuki type. Maring and Khoibu, in northeastern Manipur, are of transitional Tangkhul-Kuki type. Poeron, in the western Kuki area, approaches Tangkhul in some respects, but its correct classification remains in doubt.

Mikir (Assam), Meithei (Manipur), and Mru (Chittagong Hills Tract) all show numerous Kuki-Naga correspondences, yet are sufficiently distinct to be listed as separate linguistic entities. Mikir was originally listed as 'Naga-Bodo' by the compilers of the *LSI*, and it was left for an amateur linguist, Sir Charles Lyall,[35] to point out the basic Kuki affinities of the language. Meithei, the state language of Manipur, shows significant points of contact with Kachin as well as with Kuki-Naga, though its affinities are predominantly with the latter. Mru has obvious

34 'Zur Kenntnis der Kuki-Chinsprachen', *ZDMG* **56** (1902), 486–517.
35 See E. Stack, *The Mikirs* (edited by Lyall), London, 1908.

Kuki-Naga resemblances, but has been too scantily recorded (Lewin) to permit of detailed examination.[36]

Supergroups within Tibeto-Burman cannot safely be set up at the present level of investigation. The writer has suggested (Benedict, 1940, pp. 108–9) that a supergroup named 'Burmic', including Burmese-Lolo, Nung, and Kachin, be recognized, but further research into Kachin has brought to light unexpectedly intimate lexical contacts with Konyak and the Garo-Bodo group. It may be that all these, perhaps together with Abor-Miri-Dafla, will ultimately be brought under a single supergroup, as contrasted with the Kuki-Naga nucleus, but at the moment any unifying concept of this kind would be mere speculation. For the present, then, we must operate with nuclear or subnuclear divisions and with independent units, notably Bodish (Tibetan *et al.*), Himalayish (Kanauri *et al.*), Lepcha, Magari, Kiranti (Bahing *et al.*), Vayu, Newari, Mirish (Abor-Miri-Dafla), Kachin, Luish (Kadu-Andro-Sengmai), Burmish (Burmese-Lolo), Nung, Barish (Bodo-Garo), Konyak, Kukish (Kuki-Naga), Mikir, and Meithei.

§5. Tibeto-Burman reconstruction (history)

The reconstruction of the TB phonemic system is a task of paramount importance in the consideration of Sino-Tibetan. Some progress in this direction has already been made, yet no real synthesis of the material has hitherto been attempted. Houghton[37] pioneered in setting up equations for Tibetan and Burmese, while the first 'modern' studies in the general field of TB phonology were those of Wolfenden (see notes below). More recently R. Shafer and the writer, working in part from the same voluminous body of material,[38] have established a number of phonological generalizations in this field, with a special view to the system found in Ancient Chinese.[39] The present work may be regarded as an attempt to systematize and extend these results along phonemic and morphophonemic lines.

36 Shafer's article on Mru, 'The linguistic relationship of Mru: traces of a lost Tibeto-Burmic language', *JBRS* **31** (1941), has been superseded by L. Löffler, 'The contribution of Mru to Sino-Tibetan linguistics', *ZDMG* **116**, 1 (1966) (JAM).

37 B. Houghton, 'Outlines of Tibeto-Burman Linguistic Palaeontology', *JRAS* (1896), 23–55.

38 Material assembled on the Sino-Tibetan Linguistics Project of the Works Progress Administration, sponsored by Prof. A. L. Kroeber of the Univ. of California, 1935–40.

39 R. Shafer, 'The Vocalism of Sino-Tibetan', *JAOS* **60** (1940), 302–37;

§6. Tibeto-Burman primary sources

Our principal sources for Tibeto-Burman are listed in Appendix III. Tibetan and Burmese, the two important literary members of the family, are relatively well known (Csoma de Körös, Schmidt, Jäschke, Das, Missionaires Catholiques, and Judson), but the minor literary languages (Newari, Lepcha, Meithei) have unfortunately been so poorly described that only limited use can be made of them. A number of the non-literary TB languages, which make up the bulk of the family, have been rather fully, if not very accurately, recorded, and most of this material can be used to good advantage if sufficient judgment is exercised. Included in this group are Ahi Lolo (Liétard),[40] Ao Naga (Clark), Bahing (Hodgson, 1857–8), Bodo (Endle, Hodgson, 1847, Skrefsrud), Chang Naga (Hutton, 1929), Dafla (Bor, Hamilton), Garo (Bonnerjea, Chuckerbutty, Garo Mission, Keith), Gyarung (Edgar, Rosthorn, Wolfenden), Haka (Macnabb, Newland), Kachin (Hanson, Hertz, Needham), Kanauri (Bailey, Joshi), Lahu (Telford),[41] Lakher (Savidge), Lisu (Fraser, Rose and Brown),[42] Lushei (Lorrain and Savidge),[43] Maru (Abbey, Clerk),[44] Mikir (Neighbor, Walker), Miri (Lorrain, Needham), Nyi Lolo (Vial),[45] Nung (Barnard), Sema Naga (Bor and Pawsey, Hutton), Sho (Fryer, Houghton), Siyin (Naylor, Rundall),[46] Tangkhul (Pettigrew), Thado

61 (1941), 18–31. P. K. Benedict, 'Semantic Differentiation in Indo-Chinese', *HJAS* **4** (1939), 213–29; 'Studies in Indo-Chinese Phonology: 1. Diphthongization in Old Chinese, 2. Tibeto-Burman Final *-r* and *-l*', *HJAS* **5** (1940), 101–27.

40 A much better recent source is Yüan Chia-hua, *The Folklore and Language of the Ahi People*, Peking, 1953 (in Chinese) (JAM).

41 See J. Matisoff, Review of Burling, 'Proto-Lolo-Burmese', in *Language*, 1968; 'Glottal Dissimilation and the Lahu High-rising Tone', *JAOS* (*Festschrift for Mary Haas on her Sixtieth Birthday*), 1970 (henceforth cited as 'GD'); *Lahu and Proto-Lolo-Burmese, Occasional Papers of the Wolfenden Society* 1, Ann Arbor, Mich. 1969 (JAM).

42 See DeLagnel Haigh Roop, 'A Grammar of the Lisu Language', Yale University Dissertation, 1970 (JAM).

43 W. Bright has done fieldwork with the Lushei in Burma; see his 'Singing in Lushai', *Indian Linguistics* **17** (1957); 'Alternations in Lushai', *ibid.* **18** (1957) (JAM).

44 See R. Burling, 'The addition of final stops in the history of Maru', *Language* **42**, 3 (1966) [already noted in Benedict, 1948, who pointed out the analogy with Archaic Chinese]; also his comparative study, 'Proto-Lolo-Burmese', *IJAL* **43**, 2 II, 1967 (JAM).

45 See Ma Hsüeh-liang, *A Study of the Sani I Dialect*, Peking, 1951 (in Chinese) (JAM).

46 A modern study is provided by T. Stern, 'A Provisional Sketch of Sizang (Siyin) Chin', *Asia Major* **10** (1963), 222–78. E. J. A. Henderson, *Tiddim Chin*,

(Hodson, Shaw). In the present sketch we shall devote most of our attention to Tibetan-Kanauri, esp. Tibetan (T); Kachin (K); Burmese-Lolo, esp. Burmese (B); Bodo-Garo, esp. Garo (G); and Kuki-Naga, esp. Lushei (L). In every point under discussion, however, an attempt will be made to present all the relevant evidence, whether from these key languages or from elsewhere.[47]

§7. Tibeto-Burman consonants (general; final)

Some 16 consonant phonemes can be postulated for Tibeto-Burman, as follows:[48]

Velar: *g k ŋ h*

Dental: *d t n s z r l*

Labial: *b p m*

Semi-vowels: *w y*

Let us first examine the development of these consonants in root-final position. All except the sonants *g*, *d*, *b*, and *z*, also the aspirate *h*, appear in this position. Consonant clusters, however, are lacking here, although they occur in modern derived forms, e.g. T *-gs*, *-bs* (with suffixed *-s*). All the major TB groups exhibit a system of final stops and nasals, the former in most languages being represented by surds.[49] Many TB roots are of this type, e.g. **krap* 'weep', **g-sat* 'kill', **s-rik*

London: Oxford Univ. Press, 1965, furnishes a much needed modern description and glossary of a Kuki speech.

47 Three types of notation are employed in our analysis and must be kept distinct, viz. phonemic symbols, within diagonal lines (as generally employed by American phonemicists); phonetic symbols, within brackets; transcriptions, within parentheses. Forms cited alone are ordinarily transcribed for Tibetan and Burmese, phonemic or phonetic for other languages. The phonemic treatment of modern Burmese is based on the writer's study of this language from a native informant at Yale University, 1942, under the auspices of the American Council of Learned Societies. This treatment differs somewhat from the almost exclusively phonetic approach found in L. E. Armstrong and Pe Maung Tin, *A Burmese Phonetic Reader*, London, 1925.

48 A palatal series has now been reconstructed for TB (n. 122).

49 In Classical Tibetan these final stops are written as sonants (*-g*, *-d*, *-b*), and it has generally been supposed that they were originally sonant stops that have become unvoiced in modern Tibetan dialects. In view of the evidence from other TB languages, however, one must conclude that these stops were weakly articulated, imploded lenis surds which the Tibetan alphabet-makers likened to their initial lenis sonant rather than fortis surd stops. A similar situation exists in Siamese, in which final surd stops were written with letters for lenis rather than fortis stops.

'louse', **lam* 'road, way', **s-min* 'ripe', **ruŋ* 'horn' (cf. the many examples cited below). The final velars (*-k*, *-ŋ*) tend to disappear much more readily than do the dentals or labials, e.g. in Thebor as contrasted with Kanauri, in Dimasa as contrasted with Garo, in Kachin and Nung, and in practically all modern Burmese-Lolo languages as contrasted with Old Burmese.[50, 51]

Final stops and nasals make up distinct series in Tibeto-Burman, and most instances of interchange can readily be interpreted in terms of conditioning factors, e.g. B *yauk-má*~*yauŋ-má* 'pudding-stick', with *-k* > *-ŋ* before *-má* (cf. T *yog-po* 'poker'). Factors of this type play a prominent role in the verb paradigms of Bahing, Kanauri, Tsangla, Miri, and many other TB languages, e.g. Bahing *bap-to* 'scratch' (imperat.), *bam-so* (refl.), *bam-pato* (caus.).[52] Assimilative shifts after front vowels can be traced in several languages, notably in Burmese, where final velars are palatalized after *i* (see § **11**), and in Lushei; cf. L *mit* 'eye' < TB **mik*, L *va-hrit* 'black pheasant' < TB **s-rik*, *ti·t* 'scorpion' < TB **(s-)di·k*. The medial palatal element *-y-* sometimes exerts a similar influence, as in L *phiat* 'sweep' ~ *phiaʔ* 'broom' < TB **pyak*; cf. L *taʔ* 'weave' < TB **tak* for the replacement of final *-k* by glottal stop.

The TB series of final consonants includes also *-r*, *-l*, *-s*, *-w*, and *-y*. Final *-w* and *-y* are most conveniently considered in relation to the vowel system (see § **10**). Final *-r* and *-l* have already been studied by the writer in some detail (Benedict, 1940). These two consonant finals are retained in Tibetan, Kanauri, Lepcha,

Dr Mary Haas, in her phonemic treatment of modern Siamese, writes these stops as sonants (*-g*, *-d*, *-b*); see her article, 'Types of Reduplication in Thai', *Studies in Linguistics* **1**, No. 4 (1942).

50 Final *-k* is generally replaced by glottal stop, as in the Lolo languages (see § **12**) and probably in Kachin, e.g. Needham (1889) observes that K *mi* < **mik* 'eye' and *wa* < **pak* 'pig' are 'uttered sharply'; Jili preserves final *-k* in the latter root (*təwak*). Dimasa, however, replaces *-k* by *-u* after the vowel *a* (G *gitśak*, Dimasa *gadźau* 'red'; G *dźak*, Dimasa *yau* 'hand'); cf. Dimasa *-t* > *-i* after *a* (G *khat*, Dimasa *khai* 'run'; G *sat*, Dimasa *sai* 'sow, sprinkle').

51 There is a continuum of final-consonant attrition in Lolo-Burmese. A few languages (Bisu, Phunoi) preserve some final stops and nasals; others reduce all final stops to -ʔ (Mod. Burmese, Lahu, some Akha dialects) or to a creaky, laryngeal constriction of the vowel (Hani Lolo, Nasu, other Akha dialects) or to zero (other dialects of Akha). In many cases (e.g. Lisu) the degree of preservation of a final stop in a particular Loloish language depends on which of the two 'stopped tones' the syllable belonged to (see n. 259). Similarly, final nasals either reduce to vowel nasalization (Mod. Burmese, some Akha dialects) or disappear altogether after altering the vowel quality (Lahu, Lisu, etc.) (JAM).

52 Shafer (*JAOS* **60**, 1940, pp. 311–12 and Note 23) seems to misinterpret the Bahing phenomenon. Bahing verbal stems are well preserved in the transitive imperative forms; contrast *bap-to* 'scratch' (with stem **bap*) and *mim-to* 'understand' (with stem **mim*).

Nung, Lushei, Dimasa, Moshang, *et al.*; are replaced by *-n* in Kachin[53] and alternated with *-n* in Meithei; are merged in Garo (*-r* > *-l*); and are treated divergently in Mikir (*-l* > *-i* or dropped, *-r* retained).[54] The following pair of roots is representative:

(1) T *'bar-ba* 'begin to bloom, blossom', L *pa·r* 'flower, to blossom', Mikir *par* 'petal', *aŋphar* (< **a-iŋphar* < **a-mphar*) 'catkin, inflorescence, flower', G *bibal* 'flower', Dimasa *bar-guru* 'to blossom', Dhimal *bar* 'to flower', K *pan*, B *pàn* 'flower', from TB **ba·r*.

(2) Lepcha (*ă-)myal* ~ (*ă-)myel* < **s-mal* ~ **s-mel*, L *hmul*, Mikir *aŋmi* < **aŋmil*, Nung *mil*, G *kimil*, Moshang *mul* ~ *kəmul*, B (*ă-)mwè* 'body hair, fur, feathers',[55]

53 Kachin on occasion has final *-n* ~ *-ø* doublet for TB final **-l*; cf. K *myen* ~ *mye* 'fall into sleep', TB **myel*; K *ban* 'to be at rest', *ba* 'tired' < TB **bal*. Tibetan has final *-l* ~ *-n* alternation in several roots of this type; cf. *sril* ~ *srin(-bu)* 'worm (silk-worm)' < **zril* (n. 121); *'gran-pa* 'fight' but *ral-gri* 'sword' (= war-knife) < TB **ra·l* (n. 220); cf. also T *kun* 'all' < TB **m-kul*; *skyin* 'wild mountain goat' < TB **kye·l* ~ **kyi*[·]*l*; *smin-ma* 'eyebrow' < TB **(s-)mul* ~ **(s-)mil* (n. 56).

54 Gyarung (K. Chang, 1968) has a distinctive treatment of TB **-ul*, via **-il*; cf. Gyarung *paŋei* 'silver' < TB **(d-)ŋul*; Gyarung *khorei* 'snake', TB **b-ru·l*. Burmese shows a complex picture in its reflexes for TB final **-l* and **-r*, with vowel quality and possibly also length playing a role. In TB final **-il* there is simple loss of **-l*, but in TB **-ul* there is variation between replacement by *-n* and by *-i* (followed by **-ui* > *-we*); see n. 55; add B *tshè* 'wash' < TB **(m-)syil*; B *re* 'water' < TB **(m-)tśril* (n. 95); also B *ăkun* 'all' < TB **m-kul* (n. 64); good examples for TB **-ir* or **-ur* are not at hand. TB roots with final **-ar* or **-al* (short or long vowel) show three distinct types of reflexes in Burmese (TB roots cited in form to indicate precise vowel-length information):

(*a*) simple loss of final consonant: B *ká* 'dance' < TB **ga·r*; B *khà* 'loins' < TB **s-ga·l* (n. 66); B *bhà* (*phà*) 'frog' < TB **s-b* [*a*, *a·*] *l*; also the following root: T *gsal-ba* 'to be clear, distinct, bright', K *san* 'clear, pure', Nung *san* 'clean' (apparently a loan from Kachin), B *sa* 'clear, pleasant'.

(*b*) replacement by final *-n*: B *pàn* 'flower' < TB **ba·r*; B *swan* ~ *swàn* 'pour (out, upon)' < TB **św* [*a*, *a·*] *r*; B *san* 'louse' < TB **ś* [*a*, *a·*] *r* ~ **s* [*a*, *a·*] *r*; B *ran* 'quarrel' < TB **ra·l*; B *pàn* 'tired' < TB **b* [*a*, *a·*] *l*; B *wan* 'circular' < TB **wal*.

(*c*) replacement by final *-i*: B *wai* 'buy' < TB **ywar* (n. 170); B *khaì* 'lead', T *'khar-ba* ~ *mkhar-ba* 'bronze, bell-metal', from TB **k* [*a*, *a·*] *r*; B *khaì* 'congeal', Kuki **khal*: L *khal*, Tiddim *xal*, but the Burmese form might belong rather with L *kha·r* 'congeal, crust over, be frozen'; cf. also T *gar-ba* 'strong', *gar-bu* 'solid' = 'not hollow', *gar-mo* 'thick, e.g. soup'; cf. also B *bhaì* 'duck', apparently an early loan from an AT infixed root of the type **b/al/i(ts)bi(ts)* (reduplicated) via **baribi-* with the fore-stressing and replacement of *l/l* by *r* which is typical of these TB loans (Benedict, 1967bis).

55 B *mwè* < **mui* < **mul* (replacement by *-i*), also *mun* < **mul* (replacement by *-n*) in the phrase *pà-mùn* 'whiskers' ('cheek-hair') for *pà-mwè*. Replacement of *-l* by *-i* is the regular treatment after the vowel *u*; cf. B *ŋwe*, T *dŋul* 'silver'; B *mrwe*, T *sbrul* 'snake'. Samong and Megyaw (Phön dialects), which are closely related to Burmese, replace *-l* by *-ŋ*; cf. Samong *moiŋ* 'snake' and 'silver', Megyaw *myaiŋ* 'body hair' and 'silver' (cf. Coll. T *mul* 'silver'). Simple loss of *-l* after *a* and *i* is

K *mun*∼*əmun*, *id.*, *niŋmun*∼*nmun* < **r-mul* 'beard', from TB **(s-)mul* ∼**(r-)mul*.[56]

There is some evidence for alternation of final *-*r* or *-*l* with final vowel; cf. Kuki-Naga *hna·r* < **s-na·r* 'nose'[57] in relation to TB **s-na*, *id.*; also the following root:

(3) L *ha-hni*, Mikir *so-ni*, Dimasa *ha-rni*, G *wa-riŋ* < **wa-rni* 'gums (of teeth)' but general TB **r-nil*∼**s-nil*, as represented by T *rnyil*∼*snyil*∼*so-rnyil*, Lepcha *fo-nyăl*∼*fo-nyel* < **s-năl*∼**s-nel*, Kanauri *stil*∼*til* < **snil*, Thebor *nil*, K *wa-nin* (Assamese dial.).[58]

TB final *-*s* is maintained only in some of the northern speeches, notably Tibetan, Gyarung and Kanauri. We have reconstructed this final, on the basis of the correspondences in Kachin (-*t*) and Lushei (-ʔ), for the roots **g-nis* '2', **s-nis* '7' (originally '5+2') and **rus* 'bone'.[59]

	Tibetan	Kanauri	Gyarung	Garo	Kachin	Lushei
(4) two	*gnyis*	*nis*	*kĕnĕs*	*gni*	*ni*[60,61]	*hniʔ*
(5) seven	—	{*stis* / *tis*	*kĕsnĕs*	*sni*	*sənit*	—
(6) bone	*rus-pa*	—	—	—	*nrut*	*ruʔ*

Contrast the following root:

(7) Lepcha *tuk-păt* 'knee'; T *pus-mo* (West T *pis-mo*) 'knee'; K *phut* 'kneel', *ləphut* 'knee'; Nung *phaŋ-phit* 'knee', *ur-phut* 'elbow', *ra-phut* 'shoulder' (cf.

indicated by B *khà* 'loins', T *mkhal-ma* 'kidneys'; B *bhà* (*phà*), T *sbal-pa* 'frog'; B *tshi* 'oil', *ătshi* 'fat', T *tshil* 'fat'; B *ti*, Thado *til* 'earth-worm'.

56 T *smin-ma* 'eyebrow' belongs with this set; see n. 53 for the final -*n*; we must recognize a doublet: **(s-)mul*∼**(s-)mil*, with the typical TB (and ST) medial *u*∼*i* alternation reflected also in Chinese (n. 477).

57 Add Mikir *iŋnar* 'elephant', from **m-nar* = 'the snouted (*nar*) one (*m-*)' (Benedict, 1940).

58 Lepcha also has the triplet form -*ŋel*, which Grünwedel relates to *ă-thyok ă-ŋel* 'crown of head (*ă-thyok*)'. Possibly connected with TB **r-ni* 'red' (n. 265).

59 We can now add TB **r-tas* 'thick' (n. 63), although Nungish (Răwang) has *that* (cf. Răwang *sənit* '7'); also TB **s-nes*: Gyarung *ăśnäs* 'lip, beak'; Kuki-Naga **hneʔ*: L *heʔ*, Tiddim *nɛʔ* 'lower lip'; cf. also K *mədi* 'to be wet; wet', *mədit* 'to wet; wet', Kanauri *thi-ss* 'wet', under TB **ti(y)* 'water'.

60 K *ni* '2' has probably been derived from a form **nik* with suffixed -*k*; cf. Bahing *nik-si* '2' and B *hnats* < *s-nik* '2', paralleling *tats* < *tik* '1'. Nung shows the same development as Kadu, with *əni* '2' but *sənit* '7'. B *khú-hnats* '7' (*khú* 'unit') is of the same type as TB **s-nis*; cf. also Lepcha *nyăt* < **s-nis* '2'.

61 Maran cites K *ni* (mid tone), indicating that the earlier form was neither **nis* (which would have yielded K **nit*) nor **nik* (which would have yielded K *niʔ*) but simply **ni* (agreeing both with Karen and Chinese), the *-*s* being an old suffix: TB **g-ni-s*. The history of B *hnats* '2', however, remains obscure (probably not < **hnis*, since Burmese has *ăruì* 'bone' for TB **rus*).

Purik *pug-ma* 'collar-bone'); Burmese-Lolo _*put_ as reconstructed from Maru *pat-lau*<*put-* 'knee', Phunoi *phat tho khau*<*phut* 'kneel'; here we must reconstruct _*put_ rather than _*pus_ because of the Nung and Burmese-Lolo evidence. Replacement of final _*-s_ by glottal stop in Lushei is further attested by L *huʔ* 'wet', T *hus* 'moisture, humidity' (contrast L *hu*, West T *hu* 'breath'), and perhaps L *raʔ* 'fruit, to bear fruit', T *'bras* 'rice'.[62]

§8. Tibeto-Burman consonants (initial)

All 16 TB consonant phonemes are found in initial position, both singly and in clusters. The general equations that obtain here are indicated in the table below. These equations have been set up, insofar as possible, on the basis of roots showing a minimum of prefixation. The conditioning role of prefixes is all-important, hence it is imperative that correspondences be established for non-prefixed roots.

TB Initial Consonants

TB	Tibetan	Kachin	Burmese	Garo	Lushei
_*k_	*k(h)*	*k(h)~g*	*k(h)*	*k(h)~g*	*k(h)*
_*g_	*g*	*g~k(h)*	*k*	*g~k(h)*	*k*
_*t_	*t(h)*	*t(h)~d*	*t(h)*	*t(h)~d*	*t(h)*[63]

62 Cf. the treatment of this problem in S. N. Wolfenden, 'Concerning the Variation of Final Consonants in the Word Families of Tibetan, Kachin, and Chinese', *JRAS* (1937), 625–55, esp. pp. 647 ff. Wolfenden prefers to derive *-s* from *-ds* or *-ns* (lacking in Tibetan) in all instances. This view appears to have been suggested by the appearance of *-t* in Lepcha paralleling *-t* in Kachin, as in Lepcha *ăhrăt* 'bone', *nyăt* '2'; cf. also Lepcha *vot*<*wat*, Vayu *siŋ-wo*<*-wa* 'bee', Kanauri *wăs* 'honey'. T *pus*~*pis*<_*puds_ 'knee' (with suffixed *-s*) is supported by the West T forms *puks-mo* (Purik)~*buχ-mo* (Balti) and *pig-mo* (in Jäschke); cf. also T *mhkris-pa*, West T *ṭhigs-pa* 'bile, gall', TB _*m-kri-t_.

63 Lushei has initial *t-* for TB _*t-_ only where the initial is unaspirated (because of an earlier prefix); the aspirated initial has produced *tśh-* in Lushei, *s-* in Thado, Siyin and Tiddim; cf. L *tśhaʔ*, Tiddim *saʔ* 'thick', from TB _*r-tas_; L *tśhuak* 'free, release, come or go out', Siyin *suak* 'emerge', B *thwak* 'come out, emerge', from TB _*twak_; L *tśhu·ŋ* 'the inside (of anything)', Tiddim *suŋ* 'inside'; Bodo *siŋ*, Dimasa *bisiŋ* 'inside, within', Nungish: Rawang *əduŋ* 'in, middle', *məduŋ* 'to be perpendicular, to straighten', Trung *atuŋ* 'middle', from TB _*tu·ŋ_ (No. 390), the last supported by an excellent Ch. correspondence [a](*ti̯ôŋ/t'i̯uŋ* 'middle'); apparently to be excluded from this set are both T *gźuŋ* (perhaps from _*gdźuŋ_) 'the middle, midst' and B *twaŋ* 'in', *ăthwàŋ* (*-twaŋ*) 'within'. The initial cluster _*ty-_ apparently gave rise to Lushei and Thado *ś-*, Tiddim *s-*; cf. L *śen*, Thado *ă-śen*,

a 中

TB Initial Consonants (cont.)

TB	Tibetan	Kachin	Burmese	Garo	Lushei
**d*	*d*	*d*~*t*(*h*)	*t*	*d*~*t*(*h*)	*d*
**p*	*p*(*h*)	*p*(*h*)~*b*	*p*(*h*)	*p*(*h*)~*b*	*p*(*h*)
**b*	*b*	*b*~*p*(*h*)	*p*	*b*~*p*(*h*)	*b*
**s*	*s*	*s*	*s*	*th*	*th*
**z*	*z*	*z*~*ś*	*s*	*s*	*f*
**ts*	*ts*(*h*)	*ts*~*dz*	*ts*(*h*)	*s*~*tś*(*h*)	*s*
**dz*	*dz*	*dz*~*ts*~*ś*	*ts*	*tś*(*h*)	*f*
**ŋ*	*ŋ*	*ŋ*	*ŋ*	*ŋ*	*ŋ*
**n*	*n*	*n*	*n*	*n*	*n*
**m*	*m*	*m*	*m*	*m*	*m*
**r*	*r*	*r*	*r*	*r*	*r*
**l*	*l*	*l*	*l*	*r*	*l*
**h*	*h*	(zero)	*h*	[]	*h*
**w*	(zero)	*w*	*w*	*w*	*w*
**y*	*y*	*y*	*y*	*tś*~*dź*	*z*

Illustrations of TB initial stop consonants:

(8) T *kha-ba*, K *kha*, B *khà*, G *kha*, L *kha* 'bitter' (TB **ka*).

(9) T *bka*, B *tsa-ka* 'word, speech', K *gà*~*əgà* 'word, speech', *śəgà* 'speak', Nung *kha* 'speech, language' (TB **ka*).

(10) T *kun* 'all', B *kun* 'to come to an end, be used up', *ăkun* 'all' (TB **kun*); Lepcha *gŭn* 'all, each, whole' is probable T loan.[64]

(11) T *gar* 'a dance', K *gan*~*kəgan*~*khan* 'leap, bound, canter', L *ka·r* 'to step, pace, stride' (TB **ga·r*).[65]

(12) T *mkhal-ma*, L *kal* 'kidneys', B *khà* 'loins'; cf. T *sgal-pa* 'small of the back', Meithei *nam-gal*~*nam-gan*, Maring *nam-gal*, G *dźaŋ-gal* 'back' (TB **m-kal*).[66]

Tiddim *san* 'red', B *ta* 'very red, flaming red', *tya* 'very red' (for Ch. correspondences see n. 488). L *tśh-* can also stand for an original TB **tsy-* (= *tś-*), as in No. 353 (*tśuk* 'steep').

64 These forms appear to belong with TB **m-kul* '20' in view of Mikir *iŋkoi* (early form *iŋkol*) '20', from *koi* 'all' (see p. 119); for the final, see nn. 53, 54.

65 Also Lahu *qā* 'dance', implying PLB *ʔka (JAM). B *ká* 'dance', with loss of final *-*r* (n. 54) and Lisu *gwa-* (irreg. tone), id., suggest an early doublet form with initial **g-* in Burmese-Lolo.

66 B *khà* 'loins' belongs with a distinct TB root: **s-ga·l*, along with remaining forms cited in text, as shown by Tiddim Chin *xa:l* < **kha·l* 'groin' (tone 3), distinct from *kal* 'kidney' (tone 1); cf. also K *kan* (perhaps from **kal*) 'to put, or be, on the back'.

(13) T *dgu*, Kanauri *zgŭi*~*gŭi*, Nung *təgö*, K *dźəkhu*, B *kuì*, G *sku*, L *kua*~*pəkua* '9' (TB **d-kuw*).

(14) Kanauri *ku*, K *gau*, Nung *go*, B *khau*, Dimasa *dźuru-khau*, L *kou*, Empeo *gu* 'call' (TB **gaw*).[67]

(15) Nung *gar*, G *gal*, Dimasa *gar* 'leave, quit, abandon' (TB **gar*).

(16) Limbu *gip* (in comp.), Miju *kap*~*kyep*, Mikir *kep*<*gip*, Maring *tśip*<*kyip*, Yawdwin *gyip* (in comp.), B *ăkyip* '10' (TB **gip*).

(17) T *'thag-pa*, Magari *dak*, K *daʔ*, G *dak*, L *taʔ*, Mikir *thak* 'weave' (TB **tak*).[68]

(18) T *thab*, K *dap*, G *tśudap*, Bodo *gadap*, L *tap* 'fireplace' (TB **tap*).[69]

(19) T *sta-gon* 'preparation, arrangement', *stad-pa* 'put on, lay on', Tsangla *tha* 'put, place', Kanauri *ta* 'place, set, appoint', Vayu *ta* 'put, place; keep', Lepcha *tho-m*<**tha* 'place', K *da* 'put, place', *ta* 'to be left, placed', B *thà* 'put, place' (TB **ta*).

(20) K *dinduŋ*, L *duŋ* 'length', Mikir *diŋ* 'long' (TB **duŋ*); cf. also Lepcha (*a-*)*thŭŋ* 'height, length'.

(21) T *de* 'that, that one', K *dai* 'this, that', Nung *dɛ* 'this' (TB **day*).

(22) K *dan*, G *den*, Bodo *dan*, Dimasa *daiŋ*<**dan*, L *tan*, Mikir *than* 'cut', Nung *dan* 'reap (cut with a sickle)' (TB **dan*).

(23) T *phu-bo*, K *phu* 'elder brother', B *ăphuì* (*ăbhuì*), G *bu*, L *pu*, Mikir *phu*, Meithei *ipu* 'grandfather' (TB **puw*).[70]

(24) T *pha*~*ʔapha*~*ʔapa*, B *bhá*, *ăbhá*, G *pha*~*əpa*, L *pa* 'father', but K *wa*~*əwa*, Kadu *əwa*, Moshang *wa*, Bunan *əwa* 'father' (TB **pa*).

(25) T *ba-spu* 'a little hair (*spu*)', K *pha*, Nung *ba*, B *pà*, G *ba* 'thin' (TB **ba*).

(26) T *'ba-ba* 'bring, carry', K *ba* 'carry (child on back)', Nung *ba* 'carry (on the shoulder)', G *ba* 'carry', Digaro *ba* 'carry (a child)' (TB **ba*).[71]

(27) T *'bu* 'worm, insect' (West T *'bu-riŋ* 'snake'), Lepcha *bŭ* 'reptile, worm', B *puì* 'insect', Bahing *bu-sa*, Digaro *təbo*~*təbu*, Aka *beü*~*bü*, Miri *təbuü*, Nung *bö*, K *pu*~*ləpu*, Kadu *kəphu*, G *tśipu* 'snake' (TB **buw*).

67 Lahu has *kù* 'call', implying PLB **kru* (JAM).

68 Benedict (1967bis) has suggested a connection of this root with B *rak*, Răwang (Nungish): Mutwang dial. /*raʔ* 'weave' (Morse), from an original TB **trak* (AT loan-word).

69 Benedict (1968 paper) has suggested a connection with TB **rap* 'fireplace shelf' (No. 84), from an original **trap*/*drap* (AT loan-word).

70 For this semantic transference, see the discussion in Benedict, 1942bis, esp. pp. 319–20.

71 This root has a direct correspondence with AT; cf. IN *(*m*)*ba*/*ba*, Thai **ba* 'carry (especially on the back)' (possible early loan). Kachin has *baʔ* (low tone) (Maran) and the Mutwang dialect of Răwang (Nungish) has *baʔ* (Morse), both pointing to an earlier **bak* rather than **ba*.

(28) Lepcha *bŭ* 'carry; burden, cargo', *abŭn* 'vehicle', Miri *buü*, B *puì*, Mikir *bu*, Meithei *pu*, Ao Naga *əpu*, L *pu* 'carry (on the back or shoulders)' (TB **buw*).

(29) Bahing *bal*, B *pàn* 'tired, weary', K *ban* 'to be at rest', *ba* 'tired'(TB **bal*).

(30) K *bop* ~ *ləbop* 'calf of the leg', L *bop* 'leg, hind leg of an animal' (TB **bop*); cf. Lepcha (*ă*-)*bop* 'large (as belly)'.[72]

The significant contrast in the stop series is that between voiced and unvoiced consonants. Aspiration is clearly of a subphonemic order; unvoiced stops are aspirated in initial position, unaspirated after most or all prefixes. Tibetan faithfully reflects this pattern in most respects. Tibetan surd stops are unaspirated after the prefixes *g*-, *d*-, *b*-, *r*-, *l*- and *s*-, but are aspirated after the prefixes *m*-, and **'**-; cf. the following verb forms: *skor-ba* 'surround, encircle', *'khor-ba* 'turn round'; *gtib(s)-pa* ~ *'thibs-pa* 'gather (of clouds)', *thib-pa* 'very dark'; *dpyaŋ-ba* ~ *spyaŋ-ba* 'suspend, make hang down', *'phyaŋ-ba* 'hang down'. Tibetan does have a number of words with initial unaspirated surd stop, and thus aspiration after stops is phonemic here; yet these exceptional forms are unquestionably of secondary origin. Included in this group are (*a*) words with initial *kl*-, e.g. *klu* 'serpent-demon', *kloŋ* 'wave' (Tibetan lacks the cluster *khl*-), (*b*) reduplicated forms, e.g. *kyir-kyir* 'round, circular', *kyom-kyom* 'flexible', *kru-kru* 'windpipe' (West T), *tig-tig* 'certainly', *pi-pi* 'fife, flute' (West T 'nipple; icicle'), (*c*) forms which interchange with prefixed or reduplicated forms, e.g. *kog-pa* ~ *skog-pa* 'shell, rind, bark', *pags-pa* ~ *lpags* (in comp.) 'skin, hide, bark', *kug* ~ *kug-kug* 'crooked', *kum-pa* ~ *kum-kum* 'shriveled', and (*d*) loan-words and forms based on modern dialects, e.g. Ladakhi *ti* 'water' (a loan-word from the Kanauri group). The more important words not included here are *ka-ba* 'pillar', *kun* 'all' < TB **kun*, *krad-pa* 'shoe', *paŋ* 'bosom, lap', *pag* 'brick', *pad-ma* 'leech' < TB **r-pat*, *par* 'form, mould', *pir* 'brush, pencil',[73] *pus-mo* ~ *pis-mo* 'knee' < TB **put*. Many other TB languages, e.g. Kachin, Nung, Garo and Lushei, show much the same type of pattern, but with a tendency for sonant stops to be replaced by unaspirated surds. In Burmese this tendency reaches its full development, yielding a system based largely on the contrast between unaspirated surd stops (< surd or sonant stops) and aspirated surd stops (< surd stops, rarely sonant stops).

We must reconstruct, then, simply surd and sonant stops, and attribute differences in aspiration to conditioning by prefixed elements. In languages such as Burmese and Lushei, in which prefixes have been dropped for the most part, the presence or absence of aspiration becomes a clue in reconstructing lost pre-

72 Lahu has *khɨ-pɛ̀-qu* 'calf', from PLB **pum*/*pup* (JAM). Cf. also Kachin (Needham: Assam dial.) *bɔp* 'foam, froth' (= swelling of water), Nungish: Răwang *thi bɔp* 'bubble' (*thi* 'water'), *thil-bɔp* 'foam, bubble' (*thil* 'saliva').

73 T *pir* 'brush, pencil' has been identified as a loan from AT (n. 474).

fixes; thus, L *kal* 'kidney' in the face of T *mkhal-ma* suggests a lost prefix *m-* (cf. the discussion in §27). Burmese, unlike Tibetan, has aspirated surd stops after original prefixes *s-* and *r-*:

(31) T *skyi-ba*, B *khyè* 'borrow (something to be returned in kind)'.[74]

(32) T *stoŋ*, B *thauŋ* 'thousand'.

(33) T *rku-ba*, Newari *khul* (see n. 294), Bahing *ku*, K *ləgu*, Nung *khü*, B *khuì* 'steal'.

(34) T *rkyaŋ-pa*, B *khyàŋ* 'single'.

The tendency toward surdization of initial sonant stops can be traced throughout the TB area, but it is especially marked among the southern groups. These initials are generally preserved in Tibetan, Kanauri, Bahing, Miri and many other northern languages. Within the Kiranti group, sonants are preserved in the Bahing subtype, transformed into surds in the Khambu subtype (but note Limbu *gip* '10' in No. 16). It is evident that sonant stops are in some measure preserved in Kachin, Nung and the Garo-Bodo languages, yet the recording here has been so poor that the details are not clear. Shifts from surd to sonant initial seem to have occurred in some instances, especially in Garo; cf. K *gà*~*əgà* 'word, speech' < TB **ka*; G *dak* 'weave' < TB **tak*; G *tśudap* 'fireplace' < TB **tap*; G *bu* 'grandfather' < TB **pu*; also the following:

(35) Mikir *phek* < **phik*, G *bibik* 'bowels'.

(36) T *ʔa-phyi*~*phyi-mo*, Kanauri *a-pi*, Bahing and Vayu *pi-pi* 'grandmother', B *ăphè* 'great-grandfather', *ăphè-má* 'great-grandmother', but Lahu *a-pi* 'grandmother', G *a(m)bi*, Mikir *phi*, L *pi* 'grandmother'.

Lushei lacks initial *g-*, but has maintained *d-* and *b-* in some roots. Mikir has *k-* < **g-* (e.g. *kep* '10' < **gip*), *h-* < **k-* (e.g. *ho* 'bitter' < **ka*). Burmese has a scattering of words with sonant stop initials, but these cannot be regarded as inherited TB elements, despite the attractive comparisons:

B *bhà*, T *sbal-pa* 'frog' (cf. n. 55).

B *bhaŋ* 'ordure', T *sbaŋs* 'dung of larger animals'.

B *du* 'knee', Miri *lag-du* 'elbow'.[75]

74 Cf. also Nungish: Trung *skiŋ*~*skhiŋ* 'borrow/lend', with secondary final *-ŋ* (cf. Nos. 415 and 427).

75 Burmese sonant stops, transcribed *g*, *d*, *bh*, are uniformly pronounced in the modern language as slightly aspirated lenis sonant stops, only partially voiced in initial position. It is not unlikely that TB sonant stops were somewhat aspirated in initial position and unaspirated after prefixes, thus paralleling the treatment of surd stops. This type of argument has been forwarded for Tibetan by A. Dragunov, 'Voiced Plosives and Affricates in Ancient Tibetan', *CYYY* 7, pt 2 (1936), 165–74. The secondary development of sonant stops in Burmese is to be explained in part by the fact that in Burmese morphophonemics surds become sonants in intervocalic position; cf. *ăphuì*~*ăbhuì* 'price' (No. 41); *dyo* < *khrui* 'horn' and *ù-khrui*

In the Lolo languages, however, initial voiced stops are maintained with some regularity, so the Lolo evidence is of considerable importance:[76]

		TB	Burm.	Lisu	Ahi	Nyi
37	horn	**kruw*	*khrui*	*tśhu*	*tśhö*	*hkə*
38	foot	**kriy*	*khre*	*tśhi*	*khi*	*tshə*
39	copper	**griy*	*krè*	*dźi*	*dyi ~ dźi*	*dźə*
40	leaf	**pak*	*phak*	*phyæ*	*phye*	*phe*
41	price	**puw*	*aphuì*	*phü*	*phö ~ phu*	*phu*
25	thin	**ba*	*pà*	*ba*	*bo*	*ba*
27	insect	**buw*	*puì*	*bü*	*bö ~ bu*	*bu*
28	carry	**buw*	*puì*	—	*bö*	*bu*
169	pit, hole	**dwaŋ*	*twàŋ*	*du*	—	*du*

(37) Nung (Melam dialect) *təkru* 'horn', B *khrui ~ khyui* 'horn'.

(38) T *khri* 'seat, chair; frame', Nung *hi* (cf. No. 412), B *khre* 'foot'.

(39) T *gri* 'knife', K *məgri* 'brass, copper, tin', B *krè* 'copper'.

(*ù* 'head'), *gaṷ* < *khaùŋ* 'head' and *ù-khaùŋ*. Cf. also *thà* > *dà* 'knife' (T *sta-re* 'ax') but Lisu *atha*, Ahi *mi-tho*, Nyi *mi-tha*; *bhù* > *bù* 'gourd' but Lisu *aphü*, A *phü ~ phö*, Nyi *o-phu-ma*.

76 Actually there is now excellent evidence that a secondary voiced series of obstruents must be set up for the PLB stage, in addition to the *voiceless unaspirated (from PTB sonant) and the *voiceless aspirated (from PTB surd); also, a glottalized series and perhaps a voiced aspirated or glottalized series as well. The Lahu voiced initials /*bdjg*/ cannot be explained on morphophonemic grounds (as in Mod. Burmese) but are rather survivals of the PLB *voiced series, corresponding to Nasu voiced aspirates (Kao Hua-nien, 1958) and the voiced prenasalized aspirates described by Ma Hsüeh-liang in his study of the sacred Lolo epic 'On Offerings of Medicine and Sacrificing of Beasts' (it is convenient to refer to the dialect described by Ma in this work as 'Lolomaa'), e.g. 'drink': Lahu *dɔ̀*, Nasu *d'ɔ*, Lolomaa *nt'ɒ*. For discussion, see Matisoff, *Lahu and Proto-Lolo-Burmese* and works cited above, note 41. This does not necessarily imply that there were more than two PTB stop series (surd and sonant). The others are presumably due to the influence of various prefixes, e.g. the PLB *glottalized series derives partly from the ʔə- prefix (written *ḥ*- in Tibetan) and partly from the *s*-prefix; see also Matisoff, 'GD'.

PTB	surd	Q + stop	sonant	*s*/*ḥ* + surd	*s*/*ḥ* + sonant
	↓	↓	↓	↓	↓
PLB	aspirated	voiced	plain	glottalized	vd. glottalized
	↓	↓	↓	↓	↓
Burmese	aspirated	plain	plain	aspirated	aspirated
Lahu	aspirated	voiced	plain	plain	voiced
Lisu	aspirated	voiced	voiced	plain	plain

Q is an arbitrary symbol for a prefix which led to voicing, usually a nasal (JAM).

(40) Kiranti **phak* (Waling *suŋ-phak*, Lambichong *lăphak*, Yakha *sum-phak*, Balali *siŋ-bak*) 'leaf', B *phak* 'leaf' (considered as an article of use)', probably also K *pha* 'tea plant' (B *lak-phak* ~ *lăbhak* 'tea').[77]

(41) K *phu* 'to be of value, expensive', *dźəphu* 'price; wages', Nung *əphü* 'valuable, expensive', *dəphü* 'cost, price', B *ăphuì* ~ *ăbhuì* 'price'.

(27) (above) B *puì* 'insect; silkworm', Lisu *bü* 'silk'.

Tibetan maintains the surd vs. sonant distinction with great regularity, and strong evidence must be marshalled before reconstructing any stop initial conflicting with the evidence from that language. TB **d-kuw* '9' has been thus set up on the basis of the Lolo forms (Lisu *ku*, Ahi, Nyi, Lolopho *kö*) and K *dźəkhu*, G *sku*, in the face of T *dgu*, Nung *təgö*; here we must postulate T *dgu* < *dku* through assimilation. Bahing, which ordinarily maintains the surd vs. sonant distinction, shows a parallel shift in the following:

(42) T *skyur-ba*, Gyarung *kətśyur*, Tsangla *tśur-pa*, but Bahing *dzyur* < **sgyur* 'sour'; cf. also Kanauri *sur-k*, Rodong *sur-e*, L *thu·r*, Mikir *thor*, *id.*, from **su·r* (TB **s-kyur* and **su·r*); Lepcha has both *tśór* 'sour, acid' and *să-tsór-lă* 'sourish'.

The initial *p-* > *w-* shift shown by Kachin in No. 24 is paralleled in several TB roots. The initial stop of these roots tends to be maintained in the northern languages and in Mikir, while replacement by *w-* is common elsewhere. Here we must suppose that prefixed elements, present or discarded, have exerted an influence on the initial. Certainly nothing in our data justifies the reconstruction of a special set of stop consonants for these roots.[78] Cf. the following:

		Tibetan	Mikir	Kachin	Burm.	Garo	Lushei
43	pig	*phag*	*phak*	*waʔ*	*wak*	*wak*	*vok*
44	bamboo	*spa*	*kepho*	*kəwa*	*wà*	*wa*	*rua*
45	leech	*pad-ma*	*iŋphat*	*wot*	*krwat*	*ruat*	*vat*

77 This root has now been reconstructed **(r-)pak*, on the basis of the Burmese doublet *phak* ~ *rwak* (also *phak-rwak*), possibly also Lambichong *lăphak* (see n. 78).

78 The Chinese evidence (nn. 463, 487) unmistakably points to initial labial stop + *w* initial clusters in several ST (and TB) roots, including those for 'father' and 'bamboo' (text); also **bwâr* ~ **pwâr* (= **bar* ~ **par*) 'burn; fire' (No. 220); JAM notes that Kachin has a preglottalized form here: *ʔwan* 'fire', comparable with Garo *waʾl* (Burling), also K *ʔwa* 'father' (these are probably from TB prefixed **a-* = *ʔa-* forms). Chinese cognates also indicate an initial cluster of this type for the ST root represented in TB by the following: T *ʔa-baŋ* ~ *baŋ-po* 'father's or mother's sister's husband', Chepang *paŋ*, Limbu *am-paŋ-a*, Vayu *poŋ-poŋ* < **paŋ*, Nung *a-waŋ* 'father's brother', Lashi (B-L) *vaŋ-mo* 'father's older sister's husband, husband's father', Lisu *a-wɔ* < **-waŋ* 'father's brother', Garo *a-waŋ* 'father's younger brother' (see Benedict, 1941). The TB root for 'pig' (text) can be reconstructed **pwak*, with a parallel in the original **pwa* indicated for Chinese (n. 487); the alternation of final is to be explained by regarding these forms as very early

(43) Cf. Jili (Kachin) *təwak*, Phön (Burmese-Lolo) *təwo*, Empeo (Kuki-Naga) *gəbak* 'pig', all with prefixes.

(44) T *spa*~*sba* 'cane', K *kəwa*~*wa*, L *rua*<**r-wa* 'bamboo'.

(45) T *srin-bu pad-ma* (*srin-bu*='*bu* 'insect'), B *krwat*<**k-r-wat*, Lahu *vèʔ*, L *vaŋ-vat*; cf. Magari *ləwat*, Rangkhol *ervot*, Angami Naga *reva*, but Lepcha *fot*< **phat* 'leech'.

Both Nung and Meithei have *w*- in Nos. 43 and 44, but *ph*- in No. 45: Nung *wa*, Meithi *ok*<**wak* 'pig'; Nung *thəwa*, Meithei *wa* 'bamboo'; Nung *dəphat*~*phəphat*, Meithei *tin-pha* 'leech'. Burmese has doublet forms in the following two roots:

(46) T *phag* 'something hidden; concealment', B *phak*~*hwak* 'hide, conceal' (note the aspiration).[79]

(47) Thebor *ba-e* 'left', K *pai* 'left', *ləpai* 'left-handed, awkward', *əpai* 'to be awkward, speak with a brogue', B *bhai* 'left', *lak-waì* 'left hand', *waì* 'speak with

loans (fore-stressed, as usual) from an AT root of the type **mba*(*γ*)*mbuγu* (Benedict, 1967bis, but with reconstruction as cited above). The root for 'leech' (text) does not appear to have a Chinese cognate, but Karen has prefixed **r*- (n. 356); we reconstruct TB (and TK) **r-pat*, with **p*->*w*- generally after the prefix, but with Nung and Meithei maintaining the stop (text); Burmese has a parallel development in TB *(*r*-)*pak* 'leaf' (n. 77) (K *pha* 'tea' would be an early loan from Burmese in this analysis, since Kachin has *wot* 'leech'). A contrast is afforded by the root for 'ax', for which Chinese (n. 463) indicates an original **pwa* (cf. Vn. *bua*, also IN **rimbat'*); we can now reconstruct TB **r-pwa* rather than **r-wa* for this root (No. 441) on the basis of Gyarung *ṣarpye*<*-[*r*]-*pa* 'kind of ax'. We can also reconstruct TB *(*p*)*wa* 'man, person, husband' (No. 100) on the basis of the original **pwa* indicated by Chinese (n. 463). Gyarung (forms from K. Chang) is of special value in reconstructing TB initial **pw*- (Gyarung *ph*-) or **bw*- (Gyarung *p*-) as opposed to **w*- (Gyarung *w*-) in certain roots; cf. Gyarung *əphak*, B *ăwak* 'half', from TB **pwak*; Gyarung *tapat* 'flower', Nungish **śiŋ-wat* 'bud (Răwang); flower (Trung)' (*śiŋ* 'tree'), B-L **wat* 'flower', from TB **bwat*; but Gyarung *wyan* 'I wear', *tewyet* 'clothes'<**wat* (cf. Gyarung *syan* 'I kill', TB **g-sât*), Răwang (Nung) *nuŋ-wat* 'to cover breasts (*nuŋ*) with breast-cloth', B-L **wat* 'wear' (B *wat* 'wear', *ăwat* 'clothes'). In addition to the doublet forms in the text (Nos. 46 and 47), Burmese retains the initial cluster in TB *(*s*-)*bwam* 'plump, swollen' (No. 172) and B-L **bwa* 'grandmother' (n. 463) (possibly both with *â* in ST); for TB **pwa* 'palm, sole' (No. 418), on basis of original indicated by Chinese (n. 463), Burmese has bhăwà (*phăwà*), possibly from an original ST (and TB) prefixed form: **b-wa*. The unusually large number of these labial stop+*w* initial clusters in ST suggests a relatively late origin from a simple labial stop, as indicated by the probable loans from AT (see 'pig' and 'ax', above), but note the **mb* clusters in these AT forms.

79 Lahu has a similar doublet: *phâ*/*fâ*<**ʔpak*/*ʔwak* 'hide something', which (like Burmese *phak*/*hwak*) come from a causative **s*- prefix at the PLB stage, becoming **ʔ*- at a later stage. The simplex ('to hide oneself') is Lahu *vàʔ*, Burmese *wak*. See Matisoff, 'GD', for the Lahu tone (JAM).

a brogue', Tangkhul *wui-śoŋ* 'left', *phui kəsiŋə* 'left-handed' (cf. the Burmese initials), Lepcha *vi-m*, L *vei*, Mikir *arvi* 'left' (TB **bay*, thus explaining the Mikir form).[80]

Kachin also maintains the labial stop in the following:

(48) T *phaŋ*~*'phaŋ*, Thebor *phaŋ* 'spindle', K *kəbaŋ* 'hand-spindle', B *wáŋ* 'swing around; spin', *waŋ-rùi* 'spindle' (*rùi* 'handle'), *ăwaŋ* 'spindleful of thread' (TB **paŋ*).

The apparent loss of initial velar stops can also be traced in certain roots; cf. the following:

(49) T *skar-ma*, Kanauri *kar*, Lepcha *săhor*, Miri *təkar*, K *śəgan*, Western Kuki **s-gar* (Kwoireng *tśəgan*, Khoirao *səgan*), Khami *ka(r)-si*~*a-si*, but L (and general Kuki) *ar-śi* 'star' (TB **s-kar*).

(50) Lepcha *fo-gom*, K *u-kam* (also *wa u-kam*) 'molar tooth', G *wa-gam* 'tooth', B *àm* (also *àm-swà*) 'molar tooth' (TB **gam*, usually combined with **s-wa* 'tooth', basic meaning 'jaw').

(51) Lepcha *tăhi*<**tăkhi*, Mikir *tśehe*<**tekhe* 'crab', Tangkhul *khai* 'fish', *khai-reu* 'crab', Khoirao *tśəγai*, Khami *təai*, L *ai* 'crab' (TB **d-ka·y*).[81]

(52) T *khab*, Kanauri *keb*, B *ʔap* 'needle', from Burmese-Lolo **(t-)γap*: Phön *təγet*<**təγap*, Lahu *γòʔ*, Lisu *wɔʔ*, Ahi *woʔ*, revealing a development **k*>**g*> *γ*~*w* after the prefix (TB **kap*).[82]

80 Lahu has a labial nasal here: *mɛ̄* (JAM). This may be from a nasal cluster: **ŋw-*: **lak-bai*>**laŋwai*>**mai*>**mɛ̄*; cf. Lahu *phɨ̂* 'dog', from B-L **khwəy*.

81 Lahu *á-ci-ku* 'crab' is cognate. Final *-i* is the regular Lahu reflex for **-ai*; cf. B *tshai* '10', Lahu *chi*. The initial *c-* implies an older **ky-*, however, hence one should perhaps reconstruct TB **d-kya·y*, thus explaining the loss of initial stop (text) (JAM). K (*tśyə-*)*khan* 'crab' also belongs with this root (n. 284). The Chinese (perhaps also Karen) cognate indicates an original initial **g-* (without palatalization) for this root (n. 445), but it is possible that palatalization arose later (possibly at the proto-TB level) through influence from the final.

82 Additional data are now available on these two roots, also on 'jaw (molar teeth)' (No. 50), from Gyarung and six Ch'iang dialects (K. Chang), Trung (Nungish) and Lepcha ('needle'):

	Gyarung	Ch'iang	Trung	Lepcha
needle	*tekyep*	*xe*~*he*	*uop*	*ryŭm*
house	*ṭṣam*	*tśi*~*tśye*	*tśiəm*	*khyŭm*
jaw (molar teeth)	—	—	*skam*	*fo-gom*

Note: Trung *skam* 'molar tooth', from *sa* 'tooth'+*/kam* (<'jaw').

These roots are now reconstructed **kəp* 'needle', **kyim*~**kyum* 'house' and **gəm* 'jaw (molar tooth)', all with excellent agreement with the Chinese cognates (nn. 479, 482), the loss of the initial stop in all three roots having been conditioned by palatalization, either primary (**kyim*~**kyum*) or secondary (**kəp* and **gəm*,

Both loss of the initial and palatalization before *i* are illustrated in the following:

(53) T *khyim*, Bahing *khyim*~*khim*, Vayu *kim*~*kem*, Lepcha *khyŭm*, Miri *əkum*, Mru *kim*, Andro *kem*, Mikir *hem* < **khem*, Chairel *him*, Limbu *him*, Namsang *hum*, Chepang *kyim*~*tim*, Nung *kyim*~*tśim*~*tśum*, Kadu *tyem*, Moshang *yim*~*yüm*, Magari *im*~*yum*, Meithei *yum*, B *im*, Lahu *yɛ̀*, Chinbok *im*, L (and general Kuki) *in* (showing assimilation of the final) 'house' (TB **kim*).[82]

Lushei (and general Kuki) has also lost initial **k*- before *w* in *ui* 'dog' < TB **kwi* (below, No. 159). Note that loss of this initial, as in the above examples, cannot be explained on any ordinary phonological grounds;[83] contrast the following, showing retention of **k*- even before *i*:

(54) K *khyi*~*tsyəkhyi*~*śik-tśi*, B *khye*~*gyi*, L *sa-khi*, Southern Kuki **d-khi* 'barking deer' (TB **d-kiy*).

TB initial **t*- is generally well preserved, even before the front vowel *i*, and no instance of loss of this initial has yet been uncovered. Palatalization of **t*- before *i* does occur in Garo-Bodo, however; cf. the following:

(55) Kanauri *ti*, Manchati *ti* 'water', Kanauri *thi-ss*, Bunan *thi* 'wet', Vayu *ti*, Magari *di*, Achang (Burmese-Lolo) *ti*, Kanburi Lawa (Burmese-Lolo) *thi*, Nung *thi* 'water', K *mədi* 'moist, damp, wet', *mədit* 'to wet, dampen; wet, damp, moist'; G *tśi* 'water', from TB **ti*(*y*). By way of contrast, Garo has *t*-~*d*- for **d*- before *i*:

(56) T *sdig-pa* 'scorpion', *sdig-srin* 'crab, crawfish' (*srin* 'insect'), L *ti·t* 'scorpion', G *na-tik* 'shrimp' (*na* 'fish'), from TB *(*s*-)*di·k*; Lepcha has *dik lăŋ-fik* 'scorpion', etymologized (Grünwedel, in Mainwaring) as 'the evil one [T *sdig-pa* "sin"] that has its abode under the stones [*lăŋ*]'.

before the vowel *ə*); cf. also K-N **e·k* 'excrement', perhaps from TB **kyak* (n. 399). Benedict (1967bis) has suggested an ultimate AT source (cf. IN**d'aɣum* 'needle', **ɣumaʔ* 'house') for two of these roots, yielding an initial **ɣ*- in TB, but it is now clear that the roots are not strictly parallel in TB generally (see the above table). The view that borrowing has occurred in the root for 'needle' is greatly strengthened by Lepcha *ryŭm* (overlooked in Benedict, 1967bis), from an earlier prefix + *rum* form; cf. 'indigo': IN **taɣum*, Lepcha *ryom* < prefix + *ram*, T *rams* (Benedict, 1967bis); note that Chinese also has final -*m* for 'needle' (n. 482).

83 This is a peculiar root. Lahu has a labial initial /*phɨ̂*/ and Karen has **thw*-; evidently this was a complex, phonologically unstable initial (JAM). Tiddim Chin, probably also Siyin (Stern, *Asia Major* **10**), has an unique cluster here: *ʔwi* 'dog', indicating simple replacement of the initial **k* with *ʔ* (as found also in Chinese, but in this root Chinese indicates an original **kw*-). This development was perhaps conditioned by metanalysis: **kwi* < **k*/*wi*, with **k*- as 'animal prefix' (n. 301); cf. the Karen development of *t*- for **k*- in this same root (p. 133), apparently also through metanalysis; also B-L **la* (generally) from **kla* (B *kyà*) 'tiger', which can be identified as a loan from Mon-Khmer (*khla*~*kla* forms) (rather than vice versa) because of the presence of this root in the Munda languages of India (*kula*~*kul* forms).

Illustrations of TB initial sibilants and affricates:

(57) T *se-ba* ~ *gse-ba* ~ *bse-ba* 'rose-bush, rose', *se-ʾbru* 'pomegranate', *se-yab* ~ *bse-yab* 'fig', Vayu *se* 'to fruit', *se* ~ *si* 'fruit', Bahing *si* 'to fruit', *si-tśi* 'fruit', Nung *śiŋ śi* 'fruit', K *si* ~ *əsi* 'fruit', *əsi si* 'bear fruit', B *sì* 'bear fruit', *ăsì* 'fruit', G *the* ~ *bithe* 'fruit', Dimasa *thai* 'bear fruit', *bathai* 'fruit', L *thei*, Mikir *the* ~ *athe* 'fruit' (TB **sey*).

(58) T *gsod-pa*, Pf. *bsad*, Nung *sat*, K *sat*, B *sat*, Dimasa *thai* < **that* (see n. 50), L *that*, Mikir *that* 'kill' (TB **g-sat*).[84,85]

(59) Tsangla *za* ~ *źa*, Magari *za*, Digaro *sa*, K *śa*, B *sà*, G *bisa*, Dimasa *sa* ~ *basa*, L *fa* 'son, offspring', Nung *za-mi* 'daughter' (B *samì*) (TB **za*).[86]

(60) West T *zi* 'something of a very small size or of quantity', K *zi* 'small', *zi-zi* 'small, minute', B *sè* 'small, fine, slender', Lahu *i* < **yi* < **ʔzi* (TB **ziy*).[87]

(61) T *gzig*, Nung *khaŋ-zi* 'leopard' (*khaŋ* 'tiger'), B *sats* < **sik* 'small animal of the tiger genus' (TB **zik*).

(62) T *tsha* 'hot; illness', *tsha-ba* 'hot; heat; spice, condiment', *tshad-pa* 'heat; fever', B *tsha* 'hungry', *ătsha* 'hunger; something faulty or hurtful' (but Lolo **tsha* 'hot'), G *sa* 'ache; sick', *sa-ani* 'pain', *sa-gipa* 'pepper', Dimasa *sa* 'ache, pain', *sa-ba* 'hot (used of the heat of chillies, peppers)', L *śa* ~ *śat* 'hot', Mikir *so* 'hot, excessive; to be ill, sore' (TB **tsa*).

(63) T *ʾtshab-pa*, B *tshap* 'repay' (TB **tsap*).

(64) T *tshigs*, Kanauri *tsig*, Lepcha *(a-)tśak* < **tśik*, B *ătshats* < **ătshik*, Nung

84 G *sot* 'kill', with discrepant initial and medial elements, must be referred to a distinct root; cf. *rasot* 'clip, crop, sever', *sko rasot* 'behead'.

85 It now appears that G *sot* (= *soʔot*) 'kill' belongs with this set, with both the initial and the vowel conditioned by an original vowel *â* (n. 344).

86 Lepcha has *(ă-)zon* 'grandchild', from **za-n* (see n. 284 for this suffix), also the unusual, skewed reciprocal term: *(ă-)zo* 'great-grandfather', from **za*. B-L generally **za* 'child', with Lisu paralleling Lepcha in having a skewed reciprocal term: *za* 'child', *a-za* 'grandmother', but Maru and Atsi *tso* 'child', from B-L and TB **tsa*; cf. T *btsa-ba* 'to bear (children)', *tsha(-bo, -mo)* 'grandchild, nephew or niece', Bahing *tśa-tśa* 'grandson', Dhimal *tśan* 'son' (with suffixed *-n*, as above); Tsangla has both roots in the same basic meaning of 'child': *za* ~ *źa*, also *o-sa* ~ *ok-tsa* ~ *wok-tsa* (various sources), with both roots appearing in the single form *za-sa* 'child (baby)'. Chinese reflects the doublet exactly: *tsi̯əg/tsi*[a] and *dzi̯əg/zi* 'child', from **tsa* ~ **za* (character normally read *tsi̯əg* and is also the 1st cyclical character, but one archaic form of graph also used for *dzi̯əg/zi*,[b] the 6th cyclical character, the graph of which is 'foetus'); Chinese also has the verbal doublet with voiced affricate initial: *dzʻi̯əg/dzʻi*[c] 'to beget'. For the initial alternation in TB, cf. TB *tśi* and **źəy* 'urinate; urine' (n. 96).

87 This root is preglottalized in B-L (JAM), probably from an original form with **a-* prefix.

[a] 子 [b] 巳 [c] 字

tsi, Mikir *sek* 'joint', G *dźak-tśik* 'elbow' ('arm-joint'), *dźa-tśik* 'knee' ('leg-joint') (TB **tsik*).

(65) T *rtsi* 'all liquids of a somewhat great consistency, such as the juice of some fruits, paints, varnish', K *tsi*~*ətsi*, B *tshè* 'drugs, medicine, tobacco, paint', Nung *mətsi* 'medicine' (TB **tsiy*).

(66) Bahing *dźa*, Nagari *dźya*, K *śa*, B *tsa* 'eat', *ătsa* 'food', G *tśha* 'eat', L *faʔ* 'feed with the mouth', but T *za-ba*~*bza*~*ba*, Kanauri *za* 'eat' (TB **dza*).[88]

(67) T *mdza-ba* 'to love', K *ndźa* 'show love; affectionate', B *tsa* 'have tender regard for another' (TB **m-dza*).[89]

(68) K *dźan*, L *far-nu*, Tangkhul *əzăr-vă* 'sister (man speaking)', Meithei *itśal*~*itśan*, Kadu *san* 'younger sister' (TB **dzar*).

(69) Dimasa *dźop*, L *fo·p*, Thado *tsop*, Siyin *tuop* 'suck; kiss' (TB **dzo·p*); cf. Siyin *ta* 'child' < TB **za*.

The affricates, like the stops, show a primary division between voiced and unvoiced forms, with aspiration of secondary significance. Tibetan has the same pattern of aspiration for affricates as for stops (see above), with almost no initial unaspirated forms (*tsi-tsi* 'mouse' is the most noteworthy of the lot). Palatalization before the front vowel *i* is common throughout the TB area (see the discussion under §9). The shifts **ts-* > *s-* and **s-* > *t(h)-* mark off Garo-Bodo and Kuki-Naga from most other TB languages (Ao Naga retains *s-*), yet are curiously paralleled in Modern Burmese, which has **ts-* > *s-*, **tsh-* > *sh-*, and **s-* > *θ-* (a weakly articulated interdental stop). Meithei has **ts-* > *s-* as in Lushei (*sam* 'hair' < **tsam*, *sum-bal* 'mortar' < **tsum*, *əsa-ba* 'hot' < **tsa*), but **s-* > *h-* (*məhei* 'fruit' < **sey*, *məhau* 'fat' < **sa·w*, *əhum* '3' < **g-sum*). The latter development is found also in Chang Naga and other Konyak languages.

Tibetan has only prefixed *g-* and *b-* before *s-* and *z-*, hence sibilants are shifted to affricates after other prefixes, notably *ʼ-*, *m-* and *r-*;[90] cf. T *rtsa(-ba)* 'vein; root' < TB **r-*sa; also the following:

(70) T *rtsaŋs-pa* 'lizard', K *nsaŋ son* 'jungle lizard', B *saŋ-kyau* 'skink (earth lizard)', *saŋ-lip* 'species of skink' (TB **r-saŋ*).

88 Initial *z-* forms are also found in Lepcha: *zo* < **za* 'eat', *ăzom* 'food', *zot* 'graze', *ăzot* 'pasturage'. The Tibetan form can be derived from **b-dza* (Tibetan lacks the cluster **bdz-* and has simplified to *bz-*), and similarly for the Kanauri and Lepcha forms, but note that Chinese also has a doublet with initial **z-* (n. 452), probably of similar origin.

89 Maran cites *ndźaʔ* (high tone) for Kachin, probably from **-dźak*, hence this form may be distinct.

90 For *tśh-* < *ś-* after prefixed *ʼ-*, cf. T *śi-ba*~*ʼtśhi-ba* 'die' < **siy*; T *ʼtśhar-ba*~*śar-ba* 'rise, appear, become visible (of the sun, etc.)', *śar* 'east', Kanauri *sar* 'lift, bear, carry', *sar-sí* 'rise' (refl. form), Nung *nam sarr* 'sunrise', *nam sarr kha* 'east' (*nam* 'sun').

Tibetan has dropped the occlusive part of the affricate initial in *za-ba* 'eat' < TB **dza*, and in the following pair of roots:

(71) T *źim-pa* 'well-tasted, sweet-scented', Bahing *dźi-dźim* < **dźim-dźim* 'sweet', Aka *dźim-tśi* 'fresh (water)', B *tshím* 'pleasant to the taste, delicious, savory', from TB **dz(y)im*.[91]

(72) T *źon-pa*, Nung *zun*, K *dźon* 'mount, ride (an animal)' (TB **dzyon*).[91]

Kachin and Nung show a similar development in the following:

(73) T *ʔag-tshom* 'beard of the chin', Kanauri *tsam* 'wool, fleece', *mik-tsam* 'eyebrow', Magari *tśham* 'hair, wool', Tsangla *tśam*, Bahing *tsam*, B *tsham*, L *sam* 'hair (of head)', Dhimal *tśam* 'hide, bark', G *mik sam* 'eyebrow', but K *sam* 'hair (of head)', Nung *əŋsam* 'hide', and Ladakhi *sam-dal*, Lahuli *yar-sam* 'mustache' (TB **tsam*).[92]

The TB initial is uncertain in the following:

(74) T *sen-mo* 'finger- or toe-nail', Digaro *mśi*, Miju *msen* 'claw', Dhimal *khur-siŋ* 'finger-nail', B *ăsàń* 'nail', *lak-sàń* 'finger-nail', *khre-sàń* 'toe-nail', L *tin* 'nail, claw, hoof' (note the unaspirated initial), Khami *msiŋ* ~ *mseŋ*, Siyin *tśiŋ*, Empeo *mitśin* 'nail', perhaps also Magari *arkin* and K *ləmyin* (< **lak-myin*), Nung *nyin* (< **myin*) 'finger-nail',[93] on the strength of the Miri doublet *lag-śin* ~ *lag-yin*, *id.*; this root we have provisionally reconstructed **m-(t)sin*.[94]

Kachin appears to have *th-* for **ts-* in two roots:[95]

(75) B *tshum*, Nung *sum-phaŋ*, K *thum*, L *sum*, G *sam* 'mortar' (TB **tsum*).

91 The Tibetan forms with initial *ź-* in Nos. 71 and 72 have probably been derived from prefixed forms such as **bdź-* (cf. n. 88).

92 This root now reconstructed **tsâm* ~ *sâm* (for vocalism, see n. 344); K *sam* is probably an early loan from Burmese, but the Nung, Ladakhi and Lahuli forms all point to a doublet with initial **s-*, probably derived from the standard root in **ts-* through preglottalization as a result of prefixed **a-* = *ʔa-* (Nung *əŋsam* 'hide' shows this prefix in typical nasalized form); note that the apparent Chinese cognate (*sam/ṣam*[a] 'hair, feather') also has the initial *s-*.

93 For Nung *n(y)-* < **my-*, cf. Nung *mit* ~ *nit* 'mind, temper', K *myit*; Nung *mɛ* ~ *nɛ* 'eye' < **myak* (No. 402). Ahi and Nyi (Burmese-Lolo) regularly have *n-* < *my-*, *d-* ~ *dl-* < *by-*, *t(h)-* ~ *tl-* < *py-*; cf. B *myà*, Ahi *no*, Nyi *na* 'much, many'; B *pyà* < *byà*, Ahi *do*, Nyi *dla-ma* 'bee'; B *pyam*, Ahi *thö* ~ *thɛ*, Nyi *tlö* 'to fly'. The shift **my-* > *n-* before the high front vowel *i* appears also in Bahing (and general Kiranti) *niŋ* 'name' < **r-miŋ* (Limbu has *miŋ*); Aka *ənyin* 'to name', *ninyi* 'name' < **r-miŋ*, *ənyi* 'eye' < **mik*.

94 This root can now be reconstructed **m-tsyen* (n. 122).

95 It now appears that these roots are to be reconstructed with the initial cluster **tśr-* (*tś-* = *ć-*, a unit phoneme): **tśrum* 'mortar' (apparently an old loan from AT;

a 彡

(76) T *rtsi-ba*, K *thi*, and perhaps B *re* 'count' (TB **r-tsiy*).

This type of development, which is relatively rare in TB, appears also in Western Kuki and Digaro (*tha* 'eat' < TB **dza*, **thaŋ* 'hair' < TB **tsam*), as well as in Nung (*thil* 'spittle' < TB **m-ts(y)il*).[95]

The Lolo languages preserve the distinction between surds and sonants for sibilants and affricates as well as for stops:

		TB	Burm.	Lisu	Ahi	Nyi	Lahu
57	fruit	**sey*	*ăsì*	*si*	*sa*	*sə*	*šī*
59	child	**za*	*sà*	*ra*	*zo*	*za*	*yâ*
61	leopard	**zik*	*sats*	—	*zö*	*zə*	—
71	hair	**tsam*	*tsham*	*tśhye*	*tshə*	*tshe*	*jɨ*
66	eat	**dza*	*tsà*	*dza*	*dzo*	*dza*	*câ*

Sonant initials for Burmese-Lolo often can be reconstructed with certainty, even when cognates from other TB groups are lacking,[96] e.g. B *sak*, Lahu *yàʔ*, Lisu *ræ*, Ahi *ze*, Nyi *zə* 'descend', from Burmese-Lolo **zak*. In the following root, Burmese-Lolo shows a doublet formation:

(77) T *gtśid-pa* ~ *gtśi-ba* 'urinate', *gtśin* 'urine', K *dźit tśyi* ~ *dźit dźi* 'urinate', *dźit* 'urine', Nung *tsi* 'urine', *tsi tsi* 'urinate', B *tshì* 'urine (the polite term)', Lahu *jɨ̂*, Dimasa *si-di* 'urine; urinate' (*di* 'water'), from TB **ts(y)i*; Burmese-Lolo also has the doublet **ziy* 'urine', represented by B *sè*, Lisu *rzi*, Ahi *zö*, Nyi *zə*.

cf. N. Thai **qrum*, Mak *tśum toi* 'mortar'); **(r-)tśrəy* 'count'; **m-tśril* 'spittle'; the latter pair have significant Chinese cognates (n. 457). B *re* 'count' reflects this **tśr-* cluster rather than the **r-* prefix. This correspondence is strengthened by B *re* 'water' (also *ri* in inscriptions), from **tśril* (see n. 54 for final); Burmese furnishes a perfect semantic parallel: B *tam-thwè* 'spittle', from **ta-mthwè* = 'its (*m-*) water (*thwè*)', from TB **twəy*; cf. also Dhimal *thop-tśi* 'spittle', G *khu-tśi* 'saliva' = 'mouth (*khu*)-water', from TB **ti(y)*. T *mtśhil-ma* 'spittle' has the normal **tś(h)-* reflex here; T *rtsi-ba* 'count' stands for **rtśi-* (Tibetan lacks the **rtś-* cluster). Burmese, Nung and Lushei all show distinct reflexes in **tśrum* 'mortar', and perhaps a doublet **tsum* should be recognized, but the irregularity might also be attributed to the apparent loan-word status of this root (above).

96 Cf. also 'use': B *sùm*, Lahu *yɛ̂*; '3rd pers. prn.': B *sàŋ*, Lahu *yɔ̂*. Burmese *s-*/Lahu *y-* is usually from PLB **z-* (JAM). Lisu has initial *r-* in 'descend' (text) but *rz-* in 'urine' (text) and a doublet *rze* ~ *rö* 'use' < B-L **zum* (above). It is possible that a distinction between initial **z-* and **ź-* must be set up for B-L, paralleling the distinction between **s-* and **ś-*; we reconstruct B-L **źəy* 'urine' rather than **zəy*, in view of the doublet **tśi*, maintaining the palatal initial for this root and offering an exact parallel to TB **tsa* ~ **za* 'child' (n. 86); perhaps also **źum* 'use', with a possible cognate in Chinese: *di̯uŋ/yi̯uŋ*[a] 'use, employ', perhaps from an earlier **di̯um* (n. 479).

[a] 用

Illustrations of TB initial nasals, liquids, *h*-, *w*-, *y*-:[97]

(78) T *lŋa*, K *məŋa*, B *ŋà*, G *boŋa*, L *ŋa*~*pəŋa* '5' (TB **l-ŋa*~**b-ŋa*).

(79) T *ŋu-ba*, B *ŋui*, Nung *ŋü* 'weep, cry' (TB **ŋuw*).

(80) T *na-ba* 'to be ill', *nad* 'illness', Kanauri *na* 'to be hurt', B *na* 'to be ill', *ăna* 'pain, disease', K and Nung *əna* 'illness', L *na*~*nat* 'to be ill; illness' (TB **na*).

(81) T *nyi-ma*, L *ni* 'sun, day', B *ne* 'sun', *né* 'day', K *ni* 'day', Dimasa *di-ni* 'today' (cf. K *dai-ni*, lit. 'this day') (TB **niy*).

(82) T *rmaŋ-lam* 'dream' (*lam* 'road, way'), Miri *im-maŋ*, K *maŋ*~*yup-maŋ*, Nung *ip-maŋ*, L *maŋ*, Mikir *maŋ*, G *dźu-maŋ* 'dream', B *ip-mak* 'dream', *hmaŋ-tsa-saŋ* 'walk in sleep', *hmaŋ-tak-mí* 'to be possessed (applied to somnambulism)', Lahu *mâʔ* 'dream' (TB **maŋ*); note the use of TB **ip* 'sleep' in composition.[98]

(83) T *miŋ*, Magari *armin*, Limbu *miŋ*, Dhimal *miŋ*, K *myiŋ*, L *hmiŋ*, Rangkhol *ermiŋ* 'name', G *miŋ* 'to name', *bimuŋ* 'name', B *mań* 'to be named', *ămań* 'name', *hmáń* 'to name', but Nung *biŋ* 'name' (Nung normally retains *m*-) (TB **r-miŋ*).[99]

(84) K *rap* 'central fireplace', *kərap* 'lower screen over fireplace', Nung *mərap* 'fireplace', B *mì-rap-paùŋ* 'wooden fireplace' (*mì* 'fire'), Maru *γrɛ*<**hrap* 'fireplace', L *rap*, Mikir *rap* 'shelf over fire' (TB **rap*).[100]

(85) Vayu *ruŋ*, Bahing *ruŋ*, Lepcha *ăróŋ*, Tsangla *wa-roŋ* (*wa* 'cow'), Miri

97 Lolo-Burmese provides solid evidence for the existence of aspirated and glottalized sonorants as well as plain ones; see Matisoff, 'GD'. STL mentions Burmese *l*-/Loloish *h*- (JAM). These appear to be almost all of secondary origin; cf. the schema for reconstruction of initial stops as set up by Matisoff (n. 76).

98 Maran cites *ʔmaŋ* 'dream' for Kachin, suggesting a possible clue to the B-L development **ʔmaŋ*>**ʔmak* (see n. 242). Prefixed **r*- for this root is supported by Gyarung (K. Chang) *karmye* 'to sleep', from **-rma*[*ŋ*]; for the semantics, cf. T *rmi-ba* 'to dream'<TB *(*r*-)*mwəy* 'to sleep'. Trung (Nungish) has *mləŋ* 'dream', *mləŋ mləŋ* 'to dream', from **ləməŋ*=**r-məŋ* by metathesis; cf. Trung *a-mra* 'field', Mutwang (Răwang dial.) *rəma*, *id*. Note that in composition Burmese maintains the final nasal (*hmaŋ*-); the B-L forms in general point to an original *ʔmak* (as reconstructed by Burling and JAM).

99 Cf. the development of sonorant stops from nasals in Bisu: /*bi*/ 'fire'; this phenomenon is rare in TB generally (JAM). Nung (Răwang) *biŋ* 'name' is a pseudo-cognate here, hence does not represent this rare shift; it has been derived (regular shift) from **briŋ*; cf. Trung *aŋ-prəŋ* 'name' (with typical nasalized **a*-prefix); also Lepcha *bryaŋ*, *id*., from *sbraŋ*; a connection with TB **braŋ* 'to give birth' (No. 135) has been suggested (by JAM). Gyarung (K. Chang) has *termi* (high falling tone)<**-rmiŋ*, confirming the prefix in this root. For Kachin, Maran cites *myiŋ* (mid tone) 'name', *śəmyiŋ* (low tone) 'to name', paralleling the Burmese forms.

100 See n. 69.

əröŋ, Moshang (Konyak) *əruŋ*, K *ruŋ*~*nruŋ*, Nung *dəriŋ*~*riŋ*, G *groŋ*<*g-roŋ* 'horn' (TB **ruŋ*).[101]

(86) T *lag(-pa)*, Miri *əlak*, Chairel (Luish) *lak*, K *lə-*, B *lak* 'arm, hand' (TB **lak*).[102]

(87) T *lam*, K *lam*, B *làm*, G *ram-a* 'road', Nung *lam* 'side, direction', L *lam* 'way, direction, place', *lam-lian* 'road' (*lian* 'large') (TB **lam*).

(88) Bahing *luŋ*, Lepcha *lăŋ* (also *luŋ-* in comp.), Miri *ü-liŋ* (Abor *ö-lüŋ*), K *luŋ*~*nluŋ*, B *kyauk*<**k-lauk*, G *roŋ*, Dimasa *loŋ*, L *luŋ*, Mikir *arloŋ* 'stone' (TB **r-luŋ*).

(89) T *hab* 'mouthful', B *hap* 'bite at, as a fish or dog', L *hap* 'bite, snap'.

(90) K *wai* 'whirl, as a whirlpool; stir, as with a ladle; strike out with a sweeping movement', *phuŋ-wai* 'whirlpool', Nung *thi buŋ wai* 'whirlpool', B *wài* 'whirlpool', also 'soar around, as a bird; brandish a sword, weapon or stick', L *vai* 'row, paddle', also 'wave (the hand, arm)', Mikir *iŋvei* 'fly around (as an insect)', but cf. Meithei *pai* 'to fly' (TB **way·*).

(91) K *wan*, B *wàn*, L *val* 'circular' (TB **wal*).

(92) T *yab-mo*~*g-yab-mo* 'the act of fanning or waving; fan', Miri *məyap*, B *yap*, Mikir *hi-dźap* 'fan', L *za·p* 'fan, winnow, flap, flutter', *hmai-zaʔ* 'a fan' (*hmai* 'face'), Tangkhul *kəyap* 'to fan', G *tśo* 'row, paddle, dig', Dimasa *dźau* 'paddle, dig or root up, winnow'; cf. also K *kətsap* 'winnow' (TB **ya·p*).

(93) Bahing *yö*<**yu*, K *yu*~*yun*, Nung *yu*~*yi* [*yü*], L *sa-zu*, Thado *yu-tśa*, Mikir *phidźu*, Kanauri *pĭu* 'rat', West T (Balti) *byu-a* 'rat, mouse', T *byiu* [*byu*] 'alpine hare' (cf. L *sa-zu-pui* 'hare' = 'big rat') (TB **b-yuw*).[103]

(94) Thebor *yu*, Tsangla *yu*, Digaro *yu*, Dhimal *yu*, G *tśu*, Dimasa *dźu*, L *zu*, Meithei *yu* 'liquor, wine, beer', from TB **yu(w)*.

As indicated above, TB nasal initials are well preserved throughout the TB area. TB initial **r-* and **l-* are almost as well maintained in most TB languages, though occasional shifts are encountered, e.g. G **l->r-*, Modern Burmese and

101 This root now reconstructed **rwaŋ*, a doublet of **rwa* (n. 231).

102 The usual Kachin word for 'hand' is peculiar: *lətaʔ* (high tone), *lə-* appears as the preformative in several words relating to hands and feet. The *t* is like the *t* in T *rta* 'horse', suggesting epenthetic *t* after liquids; cf. also K *mətaʔ* (high tone) 'lick', T *ldag*; and *śəta* 'moon/month' from an *lt-* cluster) (JAM). For a different interpretation of the Kachin forms, see nn. 109 and 137; the writer considers T *rta* 'horse' as entirely distinct from other TB forms.

103 B *yun* 'rabbit' belongs with this root (cf. the Tibetan and Lushei meanings); the suffixed *-n* is the 'collective' (n. 284), appearing also in Kachin (text); the Ch. cognate compares closely with the Burmese form in all respects: *tsi̯wən/tsi̯uĕn*[a] ~ *ts'i̯wən/ts'i̯uĕn* 'hare', from **tsun*<**yun* (n. 428); T *byiu* < *byi–ba* 'rat' (No. 173).

a 㕙

Lolo *_r_- > _y_-, and _r_- ~ _l_- fluctuation in Meithei. Note Garo initial *_l_- > _r_- but final *-_r_ > -_l_. Vacillation between initial _l_- and _r_- appears in the following roots:

(95) T _ltśi-ba_ ~ _ldźi-ba_ < *_s-li_ 'heavy', _ldźid-pa_ 'heaviness, weight', Kanauri _li-k_, Manchati _hli-i_, Vayu _li-s_, Lepcha _li_(-_m_), K _li_, Nung _əli_, B _lè_, G _dźrim_, Dimasa _risi_, Bodo _illit_ ~ _gillit_, L (and general Kuki) _rit_ 'heavy' (TB *_s-liy_).[104]

(96) Lepcha _tŭk-liŋ_ ~ _tŭŋ-liŋ_, Nung _liŋ_,[105] Miri _əlüŋ_, B _lań_ < *_liŋ_, L _riŋ_ 'neck' (TB *_liŋ_).[106]

Note that Lushei has _r_- for *_l_- in both roots, perhaps because of the following _i_.

TB initial *_h_- is rare, and can be reconstructed for only a few roots of restricted range, with only *_hap_ 'bite, snap' (No. 89) represented in more than two main divisions (T, B, L). Kachin has this initial only in the loan-word _ho_ (usually pronounced _kho_) 'announce', from B _haù_ > _hɔ̀_; cf. L _hau_ 'abuse, reproach', _hauʔ_ 'bespeak'.[107] Loss of initial *_h_- is indicated in the following:

T _haŋ-ba_, K _gəaŋ_ 'pant, gasp'.

Garo has initial _h_- in a few words for which no certain cognates have been uncovered, but cf. the following:

(97) Kiranti *_kha_ (Bahing _kha-pi_, Lohorong _ba-kha_), Kadu _ka_, K _gá_ ~ _əgá_ ~ _ngá_ [_n-gá_], Nung _ga_ ~ _rəga_, Moshang _ga_, G _ha_ 'earth', from TB *_r-ka_.

Of the pair of semi-vowel initials, TB *_y_- presents relatively little difficulty. The shift from *_y_- to _z_- (Lushei) or to _dź_- ~ _tś_- (Garo, Mikir) is characteristic of both the Garo-Bodo and Kuki-Naga groups in general, although many Kuki languages

_104_ The Tibetan forms are not the product of metathesis, as this would suggest, but simply reflect palatalization of _l_- before _y_, _i_ or _e_, as follows: *_li_ > *_lyi_ > _ldźi_ 'heavy', also *_s-li_ > *_hlyi_ > _ltśi_; T _ldźi-ba_ ~ '_dźi-ba_ 'flea', from *(_ă_-)_li_, TB *_s-liy_ (the *_s_- prefix is not represented in this root in Tibetan, having been replaced by *_a_- or simply dropped); T _ltśe_ 'tongue', from *_hlye_ < *_s-le_ < TB *_s-lay_ (here the *_s_- prefix is represented by *_h_-). With prefixed *_a_-, the shift is simply to _dź_- ('_dźi-ba_ 'flea'); with prefixed *_b_-, there is further simplification to _ź_-, Tibetan lacking the cluster *_bdź_- (cf. n. 88: T *_bdza_ > _bza_ 'eat'), hence T _bźi_ '4' represents a perfectly regular development from TB *_b-ləy_ (see n. 436 for similar shift in Chinese). In addition to the 'internal' support for this suggested line of development in Tibetan, there is also 'external' support in the loan-word _ltśags_ < *_hlyag/s_ 'iron', ultimately from an AT root ending in *-_χliaq_ (Thai *_hlek_, Kam-Sui *_qhlet_, Lakkia _khyãk_), the typically TB _a_ vocalism in this instance certainly being archaic (cf. Benedict, 1967bis).

105 Nung _liŋ_ 'neck' cited in Peal, 1883, who has reversed the words _nyin_ 'nail' and _liŋ_ 'neck'.

_106_ T '_dźiŋ-pa_ ~ _mdźiŋ-pa_ 'neck' belongs with this set, since it can be derived from *_a-lyiŋ_ ~ *_m-lyiŋ_ (n. 104).

_107_ Other possible initial *_h_- words in Lolo-Burmese include 'yawn': B _hà_, Lahu _há-gə̂ʔ_, Akha _a-hà_ (prob. onomatopoetic); also 'be the case': B _hut_, Lahu _hêʔ_ (JAM).

(e.g. Thado, Sho, Kami) preserve **y*-. In addition to the correspondences illustrated above (G *tś*-, Dimasa *dź*-), Garo-Bodo has another series with G *dź*-, Dimasa *y*-:

G *dźoŋ*, Dimasa *yuŋ* 'insect'.

G *dźak*, Dimasa *yau* < **yak* 'arm, hand'.

G *dźa*, Dimasa *ya* 'leg, foot'.

These roots are perhaps to be reconstructed with initial **y*-, but the evidence here is not entirely satisfying.[108, 109] Initial **r*- ~ **y*- interchange is indicated for the following root:

(98) T *lag g-yas*, Lepcha *gyo-m* < **gya*, B *lak-ya*, but K *ləkhrá*, G *dźak-ra*, Dimasa *yau-gada* 'right (hand)' (TB **g-ya* ~ **g-ra*).

For this interchange of initials, cf. also TB **s-rak* and **g-yak* 'ashamed, shy'.[110]

TB initial **w*- presents a special problem because of the widespread **p*- ~ **b*- > *w*- shift outlined above. Tibetan has initial *w*- only in the words *wa* 'gutter', *wa* 'fox'[111] and *wa-le* ~ *wal-le* 'clear';[112] medial *wa* is regularly represented in Tibetan by *o* (see Nos. 160, 218, 221, 461). Roots reconstructed in initial **w*- on the basis of evidence from the southern TB languages alone, as Nos. 90 and 91 above, must be regarded as uncertain entities, especially when (as in No. 90)

108 G *dźak* ~ *dźa*, Dimasa *yau* ~ *ya* 'arm' ~ 'foot' belong in a curious series found in Konyak, Chairel, and Abor-Miri-Dafla; cf. Tableng *yak* ~ *ya*, Tamlu *lak* ~ *la*, Banpara *tśak* ~ *tśia*, Namsang *dak* ~ *da*, Moshang *yok* ~ *ya* (all in Konyak group), Chairel *lak* ~ *la*, Miri *əlak* ~ *əle*, Dafla *əla* ~ *al* (*a-l*) 'arm' ~ 'foot'. The root for 'arm' in final *-k* is perhaps simply a prefixed form of TB **lak* (No. 86), yet cf. Gyarung *təyăk* 'hand', L *zak* < **yak*, B *gyak-kalí* ~ *tshak-kalí* 'arm-pit', also *lak-kalí*, *id.* (*lak* 'arm').

109 These B-G sets can be reconstructed **dyuŋ* 'insect' (cf. Chinese *d'i̯ôŋ*/*d''i̯uŋ*,[a] *id.*); **dyak* 'arm, hand', from TB **g-lak*; **dya* 'leg, foot', from TB **g-la*; cf. Chepang *la* 'foot' (but Kiranti generally *laŋ*). It is now possible to bring K *ləta*ʔ 'hand' into this set, from **glak* with the prefixed **g*- being treated as the first member of a cluster; K *śəta* 'moon', from **s-gla*, furnishes an exact parallel (n. 137); in unprefixed forms, Kachin has *kr*- (*kriŋ*- 'hill' < TB **gliŋ*). A separate TB root *(*g*-)*yak* appears to be required to account for the Lushei and Burmese forms (n. 108); cf. also B-L *ʔ*gyak* 'cubit' (cited by JAM). Gyarung (K. Chang) has *tekhlye* < */*khla*[*k*] 'upper arm', apparently from TB **g-lak*.

110 We now reconstruct TB **śrak* 'ashamed, shy' for **s-rak* (n. 304), minimizing the possibility of some relationship with TB **g-yak* (text).

111 Lepcha *f*- < **sw*-, as in *fo* < **s-wa* 'tooth'. T *wa* 'fox' has been derived from TB **gwa*, as represented by Chamba Lahuli *gŭa*, Bunan *goa-nu* ~ *gwa-nu*. The initial stop appears to be preserved in the form *gaa* 'fox' cited for the Amdo dialect (Kansu) in N. M. Przhevalski, *Mongolie et pays des Tangoutes* (trans. by G. de Laurens), Paris, 1880.

112 Cf. K *wan* 'clear, pure, clean, undefiled'.

[a] 蟲

possible cognates with initial labial stop have been uncovered; cf. also the following:

(99) L *sa-va* (Kuki **wa*), Mikir *vo*, Chepang *wa*, Nyi Lolo *wa* 'bird'.

The above suggests a reconstruction in **w-* (TB **wa*), yet Bahing *ba* 'fowl' (perhaps a borrowing from T *bya* 'bird, fowl') puts us in doubt on the matter, while Lepcha *fo* 'bird' is not conclusive.[113] Where Lepcha has *v-* < **w-* we can be more certain of our reconstruction:

(100) Lepcha *əvo* < **əwa* 'husband', Dhimal *wa-dźan* 'boy', *wa-val* 'man', Kuki **wa* (Taungtha *wa*, Haka *va*, Lakher *əwa-pa*) 'husband', K *wa* 'human being', Yellow Lahu *và* 'man, person' (TB **wa*).

Prefixed **s-* aspirates (unvoices) initial nasals and liquids in Burmese, Lushei and (irregularly) in several other TB languages, including Magari, Digaro and Dhimal.[114, 115] In Lepcha prefixed **s-* palatalizes initial nasals and liquids as well as stops. The following roots are illustrative:

(101) T *sna*, Newari *hna-sa*, Magari *hna*, Dhimal *hna-pu*, Digaro *həna-gam* ~ *hnya-gom* (note the palatalization), Nung *śəna*, Kadu *səna*, B *hna*, L *hna·r* (cf. No. 3) 'nose', Lepcha *nyo* 'snot' (TB **s-na*).[116]

(102) T *snabs*, B *hnap*, L *hnap* 'snot' (TB **s-nap*).

(103) Gyarung *snom* 'sister', Magari *arnam* 'maiden', Nung *ənam* 'cousin', *ənam-mɛ* 'sister', Byangsi and Chaudangsi (Almora group) *nam-sia*, Kanauri *stem* < **snem*,[117] Lepcha *nyom*, K *nam*, G *nam-tsik* 'daughter-in-law', B *mauŋ-hnam* 'husband and wife' (archaic) (TB **s-nam*).

There is some evidence that other prefixes, notably **r-*, can produce a similar effect in Burmese and Lushei; cf. B *hrats* '8' < TB **b-r-gyat*, B *hŋà* 'borrow' < TB **r-ŋya*, also the following:

113 Lepcha has *f-* for *ph-* in a number of roots, as well as *f-* ~ *p-* alternation; cf. Lepcha *far* ~ *afar* 'price', *par* 'buy', T *phar* 'interest (on money); exchange, agio', Kanauri *be-par* 'trade', Gyarung *mphar* 'to be for sale', G *phal* 'sell'.

114 Magari is especially rich in aspirated or unvoiced initial nasals and liquids; cf. *hwak* ~ *wak* 'pig', *hmut* 'blow', *hmaŋ-naŋ daŋ* 'dream' ('see in a dream'), *hraŋ* 'horn', *hlaŋ* ~ *hluŋ* 'stone', *hla* 'leaf', and *hme* 'fire'. Magari also occasionally replaces *kh-* with *h-*, as in Mikir; cf. Magari *hrap* 'weep' < TB **krap*.

115 It now seems that the **s-* prefix served rather to glottalize the following initial at the PLB stage, e.g. Atsi *nʔap*, Maru *nʔeʔ* 'snot' < TB **s-nap* (No. 102); cf. Burling, *PLB*, on Atsi and Maru; also Matisoff, 'GD' (JAM). The writer prefers to regard glottalization and aspiration here as alternative developments from TB prefixed **s-*, since a series such as B *hnap* < **nʔap* < **s-nap* seems unlikely.

116 Cf. Lepcha *ănyo*, a semantic doublet ('expletive') of *ămik* 'eye', and B *myak-hna* 'face' ('eye-nose').

117 Kanauri regularly has *st-* < *sn-*; cf. *stil* ~ *ťil* 'gums' < **s-nil*, *stiŋ* 'heart' < **s-niŋ*, *stiś* ~ *tiś* '7' < **s-nis*, and *stam* 'give forth smell' < **s-nam*.

(104) T *rmen-pa*~*śa-rmen* 'gland, wen', *rme-ba* 'speck, mark, mole', B *hmáń* 'mole' (TB **r-men*).

In addition to the regular consonant initials described above, we must postulate a 'zero' or vowel initial for Tibeto-Burman. Tibetan distinguishes between glottalized and non-glottalized vowel approach, written ʔ and ʾ respectively.[118] Burmese has simply the glottalized variety, which we have not indicated in our transcription. We lack adequate information on other TB languages, but the material in general suggests that the glottalized approach is the normal one in the TB area. The Tibetan distinction cannot be shown to be an inherited feature, and consequently we have reconstructed TB roots with pure vowel initial, with the rule that vowels in initial position were preglottalized. Note further that Tibetan has initial *yi-* as opposed to *ʾi-* or *ʔi-* (rare) and initial *ʾu-* and *ʔu-* but not *wu-*. The same general type of relationship obtains elsewhere, hence we can conclude that Tibeto-Burman had **(y)i-* and **(w)u-* but not contrasting types (we have reconstructed these roots without the semivowel).[119]

Illustrations of TB initial vowel:

(105) K and Nung *məa*, B *á*, L *a* 'to be dumb' (TB **(m-)a*).

(106) T *ʔag-tshom* 'beard of the chin' (='mouth-hair'; cf. the resp. term *źal-tshom*, with *źal* 'mouth'), Lepcha *ók* 'to open (as door, mouth)', Bunan *ag* 'mouth', B *ak* 'crack open', *ăak* 'opening, gap' (TB **ak*).

(107) K *up*~*wup*, Mikir *up*, B *up* 'to cover', L *up* 'to shelter' (TB **up*).

(108) T *ʔum* 'a kiss', Lepcha *ŭm* 'receive into mouth without swallowing', Miri *um-bom* 'hold (as inside the mouth)', Mikir *om*<**um* 'chew; mouthful', K *məum* 'hold, as water or smoke in the mouth', Nung *im* 'mouthful' (TB **um*).

(109) T *ʔud* 'swaggering, bragging', B *ut* 'noisy' (TB **ut*).

(110) T *ʔog*, B *auk* 'below' (TB **ok*).

(111) Magari *ol* 'to finish', G *ol* 'lax, loose; relax', L *o·l* 'to have little to do' (TB **o·l*).

(112) Mikir *ik*, B *ats-kui* 'older brother' (TB **ik*).

(113) Nung *i*<*ik* 'strangle', B *ats* 'squeeze, clench (the throat), throttle' (TB **ik*).

(114) T *yib-pa* 'hide one's self', K *ip*~*yip* 'cover, conceal (information)',

118 Cf. the study by G. L. M. Clauson and S. Yoshitake, 'On the Phonetic Value of the Tibetan Characters [ʾ] and [ʔ] and the Equivalent Characters in the *h*Phags-pa Alphabet', *JRAS* (1929), 843–62; also the remarks in O. Schrader, 'Siamese Mute H', *AM* 3 (1926), 33–48.

119 See n. 339; also n. 120.

ʔyup 'sleep', and Tsangla *ip* ~ *yip*, Bunan *ib*, Bahing *ip*, Nung *ip*, B *ip*, Ao Naga *yip*, Miri *yup* (Abor *ip*) 'to sleep' ('cover the eyes') (TB **ip*); for the semantics, see Benedict, 1939, p. 224.[120]

§9. Tibeto-Burman consonant clusters

TB consonant clusters, found only in root-initial position, are of two types: (*a*) stop or nasal + liquid (*r* ~ *l*), (*b*) consonant (or cluster of foregoing type) + semi-vowel (*w* ~ *y*). The following combinations can be established for Tibeto-Burman:

Medial *r*[121]	Medial *l*	Medial *w*	Medial *y*
kr	*kl*	*kw*	*ky*
gr	*gl*	*gw*	*gy*
—	—	*tw*	(*ty*)
—	—	*dw*	(*dy*)
pr	*pl*	*pw*	*py*
br	*bl*	*bw*	*by*
—	—	*sw*	*sy*[122]
—	—	(*zw*)	(*zy*)[122]
—	—	*tsw*	*tsy*[122]
—	—	(*dzw*)	(*dzy*)[122]

(cont. on p. 38)

120 The Mutwang dialect of Răwang (Nungish) has *yɨp* 'sleep', *śəyɨp* 'put to sleep' (Morse); Burmese also has the causative form *sip* 'put to sleep by lulling', from **s-ip*; the B-L data indicate a reconstruction with initial **y-*, and TB **yip* appears to be preferable to **ip* (text), especially in view of the recognition of a separate palatal series (n. 122).

121 We must add to this table TB *tr- and *dr- (n. 135), **sr-* and **śr-* (n. 304), **źr-* (n. 156), **zl-* (n. 136), perhaps also **zr-* for the following root: T *sril* ~ *srin* (*-bu*) 'worm (silk-worm)'; Thado *til* 'earthworm' (cf. also L *til* 'testicles'); B *ti* 'earthworm', from B-L **di* (Lisu *bi-di*); Chinese has a 'triplet' for 'earthworm' (all on same tone) pointing to an original initial such as **zr-* (n. 457).

122 In view of the recognition of the initial clusters **śr-* and **źr-*, it is advantageous to recognize a separate palatal series here: **ś-* for **sy-*, **ź-* for **zy-*, **tś-* (unit phoneme = *ć-*) for **tsy-*, and **dź-* (unit phoneme = *j-*) for **dzy-*. This also makes possible a contrast with palatalized dentals throughout, e.g. the reconstruction **m-(t)sin* 'nail, claw' becomes **m-tsyen*, with the medial **-ye-* yielding *-i-* in most forms, and the initial **tsy-* generally yielding *s-* or even (with voicing) *y-*; **(t)syaŋ* 'clear, pure, clean' becomes simply **syaŋ*; **s(y)ir* 'iron' becomes **syi·r* ~ **sya·l* (n. 244).

Medial *r*[121]	Medial *l*	Medial *w*	Medial *y* (cont.)
ŋr	—	(*ŋw*)	*ŋy*
—	—	*nw*	*ny*
mr	*ml*	*mw*	*my*
—	—	*rw*	*ry*
—	—	*lw*	*ly*
—	—	*hw*	(*hy*)
—	—	(*yw*)	—

Illustrations of TB initial clusters with *r* or *l*:

(115) T *skra*, Kanauri *kra*, K *kəra* 'hair (of head)' (TB **s-kra*).

(116) T *khrab-khrab* 'a weeper', Kanauri *krap*, Thulung (Kiranti) *khrap*, Magari *hrap*~*rap*, Digaro *khro*~*kro*, K *khrap*, G *grap*, L *ṭap*, Siyin *kap* 'weep' (TB **krap*).

(117) T *'khrud-pa*~*'khru-ba*, K *khrut*, B *khyuì*, Dimasa *gru* 'bathe, wash' (TB **kruw*).

(118) K *khru*, B *khruì*~*khyuì*, Lahu *gû*, G *kru*, Khami *məkhru*, Angami Naga *mekru* 'dove', L *ṭhu-mi* 'pigeon', *ṭhu-rou* 'dove' (TB **kruw*).[123]

(119) Bahing *khrit*, K *krit*, Nung *əgyit*, B *krit*, Mikir *tśiŋkrit* 'grind; gnash (the teeth)' (TB **krit*); cf. T *so khrig-khrig byed-pa* 'grind the teeth'.

123 The voiced Lahu initial of *gû* 'dove' seems to be the result of the nasal prefix (Khami, Angami). The nasal prefix may be the usual source of the PLB voiced series, with the following correspondences: Lahu voiced/Nasu voiced aspirate/Lolomaa prenasalized, the latter with redundant aspiration (as in Tibetan after prefixed *ḥ*- and *m*-); for the mysterious connection between nasality, aspiration and glottalization, see Matisoff, 'Lahu and PLB' and 'GD'. In the following words there is a correspondence between this series and K prefixed *mə*- (rarely *n*-) (JAM):

	Kachin	Lahu	Nasu	Lolomaa	Other
door	*nkha*	—	*a-gʿu*	*ŋkʿu*	B *tam-khà* < **ta-mkhà*
yeast	*mətsi*	*dî*	—	—	—
thrust	*mədźut*	*jûʔ*	—	—	—
pillow	*məkhum*	(*ú-*)*gɛ̂*	—	*ŋkʿɤ*	Nung *məkhim*
pound, v.	*mədup*	—	—	*ntʿv*	T *mthu*
wide	*məden*	—	*dʿɯ*	*ntʿɯ*	—
side	*məga*	*jâ*	—	—	—
very	*mədźan*	*jâ*	—	—	—
bridge	*məkhrai*	*go*	*dzʿɛ*	*ntsʿe*	—
liquor	*məgyep*	*jɨ̀*	*dʐʿi*	*ntʂʿʐ*	—

We now reconstruct **m-krəw*, since there is evidence for this nasal prefix in B-L as well as K-N, as indicated clearly by the above table of correspondences assembled by JAM, which includes two general TB roots: 'door' (No. 468) and 'pillow' (No. 482).

(120) T *graŋ-ba* 'cold, cool; coldness; to get or grow cold', L *ṭaŋ* 'dry', *ṭaŋ-tho·m* 'cold (weather)', Mikir *niŋ-kreŋ* 'cold weather, winter' (*niŋ* 'season') (TB **graŋ*).[124]

(121) T *sgro-ba* 'bark of willow', *gro-ga* 'thin bark of birch-tree', K *śəgrau* 'outer skin, as of fruit' (TB **s-graw*).

(122) T *grog-po* 'deep dell, ravine', B *khyauk* (prn. *dyauʔ*) 'chasm, gulf', K and Nung *khəro* 'ravine' (TB **grok*).

(123) Lepcha *klo*<*kla*, Mikir *klo*<*kla*, K *khrat* 'fall', B *kyá* 'fall', *khyá* 'let fall', L *tla·k* 'fall', *thla·k* 'let fall' (TB **kla*).

(124) B *kyak* 'to be cooked', *khyak* 'cook', Lahu *cá* 'to boil', K *khya* 'prepare glutinous rice', Mikir *arklak*~*arklok* 'boil over', L *tlak* 'boil or cook without salt' (TB **klak*).[125]

(125) Kanauri *khö*<*kli*,[126] Bahing *khli*, Digaro *klai*<*kli*, K *khyi*, B *khyè* (prn. *thyì*)~*ăkhyè*, G *khi* 'excrement', Lepcha *təkli* 'entrails, guts; mucus of entrails', also T *ltśi-ba* 'dung' (TB **kliy*).[127]

(126) Mikir *arkleŋ*, L *thliŋ*, B *khraŋ-tshi*, Lahu *ɔ̀-chɔ-pwɛ*~*ɔ̀-cɔ-pɔ* 'marrow', Dimasa *buthluŋ*~*bithlim* 'brain' ('skull-marrow') (TB **kliŋ*).[128]

(127) T *kluŋ* 'river', K *kruŋ* 'valley, dale', B *khyuíŋ* 'concave; concave piece of ground, valley' (TB **klu·ŋ*).[129]

124 There must be a B-L variant in final **-k*: Lahu *kâʔ*, Atsi *kyoʔ*, Maru *kyɔ̀ʔ*, Akha *gáʔ*, from PLB **krak* (JAM). Lisu has *dźya* 'cold', pointing to an original voiced initial, yielding B-L **grak*, a doublet of **graŋ*. Tibetan has *khyag(s)-pa* 'frozen; ice; the frost, cold', perhaps from **khlag* (**khl-* lacking in Tibetan), another possible cognate here; Lepcha has *hyáŋ* 'cold', of uncertain derivation. A variant root **glaŋ* must be recognized, however, on the basis of Trung (Nungish) *glaŋ* 'cold', Mikir *paŋ-kleŋ* 'to freeze, congeal' (note the parallel vocalism in the two roots). Finally JAM (1970 b) cites B-L **ngraŋ* 'cold', from **m-graŋ*.

125 This is a simplex/causative pair; the Lahu *cá* form descends from the causative member (B *khyak*); these are from **-l-* clusters (JAM).

126 Kanauri *ö*<*li*~*yi*; cf. *böŋ*~*pöŋ* 'fill'<TB **bliŋ*~**pliŋ*, *pö* '4'<TB **b-liy*.

127 Our analysis of the treatment of TB **l-* before the vowel *i* in Tibetan (n. 104) furnishes a simple explanation for the Tibetan form here: **s-kli* (prefixed **s-* with roots for parts of body)>*sklyi*>*hlyi* (Tibetan lacks initial **skl-*)>*ltśi*; contrast **sgl-* (also lacking in Tibetan), which yielded TB *zl-* in 'moon' (n. 137).

128 This is a very peculiar root, probably because of the initial **rkl-* group. Lahu has a palatal affricate where a front velar is expected. Lahu *c*/*ch* indicates proto-variation between a plain and a glottalized initial (<**skraŋ*) (JAM). We now reconstruct this root **r-kliŋ* (Mikir *arkleŋ*), yielding *kr-* in B-L through assimilation to the prefix; for the final, cf. B *hraŋ* 'alive'<TB **śriŋ* (probable effect of the complex initial group); cf. also Lepcha (*ă-*)*yăŋ*~(*ă-*)*yóŋ* 'brain, marrow'.

129 T *kluŋ* 'river' has frequently been compared with similar forms in S.E. Asia, notably Siamese *klɔ·ŋ*, Cham *krauŋ* and Ch. *kŭŋ*/*kɔŋ*[a] 'river' (in China specialized in reference to the Yangtse), but the TB root (**klu·ŋ*) may well be independent of

[a] 江

(128) T *gliŋ* 'island, continent; region, country', K *kriŋ-muŋ* 'hill' (cf. *kriŋ* 'firm, stable, immovable'), B *krań* 'dry land, ground', Lahu *mì-gɨ̀* 'land' (TB **gliŋ*).

(129) Thami (Kiranti) *əpra*, Digaro *pra*, L *ṭha*, Thado *əpha* 'good' (TB **pra*).

(130) T *spro-ba* 'delight in; wish', K *pro*~*pyo*, B *pyau* 'to be pleased, enjoy one's self' (TB **pro*).

(131) K *prut* ~ *śəprut*, B *prut* 'to boil' (TB **prut*).

(132) Kanauri *bra* 'forked (of roads)', *pra* 'spread, stretch', Bahing *bra* 'scatter; to be distant', K *bra* 'scattered, dispersed', B *prà* 'divided into several parts', G *bibra* 'junction', Dimasa *bara*~*bubra* 'confluence (of rivers), fork (of tree)' (TB **bra*).[130]

(133) Kanauri *bren* 'get well', K *bran* 'become convalescent, recover; increase', Nung *ban* 'convalesce', *dəban* 'heal', B *pran* 'return; repeat; recover from fainting' (TB **bran*).

(134) T *brag*, K *luŋ-bra*, G *roŋ-brak* 'rock' (TB **brak*).

(135) T *'braŋ-ba* 'to bear, give birth', L *piaŋ* 'to be born' (TB **braŋ*).

(136) T *'broŋ* 'wild yak', B *prauŋ* 'buffalo, bison' (TB **broŋ*).

(137) B *pra*, Mikir *phelo*<*phla*, G *tapra*, Dimasa *thapla* 'ashes' (TB **pla*).[131]

(138) K *bren*~*byen* 'flat and wide', *luŋ-byen* 'slab', *phun-pyen* 'plank', Nung *śiŋ-byen* 'plank', B *pyáń* 'to be reduced to a level; plank; flat surface', *kyauk-pyáń* 'flat level stone, slab', Mikir *kapleŋ* 'plank', G *bol-pleŋ*, Dimasa *boŋ-palaŋ*~*bo-phalaŋ* 'plank' (TB **pleŋ*).

(139) K *proŋ* 'to be burned, as a house', *kəproŋ* 'parboil', Mikir *phloŋ* 'burn the dead; cremation' (TB **ploŋ*).

(140) K *phroŋ* 'flee, run away', Mikir *arploŋ* 'run', *iŋploŋ* 'run, gallop' (TB **ploŋ*).[132]

(141) Kanauri *ble* 'to slip', Digaro *ble* 'slippery' (TB **ble*).

(142) Kanauri *böŋ*<*bliŋ* 'to be full', *pöŋ*<*pliŋ* 'fill', Kanashi *plen* 'fill', Lepcha (*a-*)*blyăn*<**bliŋ*, Digaro *bloŋ* 'full', Miri *büŋ* (Abor *buüŋ*) 'full', Nung *biŋ* 'to fill, be full', K *phriŋ* 'to be full', *dźəphriŋ* 'fill', B *práń* 'to be full', *phráń* 'fill, make full, complete', Lahu *bɨ̂* 'full', Mikir *pleŋ* 'full, complete; fulfill', *pepleŋ* 'fill', Dimasa *phuluŋ* 'fill in (rice into a basket)' (TB **bliŋ*~**pliŋ*).

all these; a more likely comparison is supplied by Lepcha *kyoŋ* 'river' (usu. in comp. with *uŋ* 'water'); cf. also T *ldźoŋs*<**lyoŋ-* (n. 104) 'large valley'.

130 For Kachin, Hanson (1906) also cites *bra* 'apart, forked', but Maran cites *braʔ*~*kăbraʔ* 'forked', indicating an original **brak*.

131 R. B. Jones (*Karen Linguistic Studies*, Berkeley, 1961) reconstructs a Proto-Karenic **khlà(h)* 'ashes'. Lahu has *qhɔ̀ʔ-lá*; cf. T *gog-thal* (JAM). See n. 364 for this root, which presents many difficulties.

132 Cf. B *hrauŋ* 'flee' (JAM).

In general, TB medial *l* clusters are better preserved than medial *r* clusters, while surd stop clusters are much better represented than sonant stop clusters. The several languages differ widely in their treatment of these clusters. Tibetan maintains most stop clusters, yet lacks initial *pl-*, which presumably has become *p(h)y-* (we have no certain examples for this shift). No comparisons have been found, however, for the few Tibetan words with initial *bl-* (incl. *bla* 'superior', *bla-ma* 'lama', *blu-ba* 'ransom', *blo* 'mind', *blon-po* 'officer'), and scarcely any for those with initial *gl-* (No. 128, and cf. T *gliŋ* 'flute, fife', B *kyań* 'tube closed at one end').[133] A number of northern TB languages, including Bahing, Lepcha, and Dhimal, preserve consonant clusters as well as or better than Tibetan. Kanauri retains medial *r* but not medial *l* clusters. In Kachin both types of clusters have fallen together into a single *r* type (sometimes medial *y* in the standard Kachin dialect). Burmese commonly has *r* for medial *r*, *y* for medial *l*, but there are numerous exceptions to this generalization (Nos. 117, 122, 126, 128, 130, 137, 142).[134] Garo and Dimasa preserve medial *r*, as well as initial *pl-* in some roots (Nos. 137, 138), but Dimasa *khi* 'excrement' < **kli* (No. 125) and *buthluŋ* ~ *bithlim* 'brain' < **kliŋ* (126) present contrasting types of development. Lushei has the cerebral stop *ṭ-* for the clusters **kr-*, **pr-*, and probably **gr-* (No. 120), but *t(h)l-* for **kl-* and apparently *pi-* [*py-*] for **br-* (No. 135). TB **gr-* and **br-* are each represented by the single comparisons cited, and neither **gl-* nor **bl-* can be traced with certainty; cf., however, L *ṭe·k*, Sho *glek* 'meteorite, thunderbolt' < Kuki-Naga **gle·k* (contrast Sho *kat* ~ *kak* < **krap* 'weep'). A few Kuki-Naga roots with initial clusters can be reconstructed on the basis of data from Northern Kuki (Thado, Siyin), which has *p(h)-* < **pr-*, *k(h)-* < **kr-*, or occasionally other languages:

**krap* 'weep': L *ṭap*, Siyin and Thado *kap*, Angami Naga *kra*.

**k(h)rok* 'sour': L *ṭok* 'sour', Angami Naga *khro* 'acid'.

**khrwi* 'sew': L *ṭhui*, Siyin *khui*; from TB **krwi(y)*; cf. K *tśyəwi* ~ *tśywi*.

**u-p(h)rok* 'toad': L *u-ṭok*, Thado *u-phoʔ*.

**phra* 'good': L *ṭha*, Thado *əpha*.

133 See Matisoff, 'GD', No. 98, for *gliŋ*/*kyań*.

134 The development *r* > *y* in Burmese has badly confused the phonetic picture here, and has led to frequent interchange between the two letters for these sounds in written Burmese (cf. No. 118). Medial *l* appears in many forms from the early inscriptions, but *r* ~ *l* ~ *ly* interchange is common even at that period (ca. A.D. 1100–1500). Medial *l* in the inscriptions corresponds to TB **r* as well as **l*, hence the Burmese evidence is not of critical value in making this distinction; cf. the following early forms: *klauk* for *kyauk* 'stone' (TB **r-luŋ*), *klwat* for *kywat* 'to be freed' (TB **g-lwat*), *klya* for *kyà* 'tiger' (Burmese-Lolo **k-la*), *khlyá* for *khyá* 'let fall' (TB **kla*), *klyak* for *kyak* 'to be cooked' (TB **klak*), but *khlauk* for *khrauk* '6' (TB **d-ruk*), *phlu* for *phru* 'white' (cf. Horpa *phru-phru*), *khley* for *khre* 'foot' (TB **kriy*).

**phral* 'cold (dry) season': L *ṭhal*, Siyin *phal(-bi)*.

The Mikir evidence is of special value in establishing the difference between **r* and **l* after surd stops, e.g. in relation to Kachin, which has *r* for both (cf. Nos. 139, 140).

Clusters such as **dr-*, **dl-*, **tr-*, **tl-*, **sr-*, **sl-* need not be postulated for the parent TB speech. Tibetan has *dr-*, *tr-* (*tram-pa* 'hard', *tron* 'diligence'), *sr-*, *sl-* and even *zl-*. The combinations *dr-*, *sr-* and *sl-* are to be construed as made up of prefix + initial **r-* or **l-*.[135] Tibetan *zl-* must be derived from **s-l-* (through assimilation), as in *zlog-pa* 'cause to return', *ldog-pa* (Pf. *log*) 'return', with *z-* for the normal causative prefix *s-* (cf. *slog-pa* 'turn'). Two general TB roots bear on this point:

(143) T *zlum-pa*, K *lum*, B *lùm* 'round, globular', L *hlum* 'ball' (TB **s-lum*).[136]

(144) T *zla-ba*, Bahing *la*, Vayu *tśolo* < **tśăla*, Digaro *həla* ~ *hlo*, Nung *səla*, B *lá* (Samong *səla*, Lolo **hla*), K *śəta*, Kadu *səda* (the dental in these two languages cannot be explained) 'moon' (TB **s-la*), but L *thla* < **khla*, Meithei *tha* < **khla*, Mikir *tśiklo* (cf. *tśikli* 'flea'), from TB **g-la*, whence perhaps Magari *gya(-hot)*.[137]

Some evidence exists for the nasal clusters **ŋr-*, **mr-* and **ml-*. Tibetan has initial *mr-* in *smra-ba* 'speak, talk', *smraŋ* ~ *smreŋ* 'word, speech', *smre-ba* 'wail, lament' (cf. B *mrwak* ~ *prwak* 'utter, speak', L *biak* 'speak'), and *nr-* in *snrubs* and *snron* 'names of two of the lunar mansions', *snrel(-g)źi* 'sloping, oblique; pell-mell'. Lepcha, which is especially rich in consonant clusters (many secondary), has *mr-* ~ *mry-*, *ml-* ~ *mly-*, and even *ŋr-*, but no certain comparisons have been found for words with these clusters. Burmese has a long series of words with initial *mr-*, and several words with *ŋr-*, while a number of initial *ml-* and *mly-* forms appear in the inscriptions, e.g. *mlauk* for *mrauk* 'north', *mlauŋ* for *mraùŋ* 'ditch', *mliy* for *mrè* 'grandchild', *mlyui* for *myui* 'to swallow', *mlyau* for *myaù* 'float'. Of the modern Burmese dialects, Tavoyan has retained *ml-* in a few words, notably *mle* for *mre* 'earth' and *mlè* for *mrè* 'grandchild', while Taungyo vacillates between

135 This generalization does not hold, since there is good evidence for **drup* rather than **d-rup* 'sew' (n. 320) and for **sram* rather than **s-ram* 'otter' (n. 302); also **tr-* has now been reconstructed in the root for 'weave': **trak* (n. 68); **sl-* probably occurred in the ancestral TB speech, especially in view of **zl-* (n. 136), but has not yet been demonstrated; **tl-* and **dl-* appear unlikely candidates for TB.

136 We now prefer to reconstruct TB **zlum*, the initial cluster **zl-* yielding both L *hl-* and B *l-* (TB **sl-* should yield B **hl-*); note that the cluster *zl-* in Tibetan is original in this root, but secondary in *zla-ba* 'moon' < **s-gla* (n. 137).

137 This root has now been reconstructed **s-gla*, on the basis especially of the Mikir and Magari forms. This also serves to explain K *śəta*, from **s-kla* < **s-gla*; cf. K *lətaʔ* 'hand' < **glak* (n. 109).

mr- and *ml-*. B *mrè* 'grandchild', *hmrà* 'arrow' and *mrwe* 'snake' all seem to be made up of prefixed *m* or *b*+initial *r-* or *l-* (see §**27**);[138] cf. also the following:

(145) Kanauri *raŋ*ʿ, Manchati *hraŋ*, Bunan *śraŋs* (Himalayish **s-raŋ-s*), Chepang *sĕraŋ* 'horse', but K *kumra*~*kumraŋ*, B *mràŋ*, Haka *raŋ* (TB **s-raŋ*~**m-raŋ*).[139]

The above root has a close parallel:

Kanauri *raŋ*, B *mráŋ* 'high'.[140]

Direct comparisons of the initial cluster are also available:

(146) Murmi (Bodish) *mraŋ*, B *mraŋ* 'see', perhaps also Nung *yaŋ*, *id.* (TB **mraŋ̇*).[140]

(147) B *mrak* 'cut keenly', *mrá* 'very sharp, keen', K *mya* 'torn, ragged', *əmra*~*əmya* tear, maul, lacerate', Dimasa *dźəbrau*<**dźəbrak* 'maul, claw, scratch' (TB **mrak*).[141]

(148) T *bra-ba* 'to have or be in great plenty, abound', Kanauri *mra*, Manyak (Hsi-fan group) *təbra*, B *myà* 'much, many' (TB **mra*).

(149) Kanauri *myag*, B *mrak* 'grass' (TB **mrak*).[142]

(150) T *'bru* 'grain, seed', K *myu*~*əmyu* 'kind, sort, tribe', B *myuì* 'seed', *ămyuì* 'race, lineage; kind, class, sort' (TB **mruw*).

138 Prefixed *m*+*r*/*y* becomes a voiced initial, as above: **mr*, **my*>Lahu *m* ('monkey', etc.), but see 'grandchild': Lahu *hɔ̄*, from **ml* (<**hl*) for another development (JAM). The TB root for the latter is **b-ləy*, suggesting a development of the type: **b-ləy*>**phləy*>**hləy*.

139 T *rta* is a possible cognate of this root (n. 102) (JAM). K *kumraŋ* appears to represent the product of a double prefixation: **k-m-raŋ*, including the TB **k-* 'animal prefix' (n. 301). In Himalayish the earlier **m-* prefix was dropped (normal development here), then the TB **s-* 'animal prefix' (p. 107) was added, yielding **s-raŋ-s* (see n. 290 for the final **-s*). Inasmuch as the horse, a relatively recent arrival here (S.E. Asia), is often described in derived forms (IN has **ad'ar/an* 'the learned one'), one is tempted to relate this TB root for 'horse' to the root for 'high' (see text)='the high (*-raŋ*) one (*m-*)' (the equivalent of 'its highness'); the *auk-myit* of B *mráŋ* 'high' relates to either tone in that language, hence there is no basic tonal discrepancy here (see §**12**).

140 Trung (Nungish) has *mraŋ* 'high, long', establishing the presence of prefixed **m-* for this root (Kanauri drops most prefixes). Răwang, another Nungish language, has *haŋ* 'high' (apparently unrelated) but *yaŋ* 'long', the latter providing a parallel for Răwang *yaŋ* 'see' (No. 146), yet the loss of the prefix in this Nungish language is unexpected.

141 Trung (Nungish) has *pra*<**pra* or **prak* (Trung simply drops TB final **-k*) 'to cut with sharp instrument', suggesting the possibility of an original **pr-* or **br-* in this root or in a doublet root (note Dimasa *dźəbrau*<**dźəbrak*).

142 T *'dźag-ma* 'grass', from **a-lyag* (n. 104) belongs in this set, yielding the TB reconstruction **m-lyak* (with Tibetan substituting TB **a-* for **m-*). It can now be seen that Kanauri has *mr-* for **mr-* (No. 148) but simply *r-* for prefixed **m-r-* (No. 145 and 'high'), also *my-* for both **ml-* (No. 153) and **m-l-* (No. 149).

Note that Tibetan has developed *br-* in roots of this type. Burmese appears to have *mr-* for **br-* (cf. B *m-* < prefixed **b-* before liquids) in at least one root:

(151) T *'brub-pa* 'cause to overflow, gush, spout forth', *'brubs* 'water that has flowed over', K *phrup* 'squirt, as water with the mouth', G *brip* 'flood', *prip-at* 'overwhelm', B *mrup* 'to be submerged, overwhelmed, buried', *hmrup* 'submerge' (TB **brup* ~ **prup*).

Initial **ml-* is indicated for the following pair of roots:

(152) Mikir *mili* ~ *meli* 'sand-bank, bare ground', Nung dial. *məli* 'country; mountain', Manyak (Hsi-fan group) *məli* ~ *mli*, B *mre*, Tavoyan dial. *mle*, Phön (Samong dial.) *təmli* ~ *təmyi* 'earth' (TB **mliy*).

(153) Kanauri *myṵ* 'to swallow' (nasalization not explained), K *məyuʔ* 'throat; to swallow', B *myui* (inscriptions *mlyui*) 'to swallow' (TB **mlyuw*).[143]

Initial **ŋr-* can provisionally be reconstructed for the following roots:

(154) B *ŋrà*, K *nya* 'meet, encounter' (TB **ŋra*).

(155) B *ŋraŋ* 'contradict, deny', Nung *ŋyeŋ* 'deny', *əŋyeŋ* 'slant' ~ *əŋeŋ* 'oblique' (TB **ŋraŋ*); cf. L *ṭaŋ* < **graŋ* 'deny'.

(156) B *ŋrui* ~ *ńui* 'dark in color; darken', *hńuì* 'dull, faded, wither', K *nyui* 'faded, wilted, withered', Nung *ŋyö* 'withered', *əŋyü* 'fade' (TB **ŋruw*).

Illustrations of TB initial clusters with **w* or **y*:

(157) B *kwaì* 'dammer-bee', L *khuai* ~ *khoi*, Thado *khoi* ~ *khui-va* (*va* 'bird'), Tangkhul *khui*, Lakher *əkha* 'bee', Nung *kha* 'bee (domesticated)' (TB **kwa·y*).[144]

(158) T *rkon-pa* ~ *skon-pa* 'basket; fowler's net', Lepcha *kun* 'sort of fishnet', K *sumgon*, Nung *gun*, B *kwan* 'casting net' (TB **kwan*).[145]

(159) T *khyi*, Kanauri *kui*, Thebor *khui*, Vayu *uri*, Chepang *kwi*, Bahing *khli-tśa*, Limbu *khi-a*, Digaro *nkwi*, K *gwi*, Jili *təkwi*, Nung *təgi*, B *khwè*, 'Garo A' dialects **kui* (Koch and Ruga *kui*, Rabha *ki*), Dimasa *si*, L (and general Kuki) *ui*, Mikir *hi* < **khi* (obsolete word recorded by Robinson, 1849) 'dog' (TB **kwiy*).[146]

(160) T *bgo-ba* 'put on (clothes)', *gon-pa* 'put on (clothes); clothing', *gos* 'garment, dress', *skon-pa* 'to dress, to clothe another person', K *khon* 'wear (as bracelets)', Nung *gwa* ~ *ga* 'to dress' (intr.), *dəgwa* ~ *dəga* (tr.), *gwa-lam* 'clothes', Lisu *gwa* 'to dress', Menia (Hsi-fan) *ga-ma* 'clothes', G *gan* 'wear, dress', Mikir *kan* 'clothes, finery' (TB **gwa* ~ **kwa*).

143 Angami Naga (Burling, 1962), like Kachin, handles this root as a prefixed form: *me-zu* 'to swallow', from **m-yu*; cf. also Karen (n. 403).

144 This root is also represented by Gurung *kwe*, Thakali *koy* 'bee'; it has been identified as a possible early loan-word from AT (Benedict, 1967 bis).

145 A doublet **gwan* must be recognized here; cf. K *sumgon*, Nung *gun*, B-L **gwan* (Maru *gùm*; Atsi *sùmgòn* is a loan from Kachin); the Chinese evidence indicates that the final *-n* is an old suffix (n. 428).

146 See n. 83 for the loss of initial **k-* in Kuki.

(161) T *skyoŋ-ba*, pf. *bskyaŋs* 'guard; keep, tend (cattle)', B *kyaùŋ* 'feed, tend cattle' (TB **kyoŋ*).

(162) T *skyeŋ-ba* 'to be ashamed', K *khyeŋ* ~ *tśeŋ* 'red, crimson' (TB **kyeŋ*).[147]

(163) T *brgyad*, Kanauri *ræ*, Bahing *ya*, Thulung *yet*, Dumi *ri*, K *mətsat*, Nung *əśat*, B *hrats*, G *tśhet*, Dimasa *dźai* < *dźat*, L *riat* (Kuki **d-ryat*) '8' (TB **b-r-gyat*).[148]

(164) T *brgya*, K *lətsa*, Nung *ya*, B *ăra*, G *rittśa*, Dimasa *radźa*, L *za* < *ya* '100' (TB **r-gya*).[148]

(165) T *mtho* 'span', B *thwa* 'measure with a span', *ăthwa* 'span' (TB **twa*).

(166) K *dəwi* ~ *dwi*, G *tśi*, Dimasa *di* ~ *gidi* 'sweet', L *tui* 'nice (to taste or smell)' ('sweet' in Thado and other Kuki languages) (TB **twi(y)*).

(167) K *twi* 'suppurate (as a boil)', B *twe* 'flow moderately and incessantly' (TB **twiy*).

(168) L (and general Kuki) *tui* 'water; egg ("fowl-water")', Dhimal *tui* 'egg'; also K *məthwi* 'to spit', B *thwè* 'to spit', *tam-thwè* (perhaps from **ta-mthwè*) 'saliva, spittle' (TB **twiy*).[149]

(169) T *doŋ* 'deep hole, pit, ditch', Nung *duŋ-khr* 'hole', B *twaŋ* 'hole, pit', Lahu *γɨ-tû*, Lisu *du* 'well' (B *re-twàŋ*, lit. 'water-pit'), Lolopho *śi-du* ~ *hi-du* 'cave, hole', Nyi Lolo *fe-du* 'cave', *pu-du* 'hole' (TB **dwaŋ*).[150]

147 B *kyaŋ*, an intensive used with *ni* 'red', belongs with this root: *ni-kyaŋ-kyaŋ* 'pale red' (= color of blushing); this form supports the reconstruction of the initial cluster **ky-* in this root.

148 This pair of numeral roots presents unusual difficulties both in TB and in Chinese (n. 435). Tibetan is distinctive in having the same initial group (*brgy-*) for both roots; the *b-* is an added prefix which is matched in one root by Kachin (*mətsat* '8'). The root for '8' was metathesized in Tibetan: *brgyad* < **bgryad* (Tibetan lacks the initial group **bgry-*). The element **-gryad* represents the basic TB root **g-ryat*, whence B *hrats* via **hret*; Kachin has *mətsat* < **b-kyat* < **b-kryat* by regular shifts (treating **g-ry-* as an initial cluster); Kuki-Naga has replaced the prefix: **d-ryat* for **g-ryat*, apparently under the influence of TB **d-ruk* '6' and **d-kəw* '9'. Chinese shows a contrasting type of development (n. 435), with metathesis of the root for '100' rather than for '8' and with replacement of the prefix **g-* with **b-* (paralleling a common development in TB in the roots for '3' and '5') rather than with **d-*.

149 Cf. Benedict, 1939, p. 225, for the semantics of this root. Lushei preserves the full compound *ar-tui* 'fowl-water' only in *ke-ar-tui* 'heel' ('foot-egg'), Mikir *keŋ-ti*. TB **ti(y)* 'wet; water' (No. 55) has yielded K *mədi* 'wet', *di* 'egg', Moshang *wu-di* 'egg' ('fowl-egg'), also G *tśi* 'water', *bitśi* ~ *do-bitśi* 'egg' ('fowl-its-water'), *khu-tśi* 'saliva' ('mouth-water') and the parallel Dimasa *di* series. Dhimal distinguishes between *tui* 'egg' (TB **twiy*) and *tśi* (Toto *ti*) 'water', *thop-tśi* 'spittle', *hna-thi* 'snot' (TB **ti(y)*).

150 Tiddim Chin *wa·ŋ* 'hole; make a hole' appears to be cognate here, indicating a reconstruction **dwa·ŋ*.

(170) B *phwaì* 'husks, chaff', L *phuai* 'shavings', Pankhu *phəwai*, Thado *wai*, Rangkhol *śəbai∼səvai*, Sopvoma *upfai<əphwai* 'husks' (TB **pwa·y*).

(171) L (and general Kuki) *pui* 'feminine affix', K *wi∼yi* 'feminine affix', *śəwi∼śəyi* 'female' (TB **pwi(y)*).

(172) T *sbom-pa* 'thick, stout, coarse', K *bom* 'swell', *bom-bom* 'swelling; round and chubby', B *phwám* 'fat, plump', L *puam* 'swollen; to swell' (TB **bwam*).

(173) T *byi-ba* 'rat, mouse', B *pwè*, L *bui* 'bamboo rat' (TB **bwiy*).

(174) T *phyag-ma* 'broom', *'phyag-pa* 'sweep', L *hmun phiat* 'sweep', *hmun phiaʔ* 'broom', Empeo *piag*, Chepang *phek*, Mikir *arphek* 'broom', Miri *pök* 'sweep', *sam-pök* 'broom', K *we∼ye* 'sweep', *diŋye* 'broom' (TB **pyak*).

(175) T *dpyaŋ-ba∼spyaŋ-ba∼'phyaŋ-ba*, K *əphyaŋ* 'hang' (TB **pyaŋ*).

(176) T *'phyo-ba* 'swim, soar, float', K *pyau∼byau* 'fly, float; play, shoot, as a fish' (TB **pyaw*).

(177) T *bya* 'bird, fowl', B *pyà* (Ahi *do*, Lolopho *byo*, Nyi *dla-ma*, Lisu *byæ*) 'bee' (TB **bya*); for the semantics cf. No. 157.[151]

(178) T *'byor-ba∼'byar-ba* 'stick to, adhere to', *sbyor-ba*, pf. *sbyar* 'affix, attach; compile, compose; join, connect', Bahing *phyer* 'sew', L *phiar* 'knit, plait, be entangled; plot, conspire, plan' (TB **byar∼*pyar*).

(179) T *'byon-pa* 'go', K *byon* 'come or go out of' (TB **byon*).

(180) K *ləsəwi* 'shave or whittle off', *gəsəwi* 'rub up against (as a dog)', B *swè* 'whet, rub, polish', G *si-rok* 'shave', Dimasa *si*, L *sui* 'scrape' (TB **s(y)wiy*).

(181) T *śa* 'flesh, meat', *śa-ba∼śwa-ba* 'hart, stag', Kanauri *śya* 'flesh, meat, game', Magari *mi-śia* 'flesh, meat', Bahing *sye*, Sangpang *sya* 'flesh', K *śan* 'flesh, meat, deer flesh; deer', Nung *śa* (dial. *śia*) 'flesh, meat', B *sà∼ăsà* 'flesh', *sà* 'beast', L *sa* 'animal'∼*śa* 'flesh, meat' (TB **sya*).

(182) T *śes-pa*, Vayu *ses*, B *sí* 'know, understand', K *śi* 'news', G *masi*, Dimasa *mathi∼mithi* 'know', Bodo *mithi* 'know', *dithi∼khithi* 'show' (TB **syey*).

(183) K *mətsəwi∼mətswi* 'pus', B *tshwè* 'decayed, crumbling; rotten' (TB **tswiy*).

(184) G *gittśak* 'red', Dimasa *gadźau<gadźak* 'red; gold', L *raŋ-ka-tśak* 'gold' (cf. *raŋ-va* 'tin'), K *dźa* 'gold', Nung *za* 'silver, money' (TB **tsyak*).[152]

151 Nyi **dy-* does not occur, hence we must assume **by->* Nyi *dl-*; this is the reverse of the Tibetan development shown in 'four': TB **b-l->*by->*bź-* (JAM). Gyarung has *prye<*pra* (also *pra-* in comp.) 'fowl', *pra-khu* 'owl'; Angami Naga (Burling, 1962) has *pera<*bra* or **b-ra* 'fowl'; a doublet **bra* must be recognized on this basis; there is also a possibility that this is an old loan from AT (Benedict, 1967bis).

152 Cf. Benedict, 1939, pp. 222–3, for the semantics of this root (T *ser* 'yellow', *gser* 'gold', Gyarung *kəwurni* (<**g-rni*) 'red', *tərni* (<**d-rni*) 'gold'; Ahi Lolo *tho* 'white; silver')).

(185) T *gtśod-pa*, pf. *btśad*, L *tśat* 'break, cut' (TB **tsyat*).

(186) K *tśyap* 'to be on friendly terms; to adhere, as soot to a roof', B *tsap* 'join, unite, connect', G *tśap-tśap* 'adjacent' (TB **tsyap*).

(187) Bahing *tśyar* 'shine', K *dźan*, Moshang *roŋ-śarr*, G *sal* 'sun' (TB **tsyar*).

(188) Bahing *tśyur* 'wring', Bunan *tśhur* 'squeeze out', Kanauri *tsŭr* 'to milk', Haka *śur* 'wring' (TB **tsyur*).

(189) T *nya*, Chepang *ŋa*~*nya*, Lepcha *ŋo*, Tsangla *ŋa*, K *ŋa*, Nung *ŋa*, B *ŋà*, G *na-tŏk*, Bodo *ŋa*~*na*, L *hŋa* 'fish' (TB **ŋya*).

(190) T *brnya-ba*~*brnyan-pa* 'borrow', Nung *ŋa* 'hire, rent, lend', B *hŋà* 'borrow or lend, hire or let (the same article to be returned)' (TB **r-ŋya*).

(191) K *məni*, Bodo and Dimasa *mini*, L *nui* (Kuki **m-nui*) 'laugh' (TB **m-nwi(y)*).

(192) T *rnyab-rnyab-pa* 'seize or snatch together', K *nyap* 'squeeze; extort', B *ńap* 'to be squeezed', *hńap* 'pinch, squeeze; blacksmith's tongs' (TB **nyap*).

(193) T *nyen-pa* 'to be pained, pinched, pressed hard; to toil and moil', K *nyen* 'coax, defraud', *śənyen* 'take by force, coerce', B *ńàń* 'sigh, moan, groan; grumble or murmur at', *hńàń* 'hurt, oppress, bully' (TB **nyen*).

(194) T *snyuŋ* 'disease, illness', *snyuŋ-ba* 'to be ill', K *nyuŋ* 'sad, dejected', B *ńauŋ* 'to ache, be tired, cramped' (TB **nyuŋ*).

(195) B *hmwé* 'twirl about', L *hmui-thal*~*hmui-thlur*, Siyin *mui* 'spindle' (TB **(s-)mwiy*).

(196) T *rmi-ba* 'to dream', Magari *mi*, Miju *mui* 'to sleep', K *śəməwi* 'to be heavy with sleep', B *mwé* 'sleep, enjoy sleep' (TB **mwiy*).

(197) Bahing *myel* 'to be sleepy', K *myen*~*mye* 'fall into sleep or swoon', B *myàń* 'to be sleepy, to sleep' (TB **myel*).

(198) T *rod-pa* 'stiff, unable to help one's self', B *rwat* 'old, tough' (TB **rwat*).

(199) T *grog-ma*, Gyarung *kŏrŏk*, Lohorong and Lambichong (Kiranti) *khorok*, Miri *təruk*, Dafla *torub*, Nung *sərɔ*, B *părwak* 'ant' (TB **rwak*).[153]

(200) K *rəwi* 'gently sloping, slanting', B *hrwe* 'slant, be oblique' (TB **rwiy*).

(201) L (and general Kuki) *hrwi*, Digaro *tərui*~*təroi*, Abor *tərü* 'cane' (TB **rwi(y)*).

(202) T *gźa-ba* 'to sport, joke, play', *gźas* 'play, joke', *bźad-pa*~*gźad-pa* 'laugh, smile', Thebor *rot*, Bunan *sred*, Magari *ret*, Bahing *rit*~*ris*, Khaling *ret*, Nachereng *hres*, Nung *it*, Digaro *məra*, Aka *ra*, B *rai* 'laugh' (TB **rya-t*).

153 Labu *pú-γɔ̂ʔ* 'ant'; the first element (B *pă-*) is from the 'insect' root (No. 27); see 'GD', No. 97 (JAM). Other TB languages usually exhibit either the TB **k-* 'animal prefix' (Tibetan, Gyarung and Kiranti) or the **s-* 'animal prefix' (Nung), while Miri-Dafla has the late **d-* prefix, the root apparently never occurring without prefix.

(203) T *źag* (Lahuli *gyag*), Manchati *hrag*~*rag*, Lepcha *'ayak*, K *ya*, B *rak* 'day (24 hours)', L *riak* 'pass the night' (TB **ryak*).[154]

(204) T *źag* 'fat, grease (in a liquid state)', L *sa-hriak* 'oil, grease' (*sa* 'flesh'), B *pàn-rak*~*wat-rak* 'juice of flowers' (TB **ryak*).

(205) T *źaŋ(-po)*~*ʔa-źaŋ* 'uncle (mother's brother)', B *ăhraŋ* 'master, lord' (written *ăhsyaŋ* in addressing a monarch), Kuki **r(y)aŋ* (Chawte *raŋ*~*əraŋ*, Laiyo *raŋ*, Thado *gaŋ*, Siyin *ŋaŋ*) 'father's sister's husband' (TB **ryaŋ*).[155, 156]

(206) K *yut* 'become or grow worse, as illness', *śəyut* 'to be apathetic, indifferent', B *yut* 'inferior, mean', *hrut* 'to put down' (TB **ryut*).

(207) K *yau* 'to be mixed', *kəyau* 'mix, intermix', B *rau* 'mix, mingle' (TB **ryaw*).

(208) K *ŋəloi*, B *kywai*<*klwai*, L *loi*, Siyin *loai* 'buffalo' (TB **lwa·y*).

(209) T *hlod-pa* 'loose, relaxed', *glod-pa* 'loosen, relax, slacken', K *lot* 'escape; be free, unrestrained', *śəlot* 'set free', B *lwat* 'to be free', *hlwat* 'free, release', *kywat*<*klwat* 'loosed, freed', *khywat* 'release, free' (TB **g-lwat*).

(210) K *ləwi*~*lwi* 'flow, as water', L (and general Kuki) *lui* 'stream, river' (TB **lwi(y)*).

(211) Lepcha *lyak* 'to taste, try' (Grünwedel), B *lyak*, Nung *la*~*lɛ*, Miri *yak*, G *srak*, L *liak*, Mikir *iŋlek*, Tangkhul *khəməlek* 'lick'; Magari *let*, K *śiŋlet*~*śiŋlep* (Maran dial. *śiŋriat*), T *ldźags* (resp.) 'tongue', from TB **(m-)lyak*~**(s-)lyak*;[157] cf. the related roots: L *hliau* 'lick (as flames)', K *śiŋlau* 'tongue' (couplet form), from TB **(s-)lya·w*; Bahing *liam*, Khambu and Yakha *lem* 'tongue', B *ăhlyam* 'coruscation of flame', from TB **(s-)lyam*.[158]

(212) T *leb-mo* 'flat', *gleb-pa* 'make flat', B *lyap* 'very thin' (TB **lyap*).

154 Lahu *há* 'night; pass the night'; PLB **hr-*; see Manchati *hrag*, from TB **s-ryak* or **źryak* (T **śr-* > *ś-*, **źr-* > *ź-*). We can now reconstruct TB **s-ryak* on the basis of the above evidence (T *źag* is from **ryag*, without the prefix), and the prefix can also be reconstructed for ST itself, since it appears in the Chinese cognate (n. 457).

155 Cf. the honorific use of T *źaŋ* in early texts, e.g. *źaŋ-źaŋ* or *rgya-źaŋ* 'chief uncle', *źaŋ-loŋ* 'councillor', *źaŋ-blon* 'minister'.

156 This root has been reconstructed **źraŋ* (Benedict, 1948), with the initial cluster **źr-* contrasting with **zr-* (**zril* 'worm', n. 121); the Kuki root is **traŋ* 'father's sister's husband', as shown by Haka *(k-)traŋ* (cited in Benedict, 1941) (Lushei lacks this root); cf. also Miri *(ă-)bu riaŋ* 'father's (*ă-bu*) younger brother'.

157 Another simplex/causative pair: Lahu *lɛ̀ʔ*/*lɛ́* 'lick'/'feed an animal'<PLB **lyak*/*ʔlyak* (JAM).

158 Kanauri and Thebor *lem* 'lick' probably also belong in this set, but Lepcha *lim* 'to flame up, as fire' (*ă-lim* 'flame') points rather to a basic medial **-ya-*~**-i-* alternation in this root (see n. 251). B *hlya* 'tongue' is a possible cognate via an old suffixed form such as **hlyam-ma*, whence **hlya-ma*.

(213) Lepcha *lyop* < **lyap* 'glitter, flash, glisten', *sălyop* 'sheet-lightning', B *hlyap* 'glitter; lightning' (TB **lyap*).

TB medial **w*, found only before *a* and *i*, is well preserved in Burmese and Lushei, and appears less regularly in Kanauri, Digaro, Nung and many other TB languages. Kachin maintains **w* before *i* (often with epenthetic *ə*), with the noteworthy exception of *məni* 'laugh' < TB **m-nwi(y)*, apparently through dissimilation. Kachin and Tibetan share in the development: **wa* > *o* (Nos. 158, 160, 165, 169, 170, 198, 199, 209).[159] Lepcha has **a* > *o*, but **wa* > *u*: *kun* 'net' < TB **kwan*; *sătum* 'wolf' < TB **d-wam*. Miri also has *u* for **wa*: *təruk* 'ant' < TB **rwak*; *situm* 'bear' < TB **d-wam*. There is further evidence for this shift in Kaçhin:

B *twán* 'wrinkled; shrink', K *thun* 'shrink'.

B *lwan* 'gimlet; bore with a gimlet', K *gəlun* 'thrust, pierce, as with a spear'.

A few Tibetan words are written with a symbol called *wa-zur* ('angular *w*'), which appears only before *-a*. *Wa-zur* may have been phonetic in some instances, as argued by Laufer,[160,161] but we lack good comparative material in support of such a view. In at least two words, on the other hand, *wa-zur* seems to have functioned simply as a device for distinguishing between homonyms; cf. T *św a-ba* for *śa-ba* 'hart', from *śa* 'flesh' < TB **sya* (No. 181), and the following:

(214) T *tshwa*, Kanauri *tsa*, B *tshà* 'salt' (TB **tsa*).

This contrasts in the written language with T *tsha* 'hot' < TB **tsa* (No. 62). In view of the considerable body of material in support of the shift: TB **wa* > T *o*, we must conclude that *wa-zur* does not represent TB medial **w*.

The clusters **zw-*, **dzw-* (but note **dzyw-* in No. 242), **ŋw-*, **hw-* and **yw-* are difficult to establish for TB roots, yet it is highly likely that all five existed in the parent TB speech.[162] Initial *ŋw-* (*ŋu-*) is found both in Burmese and Lushei,

159 The *wa* > *o* shift, though especially characteristic of Tibetan and Kachin, is also found elsewhere; note L *oi* < *wai* in Nos. 157 and 208. In Modern Burmese the development has been as follows: *waŋ* > *wę* ~ *wį*, *wak* > *weʔ*, *wan* ~ *wam* > *wų*, *wat* ~ *wap* > *wuʔ* (but final *-wa* is maintained). Both medial and final *wa* interchange with *au* (> *ɔ*) in the Pagan inscriptions, e.g. *rwauh* for *rwa* 'village', *kyaun* ~ *kywaun* for *kywan* 'slave', *saun* for *swan* 'pour'.

160 B. Laufer, 'Ueber das *va zur*: ein Beitrag zur Phonetik der tibetischen Sprache', *WZKM* **12** (1898), 289–307; **13** (1899), 199–226.

161 Tibetan *wa-zur* appears to have been phonetic (for earlier *wa* or *â*) in some instances; cf. T *tshwa* 'salt' (text), Ch. *dzʻâ*,[a] *id.* (n. 487); T *rwa* 'horn' (p. 113); also T *rtswa* 'grass', with the medial *-w-* element preserved in Balti and Purik *rtswa* ~ *stswa*; cf. Ch. *dzʻwən*/*dzʻuən* ~ *dzʻiən*/*dzʻien*[b] 'grass, herb' (n. 455), but *tsʻôg*/*tsʻâu*[c] 'grass' appears to be only a pseudo-cognate.

162 TB initial **dzw-* can be inferred from one B-L root which must be reconstructed with this initial cluster: B *tswan* 'kite; (in comp.) hawk', Atsi *tsûn*, Lahu *á-cè* 'kite', Lisu *dzye* 'hawk, eagle; (in comp.) kite', with a Chinese cognate (n. 453).

[a] 鹺 [b] 荐 [c] 草

but no cross-correspondences have been uncovered.[163] Burmese appears to have shifted **ŋw-* to *nw-* in one root:

(215) K *ŋa*, Moshang *ŋa*, Nung *ŋwa* ~ *ŋa* ~ *nwa*, B *nwà* 'cattle' (TB **ŋwa*).[164,165]

The evidence of TB **hw-* is extensive but difficult to interpret. Burmese has this cluster in a few words, but it seems to be secondary here; cf. B *phwak* ~ *hwak* 'hide' (No. 46) and *khwé* ~ *hwé* 'push with the head, butt'.[166] Lushei has initial *hu-* in the following pair of roots:

(216) L *huam*, K *wam*, B *wám* 'dare' (TB **hwam*).

(217) L *huaŋ* 'yard, enclosure', K *waŋ* 'surround, encircle; circle, enclosure, compound', *śəwaŋ* 'shut in, fence in', Nung *waŋ* 'surround', B *wàŋ* 'fence made of wrought materials, forming an enclosure', Kiranti **waŋ-waŋ* 'circular' (Balali *waŋ-waŋ*, Lohorong *weŋ-weŋ*) (TB **hwaŋ*).

Another root with initial **hw-* can be set up on the basis of the Bunan correspondence:

(218) Bunan *hwaŋs* ~ *hoaŋs* 'come out, go out', T *'oŋ-ba* < *'*waŋ* 'come', Dhimal *waŋ*, B *waŋ* 'enter' (TB **hwaŋ*).

Nung has initial *hw-* in the following pair:

(219) Nung *hwap* (dial. *ab*), Bahing *ap*, Miri *ap*, Lepcha *óp* < **ap*, Vayu *wop* < **wap* 'shoot (bow, gun)', but Tsangla *gap*, Magari *ŋap*, K *gap*, Go *go*, Dimasa *gau* < **ga·p*, L (and general Kuki) *ka·p*, *id.* (TB **ga·p*).

(220) Nung *hwar* 'burn, kindle', K *ʔwan*, Moshang *var*, G *waʔl* 'fire', but Chairel *phal* < **phar*, *id.*, and T *'bar-ba* 'burn, catch fire, be ignited', *sbor-ba* (pf. *sbar*) 'light, kindle', Kanauri *bar* 'burn' (intr.), *par* (tr.), Miri *par* 'light (as a fire), ignite' (TB **bar* ~ **par*).[167]

Both these roots probably illustrate loss of initial stop, as described above (§ **8**), although the latter might be prefixed, e.g. **g-a·p* or **g-(h)wa·p*.

The cluster **hw-* has been reconstructed for the additional pair of roots:

(221) Bahing *hwa* 'light', Lepcha *o-m* 'shine', *om-bo* 'illuminating', *a-om*

163 TB also has initial **ŋw-* in the following root of limited occurrence: Bahing *ŋwap* 'cousin', Lepcha *ă-ŋop* 'levirate or sororate spouse (marriageable affinal kin)', from TB **ŋwap*.

164 Note the restricted eastern distribution of this root, which is to be regarded as an early loan from Thai **ŋua*. Chinese *ŋi̯ŭg* > *ŋi̯ə̯u*[a] is distinct from this series.

165 This has been identified as an early loan from AT (Benedict, 1967bis); cf. also Gyarung (K. Chang) *ńiŋwye* < **ńiŋwa*, and Trung (Nungish) *ŋuŋ ŋua*; Tibetan has *nor* 'cattle' (used mainly in derived meanings of 'property, wealth' and even 'money'), apparently from **nwar* (cf. the Burmese form), but the final *-r* is enigmatic.

166 For 'hide' see n. 88; Lahu has *gûʔ* 'butt with head' (JAM).

167 See n. 78 for the present analysis of this root.

[a] 牛

'light, brightness', T *'od* < **ʔwad* 'light, shine, brightness', *nyi-ʔod* 'sunlight', B *ne-at* 'sunlight' (archaic), Thado *wat* 'shine' (TB **hwa-t*).

(222) Kanauri *śui*, Bunan *śu*, Chepang *wi* ~ *wei*, Vayu *vi*, Tsangla *yi*,[168] Magari *hyu* [*hü*] < **hwi* (cf. *tśhyu* 'dog' < **khwi*), Lepcha *vi*, Bahing *hu-si*, Dumi, Sangpang, Waling, Dungmali *hi*, Lohorong *həri*, Lambichong and Chingtang *həli* < **hwi* (cf. Vayu *uri*, Bahing *khli* 'dog' < **khwi*), Digaro *həroi* ~ *hrwei*, Miri *iyi*, K *sai*, Nung *śö*, B *swè*, G *antśi*, Dimasa *thi*, L *thi*, Mikir *vi*, Meithei *i* 'blood' (TB **s-hwiy*).[169]

In the latter root, note K *sai* rather than the anticipated **swi* ~ **səwi*, and L *thi* rather than **thui* (contrast No. 168), perhaps as a result of the aspirated cluster. Initial **yw-* has not been established for any general TB root but appears in at least two Kuki-Naga roots:

**ywar* 'sell': L *zuar*, Mikir *dźor*.[170]

**ywi* 'follow': L *zui*, Siyin *yui*.

Clusters of the type: velar stop + *y*, labial stop + *y* can be established with some precision, with Tibetan furnishing the most valuable data here. Kachin preserves initial **ky-* only by exception and as a doublet form (No. 162), normally shifting to a palatal affricate:[171]

(223) T *mkhyen-pa*, K *tśyeŋ* ~ *tśye* 'know', from TB **(m-)kyen*.

(224) K *khyen* ~ *gyen* ~ *tśen* 'snow, ice', B *khyàm* 'cold' (TB **kyam*).

168 The appearance of this root in Tsangla suggests that T *yid* 'soul, mind', and *yi-* ~ *yid-* in compounds such as *yi-ga* 'appetite', *yi-dam* ~ *yid-dam* 'oath', are directly cognate (both K *sai* and B *swè* are used in the derived meaning 'disposition, spirit'). *T khrag* 'blood' is isolated in Tibeto-Burman.

169 TB **s-hywəy* is now preferred as the reconstruction for this root; the initial cluster **hyw-* is paralleled by TB **kywəy* 'yam' (No. 238), and this reconstruction serves to explain forms such as Tsangla *yi* and L *thi*, the latter via **si* < **s-yi* < **s-hywi*.

170 This root is also represented by Meithei *yol* ~ *yon* 'sell'; it is definitely a loan from AT; cf. IN **d'ual, id.*, with TB showing the characteristic *r* = *l* equation (Benedict, 1967bis). B *wai* 'buy' also belongs here, the same semantic shift occurring in AT (the Ong-Be language of Hainan); see n. 54 for the final. Răwang (Nungish) has *wan* 'buy' rather than the anticipated **war*.

171 Doublet forms are common in Kachin, e.g. *khyun* ~ *śun* 'kidneys', *khye* ~ *dźe* 'to tear'. Initial affricate forms are more often cited by Hertz than by Hanson or Needham, and are especially characteristic of the Khauri dialect recorded by Cushing ('Grammatical Sketch of the Kakhyen Language', *JRAS* **12** (1880), 395–416), e.g. *lətśauŋ* for *ləkhoŋ* '2', *tśaum* for *khom* 'to go', *dźətśu* for *dźəkhu* '9'. For the assimilative *-yam* > *-en* shift of No. 224, cf. B *pyam*, K *pyen* 'to fly'; B *kràm* 'rough, coarse', K *gren* 'raw-boned, razor-backed', *məgren* ~ *diŋgren* 'sharp', *tiŋgren* 'rough'; B *ăsam* 'sound' (used in meaning 'voice'), K *niŋsen* ~ *nsen* 'sound, voice'; also Bahing *sam* 'breath, life', T *sem(s)* 'soul, spirit', *sem(s)-pa*, pf. *sems* ~ *bsams* 'think', *bsam-pa* 'thought', Lepcha *a-sóm* < **/sam* 'spirit, breath'.

The parallel K *ts*- < **gy*- development is illustrated by Nos. 163 and 164;[172] note also G *tś*-, Dimasa *dź*- in the same pair of roots. It is reasonable to suppose that the parent TB speech had initial **ty*- and **dy*-, paralleling the other stop clusters, as well as **ny*-, yet our evidence here is of the scantiest sort. Most TB languages, including Tibetan, lack these dental stop clusters. Burmese has *ty*- only in rare doublet forms; cf. *ta* ~ *tya* 'very red' (n. 429); also the following:

B *tak-tak* ~ *tyak-tyak* 'very'; T *thag-pa* 'to be sure, decided, certain', *tig-tig* 'certainly', L *tak* 'very, real, exact', Mikir *ăthik* 'just', from TB **tyak*.[173]

Lepcha has *ty*- or *dy*- in a few words; these are probably secondary for the most part (see §**22**), but cf. the following:

(225) Lepcha *tyaŋ* 'dark', Tsangla *tsaŋ*, K *tśyaŋ* ~ *mətśyaŋ* 'black' (TB **tyaŋ*).

Bahing has a number of words with initial *ty*- or *dy*-, and several roots of this type can be set up for Kiranti:

Kiranti **dyal* 'village': Bahing *dyal*, Dumi *del*, Nachereng *tyal*, Kulung *tel*; cf. Lepcha *tyol* < **tyal*, *id.*

Extra-Kiranti comparisons are also available for the following pair of roots:

(226) Bahing *dyam* 'to be full (as a vessel)', Vayu *dam* 'to be full', *tam* 'fill', T *ltam-pa* 'state of being full, e.g. a vessel full of water', *ltam*(*s*)-*pa* 'to be full', *gtam*(*s*)-*pa* 'full', *tham-pa* ~ *them-pa* 'complete, full' (TB **dyam* ~ **tyam*).[174]

(227) Bahing *dyam* 'to be straight', T *ldem-pa* 'straight, upright', B *ătam* 'a straight, long piece'; probably also Nung *ədam* 'plain (level ground), flat', *hi-dam* 'foot' (= 'flat of leg'), Gyarung *təmi dam-dam* 'lower leg' (TB **dyam*).[175]

Tibetan shows the shift: **ya* > *e* in the above roots and elsewhere, while West T dialects tend to retain *ya* or *a*:

Bodish **thyak*: T *theg-pa* 'lift, raise, bear, endure', Ladakhi *thag* 'bear', Purik *thyak* 'lift', Balti *thyak-pa* 'patience'.[176]

Bodish **styaŋ* 'upper part': T *steŋ*, Ladakhi *staŋ*; possibly related to Limbu *thaŋ* 'above', general Kiranti **taŋ* 'horn'.

Lushei has *thi*- in the following root, which appears to have had a cluster with *y* as initial:

T *'tsaŋ-ba* ~ *saŋ-ba* 'make clear, cleanse', *seŋ-po* ~ *bseŋ-po* 'clean, white, thin, airy' (note the *a* ~ *e* alternation), West T *siŋs-po* 'thin, clear' (West T lacks **sya*-),

172 Cf. also K *tsap* 'stand' < TB **g-ryap* (No. 246); cf. also n. 148.
173 Tiddim Chin has *tak* 'to be right, correct', also 'right (side)'.
174 This root also appears in K-N: Tiddim *dim* 'to be full'.
175 Tiddim (K-N) has *tam* 'to be level'.
176 Cf. n. 338: TB *(*l*-)*tak* 'ascend; above'.

B *tsaŋ* 'clear, pure', Lushei *thiaŋ* 'clear, clean', Thado *əteŋ*, *id.*, Meithei *əseŋ-ba* 'clean', from TB **(t)syaŋ*.[177]

TB medial **y* after sibilants and affricates is best preserved in Tibetan, which makes a sharp distinction between *s* and *ś*, *z* and *ź*, *ts* and *tś*, and *dz* and *dź*. The palatalized forms can phonemically be written: /*sy*, *zy*, *tsy*, *dzy*/. Burmese retains no trace of this distinction, but many Lolo languages have a distinctive set of correspondences for TB **sy-*:[178]

		TB	Burm.	Lisu	Ahi	Nyi
57	fruit	**sey*	*asì*	*si*	*sa*	*sə*
181	flesh	**sya*	*sà*	*hwa*	*ho~hu*	*ra*
228	iron	**syam*	*sam*	*hɔ*	*hö*	*rə*

(228) Gyarung *śom* (possible effect on vowel), Nung *śam* (dial. *śĭam*), B *sam* 'iron' (TB **syam*).[179]

Lushei has *s-~ś-* < TB **sy-* as contrasted with *th-* < TB **s-*, and *ts(h)-* < TB **tsy-* as contrasted with *s-* < TB **ts-*; cf. the following root with a parallel in Mikir:

Kuki-Naga **tsyuk*: L *tśuk* 'knock against', Mikir *tśok* 'hit, strike'.

This correspondence may represent a secondary palatalization before front vowel in some roots, or perhaps an influence from final **-y*; cf. K *tśyai*, L *tśai* 'to

177 This root can now be reconstructed **syaŋ* (n. 122). West T *siŋs-* (rather than **seŋs-*) indicates an old medial *-ya-~-i-* alternation (n. 251).

178 Burling has *xwō* 'iron' for Lisu. In several Loloish languages the *s*/*š* distinction is breaking down; Lahu has only /*š*/, with *s* as an allophone before /*ɨ*/; Akha preserves the distinction, with some confusions, in most dialects: *šḿ* 'iron', *šàʔ* 'meat', *si* 'fruit' (JAM).

As Matisoff (*Lahu and PLB*, 1969) has shown, a distinction between B-L (and TB) **ts-* and *tsy-* (= *tś-*, *c-*) must also be recognized; cf. **tsh-* in B *tshu* 'fat', Atsi *tshú*, Maru *tshaù*, Lahu *chu*, Lisu *tshə̄*, as opposed to **tśh-* (= *ch-*) in B *tshuì* 'widow', Atsi *chú*, Maru *chúk*, Lahu *chɔ̂*, Lisu *chɨ* (note that Lahu does not maintain the distinction). Roots with palatal initials of this type are relatively uncommon, and only one comparison outside B-L has been uncovered; cf. B-L **dźuk* 'vulva': B *tsauk*, Atsi *dźuʔ*, Maru *dźok*, Chang Naga *su·k*, *id.*; the vowel length appears to be secondary, but Lushei has *tśhu* 'to notch; vulva', possibly from **tśhu·k*, since this language tends to drop final **-k* after long vowels or diphthongs, e.g. Burling cites *hru* 'rub' for *hru·k* 'rub, wipe' (possible dialectical variation).

179 The Tsuta dialect of Gyarung (K. Chang) has the doublet *ṣam~ṣom*; Trung (Nungish) has *śyam*; the root is also represented by Ch'iang (K. Chang) *śi~śyi~śye* (see n. 251 for a discussion of this distribution). The Nung (Răwang) meaning of *śam* is 'sword' as well as 'iron', and a relationship with the K-N root **hryam* is possible: TB **sry-* > *ś-* (we have no other examples); cf. L *hriam* 'sharp; weapon, tool', Thado *ăhem* 'sharp'. Gyarung has initial *ṣ-* for TB **ś-* in this root, but has *sar* 'louse' corresponding to B-L **śan* (n. 251), hence a doublet **sar~*śar* must be recognized for the latter.

play', from **tsya·y* (No. 289), but T has *rtse-ba* < **rtsay* 'to play, frolic, joke', which has possibly retained the original non-palatalized initial.[180]

Lakher, in the Kuki group, seems to reflect TB medial **y* in its vocalism; cf. Lakher *pəŋɔ* '5' < TB **b-ŋa* and *sɔ* 'child' < TB **za*, but *ŋa* 'fish' < TB **ŋya* and *sa* 'flesh' < TB **sya*.[181] Kachin and Bahing also retain at least in part the distinction between palatalized and non-palatalized forms (see Nos. 186, 187 and 188). Garo parallels Lushei at least in part; note especially G *masi* 'know' < TB **syey*.

TB initial **dzy-* and **zy-*, like **dzw-* and **zw-*, are scarce at best; cf. **dzyon* 'ride' (No. 72) and the following:

(229) Moshang *ədźal*, K *tsan*, G *tśel* < **tśal*, Dimasa *gadźaiŋ* < **gadźa(i)l* 'far', L *fa·l* 'apart, isolated, detached' (TB **dzya·l*).

T *'dźu-ba* ~ *źu-ba* 'melt; digest', G *so* 'rot, decay', Dimasa *sau* 'rot, decay', *gasau* 'rotten', *masau* 'digest, disintegrate, rot in water', perhaps from TB **zya·w*, but note L *thu*, Mikir *thu* 'rot, decay' < Kuki-Naga **su* (possible vowel gradation, see below).

Medial **y* after *n-* and *m-* is in general well preserved, but the cluster **ŋy-* can be established only inferentially on the basis of the correspondence: T *ny-* = B *ŋ-* (Nos. 189, 190). Most TB languages follow Burmese in simply dropping *y*, but note G *na-tŏk* 'fish' < TB **ŋya*.

TB **ry-* is maintained in Lushei (*ri-*) and appears also in the early Burmese inscriptions,[182] but has become simply *r-* in Modern Burmese, *y-* in Kachin and *ź-* in Tibetan (Nos. 202–7). An additional Kuki-Naga root with initial **ry-* can be reconstructed:

Kuki-Naga **ryal* 'hail': L *rial*, Thado *giel*, Lakher *pərei*, Rangkhol *ril*, Ao Naga *rer* ~ *rər*, Meithei *lel*, Mikir *herei*.

Both Burmese and Lushei retain TB **ly-*, while Tibetan normally has **ya* > *e*, as in No. 212; cf. also T *legs-pa* ~ *legs-mo*, Ladakhi *lags-pa*, Balti and Purik *lyaχ-mo* 'good', showing retention of the *a* vocalization in these West T dialects.[183] A parallel **ya* > *e* shift also occurs in Kachin and Mikir (Nos. 174 and 211), also in

180 The reconstruction of this root remains **(r-)tsya·y*, with **tsy-* standing for a dental affricate + *y* cluster rather than for the palatal **tś-* (n. 122); Tibetan lacks the cluster **rtś-*, however, so that an original TB **(r-)tśa·y* is also possible here, with Tibetan substituting *rts-* (as in *rtsi-ba* 'count'; see n. 95).

181 Atsi (B-L), as recorded by Hanson (1906, Appendix), makes an identical distinction: Atsi *ŋa* 'fish' but *ŋɔ* '5'.

182 The inscriptions have *ryak* for *rak* 'day', *rya* for *ra* '100', and *hsyats, syats, hyats, hyat, het* for *hrats* '8'; cf. *ăhsyaŋ* for *ăhraŋ* 'lord' (No. 205).

183 Tibetan also has the doublet: *yag-po* ~ *'dźag-po* 'good', from **(a-)lyag-* (n. 104).

Magari and Tangkhul (No. 211) and in Chepang (No. 174). TB **mly-* yields B *mly-* (archaic)~*my-*, Kanauri *my-*, K *məy-* (No. 153).

The TB cluster **hy-* is retained in Lushei (*hi-*), and appears occasionally in other languages, e.g. Bahing *hyal* 'heavy'. It has been reconstructed for the following root:

(230) L *hiat* 'to scratch' (*-iat* < **-yak*, as in No. 174), B *yak* 'strike with a stroke toward one's self, scratch' (TB **hyak*).

TB medial **y* before the front vowel *i* is as uncertain an entity as initial **y-* before *i* (see above). Tibetan regularly palatalizes velars and dentals before this vowel, e.g. *khyi* 'dog' rather than **khi*, *nyi-ma* 'sun' rather than **ni-ma*; comparable forms with initial labials appear in the older texts, e.g. *myig* 'eye' for *mig*. Tibetan does, however, distinguish between palatalized and non-palatalized sibilants and affricates even before *i*, hence we have some basis for at least indicating medial *y* in some of these roots: T *gtśi-ba* 'urinate' from TB **ts(y)i*, contrasting with T *rtsi-ba* 'juice; paint' from TB **tsiy*. In the following root Nung has *th-*, contrasting with *ts-* in *tsi* 'joint' < TB **tsik* (T *tshigs*):

(231) T *mtśhil-ma*, L *tśil* 'spittle', Nung *thil* 'spittle', *thil thil* 'to spit', from TB **m-ts(y)il*.[184]

The following roots in initial **s-* before *i* have been reconstructed without the medial element:

(232) T *śi-ba*~*'tśhi-ba*, Kanauri *śi*, Magari *śi*, Limbu *si*, Miri *śi*, Nung *śi*, K *si*, B *se*, G *si*, Dimasa *thi*, L *thi*, Mikir *thi* 'die' (TB **siy*).

(233) T *śiŋ*, Kanauri *śiŋ*, Magari *śiŋ*, Vayu *siŋ*, Bahing *siŋ*, Miri *ö-śiŋ*, Nung *śiŋ*~*thiŋ*, B *sats*, L *thiŋ*, Mikir *theŋ* 'tree, wood' (TB **siŋ*).

(234) T *mtśhin* < *mśin*, Kanauri *śin*, Miri *əśin*, Nung *phəśin*, K *sin*~*məsin*, B *ăsàñ*, L *thin*, Mikir *iŋthin* 'liver' (TB **m-sin*).

Note that Tibetan, Kanauri, Magari, Miri, and Nung regularly have *ś-* in the above series, while Kachin has *s-* and Lushei and Mikir have *th-* < **s-*. G *si*, Dimasa *thi* 'die' parallel G *masi*, Dimasa *mathi* 'know' < **syey* (No. 182). Meithei has *hak-śa* 'flesh', *śa* 'animal' < **sya*, as well as *si* 'die' < **siy* and *siŋ* 'tree, wood' < **siŋ*, as contrasted with *h-* < **s-* (see above). Burmese has perhaps preserved medial *y* before *i* in the following roots, though it must be observed that Burmese sometimes shows interchange here, as in *hmáñ*~*hmyáñ* 'ripe' < TB **s-min*.

(235) T *nyag-nyig* 'filth, dirt', *snyigs-pa* 'degenerated', *snyigs-ma* 'impure sediment', B *ńats* 'dirty, filthy', G *antśnek* 'dirt', *snek* 'sloppy' (in comp.), Dimasa *dźini* 'dirt', K *nyi*~*nye* 'evacuate the intestines', Nung *ni* 'excrement' (TB **n(y)ik*); the G and K forms suggest a variant form **s-n(y)ek*.

184 This root has now been reconstructed **m-tśril* (n. 95).

(236) T *gnyid* 'sleep', *rnyid-pa* 'wither, fade' (cf. *g-yur* 'sleep', *g-yur-ba* 'droop, hang (of fading flowers); recline, repose'), B *ńit* 'nod the head; lean a little, as a post' (TB **n(y)it*).

(237) T *smyig-ma*~*smyug-ma* 'cane, bamboo', B *hmyats* 'bamboo sprout', G *bimik* 'sprout, germ, blade' (TB **s-m(y)ik*); cf. T *mig*, G *mik* 'eye' (West T *mig-tśan* 'having seeds or grains' = Classical T 'having eyes'); also Lepcha *yăŋ-miŋ* 'knot on joint of bamboo'.

Clusters with medial **yw* must also be recognized, as shown by the following roots:

(238) T *skyi-ba* 'medicinal plant; potato', Kiranti **k(w)i* 'yam' (Dumi *ki*, Sangpang *khi*, Limbu *khe*, Balali *khu*), Digaro *gi* 'yam', Nung *gi* 'yam, root', B *kywè* 'wild yam' (TB **kywiy*).[185]

(239) L *tśuap*, G *kasop* 'lungs' (TB **tsywap*).

(240) Bahing *tśwar* 'cut with a knife by one stroke', Mikir *tśor* 'cut, chop' (TB **tsywar*).

(241) T *'tśhor-ba*, pf. *śor* 'escape; flow out, run over', Lepcha *tśhor* 'the pouring of water', G *sol-aŋ* 'flow', *sol-gipa* 'current', Dimasa *di-sor* 'flow', K *śon* 'flow, as tears, sweat, or water poured on the ground', B *swan* 'pour out, spill, shed', *swàn* 'pour upon, cast by pouring liquid into a mold' (TB **sywar*); cf. also T *gśo-ba*~*bśo-ba* 'pour out', K *dźo*~*tśyo* 'pour out, cast, enamel, dye' (see §7 for alternation of final vowel with **-r*).

(242) T *'dźol-ba* 'hang down (of cow's udder, of the long hair on a yak's belly, of tails, etc.); trail, train, retinue', *'dzol-'dzol* 'hanging-belly, paunch', L *fual* 'sag, hang low; to be loose or long (as a coat, etc.)' (TB **dzywal*).

Clusters consisting of stop + liquid + *w* or *y* are rare but do occur in some roots; cf. **krwi(y)* 'sew', also the following:

(243) B *krwap-krwap* 'rustlingly', K *krop* 'rustle' (TB **krwap*).

(244) B *khrwè-má* 'daughter-in-law', K *khri* 'paternal aunt's daughters, sister's children; son-in-law' (TB **krwiy*).

In the following pair of roots, the initial velar element has been reconstructed as a prefix:

185 Trung (Nungish) has *gui* 'taro', contrasting with *dəgei* 'dog', apparently reflecting the distinction in initials in these two TB roots (**kywəy* vs. **kwəy*). Nungish in general simplifies TB final **-wəy* or **-wi(y)* in one way or another; in Răwang they fall together with TB final **-i*: *gi* 'yam, root', *dəgi* 'dog', also *təri* 'cane' [TB **(s-)rwi(y)*] while in Lungmi (forms from N. Bodman) they are represented by *-ṳ*: *agṳ* 'dog', *tərṳ* 'cane' (contrast treatment on p. 137). Chepang also distinguishes between the two roots: *goy* < **[k]i* 'root; sweet potato', *kuy* < **[khw]i* 'dog'. This root (No. 238) has been considered (Benedict, 1967bis) an early loan from AT but this now appears unlikely (Benedict, 1972).

(245) Kiranti **rum* (*rum*~*yum*) 'salt', K *dźum* 'salt', *śum* 'to be salt; saltish', Kadu *sum*, Moshang *śum*, G *khari-tśham* (but *sum* as early form), Dimasa *sem*, Meithei *thum* (cf. *tha* 'moon' < **g-la*) 'salt' (TB **g-ryum*).[186]

(246) Lepcha *hryăm* < **hryăp* 'stand on tip of toe, rise', Kiranti: *rap* (Bahing), *rep*~*reb* (Khaling *et al.*), *yeb* (Balali *et al.*) and *rip* (Sangpang), Vayu *yep*~*ip*, Nung *rip*, B *rap*, Meithei *lep* (Old Meithei *tśərep*) Dhimal *dźap*, K *tsap*, Moshang *tśap*, Mikir *ardźap*, Empeo *sap* 'stand' (TB **g-ryap*).[186]

In the latter root, Kachin has *ts-* < **g(r)y-*, as in Nos. 163 and 164. Mikir *ardźap* < **r-yap* has a parallel in the following root:

Mikir *ardźu* 'ask, enquire', T *źu-ba* < **ryu* 'request, put a question', from TB **r-yu(w)*.

The influence exerted by prefixes is further shown in Nos. 163 and 164, which parallel No. 246 in some languages: K *mətsat* '8', *tsap* 'stand'; Empeo *təsat* '8', *sap* 'stand'; Meithei *təret* '7', *tśərep* 'stand' (Old Meithei form).

§10. Tibeto-Burman vowels (finals; diphthongs)

The TB vowel system[187] is made up of the five phonemes[188] /*a*, *o*, *u*, *i*, *e*/, which appear both in medial and final position. With the exception of *a*, however, pure vowels in final position are rare, while combinations of vowel + *w* or *y* are charac-

186 PLB **hrap* 'stand' (JAM). This reconstructed form should be compared with B *hrats* '8' < **g-ryat*. Nos. 245 and 246 (text) are now reconstructed **gryum* 'salt' but **g-ryap* 'stand', thus explaining the contrast in development; note especially K *dźum*~*śum* 'salt; salty' (the latter perhaps from a doublet form **kryum*) but *tsap* < **kyap* < **kryap* 'stand' (cf. K *mətsat* < */*kyat* < */*kryat* '8'). Tibetan has *rgyam-tshwa* 'a kind of salt, like crystal' (*tshwa* 'salt'), apparently a metathesized form from **gryam* (cf. T *brgyad* '8' for **b-gryad*); this is a rare medical term (cited by Csoma de Körös) and may be an early loan from Chinese, in which the indicated vowel shift **u* > *a* is regular (n. 479).

187 See Shafer's studies of the ST vowel system: 'The Vocalism of Sino-Tibetan', part I, *JAOS* **60** (1940); part II, *JAOS* **61** (1941) (JAM).

188 It now appears preferable to recognize the vowel *ə* for TB, but only in non-final position. This is especially indicated for the finals **-əw* and **-əy* (preferable to **-uw* and **-iy*), and there are also indications that medial **ə* still existed in certain positions at the reconstructed TB level, e.g. it explains vocalic alternation in Tibetan verbs (n. 344). Inasmuch as we probably should recognize the vowel *ə* in any event, it is advantageous to analyze prefixes along these lines, e.g. prefixed **b-* is /*bə*/ rather than /*bă*/ (with phonemic zero stress); **g-ryap* 'stand' is **gəryap*, contrasting with **gryum* 'salt'.

teristic of the system as a whole. The following finals occur (rare finals are enclosed in parentheses):

(*-u*)	(*-o*)	*-a*	(*-e*)	(*-i*)
-uw	*-ow*	{ *-aw* / *-a·w* }	(*-ew*)	—
—	(*-oy*)	{ *-ay* / *-a·y* }	*-ey*	*-iy*

TB *-*a*, the most common final in the system, is retained in most groups: cf. T, K, G, L *kha*, B *khà* 'bitter' < TB **ka* (No. 8). Lepcha, Abor-Miri, and Mikir have *-*a* > -*o*, and similar shifts appear in other groups, e.g. Maru -*ɔ*, Ahi and Nyi -*o*, Ulu -*u* in the Burmese-Lolo group. Chang (Konyak) has developed the diphthong -*au* ~ -*ou* from TB *-*a*, as in *nou* 'ear' < **g-na*, *ŋau* 'fish' < **ŋya*; *sau* ~ *śau* 'eat' < **dza*; cf. also Chang *hai* ~ *hei* 'die' for TB **siy*. Note also the bizarre set of correspondences in the Western Kuki group, with Khoirao alone maintaining the -*a* vocalization:

	TB	Khoirao	Empeo	Kabui	Maram	Kwoireng
father	**pa*	*əpa*	*əpeu*	*əpu*	*əphu*	*əpyu*
five	**b-ŋa*	*məŋa*	*miŋeu*	*pəŋu*	*miŋu*	*məŋyu*
eat	**dza*	*ta*	*teu*	*tu*	*tu*	*tyu*

Final -*o* and -*e* are found in numerous TB languages, but in most instances (as in Tibetan) can be shown to be secondary. Lushei final -*o* [-*ɔ*] interchanges with -*ou* as well as with -*wa*, -*wat*, and -*wak*, while Lushei -*e* interchanges with -*ia*, -*iak*, -*iat*, and -*ial*. Both vowels are found in a few roots with some extension in Kuki-Naga, e.g. L *pho*, Lakher *veu-phɔ*, Bete *ipho* 'shield', but present extremely few general TB correspondences. Kachin likewise has both -*o* [-*ɔ*] and -*e*, for which a few Tibetan or Burmese comparisons have been uncovered; cf. **pro* 'delight' (No. 130) and the following:[189,190]

189 The loss of final -*k* in Kachin makes for uncertainty in some comparisons of this type, e.g. K *mətho* 'to spit' is best compared with Mikir *iŋthok* < **m-thok* 'to spit, dart, peck, bite (as a snake); spittle', despite T *tho-le* *ʼdebs-pa*, West T *thu gyab-tśe* 'to spit' (lit. 'throw spittle'), which belong rather with G *stu*, Dimasa *khu-di thu* 'to spit' (*khu-di* 'spittle').

190 The problem indicated in n. 189 has now been greatly clarified with the aid of modern data on Kachin supplied (personal communication) by L. Maran, who records the final glottal stop (from TB *-*k*). K *mətho* 'to spit' is to be grouped with T *tho*-, West T *thu*, and G *stu*, Dimasa *thu* (n. 189), also Kanauri *thu* 'spit' (in comp.), *tu-kəŋ* 'spittle'; Răwang (Nungish) *du* 'vomit'; Kachin also has *məton* ~ *mədon* 'throw up', probably from **m-to-n*; TB *(*m*-)*twa* ~ *(*s*-)*twa*. For Mikir *iŋtok* < TB **m-tuk*, see n. 231. Two of the comparisons cited in the text (Nos. 248

(247) T *mtho-ba*~*mthon-po* 'to be high', K *mətho* 'high; pinnacle' (TB **m-to*).

(248) T *'phro-ba* 'proceed, issue, emanate from', *spro-ba* 'make go out, disperse', K *pro* 'bring out; come out', *śəpro* 'bring out, exhume, contribute' (TB **pro*).[190]

(249) K *do*, B *tau* 'to be related by birth or marriage' (TB **do*).

(250) K *pyo* 'to be boiled and thus soft, tender', *śəpyo* 'to boil', B *prau*~*pyau* 'quite ripe, very soft', *praú* 'soft, tender', *phraù* 'to parboil' (TB **pryo*).

(251) T *ske* 'neck, throat', K *ke* 'to be or make neck-shaped' (TB **ke*).[190]

(252) T *nye-źo* 'mishap', *nyes-pa* 'calamity; punishment', K *nye* 'punish; cause woe' (TB **nye*).

Burmese appears to have diphthongized final *-*o* to -*au* (Modern -ɔ), as in Nos. 249 and 250; also final *-*e* to -*ai* (Modern -ɛ), though the evidence for the latter shift is less substantial (the retention of *-*e* in Lushei):

(253) L *be*, Dimasa *sabai*, B *paì* 'peas, beans, lentils' (TB **be*).

(254) L *peʔ* 'to break or be broken', B *paí* 'to be broken off, chipped', *phaí* 'break off a small piece from a larger, crumble', G *be* 'break; broken', *pe* 'break down', Dimasa *bai* 'break, get broken', *sabai* 'break', *gabai* 'broken', *phai* 'hatch', *do-phai* 'break with some instrument' (TB **be*~**pe*).

Most reconstructions in final *-*o* or *-*e*, e.g. **ble* 'slip' (based on Kanauri and Digaro forms), must be regarded as provisional.

Most TB languages have a pair of high vowels which might readily be reconstructed simply as *-*u* and *-*i*. Burmese, however, has both -*u* and -*ui* < *-*uw*, -*i* and -*e* < *-*iy*, all of which correspond to high vowels elsewhere. The earlier Burmese vowel system, as represented in the inscriptions,[191] forms a symmetrical phonemic system of three vowels and the semi-vowels *w* and *y*:

-*u*	-*a*	-*i*
-*uw* (-*ui*)	-*aw* (-*au*)	—
—	-*ay* (-*ai*)	-*iy*

and 251) must now be considered problematical; Maran cites *proʔ* (high tone) 'bring out; come out', *śəproʔ* 'bring out, exhume, contribute', from **prok* and **s-prok*; also *keʔ* (high tone) 'to be or make neck-shaped', from **kek*; we reconstruct these roots TB **pro*(*k*) and *(*s*-)*ke*(*k*), respectively; it is possible that the glottal stop represents a glottal accent in some roots (n. 198); cf. also K *dźit tśyiʔ* (*dźiʔ*) (high tone) 'urinate' (No. 77), apparently through assimilation to the final -*t* of *dźit*.

191 For the Burmese inscriptions, see Ch. Duroiselle, 'The Burmese Face of the Myazedi Inscription at Pagan', *Epigraphia Burmanica* **1**, pt. 1 (1919), 1–46; K. Seidenstücker, 'Beiträge zur altbirmanischen Wortkunde', *AM* **4** (1927), 1–16; Pe Maung Tin, 'Philological Features of the Inscriptions', *JBRS* **19** (1929), 78–9.

Both *-u* and *-i* are written with symbols for long vowels, while *-u-* in *-uw* is written '*ui*' to indicate the special phonetic value (probably mid-unrounded) of this phoneme before the labial (*-w*) as well as before velars (*-k*, *-ŋ*). Final *-aw* is generally written with a special symbol '*e-a*', but occasionally as *a*+*w*, as in *uwaw* 'cuckoo' (*ú-aù*), *taw* 'forest' (*tau*). Modern Burmese retains the pure vowels *-u*, *-a*, and *-i*, but has *-o* for *-uw* (transcribed *-ui*), *-e* for *-iy* (transcribed *-e*), *-ɔ* for *-aw* (transcribed *-au*), and *-ɛ* for *-ay* (transcribed *-ai*), i.e. all diphthongal combinations have been leveled off to pure vowels (*u* and *i* are lowered, *a* is raised).

The Burmese-Lolo languages in general reflect the distinction between *-u* and *-ui*, *-i* and *-e*, while Nung distinguishes between the *-u* and *-ui* types. Maru has developed the secondary consonants *-k* (sometimes recorded as *-p*) and *-t* (sometimes recorded as *-k*) from the finals **-uw* and **-iy*, respectively, while the Lolo languages, as well as Nung, have various types of mid- or front-rounded vowels for **-uw*.[192,193] Contrast the following sets (Maru **-u*>*-au* except after *y*):

	Burmese	Maru	Ahi	Nyi	Lahu
sweet	*khyui*	*tśhuk*	*tśhö*	*tshə*	*chɔ*
weep	*ŋui*	*ŋuk*	*ŋö*	*ŋə*	—
steal	*khuì*	*khuk*	*khö*	*khə*	*qhɔ̂*
thick	*thu*	*thau*	*tho*	*thu*	*thu*
take	*yu*	*yu*	*yo*	*yu*	*yù*
white	*phru*[194]	*phyu*	*tho*	*ślu*	*phu*

192 The writer (1939, p. 215, note 5) originally regarded Maru final *-k* and *-t* as reflexes of an archaic TB set of finals (*-g* and *-d*), but this view now appears quite untenable. S. N. Wolfenden, 'On the Restitution of Final Consonants in certain Word Types of Burmese', *AO* **17** (1938), 153–68, grievously misinterprets these Burmese and Maru finals, reconstructing **-uts* and **-its* on the misleading analogy of Burmese *-ats* (<**ik*, see below).

193 Benedict, 1948; later rediscoveries of this include Burling, *Language* **42**, 3 (cited above) and A. Lyovin, 'Notes on the addition of final stops in Maru', *POLA* **7**, Berkeley, June 1968; also R. A. Miller, 'Once again, the Maru final stops' (paper read at *First Conference on Sino-Tibetan*, Yale University, October 1968) (JAM). Cf. also Miller's review of Burling ('Proto-Lolo-Burmese', 1967) in *Indo-Iranian Journal*, **12**, No. 2 (1970), esp. pp. 151 ff. The majority of the Chinese forms adduced by Miller to refute 'Burling's theory of spontaneous generation of final stops in Maru' appear to be non-cognate, while the possibility of parallel development in Chinese and Maru (Benedict) is overlooked. It is ironic that one of Burling's constructive contributions (independent of Benedict, 1948) should have become a special target in an extended review which generally (and with good reason) castigates Burling's work; for a somewhat different approach to Burling's study see the detailed review by JAM (*Language*, 1968), who points out other contributions made by Burling.

194 B *phlu* 'white' in inscriptions (n. 134); cf. also Hani *-phulu* (cited by K.

For the Maru development of secondary stops after *-i* (TB **-iy*) cf. B *krè*, Maru *kyik* 'copper'; B *lè*, Maru *pyit* '4' (TB **b-liy*); B *re*, Maru *rit* 'water' (Lolo has *-i* or *-ə* in this series). Maru has *-a* after *l* or *w*, however, as in B *lè*, Maru *la* 'heavy'; B *hle*, Maru *la* 'boat'; B *wè*, Maru *wa* 'far'; B *khwè*, Maru *kha* 'dog'; B *swè*, Maru *sa* 'blood'.[195]

TB **-iy* has been reconstructed for roots in which Burmese has *-e* < **-iy* corresponding to *-i* in Tibetan, Kachin, Garo, Lushei and most other TB languages, e.g. T *śi-ba*, K *si*, B *se*, G *si*, L *thi* 'die' < TB **siy* (No. 232). The form **-i(y)* has been used for roots for which no Burmese-Lolo cognate has been found, e.g. Nos. 166, 171, 191, 201, 210. Similarly, TB **-uw* has been reconstructed for roots in which Burmese has *-ui* < **-uw* corresponding to *-u* elsewhere, e.g. T *dgu*, K *dźəkhu*, B *kuì*, G *sku*, L *kua* (with suffixed *-a*) '9' < TB **d-kuw* (No. 13). Nung has *-ö* (Nos. 13, 27) or *-ü* (Nos. 33, 41, 79, 156) in this series; cf. also the following pair of roots:

(255) T *ʔakhu ~ khu-bo*, Vayu *ku-ku*, Bahing *ku-ku*, Digaro *(na-)ku*, Mikir *ni-hu* < **-khu* 'uncle'; Nung *əkhö*, Miri *əkü*, Ao Naga *okhu* 'uncle, father-in-law' (wife's father under system of cross-cousin marriage); K *ku*, Meithei *iku* 'father-in-law', B *kui* 'honorific affix', as in *ats-kui* 'older brother' (*ats-* < TB **ik*, No. 112); TB **kuw*.

(256) Tsangla *mu-gu*, Thebor and Bunan *khu*, Vayu *ku-lu*, Bahing *ku-ni*, Limbu *me-ku*, Digaro *nəmiŋ-khu ~ -khau*, Miri *mikki* (Abor *muikü*), Nung *məö* (unexplained loss of initial), B *mì-khuì ~ ăkhuì*, G *wal-ku*, L *mei-khu* 'smoke', K *wan-khut* 'smoke', *wan-khut khu* 'to smoke'; TB **kuw* (note general use in composition with words for 'fire').

The reconstruction of TB **-uw* can sometimes be made on the basis of the Nung evidence alone, as in TB **b-yuw* 'rat' (Nung *yü*) and the following root:

(257) Miri *pəmuü*, Nung *thəmö*, Mikir *vo-mu*, L *mu*, Lakher *pəhmo*, Khami *əhmo*, Sho *əhmü*, Angami Naga *re-mu ~ mu-vi* 'eagle, hawk, kite' (TB **muw*).

Where both Burmese and Nung forms are lacking, as in TB **yu(w)* 'liquor' (No. 94), the form with parentheses must be employed.

The reconstructions **-u* and **-i* have been reserved for roots showing this

Chang, 1967); Horpa has *phru-phru*, but we must reconstruct TB **plu* on basis of Anong (Nungish speech recorded almost 100 years ago) *pulu maŋ* 'white' (see STL, Vol. VII); the root commonly has the meaning 'silver' in the B-L languages (Benedict, 1939).

195 Lahu and Akha have an interesting darkening of **-iy* (= **-əy*) after **l* to *ɔ*, which is then fronted in Akha: 'four' *ɔ̂/ȍ*; 'heavy' Lahu *hɔ̂*; 'bow' *hɔ̂/ȍ*; 'wind' Lahu *mû-hɔ*; 'boat' Lahu *hɔ-lɔ̀ʔ-qō* (Akha *lɔ̀* does not front the vowel as expected); 'grandchild' *hɔ̄/ȍ* (see n. 263) (JAM).

correspondence in Burmese (or *-u* in Nung), provided that TB **-ow* (> B *-u*) or **-ey* (> B *-i*) can be ruled out. The following are representative:

(258) Gyarung *tu*, Vayu *du*, Digaro *thu*, Nung *du*, K *thu*, B *tu* 'dig' (TB **tu*).

(259) Nung *phədu*, L *tu*, B *tu* 'nephew' (TB **tu*).[196]

(260) T *'bu-ba* 'open (of flowers)', Nung *phu* 'open', *nam-phu* 'blossom, bud', K *pu* 'to bloom, bud', *əpu* 'blossom, bud', B *phù* 'to bud, swell', *ăphù* 'bud, swelling', Mikir *iŋpu* 'open, dilate', *phu* 'bud' (TB **bu* ~ **pu*).

(261) K *wu* 'murmur, mumble, mutter', B *u* 'howl (as a dog)', L *u* 'whine (as a dog)', Mikir *iŋu* 'bark (as a dog), grumble, growl' (TB **u*).

(262) Kanauri *kut-li*, Bahing *bli*, B *lì*, G *ri-gaŋ*, Dimasa *li* 'penis' (TB **li*).[197]

(263) Vayu *ri* 'decay', Miri *təri* 'wound, ulcer, sore', K *ri* 'to gleet', *əri* 'gleet', *nyi* (*n-yi*) 'matter, purulent discharge', B *rí* ~ *yí* 'to be rotten (of cloth), to gleet (as pus)', *ărí* 'any slimy discharge' (TB **ri*).[198]

(264) T *srid-pa* 'existence' (with suffixed *-d*), B *hrí* 'to be' (TB **s-ri*).

(265) Nung *khri* 'tickle' but *ra-kyi tśip* 'armpit' < **ra-kli* (*ra-* 'shoulder'), B *kăli* 'tickle', *gyak-kăli* ~ *tshak-kăli* ~ *lak-kăli* 'armpit' (*lak* 'arm'), Lakher *kili* 'tickle', *ba-kəli* 'armpit' (TB **g-li*); cf. Dimasa *sisi-khai* 'tickle', *sisi-khor* 'armpit' (= 'tickle-hole').[199]

The low vowel *a* (short or long) combines freely with *-w* or *-y*, while the mid-high back vowel *o* combines with *-w* (rarely with *-y*) and the mid-high front vowel *e* combines with *-y* (very rarely with *-w*). The general correspondences are as follows:

TB	Tibetan	Kachin	Burmese	Garo	Dimasa	Lushei
**-aw*	*-o*	*-au*	*-au*	*-o*	*-au*	*-ou*
**-a·w*	*-u* ~ *-o*	*-au*	*-au*	*-o*	*-au*	*-au*
**-ow*	*-o*	*-u* ~ *-au*	*-u*	*-o*	*-au*	*-ou*
**-ay*	*-e*	*-ai*	*-ai*	*-e*	*-ai*	*-ei*
**-a·y*	*-e*	*-ai*	*-ai*	*-e*	*-ai*	*-ai*
**-ey*	*-e*	*-i*	*-i*	*-e*	*-ai*	*-ei*

196 B-L **du* (Lisu *-du*), hence we must reconstruct TB **tu* ~ **du*. Gyarung (K. Chang) has *temdau* 'nephew', perhaps from **te/mdou*, with vowel gradation.

197 T *mdźe* 'penis', from **m-lye* < **m-ley* (n. 104) belongs with this set, but shows vowel gradation.

198 Maran cites K *riʔ* and *əriʔ* (low tone) 'gleet' but *nyi* (high tone) 'matter'; the glottal stop of the first two forms possibly reflects a glottal accent; cf. B *rí* ~ *yí* (all these forms possibly glottalized by the non-phonemic ʔ of an original **a-* prefix).

199 Lahu *gɨ̂-li-yá* 'tickle', *pɛ̀-lí-kā* 'armpit' (JAM). This 'funny' root possibly is to be considered a legitimate TB disyllabic root: **k(a)li*, with the first vowel either lost (Nungish), assimilated (Lakher) or unstressed (Burmese), the last

Illustrations:

(14) (above) K *gau*, B *khau*, Dimasa *dźuru-khau*, L *kou*, Mikir *ku*, Empeo *gu* 'call' (TB **gaw*).

(266) B *khaù* 'small basket for presenting offerings', L *khou* 'kind of basket' (TB **kaw*).

(267) T *sdo-ba* 'to risk, hazard, venture; to bear up against, bid defiance', B *taù* 'resent an insinuation, interfere in a quarrel', L *dou* 'to be at enmity with', also 'to prop up' (TB **daw*); K *tau* 'to have premonitions, anticipate, foresee' and B *tau* 'guess, presume' may also belong here.

(268) T *ro* 'corpse, carcass; residue, sediment', Lepcha *hryu* < */*sru* 'to be dry, dead (as leaf)', B *rau* 'very old, near withering (as leaves)', L *rou* 'dry, dead' (TB **raw*).

(269) K *krau* 'dig out, as worm's or a bee's nest from a hollow tree', L *thlou* 'to weed' (TB **klaw*).

(270) T *ŋod-pa* ~ *ŋo-len-pa* 'parch, roast, fry', K *kəŋau* 'fry', Mikir *arnu* < *arŋu* 'roast, bake, fry, grill', Tangkhul *khəŋui* 'fry' (Naga-Kuki **ŋou*) (TB **r-ŋaw*).

(271) T *nu-bo* 'younger brother', *nu-mo* 'younger sister' (West T *no* and *no-mo*), Lepcha *nŭm-nu* 'blood relation', K *nau*, L *nau* 'younger sibling', G *no* 'younger sister', Bodo *bina nau* 'sister' (TB **na·w*).

(272) K *sau* 'oil, fat, grease; oily, savory', L *thau* 'fat, grease; to be fat', G *tho*, Dimasa *thau* 'oil', Bodo *thau* 'oil', *gathau* 'sweet to taste; savor' (TB **sa·w*).

(273) B *au* 'cry out, bawl, howl', L *au* 'scream, cry out', perhaps also Dimasa *hau* 'shout in chorus' (TB **a·w*).

(274) Nung and K *nu* 'tender, soft', B *nú* 'young, tender', *nù* 'to be made soft', L *nou* 'young, soft, tender' (TB **now*).

(275) T *'tshod-pa* ~ *'tsho-ba* 'cook in boiling water, bake', K *dźu* 'burn, roast, broil, bake', Nung *əsu* 'boil', *thi su* 'boiling water', B *tshu* 'boil, bubble, effervesce', G *so*, Dimasa *sau* 'burn', L *śou*, Lakher *śaeu* 'boil', Meithei *əsau* 'heat' (TB **tsyow*).

(276) Kanauri *tso* 'thorn',[200] Lepcha *dźu* 'thorn', K *dźu* 'thorn; prick with a thorn', *ədźu* 'thorn, sharp spike of any kind', B *tshù* 'thorn, sting of an insect',

naturally having 'creaky tone' (cf. discussion on p. 88). This is very similar to the AT root, which also has semantic associations for 'armpit'; cf. IN **gəli* 'ticklish', **kili* 'shoulder' (Fiji 'armpit') and **kilit* 'shoulder; carry under the arm' (Hova 'armpit'); this root is very widespread in AT, often reduplicated, sometimes with an added *-t* of uncertain significance, e.g. Shan *sok kălit* 'tickle'; borrowing of the TB forms from Western Thai, specifically Khamti, is a possibility here; Khamti has *kăle* (prn. *kăli*) and *kap kăle* 'armpit', also *tśuŋ kări* 'tickle' (cf. the Nung form).

200 T *mtshon* 'any pointed or cutting instrument; forefinger' has perhaps been developed from this root.

tsù 'prick, pierce; piercer, awl', G and Dimasa *su* 'pierce', *busu* 'thorn' (with vowel gradation), Meithei and Thado *sou*, Lakher *seu* 'panji (spike planted in ground in warfare)' (Kuki **sow < tsow*), Mikir *su* 'thorn, sting, panji', *iŋsu* 'thorn', Tangkhul *kəsui* 'thorn' (TB **tsow*).

(277) T *tsho-ba*, B *tshu* 'fat', adj. (TB **tsow*).

(278) Central T and West T *sro-ma*, K *tsiʔ-ru* (*tsiʔ* 'louse') 'nit' (TB **row*).[201]

(279) K *gəlu* 'long', B *lu* 'disproportionately tall', G *ro*, Dimasa *galau ~ lau-ba* 'long' (TB **low*).

(280) K *mu ~ əmu* 'work, labor; affair, matter', *śəmu* 'move, stir', Nung *əmu* 'labor, business, matter', B *mu* 'do, perform', *ămu* 'deed, action', *ăhmú* 'business, work, affair', G *mo* 'move', Dimasa *mau* 'move', *samau* 'move, shake' (TB **mow*).

(281) T *ltśe < *s-le* 'tongue', *me-ltśe* 'flame', Kanauri *le*, Lepcha *ăli*, Vayu *li*, Limbu *le-sot* 'tongue' (cf. Lepcha *lin-śet*), Nung *phəlɛ* 'tongue', *thəmi-səlɛ* 'flame', K *lai* 'tongue' (couplet form), G *sre* 'tongue', *wal-sre* 'flame', Dimasa *salai* 'tongue', *wai-slai* 'flame', L *lei* (Kuki **m-lei*), Mikir *de* 'tongue' (TB **m-lay ~ *s-lay*).[202,203]

(282) Gyarung *tĕmĕ*, Thebor *me-kon*, Magari *me-me*, Bahing *me-ri*, Digaro *ləmi ~ ləmiŋ*, K *mai ~ nmai*, Aka *ərim*, B *ămrì* (cf. the Bahing form), G *kime*, Dimasa *khermai ~ bermai*, L *mei*, Aimol *rəmai*, Mikir *arme* 'tail' (TB **r-may*).[204]

(283) K *lai* 'to be changed', *gəlai* 'change, exchange; barter', *məlai* 'change, repent; substitute', Nung *thəlɛ* 'alter, change, exchange', B *laì* 'change, exchange', G *sre* 'change, exchange', Dimasa *salai* 'alter, change, exchange', *salai lai* 'interchange, exchange', L *lei* 'buy, barter' (TB **lay*).[205]

201 A rare root, represented also by Gyarung (K. Chang) *dẓəru* 'louse egg'; the *dẓ-* element of this form, along with the *s-* of T *sro-*, perhaps stand for TB **śrik* 'louse', as in Kachin.

202 Kachin also has the couplet forms *śiŋli* and *śiŋlau*, the regular word being *śiŋlet*, which we have assigned to TB **lyak* 'lick' (No. 211). B *hlya* 'tongue' appears to have been influenced by the latter root.

203 Lahu has *ha-tɛ̀* 'tongue', *à-mī-ha* 'flame' (JAM). This is cognate of B *hlya* 'tongue', probably from a distinct root (n. 158).

204 One is tempted to interpret the Bahing and Burmese forms in terms of metathesis, but there is no analogy whatsoever for this shift in either language. The Burmese form must therefore be regarded as a contraction of **a-mai-ri*, with the regular *-ai* correspondence.

205 Two distinct roots must be recognized here, viz. TB **lay* 'change, exchange' and **(r-)ley* 'barter, buy', the latter apparently related to TB **b-rey* 'buy' (No. 293), which has been identified as a loan-word from AT (n. 207). For Kachin, Maran distinguishes between *lai ~ gəlai* (mid tone) 'change' and *gəlai* (high tone) 'exchange'; Tiddim Chin has *laiʔ* 'change', *lei* 'buy'. Tibetan, which has *-e* for TB **-ay* and **-ey*, combines both sets of meanings: T *rdźe-ba < *r-lye < *r-le* (n. 104) 'barter', also 'change (name, clothes)' (this range of meanings also present in the AT counterparts).

(284) K *dai*, L *tei* 'self' (TB **tay*); cf. TB **s-tay* 'navel' (No. 299).

(285) T *ŋed* (with suffixed *-d*) 'I, we' (elegant), K *ŋai* 'I', L *ŋei* 'self' (TB **ŋay*).

(47) (above) K *pai*~*ləpai*, B *bhai*, *lak-waì*, L *vei*, Mikir *arvi* (with vowel gradation) 'left (hand)' (TB **bay*).

(286) K *mənai* 'twist', B *nai*, Tangkhul *khənai* 'knead' (TB **na·y*).

(287) B *ălai*, L *lai* 'middle, center; navel' (TB **la·y*).

(288) K *lai* 'dig up', L *lai* 'dig, hoe' (TB **la·y*).

(289) K *tśyai*, L *tśai* 'to play' (TB **tsya·y*); cf. also T *rtse-ba* 'to play, frolic, joke' (see above).

(290) T *me*, Kanauri *me*, Gyarung *timi*, Bahing *mi*, Nung *thəmi*, B *mì*, L *mey*, Mikir *me* 'fire', K *myi-phrap* 'lightning' ('fire-flashing'), *myi-than tu* 'fire-fly' (TB **mey*).

(291) T *nye-ba*, K *ni*, B *nì*, L *hnai* (with vowel gradation) 'near' (TB **ney*).

(57) (above) T *se* (in comp.), Vayu *se*, Bahing *si*, Nung *si*, K *si*~*əsi*, B *sì*~*ăsì*, G *the*~*bithe*, Dimasa *thai*~*bathai*, L *thei*, Mikir *the*~*athe* 'fruit' (TB **sey*).

(182) (above) T *śes-pa*, Vayu *ses*, B *śi*, G *masi*, Dimasa *mathi* 'know', K *śi* 'news' (TB **syey*).

Tibetan and Garo have leveled off diphthongal finals (**-au* and **-ou* > *-o*, **-ay* and **-ey* > *-e*), while Dimasa has merged **-aw* and **-ow* in *-au*, **-ay* and **-ey* in *-ai*. Kachin and Burmese have *-u* for **-ow*, *-i* for **-ey*, and *-au* and *-ai* (without length distinction) for the low vowel combinations. Lushei, on the contrary, has retained the long *a* vowel (**-a·w* > *-au*, **-a·y* > *-ai*), but has raised the short *a* vowel (**-aw* > *-ou*, **-ay* > *-ei*), thus causing **-aw* to merge with **-ow*, **-ay* to merge with **-ey*. The distinction between short and long *a*, which appears also before final stops and nasals (see below), thus can be reconstructed on the basis of the Kachin, Burmese, and Lushei material. Nung, which has *-i* < **-ey* but *-ε* < **-ay*, is also of help here. Reconstructions can sometimes be made on the basis of the Nung or Kachin forms alone:

(292) Gyarung *rni*, Nung *əni*~*təni*, Garo *khəni*,[206] Dimasa *khanai* 'hair (of head)' (TB **ney*).

(293) K *məri*, Miri *re*, Garo *bre*, Dimasa *barai* 'buy' (TB **b-rey*).[207]

Mikir and many other TB languages follow Tibetan, Garo, and Dimasa in

206 Note G *-i* rather than *-e*, which is paralleled in G *ni*, Dimasa *nai* 'look, see'; G *mi* (also *me-* in comp.), Dimasa *mai* 'rice, paddy'; G *attśi*, Dimasa *hadźai* 'give birth'. G and Dimasa *-i* in No. 182 (**syey* 'know'), however, is to be explained on the basis of the medial *y* element of this root (*e* dropped between *y*'s).

207 This root has been identified (Benedict, 1967bis) as a loan-word from AT; cf. IN **bəli* ~ **bili*, from AT *(*m*)*baḷi*; the TB form shows the typical *r* = *l*/*ḷ* equation, with handling of the **b-* as an ordinary TB verbal prefix; a separate (but related) loan perhaps yielded TB *(*r-*)*ley* 'barter, buy' (n. 205). Chinese has a possible loan

merging **-aw* and **-ow*, **-ay* and **-ey* (> *-u* and *-e*, respectively, in Mikir), but occasional distinctions are made in a few languages, e.g. Bahing *mi* 'fire' but *me-ri* 'tail'; Gyarung *timi* 'fire', *tĕmĕ* 'tail' (contrast Vayu *me* 'fire', *li* 'tongue'); Abor *ömö* 'fire', *teme~eme* 'tail'. The Bahing distinction allows us to reconstruct:

(294) Bahing (and general Kiranti) *ne* 'take', T *rnyed-pa* (with suffixed *-d*) 'get, obtain', L *nei* 'get, have, obtain', from TB **(r-)ney*.

The Lushei distinction between *-ou* and *-au* is reflected in most Kuki languages:

	Lushei	Lakher	Thado	Bete	Empeo	Tangkhul
call	*kou*	—	*kou*	*koi*	*gu*	—
fly, n.	*thou*	*mətheupa*	*thou*	*ithoi*	—	—
field	*lou*	(*lo*)	*lou*	*loi*	*lu*	*lui*
fat, n.	*thau*	*thɔ*	(*thou*)	*thai*	*pəthau*	*thau*
younger sibling	*nau*	*nɔ*	*nau*	*nai*	—	*nau*
grasshopper	*khau*	*khɔ-śu*	*khau*	—	—	*khau*

Kuki-Naga roots in **-ou* yield provisional TB reconstructions in **-ow* in the absence of Kachin or Burmese cognates:

(295) Dimasa *masau*, L *thou*, Lakher *pətheu*, Ao Naga *meso* 'arise, awake' (TB **m-sow*).

(296) T *sŋo* 'blue, green', L *ŋou* 'white', Thado *ŋou* 'clean', Sho *nau* 'green', Bete *əŋoi* 'yellow' (TB **ŋow*).

(297) T *mo* 'woman, female', L *mou* 'bride, son's or brother's wife', Meithei *imau* 'daughter-in-law', Thado *mau* 'woman' (TB **mow*).

Similarly, TB roots lacking Lushei or other significant Kuki cognates are reconstructed simply with short *a* vowel, e.g. **pyaw* 'fly, swim', **ryaw* 'mix', **day* 'that, this'; also:

(298) T *mthe-bo* 'thumb', Nung *thɛ*, Mikir *the* 'big, large, great' (TB **tay*).[208]

(299) T *lte-ba*, K *dai~śədai* 'navel', G *ste* 'abdomen' (TB **s-tay*).

(300) K *mai*, Nung *mɛ*, Mikir *me* 'good, well' (TB **may*).

(301) K *lai~śəlai* 'pass; exceed', Nung *lɛ~səlɛ* 'pass', G *re*, Dimasa *lai* 'pass', Mikir *le* 'over, excess, profit' (TB **lay*); cf. L *lei* 'fine, debt, tax'.

A few roots in **-oy* have been reconstructed on the basis of Kachin and Lushei material. This final appears in both these languages, but in some instances can be

from the same general AT source: *mai*[a] (tone B) 'buy', *mai*[b] (tone C) 'sell', possibly from **mlay* (*GSR* does not cite Ar. Ch. form); *mai* (tone C) is from *mai* + transitive suffix (n. 494).

208 The reconstruction for this root is supported by B *tai* 'very'; cf. the Ch. cognate *tʻâi*,[c] with identical semantic development.

[a] 買 [b] 賣 [c] 太

referred back to TB **-wa[·]y*; cf. L *khoi*∼*khwai* 'bee' < TB **kwa·y* (No. 157); L *loi*, K *ŋəloi* 'buffalo' < TB **lwa·y*; also the following:

(302) Bunan *lo-i*, K *loi*∼*lwe*, B *lwai* 'easy' (TB **lway*).[209]

(303) K *koi* 'shun', *məkoi* 'hide, conceal', B *kwai* 'conceal, keep out of sight' (TB **kway*).

Where evidence for TB **-way* is lacking, however, roots of this type have been reconstructed in **-oy*:

(304) K *moi* 'perfectly, beautifully' (couplet form), L *moi* 'pretty, beautiful' (TB **moy*).

(305) K *nmoi* 'blossoms, as of grain; spikes, spikelets', L *moi* 'beginning to form in the bud (as rice)' (TB **(r-)moy*).

(306) K *soi* 'graze, almost hit', L *thoi* 'slightly graze, go or pass close by' (TB **soy*).

Burmese appears to have merged **-oy* with **-wiy* in the final *-we*:

(307) B *kwé* 'bend round, be curved', *kwè* 'to bend, curve', *khwe* 'to curve, curl, coil, wind into a ring; a coil', *khwè* 'flat ring, ferrule', L *koi*, Siyin *kauyi*∼*koi* 'crooked, bent', Dimasa *sugui* 'to bend', *gugui* 'bent' (T **koy*).[210]

(308) K (Khauri dial.) *boi* 'to have a flexure or cowlick', B *bhwe* 'circular flexure in the hair of animals' (TB **boy*).

(309) K *śədoi* 'last born child in a family', *wa-doi*∼*wa-dwe* 'father's younger brother; stepfather', *nu-doi*∼*nu-dwe* 'mother's younger sister; stepmother', B *thwè*∼*ăthwè* 'youngest', *mí-thwè* 'mother's younger sister; stepmother', *bhá-thwè* 'father's youngest brother; stepfather', G *ma-de* 'aunt, stepmother', Bodo *udui* 'to be young', *ma-doi* 'mother's sister', Dimasa *gidi* 'younger (child)', *bidi* 'father's younger brother', *ma-di* 'father's younger sister' (TB **doy*∼*toy*).[211]

(310) K *goi* 'crow, as a cock; squeak, as some kinds of snakes; laugh loudly', *məgroi* 'howl, scream', B *krwè*∼*kywè* 'call out, halloo, shout; screech and scream in large numbers, as birds' (TB **groy*).

(311) K *khoi*, B *krwe* 'shellfish, shell' (TB **kroy*).[212]

209 TB **lway* rather than **lw[a, a·]y* by convention (we write short vowel in roots for which length cannot be determined).

210 For Siyin, Stern, *Asia Major* **10** (1963), cites *kui* (low tone) 'bend' (intr). and *kuei* (high tone) 'bend' (tr.); Tiddim Chin has *kuai* 'bend'; these forms probably represent an original **koi* (as in Lushei) rather than **kway*.

211 Add Trung (Nungish) *ik-ra a-dəi* (tone A) 'younger brother (*ik-ra*)', *a-la a-dəi* 'younger uncle (*a-la*)'; cf. *dəi* (tone A) 'short', *a-dəi* (tone B) 'small (persons)', also Lepcha *di(-m)* 'small'.

212 TB **kroy* rather than **krwəy*, since Kachin has *khri* 'son-in-law' for TB **krwəy* (No. 244). This reconstruction is strikingly confirmed by the finals in Thai (**-oy*) and Kam-Sui (**-ui*) in the apparently related AT root; cf. the following pair

(312) K *khoi* 'borrow or lend (presupposes a return in kind)', B *krwè* 'debt', *ăkrwè* 'on credit' (TB **kroy*).

(313) K *khoi* 'surround, enclose', B *khrwe-ram* 'surround, attend' (TB **kroy*).

Note that Siyin has *kauyi* ~ *koi* < **koy* (No. 307) as opposed to *loai* 'buffalo' < TB *lwa·y* (No. 208). Dimasa has *-ui* < *-*oy* in No. 307, paralleling the Burmese development, but simply *-i* in No. 309 (possibly because of the initial dental). Kachin, which shows loss of medial *r* in this group of roots (Nos. 310, 311, 312), alternates between *-oi* and *-we* for TB *-*oy*, as in Nos. 302 and 309, as well as the following:

(314) K *woi* ~ *we*, Jili *təwe*, Kadu *kwe* < **k-we*, Nung *əwɛ*, Moshang *vi-sil*, Shangge *yok-vi* 'monkey' (TB **woy*).[213]

The following root shows much fluctuation in final:

(315) K *ŋwi* 'gentle, mild, peaceful, quiet', *əŋwi-śa* ~ *əŋoi-śa* 'gently, peacefully, moderately', B *ŋwé* 'appear in small measure; gentle, moderate', L *ŋoi* 'quiet, silent', *ŋui* 'downhearted, sad', *ŋuai* 'listless, quiet, silent' (TB **ŋoy*).

Final *-*ew*, the front vowel + *w* combination analogous to *-*oy* (back vowel + *y*), cannot be reconstructed for any TB roots, yet does appear in Kuki-Naga (L *-eu*, Lakher *-ei* or *-ua*, Mikir *-e*):

**d-k(h)ew*: L *kheuʔ* ~ *khei*, Lakher *tśəkhei* 'pick (as a sore), dig out (as a thorn)', Mikir *arke* 'scratch the soil for grain (in birds)'.

**hrew* 'burrow': L *hreuʔ*, Lakher *rei*.

**ew* 'lean back': L *eu*, Lakher *əua*.

**m-hew*: L *heu* 'spoiled, wasted', Lakher *pəhua* 'waste away'.

Vowel gradation must be taken into account for a few TB roots, e.g. Mikir *arvi* < TB **r-bi(y)* 'left' for TB **bay*; L *hnai* 'near' < TB */na·y* for TB **ney*;

of correspondences (from Benedict, 1967bis, with corrections); aspiration is indicated for the TB roots, and *-*uw* is written *-*əw* (n. 188):

	TB	Thai	Kam-Sui	Oceanic
shellfish	*k(h)roy*	*hoy*	*qhui*	*kway*
dove	*m-khrəw*	*khraw*	*qwaw*	*kwəw-*

It is possible that the velar + *r* clusters in these roots represent an archaism; cf. I Miao, which has initial *q-* = /*kr*/- (phonemic interpretation by K. Chang); it is also possible that the medial *-r-* of Thai **khraw* 'dove' is an old infixed /*l̥*/, as found in other roots, in which event TB **k(h)roy* is to be interpreted as a loan from an AT infixed form preserved only in this loan.

213 Trung (Nungish) has *a-koi* 'monkey', with prefixed *k-*, as in Kadu. Mikir *ki-pi*, Miri *si-be* 'monkey' perhaps belong with this set; we now reconstruct TB **(b)woy*, although Chinese has a possible cognate which points to ST initial **w-*: *gi̯wăn/yi̯wɒn*[a] 'monkey' (with suffixed *-n*).

[a] 猿

Dimasa *busu* 'thorn' < TB **tsu*(*w*) for TB **tsow*; Dimasa *khau* 'steal' < TB **kow* for TB **r-kuw*. This feature also appears in the following pair of roots:

(316) T *ʔane* ~ *nene-mo*, Tsangla *ənye*, Kanauri *əne* < TB **ney*, but Gyarung *əni*, Miri *ənyi*, Nung *əni*, K *ni*, G *ma-ni*, L *ni*, Mikir *ni* 'aunt (father's sister); mother-in-law', from TB **ni*(*y*).

(317) L *tu-bauʔ* ~ *tu-bouʔ* 'hammer' < TB **tu*(*w*), but T *mtho-ba* ~ *tho-ba* 'large hammer', Thebor *tho-a* 'large hammer', *tho-ro* ~ *tho-tśuŋ* 'small hammer', Nung *du-ma*, K *sumdu*, B *tu*, Dimasa *dau-bu* 'hammer', K *thu*, B *thú* 'to pound, hammer' (TB **tow*).[214]

Kachin has *-au* (rather than *-u*) for TB *-*ow* in several roots:

(318) K *gau*, B *kù* 'cross over' (TB **gow*).

(319) K *dau*, B *thu* 'thick' (TB **tow*).

(320) K *mərau*, Nung *śəru thiŋ*, B *thàŋ-rù* 'pine, fir' (TB **row*).[215]

Generally speaking, TB vowel gradation is sporadic and irregular, and can hardly be compared with that found in Indo-European, as Shafer has attempted to do.[216, 217]

214 Kanauri has *tho-ro* 'small hammer', *gon-to* 'large hammer'. A doublet with initial **d*- must be recognized in this root: cf. Kanauri *sdo*, Thebor *do* 'mallet'; Nungish (Răwang) *du-ma*, K *sumdu*, Dimasa *dau-bu*, B-L **du* (Maru *dau*) 'hammer'. The Kanauri and Thebor *tho*- forms are likely loans from Tibetan, and the irregular L *tu*- is perhaps to be explained as a loan from Burmese (Karen has a loan here from Burmese; see p. 147).

215 For the first element of B *thàŋ-rù*, cf. T *thaŋ-tśhu* 'resin, gum' (*tśhu* 'water'), *thaŋ-śiŋ* 'fir, pine' (*śiŋ* 'tree'), Vayu *thoŋ* < **thaŋ* 'pine'; also B *thàŋ* 'firewood'.

216 'The vocalism of Sino-Tibetan', *JAOS* **60** (1940), **61** (1941); esp. the discussion on pp. 312–14. Shafer's over-simplified scheme of TB vowels fails to take into account the distinction between short and long *a*, and in general is unsatisfactory from a phonemic point of view. Shafer's *-ui* for *-*uw* rests on a misconception of the phonemic value of the form *-uiw* found in the early Burmese inscriptions (*ui* is allophone of *u* before *w*).

217 R. A. Miller, 'The Tibeto-Burman Ablaut System', *Papers of the First Congress of Foreign Orientalists in Japan*; E. J. Pulleyblank, 'Close/open ablaut in Sino-Tibetan', *Lingua* **14** (1965), 230–40 (JAM). Miller operates with a six-vowel system (with *-*ü* for our *-*uw* = *-*əw*, but only *-*i* for both our *-*i* and *-*iy* = *-*əy*) and recognizes two sets of ablaut relationships: *a* ~ *e* ~ *o*; *i* ~ *ü* ~ *u*. This scheme includes the medial **u* ~ **i* alternation in Tibetan and elsewhere (see pp. 83 and 84) but neglects the basic medial **ya* ~ **i* alternation (see pp. 84 and 85); it also encompasses the medial *a* ~ *o* and *a* ~ *e* alternations in Tibetan verbs but hardly serves as an explanation (n. 344); the material cited for vocalic ablaut in root-final position is scarcely convincing, e.g. B *ni* 'red', *na* 'ill' and *nu* 'leprous' (it seems highly unlikely that these forms are related in any manner whatever). Pulleyblank adduces material to show a distinction between intransitives and transitives based on medial vowel quality, e.g. Ch. *d'âm*[a] 'to talk' (intr.), *d'əm*/*d'ậm*[b] (same tone) 'to

a 談　　b 譚

§11. Tibeto-Burman vowels (medials)

All five vowel phonemes occur in medial position. Lushei distinguishes between short and long vowels in this position, and this distinction is reflected in Haka and other Kuki-Naga languages. Other TB languages, insofar as they have been recorded accurately, do not show this feature in any consistent way, although vowel length is sometimes marked. The Lushei distinction between *a* and *a·*, and between *u* and *u·*, is reflected in certain correspondences in Bodo-Garo and Burmese-Lolo (see below), hence we must suppose that the distinction obtained also for *o* and *o·*, *e* and *e·*, *i* and *i·*, although it is possible that the TB vowel system was asymmetrical. Lushei has relatively few forms with long vowels connected with general TB roots, and it would appear that TB medial vowels were 'normally' short (all final vowels were phonemically long). Numerous examples of roots with short medial vowel are scattered throughout the preceding pages; in the discussion below emphasis is placed on roots with long medial vowel.

Medial *a* is preserved before all types of finals in Tibetan, Kachin, Burmese, Garo, Lushei and most TB languages. Lepcha, which has *-o* for TB final **-a*, normally shifts to *o*, e.g. *ătsom* 'hair' < TB **tsam*, *lom* 'road' < TB **lam*, but *tyaŋ* 'dark' < TB **tyaŋ*. Mikir, however, with *-o* for TB final **-a* as in Lepcha, retains medial **a* with the exception of a curious shift to *e*∼*i* before final *-m*, as in *nem-po* 'sesame' < TB **s-nam*, *serim* 'otter' < TB **s-ram*, *iŋnim* 'to smell', *nem-so* 'slight smell, stink' < TB **m-nam*.[218] This shift is partially paralleled in Himalayish: Kanauri *keb* 'needle' < TB **kap*, *stem* 'daughter-in-law' < TB **s-nam*; also *bren* 'get well' < TB **bran*. Occasional shifts to *o* or *e* are encountered elsewhere; cf. T *ʔag-tshom* 'beard of the chin' < TB **tsam*, and the following:

(321) West T *lob-ma* (cf. T *lo-ma*), Kanauri *lab*, Takpa *blap*, K *lap* 'leaf', Nung *śəlap* 'leaves for packing food' (TB **lap*).

talk about' (tr.) (*GSR* glosses both as 'speak'), T *gtam* 'talk, discourse, speech', *gtom-pa* 'to talk, speak' (see n. 488 for the ST reconstruction), but much more evidence would be required to establish this point (Pulleyblank describes a study in progress).

218 Mikir also has *e* for **a* before final *-ŋ*; cf. *-kreŋ* 'cold' < TB **graŋ*; *-kleŋ* 'congeal' < TB **glaŋ*; *keŋ* 'leg, foot', T *rkaŋ(-pa)* 'foot, leg; stem, stalk'; note also Thado *keŋ* 'leg, foot' but L *ke* and Tiddim *xɛ* < **khe, id.*, possibly from a doublet root: TB **keŋ*; cf. Ch. *gʿieŋ*/*γieŋ*[a] 'leg, shank', *gʿĕŋ*/*γɛŋ*[b] 'stalk', with semantic development as in Tibetan (the Chinese vocalism suggests an original **gi*[·]*ŋ* rather than **geŋ* or **gaŋ*).

[a] 脛　　[b] 莖

(322) K *dźi-groŋ* (*dźi* 'winged insect'), B *khraŋ*, Mikir *tim-kraŋ* (*tim* 'gnat, midge') 'mosquito' (TB **kraŋ*).[219]

Long medial **a·* appears in TB **ba·r* 'flower', **ga·r* 'dance, leap, stride', **ya·p* 'fan; winnow; paddle', *dzya·l* 'far' (see above) and the following roots:[220]

(323) B *hak* 'hawk, raise phlegm', also 'stretch (the mouth), gag', L *ha·k* 'choke' (TB **ha·k*); cf. also Mikir *tśiŋ khak* 'expectorate, clear throat, cough up; phlegm, sputum', L *kha·k* 'phlegm'.

(324) T *mag-pa*, Lepcha *myok* < **s-mak*, Dhimal *hma-wa*, Miri *mak-bo* ~ *mag-bo*, K *da-maʔ*, B *sa-mak*, Lahu *ɔ̀-má-pā*, L *ma·k-pa* 'son-in-law' (TB **ma·k*).[221]

(325) G *do-bak* (*do* 'bird'), L *ba·k* 'bat' (TB **ba·k*).

(326) K *than* 'hang, as a sword at the side', *məthan* 'impale', L *ta·r* 'stick on a pole, make or set up a landmark, hang up', Mikir *tar* 'impale' (TB **ta·r*).

(327) B *khak-raŋ* 'fork', *ăkhak* 'branch', Lahu *ɔ̀-qá*, L *ka·k* 'fork (of tree); to be forked' (TB **ka·k*).[222]

(328) T *yaŋ-po*, K *tsaŋ* < **g-yaŋ* (cf. Nos. 163, 164), G *rittśeŋ*, Dimasa *redźeŋ* < **r-yaŋ* (cf. No. 164), L *za·ŋ* < **ya·ŋ*, Mikir *ardźaŋ* < **r-yaŋ* 'light (not heavy)' (TB **r-ya·ŋ*).

Lushei vacillates between short and long *a* in the following root:

(329) K *ngam* (*n-gam*) 'precipitous; precipice', *kha ningam* 'bank of a river (*kha*)', B *kàm* (archaic *khàm*) 'bank of a river or sea', *knut-khàm* 'lips' (= 'mouth-bank'), G *rikam* 'bank, margin, rim', L *kam* 'bank, shore, mouth', *kha·m* 'precipice' (TB **r-ka[·]m*).

The following pair appear to reflect an archaic TB doublet:

(330) K *kaŋ* 'to be hot; emit heat, as the sun or a flame', *kəkaŋ* 'roast, toast, bake', Nung *dəgaŋ* 'toast', B *kaŋ* 'broil, roast, toast', L *ka·ŋ* 'burn' (TB **ka·ŋ*).[223]

219 Further support for an original **a* vocalism in this root is furnished by Nungish: Răwang *məgaŋ* < **m-graŋ* 'mosquito', Trung *kraŋ* 'fire-fly'.

220 Add the following pair of roots: K *lam* 'to measure by fathoms', *ləlam* 'fathom'; B *lam* 'to encompass with the arms', *ălam* 'fathom'; L *hlam* 'arm span' but Tiddim *la·m* 'fathom'; TB **la[·]m*; T *'gran-pa* 'vie with, contend for, strive; (in general sense) fight', from **g-ral* (see n. 318 for initial, n. 54 for final), *ral-gri* 'sword' (=war-knife); B *ran* 'quarrel'; L *ra·l* 'war against, warrior', Tiddim *ga·l* < **ra·l* 'battle, war, enemy', Angami Naga (Burling) *te-hrə* 'war'; TB **(g-)ra·l*.

221 **s-mak* (cf. Burmese) > **ʔmak* in Proto-Loloish; Lahu reflects this with a high-rising tone; the first element is **za* 'child, son'; Modern Lahu has a re-prefixed form: *ɔ̀-má* (JAM).

222 Also a glottalized root in PLB: **ʔkak* < **ʔəkak*. The *a-* in Burmese is thus a re-prefixation after the original prefix had fused with the root (JAM). K *khaʔ* 'to be parted, separated, open', *dźəkhaʔ* 'to part, separate' (Maran), probably also belongs with this set.

223 Tiddim Chin has *kaŋ* (rising tone) 'to dry up', contrasting with *kaŋ* (level tone) 'to fry', also *ka·ŋ* (level tone) 'to burn'. Both these roots (Nos. 330 and 331)

(331) K *kaŋ* 'to be dry, as paddy, garments or the like', L *kaŋ* 'evaporate, dry up', also 'fry' (TB **kaŋ*).[223]

TB medial **a* is in general preserved in Bodo-Garo as elsewhere, although shifts to *i* or *e* (also *o* in Dimasa) frequently occur, especially after *r-* or *l-*; cf. No. 328 (above) and the following trio of roots:

(332) Mikir *praŋ* 'dawn', G *phriŋ*, Dimasa *phoroŋ* 'morning' (TB **praŋ*).[224]

(333) K *laŋ* 'bird of the falcon family', *gəlaŋ* 'eagle, kite, hawk', *laŋ-da*~*laŋ-daŋ* 'vulture', B *làŋ-tá* 'vulture', *hrwe-làŋ-tá* 'eagle' (= 'golden vulture'), *làŋ-yun* 'species of hawk', G *do-reŋ* 'falcon, kite', Bodo *dau-leŋ-a* 'eagle', Dimasa *dau-liŋ* 'kite' (TB **laŋ*).[225]

(334) K *naŋ* 'follow', *mənaŋ* 'companion', *śənaŋ* 'adhere to, follow up'; B *hnáŋ*<**s-náŋ* 'with, together with', *hnaŋ-hnaŋ* 'common, ordinary', G *sniŋ* 'follow, imitate', *sniŋ-gipa* 'apostle', Dimasa *phanaŋ* 'attach, set anything to another thing' (causative form) (TB **naŋ*).

Before final labial stop, however, the Bodo-Garo development of medial *a* has been as follows:

TB **-ap*>*-ap* (*-p* sometimes dropped in Dimasa)

TB **-a·p*>**-a·w*>*-au* (Dimasa)~*-o* (Garo)

show unaspirated initials everywhere, indicating an earlier prefix (see p. 20); in cases of this kind, we write by convention TB **ka·ŋ* and not *[ ]*ka·ŋ* or */*ka·ŋ*; Nungish (Răwang) has *dəgaŋ* 'toast' (text) but the prefixed **d-* here appears to be of late origin and accordingly has not been included in the reconstruction, even in the provisional form *(*d-*).

224 Lahu *š̀ɔ́-pɔ̄* 'tomorrow' (*š̀ɔ́* 'morning') (JAM). This is possibly a prefixed root: **b-raŋ*; Trung (Nungish) has *sraŋ* 'morning', probably from an original **s-raŋ*.

225 This root appears to be a loan-word in TB, probably from an Austro-Asiatic source (Benedict, 1968 paper); Mon-Khmer shows forms of *klaŋ* type (Bahnar *klaŋ*) but Khasi has *kliŋ*; closely similar forms appear in Miao (Hua Miao *klaŋ*, I Miao *qloŋ*) but not elsewhere in AT. Forrest (*JAOS* **82**, 1962) cites Lepcha *kălyŭŋ* 'sp. of eagle' but this would indicate an original long medial *u·* (n. 231); the Lepcha cognate is perhaps the standard term *kum-thyóŋ*~*pun-thyóŋ* 'eagle, kite' (with palatalization of the original velar + *l* initial cluster). Forrest analyzes the first element as the **k-* 'animal prefix' (n. 301) and it clearly is so handled in TB, but this might be the product of metanalysis (n. 83). The Ch. cognate shows a similar initial cluster: *·i̯əŋ*[a](= *ʔi̯əŋ*) 'eagle, falcon', from *ʔli̯əŋ* (n. 419), with *ʔ* standing for **k* or even **q* (indicated by Miao forms). Tibetan has *glag* 'eagle, vulture', which has been compared (p. 178) with Ch. *glâk*/*lâk*[b] 'kind of bird' but which might represent an old doublet of our general ST root here: **g-ləŋ*~**g-lək*; cf. Ch. *di̯ək*/*i̯ək*[c] 'hawk, kite', from **li̯ək* (n. 458); this reading for the Ch. graph is based on the use of *di̯ək*/*i̯ək*[d] 'stringed arrow' as phonetic, the graph then having been applied to another root (n. 453).

[a] 鷹　[b] 雒　[c] 鳶　[d] 弋

		TB	Lushei	Garo	Bodo	Dimasa
116	weep	**krap*	*ṭap*	*grap*	*gap*	*gara*
118	fireplace	**tap*	*tap*	*tśudap*	*gadap*	*gap*
219	shoot	**ga·p*	*ka·p*	*go*	*gau*	*gau*
92	fan, winnow, paddle	**ya·p*	*za·p*	*tśo*	*dźau*	*dźau*

The Bodo-Garo evidence permits the reconstruction of long medial *a·* in the following roots:

(335) K *məlap*, Dimasa *balau* 'forget' (TB **b-la·p*).

(336) B *khap* 'dig up, take out of, draw, as water', G *ko* 'draw water', Dimasa *khau* 'fill, gather, pluck', *di khau* 'draw water' (TB **ka·p*).[226]

(337) K *thap* 'capable, quick, useful' (Needham), 'beautiful' (Hertz), G *ni-to* 'beautiful, fit' (*ni* 'look'), Dimasa *thau* 'to be fit for, suitable for' (TB **ta·p*).[227]

The correspondence for short medial *a* is further supported by the following:

(338) L *kap* 'fork of the legs', also 'to gag, wedge open', Dimasa *ya-khap* 'groin, fork' (*ya* 'leg') (TB **kap*).

The mid-high medial vowels **o* and **e* of TB are well preserved in Tibetan, Kachin and Lushei, but are not nearly so well represented as are **a*, **u* and **i*. Long medial **o·* appears in **dzo·p* 'suck, kiss' and **o·l* 'finish; relax' (above), while long medial **e·* occurs in the following pair of roots:

(339) Jili *təkhyen*, L *ke·l* 'goat' (TB **ke·l*).[228]

(340) Dimasa *gepher* 'flat', L *pe·r* 'flat and thin' (TB **pe·r*).

Burmese, which lacks both these medial vowels (*o*, *e*), has merged medial **o* with short medial **u* in medial *au* before velars (*-auk*, *-auŋ*) but with *a* before other finals (*-at*, *-an*; *-ap*, *-am*):

(341) T *mdoŋs* 'eye in peacock's feather', K *u-doŋ*, B *ú-daùŋ* 'peacock' (TB **doŋ*).

226 Lahu has *qho* < **kham*, indicating a doublet with final nasal (the reverse of the usual B-L situation) (JAM).

227 For Kachin, Hanson has *thap tsiŋ* 'beautiful' but defines *thap* as follows: 'to be of a deep, black or red colour; to be ruddy, and thus beautiful; to be pleasing, agreeable, delightful' (suggesting that this is basically a color name). In Tibetan the root is perhaps represented by *thabs* 'opportunity, chance, possibility' = 'the fit (*thab-*) place or time (*-s*)'; cf. also T *stabs* 'mode, manner, way, measure'. The Bodo-Garo forms can be compared directly with B *tau*, Lahu *dɔ* 'to fit, be suitable' (JAM, 1969), but the latter pair might also be from a root such as **m-da·p*, yielding **m-daw*, with development as in B-G.

228 This root now reconstructed **kye·l*, since Jili (in Kachin group) preserves medial *-y-* before *e*; a doublet **kyi*[·]*l* is represented by T *skyin* 'wild mountain goat' (n. 53).

(342) T *skog-pa* ~ *kog-pa* 'shell, rind', *phyi-kog* 'bark' (*phyi* 'outside'), Bahing *kok-te* 'skin', B *ăkhauk*, Lahu *ɔ̀-qú* 'bark' (TB **kok*).[229]

(343) K *on-on* ~ *go-on* ~ *won* 'feel squeamish, nauseated', B *an* 'retch, vomit' (TB **on*).

(344) T *gtsod* ~ *btsod* 'Tibetan antelope', B *tshat* 'sambhur' (TB **tsot*).

(345) L *pop* 'hole, aperture', B *pap* 'to be a crevice, crack open' (TB **pop*).

TB medial **e* before final velars and dentals has fallen together with **i* in Burmese *-ats* and *-ań*, and before labials in Burmese *-ip* and *-im*; cf. B *hrats* '8' < **/ret* < **/ryat* (TB **b-r-gyat*); B *hmáń* 'mole' < TB **r-men*; B *pyań* 'plank' < TB *pleŋ*; also the following:

(346) K *ren* 'to be equal', *diŋren* 'place in a long, even row'; B *rań-tu* 'to be equal', *hrań* 'put together side by side'; Dimasa *ren* 'line' (comp.), Mikir *ren* 'line, range, row' (TB **ren*).

(347) Kiranti **khrep* 'ant', K *krep* ~ *śəkrep* 'bug', B *khrip* 'lac' < 'lac insect' (TB **krep*).[230]

(348) K *nem*, Nung *ənem*, B *ním* 'low' (TB **nem*).

TB medial **o* and **e* are represented in a few Bodo-Garo forms:

(349) T *kor* 'round, circular', West T *kor* 'hollow in the ground, pit', L *kor* 'small valley, ravine', G *a-khol*, Dimasa *ha-khor* 'cave', Bodo *ha-khor* 'hole; valley' (*a* ~ *ha* 'earth') (TB **kor*).

This root is to be kept distinct from the following:

(350) L *khuar* ~ *khur* 'hole, cavity', Nung *duŋ-khr* [*-khər*] 'hole' (for *duŋ-*, see No. 169) (TB **kwar*).

229 Another glottalized PLB root (note Tibetan prefixed *s-*): **ʔkuk* 'outer covering' (JAM). Bahing also has *siŋ-kok-te* 'bark' (*siŋ* 'tree'). Two little known Himalayan languages indicate an original **kw-* initial cluster: Chourasya *kwak-te* ~ *kok-te*, Thulungya *kwok-si* ~ *kok-si* 'skin', and this appears significant in the light of Gyarung (K. Chang) *werkhwak* 'its skin', from **-rkhwak*. We can now reconstruct TB **(r-)kwâk*, yielding B *-khauk* via **-khok*, theoretically contrasting with TB **kwak* yielding B *k(h)wak* (we have no comparisons for this). This reconstruction is supported by the Chinese cognate, viz. *kʻwâk*[a] 'leather'. Chinese also has an apparent doublet showing loss of the medial *-w-*, viz. *kɛk*[b] 'hide, skin; (flay, peel) take away' (but the vowel is anomalous). Karlgren suggests that the verbal meaning is derived, but in TB the opposite development might have occurred: 'to peel or skin off' > 'something peeled or skinned off'; cf. L *khok* 'peel off, pull off (skin, bark)', Chang Naga (Konyak group) *kwok-* 'to strip (as fibres)' (note the initial *kw-* cluster, again suggesting an original **kwâk*).

230 Lahu *a-kɨ* 'lac' indicates PLB **ʔkrip*, as does B *khrip* (JAM). For the semantics of this root, see Benedict, 1939. Răwang (Nungish) has both *rap* 'lac insect' and *rip* 'flying ant', the latter from **khrip*; cf. Răwang *rap* 'winnow' < **khrap* (n. 382); for the relationship in meaning, cf. Miri *təruk* 'ant', also 'lac insect' < TB **rwak* 'ant'.

a 鞹 b 革

(351) K *lep*, G *rep*, Dimasa *lep*, L *hlep* 'slice, pare, cut off' (TB **lep*), but Lepcha has *lip* 'to slice, cut in slices'.

(352) K *preŋ*, G *diŋ-breŋ* 'straight', Dimasa *beleŋ* 'to be erect, straight', *gibleŋ* 'erect, straight', *si-phleŋ* 'straighten out' (TB **bleŋ ~ *pleŋ*).

The high medial vowels **u* and **i* of TB are well maintained in Tibetan, Kachin and Lushei, but partial or complete replacement by lower vowels (*o ~ e ~ a*) is characteristic of Burmese, Garo and many other TB languages. General replacement by *a* is found in Magari, Lepcha, Digaro, Chang Naga and Maru. Lepcha typically has short *ă* as opposed to long *a* (from TB **a*): *hrăt* 'bone' < TB **rus*, *lăŋ* 'stone' < TB **r-luŋ*, *nyăt* '2' < TB **g-nis*, *nyăl ~ nyel* 'gums' < TB **r-nil*; Lepcha also has forms with medial *u*, which in at least three roots appear to reflect TB long **u·*: *tăfuk* 'stomach' < TB **pu·k*, *kuŋ* 'tree' < TB **ku·ŋ* and *muk* 'weeds' TB **mu·k* (see below).[231]

Burmese maintains high vowels, long or short, before labials, also when long before velars (no examples of long **i·* here) and dentals, but short **u* before velars,

231 Lepcha often has medial *ă ~ u* interchange, e.g. *măt* 'to blow', *sŭŋ-mut* 'wind'; cf. Bahing *hmut ~ mut*, Gyarung *-mut*, Kachin (Assam dial.) *mut*, Miri *mut*, B *hmut* 'to blow (mouth, wind)', from TB **(s-)mut*. Further analysis of the Lepcha material shows that this language regularly has medial *a* or *ă* for TB medial **u*, and medial *u* or *ŭ* for TB medial **u·*; in addition to the three roots cited in the text, cf. the following: *tŭk-păt* 'knee' < TB **put*; *tărăk* '6' < TB **d-ruk*; *tuk-tsam* 'mortar' < TB **tśrum* (or **tsum*); *sam* '3' < TB **g-sum*; *lyam* 'to warm up food', from **s-lam* < TB **lum*; *(a-)myal ~ (a-)myel* 'body hair' < TB **(s-)mul*; *khlyam* 'sweet', from **s-klam* < TB **klum* (L *thlum*, Siyin *thum*, Meithei *thum*), as contrasted with *muk* 'foggy, misty', *muk-muk* 'dullness, darkness' < TB **r-mu·k*; *muŋ* 'overclouded, overcast' < TB **mu·ŋ*; *kuk* 'to rake, scrape', etc. < TB **ku·k*; *kum* 'arched, concave, vaulted' < TB **ku[·]m*; cf. also *ryŭm* 'needle', an apparent loan from AT (n. 82, citing IN **d'aγum*). The Lepcha correspondence permits the reconstruction of long medial **u·* in TB **nu·p ~ *ni[·]p* 'sink': Lepcha *nŭp* 'to be covered with water', also **(m-)u·m* 'hold in the mouth': Lecha *ŭm* 'receive into mouth without swallowing'. Complex doublets must be recognized in some instances: TB **(m-)tuk ~ *(s-)tu·k ~ *(s-)du·k*: Mikir *iŋtok* 'to spit; spittle' (n. 189); Maru *tauk* 'vomit, spew'; Lepcha *tyuk* 'to spit', *dyuk* 'spittle'; TB **duŋ ~ *tu·ŋ* 'long, length' (Lepcha *ă-thŭŋ* 'height, length'); also TB **pu·k ~ *buk* 'cave; belly' (Lepcha *tăfuk ~ tăbok ~ tăbak*), with Chinese showing forms derived from **puk ~ *buk* (n. 479). Lepcha, finally, has medial *o* or *ó* in three roots: *-tok* 'neck' < TB **tuk*; *(ă-)róŋ* 'horn' < TB **ruŋ*; *tśór* 'sour, acid' < TB **skyur*, the last root apparently related to TB **su·r* 'sour', Ch. *swân/suân*;[a] this suggests the reconstructions **twak* 'neck', **rwaŋ* 'horn' (a doublet of **rwa*) and **s-kywa·r* and **swa·r* 'sour'. One would anticipate that Lepcha might make a similar distinction between medial *ă* < TB **i*, and medial *i* (or *e*) < TB **i·*, but this cannot be established on the basis of the material now at hand, although Lepcha *kil* 'screw' < TB **ki·l*, and Lepcha *hlet-bŭ* 'leech' < TB **(m-)li·t* are suggestive here.

a 酸

and short **i* before velars and dental nasal (but not stop) show the development of diphthongs:

TB **-uk*, **-uŋ* > B *-auk*, *-auŋ* but **-u·k*, **-u·ŋ* > B *-uik* /*-uk*/, *-uiŋ* /*-uŋ*/.

TB **-ik*, **-iŋ* > B *-ats*, /*-ait*/, *-ań* /*-ain*/.

TB **in* > B *-ań* /*-ain*/ (but **-it* > B *-it*).

As noted above, B *ui* here is simply a positional variant (allophone) of the phoneme *u* before *-k*, *-ŋ* and *-w*. TB long medial **u·* has developed in the same manner as final **-u(w)*, while short medial **u* has fallen together with medial **o* in the diphthong *au* (see above).[232] In addition to B *khrauk*, L *ruk* '6' < TB **d-ruk*, the following cross-checks with Lushei are available:

(353) B *tsauk* 'steep', L *tśhuk* 'descend, steep (downwards), down' (TB **tsyuk*).

(354) B *hnaùŋ* 'to be after', *ăhnaùŋ* 'coming after, last', *ăhnaúŋ* 'back (of a knife)',[233] L *hnuŋ* 'the back', *hnuŋ-a* 'after, behind', Mikir *ənuŋ* 'back' (TB **s-nuŋ*).

(355) B *lak-khyaùŋ* < **lak-(k)yaùŋ* 'finger' (*lak* 'hand'), *khre-khyauŋ* 'toe'

232 Lahu and probably other Loloish languages have two correspondences to Burmese final *-auk*; we reconstruct **-ok* and **-uk*:

*Final *-ok*

	Lahu	Burmese	Tibetan		Lahu	Burmese	Tibetan
fear	*kɔ̂ʔ*	{*krauk* / *khrauk*}	*dogs*	poison	*tɔ̀ʔ*	*tauk*	*dug*
flint	*mí-jɔ̀ʔ*	*mì-kyauk*	—	behind	*-nɔ́*	*nauk*	—
below	*hɔ́*	*ʔauk*	*og*	project	*ŋɔ́*	*ŋauk*	—
morning	*šɔ́*	*sauk*	—	six	*khɔ̀ʔ*	*khrauk*	*drug*
hit	*dɔ̂ʔ*	*tauk*	—				

*Final *-uk*

	Lahu	Burmese	Tibetan		Lahu	Burmese	Tibetan
catch fire	*tòʔ/tú*	*tauk*	*dugs-pa*	mane	*ɔ̀-kú-mu*	—	*rŋog-ma*
outer covering	*qú*	*khauk*	*skog*	dry	*hú*	*khrauk*	—
scoop	*lú*	*hauk*	*skyogs*	drink	*šú*	*sauk*	—

In addition to the above, we reconstruct final **-u·k* for 'erect; prick': T *ʾdzug*, Burmese *tsuik*, Lahu *jûʔ* (JAM).

One would anticipate that the Lahu distinction detailed above might point to TB **-ok* and **-uk*, which in Burmese have fallen together in final *auk* (text), but this does not appear to be the case; much additional material from other Loloish languages will be needed to clarify this matter.

233 Also B *nauk* 'behind', Lahu *qhɔ̀ʔ-nɔ́*. The aspirated Burmese variant confirms the glottalized initial (see 'GD') (JAM).

(*khre* 'foot'), K *yuŋ*~*ləyuŋ*<**lak-yuŋ*, L *zuŋ*<**yuŋ*, Khami *məyuŋ*~*məzuŋ* 'finger, toe', from TB **(m-)yuŋ*.[234]

(356) T *'thug-pa*~*mthug-pa* 'thick', *stug(s)-pa* 'thickness', B *thuik-thuik* 'thickly', L *thu·k* 'deep' (TB **tu·k*).[235]

(357) T *rmugs-pa* 'dense fog; inertness', *smug-po* 'dark red, purple-brown'; Lepcha *muk* 'foggy, misty', *muk muk* 'dullness, darkness'; B *muik* 'dark; ignorant', L *mu·k* 'dull (color)' (TB **mu·k*).[236]

(358) T *phug(s)* 'innermost part', *phug-pa* 'cavern'; Miri *sap-puük*, Abor *rak-puük* 'cave' (cf. T *brag-phug* 'rock cavern'); Nung and K *luŋ-pu* 'cave' (with *luŋ* 'rock'=T *brag*); Lepcha *tăfuk*<**-phu·k*, also *tăbak*~*tăbok*<**-buk*, Gyarung *tĕpŏk*, Limbu *səpok*~*səpu*, Sho *pük*, Kabui *puk*, Maring *uk*, Meithei *puk*, Mikir *pok* 'belly', Ao Naga *tapok* 'cave', *tepok* 'belly', B *wàm-puik* 'outside of belly' (cf. *puik* 'pregnancy'), G *ok* 'belly', L *pu·k* 'cave' (TB **pu·k*~*buk*).[237]

(359) Lepcha *kuŋ* 'tree', *ăkuŋ* 'bush'; K *kuŋ* 'to branch; a branch', *ləkuŋ* 'limb, branch'; B *ăkhuiŋ* 'stalk, branch', also *ăkuìŋ* 'large branch, bough' (apparently from *kuìŋ* 'hang over in a curve, bend downwards'); L *ku·ŋ* 'plant, tree, trunk of tree, stem of plant' (TB **ku·ŋ*).

Burmese also offers evidence for short medial **u*, but with change of final, in B *kyauk*<**k-lauk*, L *luŋ* 'stone'<TB **r-luŋ* (above); cf. also B *kauk*<TB **guk*~**kuk* 'bend, crooked'.

Burmese and Lushei show different vowel length in the following root:

(360) T *'dzug-pa*~*zug-pa* 'prick or stick into; plant; erect'; B *tsuik* 'erect, set

234 Cf. also 'finger': B *lak-hnuì*, Atsi *nʔyuì*, Maru *nʔyuk*, Lahu *làʔ-nɔ*, Akha *làʔ-nǒ*, Bisu *là-hñuŋ*, all related. Perhaps the prototype is something like **lak-sənə-yuŋ*, since there is an additional second element in the compound; the *sə-* could be related to the second element in Lahu *làʔ/khɨ-šɛ* 'hand/foot'; see TB **s-* prefix for body parts (JAM).

Add Lisu *læʔ-ńi* 'finger' to the above. Bisu *-hñuŋ* suggests a derivation from **(s-)m-yuŋ* (cf. the Khami prefix).

235 There is an open-syllable variant here: B *thu*, Lahu *thu* 'thick'; see No. 319 (TB **tow* 'thick'); from a long vowel (?) (JAM).

236 The Kachin and Nung forms cited under No. 488 (**r-muw*) apparently belong here, since Maran cites K *muʔ* (high tone) 'thunder, cloudy', also *ləmuʔ* (low tone) 'sky' (Khauri=Gauri dialect), allowing the reconstruction TB **r-mu·k* (an archaic doublet of **(r-)muw*=**(r-)məw*). Nungish (Răwang) has *mu*<**mu·k* 'sky' (*mu ru* 'to be struck with lightning'), contrasting with *thəmö* 'eagle, hawk, kite'<TB **muw*=**məw*; cf. also Nutwang dialect of Răwang *muʔ laŋ* 'heaven' (Morse). Angami Naga (Burling) has *hmuu-tśa* 'fog', probably from **s-muk*; cf. also n. 308.

237 A doublet form in initial *b-* is indicated by Lepcha, as well as by T *bug-pa* 'hole', *sbug(s)* 'hollow, cavity, excavation, interior space', and *'bug(s)-pa*~*'big(s)-pa*, *phug-pa*~*phig-pa* 'sting, pierce, bore, make a hole'.

upright, plant', Lahu *jûʔ* 'pierce, stab, implant'; L *fuk* 'to erect, be erect' (TB **dzu*[·]*k*).

Long medial **u·* can at times be reconstructed on the basis of the Burmese forms alone, as in **klu·ŋ* 'valley, river' (B *khyuiŋ*) (above); cf. also the following:

(361) K *duŋ*, Namsang (Konyak group) *toŋ*, B *thuiŋ* 'sit' (TB **tu·ŋ*~**du·ŋ*).

(362) Lepcha *so muŋ* (= *so muk*) 'cloudy weather'; K *muŋ* 'cloudy; sullen, sulky', B *hmuiŋ* 'dull, downcast', *hmuìŋ* 'very dark', from TB **mu·ŋ*, a doublet of **mu·k* (No. 357).

(363) Lepcha *muk* 'weeds, rubbish', Miri *pömuk* 'dust', B *ăhmuik* 'refuse, dust' (TB **mu·k*).[238]

TB long medial **u·* also appears in TB **su·r* 'sour', **b-ru·l* 'snake' (above) and the following roots:

(364) B *mum* 'begin to form, as a bud', *ămum* 'incipient bud', L *mu·m* 'close (as a flower)', *kuʔ-mu·m* 'bud; to bud' (TB **mu·m*).[239]

(365) K *nun* 'to be worn, threadbare', *kənun* 'rub', *mənun* 'rub with the fingers', G *nol* 'rub, knead', L *nu·l* 'brush past, rub against' (TB **nu·l*).

(366) T *mur* 'gills', *mur-goŋ* 'temples', *mur-ʾgram* 'jaw' (cf. *mur-ba* 'gnaw, masticate'), Nung *mr* [*mər*] 'face', L *hmu·r* 'point, tip, prow', Thado *mu* < **mur* 'beak', Khoibu *mur*, Tangkhul *khəmor* 'mouth' (TB **mu·r*).[240]

Burmese fails to distinguish between short and long medial **u* before final dentals and labials, having simply *u* for both series: B *tshum* 'mortar' < TB **tsum*; B *mum* 'form bud' < TB **mu·m*; cf. also:

Lepcha *kŭm* 'arched, concave, vaulted', B *khùm* 'convex, arched', L *kum*~*ku·m* 'concave' (TB **ku*[·]*m*).

B **-ats* (< TB **-ik*) and *-ań* (< TB **-iŋ*) can phonemically be written /*-ait*/ and /*-ain*/,[241] thus paralleling B *-auk* < TB **-uk* and **-auŋ* < TB **-uŋ*. For this develop-

238 B-L **muk* 'weeds, grass' (JAM) ties in semantically with Lepcha (see n. 232 for the vocalism).

239 Kachin has both *mu-um* 'to bud; a bud' and *məum*, *id.*, derived by Hanson from *um* 'to be puckered up'; it would appear that these forms represent specialized reflexes for the TB long medial **u·*, with metanalysis of the initial **m-* as the common TB **m-* prefix.

240 Nung (Răwang) *mr* also glossed as 'mouthful', which is nearer the apparent basic meaning of 'mouth' for this root, with the likely Ch. cognate *mwən*/*muən*[a] 'gate, door' (n. 479).

241 In Modern Burmese final *-ań* represents *-i*, *-e*, *-ɛ*, and *-ɛ̨*. These differences can scarcely be correlated with any distinctions in TB vocalism and must be regarded as of relatively recent origin, especially in view of instances of interchange such as *mań* > *mi* 'to be named', *hmáń* > *hmɛ̨* 'to name' < **miŋ*; cf. also *kràń* > *tyì* 'ground' < **gliŋ*, *myàń* > *myì* 'sleepy' < **myel*, *asàń* > *əθì* 'nail' < **m-(t)sin*, *hrań* > *hye* 'long' < **s-riŋ*, *pyáń* > *pyé*, *phyáń* > *phyé* 'full' ~ 'fill' < **bliŋ* ~ **pliŋ* (Judson

a 門

ment, cf. B *ats-kui* 'older brother' < TB **ik*, *hmyats* 'bamboo sprout' < TB **s-m(y)ik*, *ńats* 'dirty' < TB **n(y)ik*, *sats* 'small animal of tiger genus' < TB **zik*, *ătshats* 'joint' < TB **tsik*, *práń* 'full', *phráń* 'fill' < TB **bliŋ ~ *pliŋ*, *lań* 'neck' < TB **liŋ*, *mań* 'to be named', *ămań* 'name' < TB **miŋ* (above). The nasal > stop shift in final characteristic of Burmese[242] (cf. *ip-mak* 'dream' < TB **maŋ*, *kyauk* < **k-lauk* 'stone' < TB **r-luŋ*) is especially in evidence here; cf. B *sats* 'tree' < TB **siŋ* (above) and the following pair of roots:

(367) T *snyiŋ* 'heart, mind', Kanauri *stiŋ*, Limbu *niŋ-wa*, B *hnats* < **hnik*, Lushei (Ngente dial.) *niŋ* 'heart', Mikir *niŋ* 'heart, mind', Nung *əniŋ*, G *təniŋ* 'brains' (TB **s-niŋ*).

(368) T *na-niŋ* 'last year', *gźi-niŋ ~ źe-niŋ* 'two years ago', also *lo-rnyiŋ ~ na-rnyiŋ = na-niŋ* (cf. *rnyiŋ-pa* 'old, ancient'), Tsangla *niŋ*, Miri *nyiŋ* (in comp.), Nung and K *niŋ*, B *ăhnats* < **ăhnik*, Mikir *niŋ* 'year' (TB **niŋ*).[243]

Burmese retains final **-it* (Nos. 119, 236), final **-ip* (Nos. 16, 114) and final **-im* (Nos. 53, 71). Final **-in*, however, is represented by **-ań*, as in B *ăsàń*, L *thin* 'liver' < TB **m-sin*; B *hmáń ~ hmyáń*, L *hmin* 'ripe' < TB **s-min*.

TB long medial **i·* is rare, especially before final velars, but can be established for a few roots, including **(s)di·k* 'scorpion' (above). Burmese, which has **-ań* for TB **-in* (see above), has *-in* for TB **-i·n*:

(369) K *śin ~ śen ~ tśen* < **kyin*, B *khyin*, L *khi·n* 'weigh' (TB **ki·n*).

indicates final *-i* for these two words); *hmáń* > *hmɛ́* 'mole' < **r-men*, *hmáń* > *hmɛ́* 'ripe' < **s-min*, *asàń* > *əθɛ̀* 'liver' < **m-sin*, *lań* > *lɛ* 'neck' < **liŋ*; *hńàń* > *hnyɛ̨̀* 'hurt, oppress' < **nyen*, *pyań* > *pyɛ̨* 'plank' < **pleŋ*, *hrań* > *hyɛ̨* 'put together side by side' < **ren*. The nasalized final *-ɛ̨* appears to be correlated in some measure with TB medial **e*; cf. also T *sre-moŋ ~ sre-mo* 'weasel', Mikir *iŋren* < *m-ren* 'mongoose', B *hráń* > *hyɛ́* 'squirrel'.

242 Indeed, of B-L in general (JAM). Cf. Trung (Nungish) *śiŋ* 'tree', *śiŋ-lap* 'leaf', *śiŋ-wat* 'flower' but *śiŋ ~ śik* 'firewood', *śik-śi* 'fruit'. The Mutwang dialect (Morse) of Răwang (Nungish) has a highly idiosyncratic final cluster *-nt* in two items, including *nönt* 'heart', from TB **s-niŋ*; the standard Răwang dialect (Barnard) has *əniŋ* 'brains', and it would appear that the Mutwang form is a derivative of TB **a-niŋ = ʔa-niŋ* via **ʔniŋ > ninʔ* (essentially a suprasegmental glottal accent) > **nint*. This development is closely paralleled in Gyarung (K. Chang) *teṣńit* 'heart', identical in form with *teṣńit* '7' < **te/snis* (TB **s-nis*). The Burmese-Lolo shift, which probably has a similar origin, cannot be assigned to the proto-B-L period, since an original final nasal in the root for 'tree' (TB **siŋ*) is retained in some Loloish languages (JAM) and the root for 'heart' (TB **s-niŋ*) shows forms very close to the original in two Chinese transcriptions for early B-L languages: Hsi-hsia (eleventh and twelfth centuries) *nieŋ*;[a] Pai-lang (third century) *ńi̯əŋ/ńźi̯əŋ*.[b]

243 This root now reconstructed **s-niŋ*; Kachin has both *niŋ* and *śəniŋ*, and Pyu has *snì* < **snìŋ*, both agreeing with B-L initial **hn-* (and note Karen **hneŋ*).

[a] 寧 [b] 仍

The following roots also have this long medial vowel:

(370) L *tśi·p*, G *tśip* 'shut, close', from TB **ts(y)i·p*.

(371) B *rit* 'reap, mow, shave', L *ri·t* 'scrape with a hoe', Mikir *ret* 'scrape, shave', Miri *rit* 'cut' (TB **ri·t*).

(372) Dhimal *śir*, G *sil*, Dimasa *śer*, L *thi·r* 'iron', from TB **s(y)i·r*.[244]

(373) T *skyil-ba* 'to bend', *'khyil-ba* 'wind, twist, roll', Lepcha *kil* 'a screw', K *kyin* 'to be soft and easily twisted', *əkyin* 'roll, as a turban, into a ball', *gyin* 'roll, fashion, as mud pellets', L *ki·l* 'corner, angle' (TB **ki·l*).

TB medial **u* and **i* are only partially maintained in Bodo-Garo. Garo regularly preserves medial **i*, but in Bodo and Dimasa this medial tends to be merged with **u* (often with loss of final consonant). Doublet forms in Dimasa, with the Hills dialect having medial *i* and the Plains dialect medial *u*, are characteristic, and some *i*∼*u* alternation appears also in Garo; cf. G *mik*, Dimasa *mu* 'eye' < TB **mik*; G *na-tik* 'shrimp', Dimasa *na-thu* 'prawn' < TB **(s-)di·k*; G *bibik*, Dimasa *bubu* 'bowels' < TB **pik*; G *miŋ* 'to name', *bumuŋ* 'name', Dimasa *bumu* (in comp. *muŋ*) 'name' < TB **r-miŋ*; Dimasa *phuluŋ* 'fill in' < TB **pliŋ*; Dimasa *bithlim*∼*buthluŋ* 'brain' < TB **kliŋ*; G *min*, Dimasa *min*∼*mun* 'ripen' < TB **s-min*; also the following roots:

(374) Abor-Miri *mit*, Nung *śəmit*, K *simit* (Assamese dial.), L *timit*, Tangkhul *khəśimit*, Mikir *met*, G *kimit* 'extinguish', Dimasa *khumu* 'destroy' (TB **mit*).

(375) K *phuŋ-lip* 'dive' (*phuŋ* 'water') (Hertz: *kha phun-lip si* 'drown'), G *tśi rip* 'dive' (*tśi* 'water'), *srip* 'sink', Bodo *thrup* 'sink', Dimasa *lip*∼*lup* 'dive', *gilib*∼*gulub* 'drown' (TB **lip*), perhaps also Lepcha *lap* 'bury'.

(376) T *byib-pa* 'cover, wrap up; hide, conceal', Bodo *phop*∼*fop* 'bury', Dimasa *bib*∼*bub* 'conceal oneself, hide', *phip*∼*phup* 'bury', Mikir *pip* 'bury' (TB **bip*∼**pip*).

(377) K *phriŋ* 'bark', Dimasa *biriŋ*∼*buruŋ* 'bark, call (as an animal)' (TB **priŋ*).[245]

(378) Nung and K *məliŋ*, G *buruŋ* (Garo Mission)∼*briŋ* (Chuckerbutty) 'forest', Dimasa *ha-bliŋ* 'jhum field in second year of cultivation' (*ha* 'earth') (TB **b-liŋ*).[246]

244 The Kiranti group has **sya·l* 'iron': Bahing *sya·l*, Sangpang *syel*∼*sel*, Dumi *sel*, pointing to an archaic doublet in this root: TB **syi·r*∼**sya·l* (see p. 84 for the medial alternation); the alternation of finals suggests that this is an old loan-word from AT.

245 Chang Naga (Konyak group) has *lăŋ* 'to bark', from **riŋ*, suggesting that this might be a prefixed root: **b-riŋ*, although this should yield K **məriŋ* (cf. No. 378) rather than *phriŋ*; cf. also Ch. **srieŋ/sieŋ*[a] 'to bark' (not in texts), probably from **s-ri·ŋ* (see n. 457 for the initial cluster here).

246 T *źiŋ* 'field, ground, soil, arable land' may belong with this set, since it

[a] 猩

(379) K *khrim* 'threaten', *məkrim* 'smart, as the eyes; be on edge, as the teeth', B *krìm* 'to be terrified' (obsolete), *khrìm* 'threaten, terrify', Dimasa *migrim* 'fear, be anxious about something, set the teeth on edge, have gooseflesh' (TB **krim*).

(380) G *sim*, Dimasa *sim-ba* ~ *sum-ba*, *gisim* ~ *gusum* 'black, blue, dark', L *thim* 'dark; darkness', from TB **s(y)im*.

Medial **i* is rarely replaced by *a* (there are a few instances in Bodo), whereas the **u* > *a* shift is often encountered in Bodo-Garo, e.g. G *githam*, Dimasa *gatham* (but *thim-dźi* ~ *thum-dźi* '30') '3' < TB **g-sum*; G *sam*, Dimasa *sam-tho* 'mortar' < TB **tsum*; also the following pair of roots:

(381) Lepcha *lyam* < **s-lam* 'to warm up food' (cf. K *śəlum*, B *hlúm*), K *lum* 'warm', *məlum* 'simmer, heat', *śəlum* 'heat, warm, as food', Nung *lim* 'warm', B *lum* 'warm', *hlum* 'warm oneself by a fire', *hlúm* 'heat again, warm over', Bodo *lum-doŋ* (Hodgson) ~ *lam* (Endle) 'fever', Dimasa *lim* ~ *lum* 'to be hot, have fever', *lim-ba* 'illness, fever', also G *gram tśi* 'sweat', Bodo *galam* 'to sweat', *galam doi* 'sweat', Dimasa *gilim di* ~ *gulum di* 'sweat' (= 'heat-water'; cf. Siyin *kwo-ul* 'sweat' ~ 'warm') (TB **lum*).

(382) T *'khruŋ-ba* 'to be born; shoot, sprout, grow (of seeds and plants)', K *khruŋ* 'live, be alive', *məkruŋ* 'fresh sprouts, new twigs', Bodo *gakhraŋ* 'fixed, firm, healthy', Dimasa *gakhraŋ* 'green' (TB **kruŋ*).[247]

Before labials and dentals, medial **u* usually falls together with medial **i* in Bodo-Garo; cf. G *brip* 'flood' < TB **brup*, and the following roots:

(383) Lepcha *kut* 'to rule a line', *ă-kut* 'strake', *hut* < **khut* 'to scratch, as body or earth', *ă-hut* 'scratching; a rake', K *khut* 'scrape, rub', Nung *tśəkut* 'itch', B *kut* 'scratch', *khut* 'gash, chop, cut, beat (metal)', G *kit* 'carve', *ka-kit* 'itch', Dimasa *khu* 'engrave on wood or stone' (TB **kut*).

(384) B *hrup* 'snuff up, sip, sup', Dimasa *surup* 'sip, lap, smoke', *khu sirip* 'gargle' (*khu* 'mouth'), perhaps also Manchati *srub* 'spittle' (TB **s-rup*); cf. also Lepcha *hŭp* 'a sip, gulp', *háp* 'to suck'.

(385) K *phun* 'put on and wear, as a coat; cover, as with a blanket', G *pin-dap* 'cover', Dimasa *phin* ~ *phun* 'put on, wrap, cover' (TB **pun*).

Bodo-Garo closely parallels Burmese in having two distinct sets of correspondences for TB medial **u* and **u·* before velars:

TB medial **u* = L *u* = B *au* = Garo and Dimasa *o*.

TB medial **u·* = L *u·* = B *ui* = Garo *i* = Dimasa *i* ~ *u*.

appears to be from **lyiŋ* (n. 104), as indicated by Lepcha *lyăŋ* 'land, field' (cited by Forrest, *JAOS* **82**, 1962). The basic meaning is distinct, however, despite the semantic extension found in Dimasa, and the forms cannot be related with any confidence.

247 Cf. the closely similar semantic development shown by TB **s-riŋ* ~ **s-raŋ*, and Nung *əzim* 'raw', B *tsìm* 'green; unripe' (TB **dzim*).

Several cross-checks with Lushei and/or Burmese are available; cf. L *ruk*, B *khrauk*, G *dok*, Dimasa *do* '6' < TB **d-ruk*; L *luŋ*, B *kyauk* < **k-lauk*, G *roŋ*, Dimasa *loŋ* 'stone' < TB **r-luŋ*; L *thu·k* 'deep', B *thuik-thuik* 'thickly', G *dik*, Dimasa *dib-bi* ~ *dub-ba* ~ *gidip-ba* 'thick' < TB **tu·k*; also the following roots:

(386) G *mattśok* ~ *mattśak*, Dimasa *moso*, L *sa-zuk* < *-*yuk*, Mikir *thidźok* < *-*yok* 'deer (sambhur)' (TB **d-yuk*).

(387) B *tauk* 'fillip; cut by a single, light blow', Lahu *dɔ̂ʔ* 'hit, beat', G *dok* ~ *dak* 'knock, pound', Dimasa *do* 'knock, hit down, hammer down, stamp', L *tuk* 'cut, chop' (TB **tuk*); cf. also Lepcha *tyók* < **s-tók* 'come into collision with, hit against, knock against (as egg in breaking)'.

(388) B *kuik* 'bite with the teeth or an instrument; shear', G *kik* 'strip', Dimasa *khu* 'pare off (rind of fruit), strip' (TB **ku·k*); cf. also Lepcha *kuk* 'to rake, scrape or draw towards self as with a stick; to hoe superficially; to pull upwards with hook; to ladle, spoon out; to toss, as bull with horns'.

(389) B *khrúiŋ* ~ *khyúiŋ*, G *griŋ* 'cage' (TB **kru·ŋ*).

(390) L *tśhu·ŋ* 'the inside (of anything)', Bodo *siŋ*, Dimasa *bisiŋ* 'inside, within' (TB **tsyu·ŋ*).[248]

Bodo-Garo and Burmese differ with regard to vowel length in the following root (reconstructed on basis of Burmese):

(391) T *'phrug-pa* 'scratch oneself', B *phrauk* ~ *phyauk* 'scratch in order to allay itching', G *brik*, Dimasa *buru* 'scratch' (TB **pruk*).

Where Burmese and Lushei cognates are lacking, Bodo-Garo evidence is of value in reconstructing vowel length for this medial; cf. Dimasa and G *groŋ* 'horn' < TB **ruŋ* (above) and the following:

(392) K *du* < **duk*, G *gitok*, Dimasa *godo*, Mikir *tśethok*, also Lepcha *tŭk-tok* (*tok* in comp.) 'neck' (TB **tuk*).

(393) T *khug-ma* 'pouch, little bag', G *khok* 'basket', Dimasa *baiŋ-kho* 'basket carried on a load', *bokho* 'receptacle', Mikir *hok* < **khok* 'small hanging basket' (TB **kuk*); cf. also Lepcha *kóm ba-gŭk* 'purse' (*kom* 'silver, money').

(394) Kiranti **muk* (Lambichong, Chingtang, Yakha *muk*) 'arm, hand', G *mik* 'cubit', Bodo *mu* 'arm-length', perhaps also B *muik* 'measure with breadth of fist' (TB **mu·k*).

(395) K *nguŋ* (*n-guŋ*) 'back of a blade', G *rikiŋ* 'edge', *dźa-rikiŋ* 'shin' (='leg-edge'), Bodo *giŋ* 'side', Dimasa *ruguŋ* 'near, by the side of', *burguŋ* 'margin, edge, rim; blunt edge of a knife' (but *di-rgoŋ* 'bank of a river'), Mikir *kuŋ* 'side, edge, border, brim, bank, rim', *arkoŋ* 'shin' (TB **r-gu·ŋ*).

The distinction between short and long medial **u* cannot be established for any languages other than Lushei, Burmese and Garo-Bodo, possibly also Lepcha, yet

248 This root has now been reconstructed **tu·ŋ* (n. 63).

indications of this feature elsewhere are not lacking. Thus, Sho (Southern Kuki) distinguishes between *sok* '6' < TB **d-ruk* and *pük* 'belly' < TB **pu·k*, *thük* 'deep' < TB **tu·k*, *müg* 'dull' < TB **mu·k*. Mikir retains medial **u* rarely (No. 107) and medial **i* somewhat more commonly (Nos. 112, 119, 234, 367, 368, 376), the characteristic developments being **u > o* (Nos. 42, 88, 108, 358, 386, 392, 393, also 395 with *u ~ o* alternation), **i > e* (Nos. 16, 35, 53, 64, 126, 142, 233, 374, 402, 404). Mikir vacillates between *e* (No. 371) and *i* as reflexes for TB long medial **i·*; cf. the following root:

(396) Lepcha *hlet-bŭ* (*bŭ* < TB **buw* 'insect, snake'), L *hli·t*, Mikir *iŋlit* 'water leech', Ao Naga *melet* 'horse-leech (usually found near water or in very damp localities)', K *lip* 'sp. of horse-leech' (cf. K *śiŋlet ~ śiŋlep* 'tongue'), from TB **(m-)li·t*.

Mikir reveals an interesting agreement with Bodo-Garo in the following root:

(397) K *khun*, G *khol ~ khal*, Dimasa *khon*, Mikir *iŋkol ~ iŋkoi*, Siyin *kul*, Haka *kul ~ kwe* '20', from TB **(m-)kul*.

The above root contrasts with G *kimil*, Dimasa *bikhimi*, Mikir *aŋmi* < **aŋmil* 'body hair' < TB **mul*. Both roots, however, appear to have short medial vowel (cf. L *hmul* 'body hair'), and the **u > i* shift is perhaps the result of dissimilation; cf. Mikir *vi* 'tend, graze (flocks)', L *vul* 'keep or rear (domestic animals)'. Mikir has *u* for TB long medial *u·* in *phurul ~ phurui* 'snake' < TB **b-ru·l*, while Meithei offers a contrast between *lil* 'snake' < TB **b-ru·l*, and *kul* '20' < TB **kul*.

Alternation between the high vowels *u* and *i*, though especially characteristic of Bodo-Garo, is not uncommon elsewhere; cf. Nos. 53 and 114 (above), also T *pus-mo ~ pis-mo* 'knee', *smyig-ma ~ smyug-ma* 'cane', *phug-pa ~ phig-pa* 'bore' (n. 237), T *sbud-pa*, Central T *sbid-pa* 'bellows' (note that all these have labial initials). Medial **u ~ *i* alternation must be set up for the following TB roots:

(398) T *'phur-ba*, Central T *'phir-ba* 'to fly', Nung *əphr* [əphər] 'shake (as a cloth)', *khoŋ-phr* 'moth', G *bil*, Dimasa *bir* 'to fly' (TB **pur ~ *pir*); cf. Bahing *byer*, Abor-Miri *ber* 'to fly'.[249]

(399) Bahing *tyup ~ töp ~ tip*, Sunwari *tup*, K *dup* 'beat, strike', *mədup* 'pound, hammer', Nung *dip* 'beat', *əthip* 'strike against', Mikir *dip-dip* 'beat (heart, pulse)', *thip* 'beat (drum)' (TB **dup ~ *dip*, **tup ~ *tip*).

(400) T *nub-pa* 'fall gradually, sink; set (sun, moon); decay, decline', *nub* 'west; evening', *snub-pa* 'cause to perish, suppress', K *nip* 'shade, cast a shadow; be overcast, dim', *śiŋnip* 'shadow', Nung *nəm nip lam* 'west' (*nəm* 'sun', *lam* 'side'),

249 A distinct root **byer* must be recognized for TB on the basis of the Bahing and Abor-Miri forms, along with Trung (Nungish) *biel* 'to fly' (in comp. 'airplane'), from **byer*; Chinese appears to have cognates for both roots (nn. 443 and 460).

Bahing *nip* 'compress, express', B *nip* 'to be kept down', *hnip* 'crush, put down, oppress' (TB **nup* ~ **nip*).[250]

(401) T *rum* 'darkness, obscurity', K *rim* 'to be dusk, dark', *nrim* 'evening', *niŋrim rim* 'twilight', *sərim* 'twilight', Nung *rim-rim na* 'grey' (*na* 'black'), *rim-rim wɛ* 'twilight' (TB **rum* ~ **rim*).

Nung regularly shows preference for medial *i*, as in *mil* 'body hair' < TB **mul*, *riŋ* 'horn' < TB **ruŋ*, *im* 'mouthful' < TB **um*, *lim* 'warm' < TB **lum*.

Alternation between medial **ya* and **i* is indicated for the following pair of roots:

(402) T *mig*, Kanauri *mik*, Lepcha *ămik*, Vayu *mek*, Magari *mik*, Bahing *mi-tśi*, Thulung, Dumi, Rai *mik-si*, Limbu *mik*, Dhimal *mi*, Miri *əmik*, K *myi*, G *mik*, L *mit*, Mikir *mek*, but Burmese (and general Burmese-Lolo) *myak*, Nung *mɛ* ~ *nɛ* < **myak* (see n. 93), perhaps also Gyarung *tĕmńăk* 'eye' (TB **mik* ~ **myak*).[251]

(403) K *u-ri* < **-rik* 'pheasant' (*u* 'bird'), B *rats* 'pheasant', G *grik* 'pheasant',

250 The Bahing and Burmese forms are preferably analyzed as part of a distinct set: TB **nip* 'crush, compress'; cf. Ch. *ni̯ap/ni̯äp*[a] 'trample', from ST **nep*. TB **nu·p* ~ **ni[·]p* 'sink', with long medial *u·* on basis of Lepcha *nŭp* (n. 231); add B-G **(h)nap* < **(h)nup* 'set (sun), sink, drown', also 'enter, penetrate', thus tying in directly with the principal Ch. cognate: *ńi̯əp/ńźi̯əp*[b] 'enter' (n. 479). The initial cluster in B-G is probably from **sn-*; cf. the following (the first entry from TB **s-nam*):

	Garo	Bodo	Dimasa
daughter-in-law	*nam*	*ham*	*ham*
enter, etc.	*nap*	*hap*	*hap*
good	*nam*	*ham*	*ham*

251 The **myak* form for this root must now be regarded as the earlier in view of the evidence not only from Karen (**mɛ* < **myak*) but also from Ch. (n. 488). Nungish stands closest of all other TB groups to the B-L family, while Gyarung also shares in a number of roots found only here, e.g. **śam* 'iron' (*n*. 179) and the following root: Gyarung (K. Chang) *sar* 'louse', B *san*, *id.*, from B-L **śan* (Maru *śin*, Lahu *śe*, Lisu *hü*); TB **sar* ~ *śar*. The evidence from this one root ('eye') speaks strongly in favor of a BL-Nungish-Gyarung supergroup, which alone in TB has retained the archaic form: **myak*. There is considerable evidence for medial *ya* ~ *i* alternation in ST itself; cf. ST **tyik* ~ **tyak* '1' (n. 271); **(m-)lyat* ~ **(m-)li·t* 'leech' (n. 398); also **(m-)syil* ~ **(m-)syal* 'wash' (n. 462). The medial *ya* form is the more archaic, as shown by Miao-Yao **nyaŋ* 'year' (approximate reconstruction), a very early loan from a doublet: **(s-)nyaŋ* of ST **(s-)niŋ*, as reconstructed on the basis of TB, Karen and Chinese; Ch. retains an indication of the early vocalism in *nâŋ*[c] 'in past time, formerly', a related form; cf. T *rnyiŋ-pa* 'old, ancient', *lo-rnyiŋ* 'last year'. Chinese perhaps also reflects an archaic doublet: **syaŋ* of ST **siŋ* 'tree' in *si̯aŋ*[d] 'look at, see', the graph showing an 'eye' and a 'tree', the latter probably as a phonetic (better than Karlgren's suggestion in *AD*, viz. 'an eye, spying, looking out from behind a tree').

[a] 躡 [b] 入 [c] 曩 [d] 相

do-grik 'black pheasant' (*do* 'bird'), L *va-hrit* 'black pheasant' (*va* 'bird'), but T *sreg-pa*, West T *śrag-pa* 'pheasant', Lepcha *kəhryak fo* 'kaliy-pheasant' (*fo* 'bird') (TB **s-rik*~**s-ryak*).

TB shows a similar medial **ya*~**e* alternation in L *hniam*<**hnyam* 'low, short', TB **nem* (above). The following root has medial **a* (rather than **ya*) alternating with **i*:

(404) Kanauri *śöŋ*<**sriŋ* (see n. 126), Manchati *sriŋ*, Chamba Lahuli *sriŋ*~*śiŋ* 'live, be alive', L *hriŋ* 'fresh, green', *hriŋʔ* 'bear, beget', Meithei *hiŋ* 'be alive', Mikir *reŋ* 'live, come to life', *reŋ-seŋ* 'green, verdant' (an apparent couplet from **s-reŋ*), K *tsiŋ*<**śriŋ* 'grass; grassy, green', *kətsiŋ* 'fresh, green, raw, unripe', Nung *məśiŋ*<**m-śriŋ* 'green (color)', *śin* 'grass' (possible loan from Kachin), also *əthiŋ* 'unripe, uncooked' (cf. No. 231), but B *hraŋ* 'live, be alive', G *thaŋ*<**sraŋ* 'live', *gathaŋ* 'green', Dimasa *gathaŋ* 'alive, living; green, unripe' (TB **s-riŋ*~**s-raŋ*).[252]

Burmese has medial *a* for TB **i* in *khraŋ-tshi* 'marrow' < TB **kliŋ* (above), and for TB **u* in the following root:

(405) T *bsuŋ* 'smell, esp. sweet smell', K *suŋ* 'scent, odor, smell', but B *sàŋ* 'emit a pleasant odor' (TB **suŋ*).

§12. Tibeto-Burman tones

Tones probably occur in most TB languages, yet our information on this point is meagre.[253] The archaic West T dialects (Balti, Purik) appear to lack tones

252 Now reconstructed **śriŋ* (n. 305); the aberrant vocalism of B *hraŋ* has probably been conditioned by the initial cluster (n. 128).

253 It is perhaps in the area of tone-reconstructions that the most dramatic progress has been made in TB studies over the past few years, as more and more accurate data become available. The most important general articles on S.E. Asian tones to appear since Benedict, 1948 ('Tonal systems in Southeast Asia', *JAOS* **68**, 184–91) are Haudricourt, 'De l'origine des tons en viêtnamien', *JA* **242** (1954); 'Bipartition et tripartition des systèmes de tons dans quelques langues d'Extrême-Orient', *BSLP* **56** (1961). The best tonal data to date are on Loloish; Chinese linguists like Ma Hsüeh-liang, Yüan Chia-hua, Wen Yu, Hu T'an and Kao Hua-nien have painstakingly recorded many Loloish dialects of Yünnan, not only indicating tones in isolation but also in many cases describing sandhi phenomena in syllable-sequences (see List of Sources). The Japanese scholar, T. Nisida, has used this material (and his own) in his important article, 'Burmese and the Lolo languages: a comparative study of their tone-systems' (*Biruma-go to Roro syogo: sono seityoo taikei no hikaku kenkyuu*), *TAK* **4**, 1, June 1964. See also his 'Tonemic

altogether (Read, Bailey, 1908), while the two-tone system of Central T dialects can be interpreted in terms of the initials of Classical Tibetan (high tones from original surds, low tones from sonants).[254] Simple tonal systems of Tibetan type have been incompletely recorded for several TB languages, including Kadu (R. G. Brown, 1920), Sho (Fryer), Tangkhul (Pettigrew, 1918), Thado (Shaw), Chang (Hutton, 1929), Khami (Houghton, 1895), and Sema Naga.[255] Note also the interesting pair of words cited for Taman by R. G. Brown (1911), viz. *thi* 'water' (high tone), *thi* 'egg' (low tone), both from TB **ti(y)* (see n. 149). Comparative work on the scantily recorded tones of these languages cannot be pursued with any degree of success. Kachin and Nung both appear to have more complicated tonal systems, but unfortunately these tones have not been recorded.

The Burmese-Lolo tonal system alone offers an opportunity for comparative study. In addition to Burmese itself, tones have been recorded for Phunoi and Akha (Roux), Black Lolo, White Lolo, and Müng (Bonifacy), Lahu (Telford), Lisu (Fraser), Ahi and Lolopho (Liétard), Nyi (Vial), and Moso (Rock). A partial

correspondences between Tibetan and Burmese', *Gengo Kenkyuu* **34**, 90–5 (1958). R. Burling has worked out the basic tone-correspondences for Burmese, Atsi, Maru, Lahu, Lisu and Akha in a generally satisfactory manner in his *PLB*. Further investigations have been carried out by Matisoff, *opera citata*. P. Lewis, *Akha–English Dictionary*, 1968 (reviewed by Matisoff, *JAS* **28**, 3, 1969) has recorded the tones of that language accurately. It remains to be seen whether the tones of B-L can be related systematically to those of Kachin or whether the two systems arose independently. The most serious problem yet unsolved in B-L tone-studies is the elucidation of the conditioning factors for the development of the two distinct stopped tones in Loloish. Another important desideratum is a clarification of the origin of the Burmese 'creaky tone' and its Loloish cognates; this is by far the rarest of the three open tones, and is clearly secondary in some sense, though its development antedates the split-up of Common B-L (see n. 260) (JAM).

We now have much material on various B-L tonal systems, as described above by JAM, but very little on tones elsewhere in TB, with the conspicuous exception of the Kachin system (Maran). Our more recent sources here are noted in n. 494, which considers TB tones in relation to those of Karen and Chinese. Detailed studies of the tonal systems of several Nepal languages: Gurung, Tamang, Thakali, Chepang, Newari, Sunwar and Sherpa (a Tibetan dialect) have recently been published; see Austin Hale and Kenneth L. Pike, *Tone Systems of Tibeto-Burman Languages of Nepal*, Occasional Papers of the Wolfenden Society on Tibeto-Burman Linguistics, Univ. of Illinois, Dept. of Linguistics, Urbana, 1970.

254 The only adequate description of Tibetan tones, from a phonemic point of view, is that found in Yü Tao-ch'üan[a] and Chao Yüan-jên,[b] 'Ts'ang-yang-chia-ts'o ch'ing ko'[c] ('Love Songs of Tshangs-dbyangs-rgya-mtsho'), *CYYY*, Monographs, A-5 (1930). Cf. also G. de Roerich, 'Modern Tibetan Phonetics, with special reference to the Dialect of Central Tibet', *JASB* (n.s.) **27** (1931), 285–312.

255 See N. L. Bor and J. H. Hutton, 'The Use of Tones in Sema Naga', *JRAS* (1927), 103–9.

[a] 于道泉 [b] 趙元任 [c] 倉洋嘉錯情歌

examination of Phunoi and Akha by Shafer[256] suggests that some tonal agreement with Burmese exists. Further investigation has shown that the tones of the best recorded languages (Maru, Lisu, Ahi, Lolopho, Nyi) together form a tonal pattern more complex than that of Burmese, yet agreeing with the latter in fundamental respects. Burmese distinguishes between a low-level tone (unmarked) and a high-falling tone (×̀), and has in addition an 'intermittent voice' or 'creaky voice' tone (written ×́).[257] Only words ending in a voiced element (vowel or nasal) are affected by these tones. Words ending in an unvoiced element (surd stop) are not subject to tonal differentiation, Burmese in this respect thus paralleling both Chinese and Thai (as reconstructed). Modern Burmese, as well as Lahu, Phunoi and Akha (see n. 256), and most Lolo languages, replace final stop by glottal stop:[258]

	Burmese	Lahu	Lisu	Ahi	Lolopho	Nyi
hand, arm	*lak* > *lɛʔ*	*làʔ*	*læ̂ʔ*	*lyeʔ*	*lɛʔ*	*lè*
pig	*wak* > *wɛʔ*	*vàʔ*	*væ̂ʔ*	*vyeʔ*	*vɛʔ*	*vè*
descend	*sak* > *θɛʔ*	*yàʔ*	*ræ̂ʔ*	*zeʔ*	—	*zə́*
sharp	*thak* > *thɛʔ*	*thâʔ*	*tshyæ̌ʔ*	*thyeʔ*	—	—

(*cont. on p.* 88)

256 'Phunoi and Akha Tones', *Sino-Tibetica* **4** (Berkeley, 1938). Shafer writes $×_1$ (= low-level) for the Akha tone represented by the tone-mark *nang* (subscribed dot) of the Annamite transcription adopted by Roux. This Akha tone is best interpreted as low tone with glottal stop (as in Annamite), especially in view of its correspondence with final stop consonants in Burmese, e.g. B *wak*, Akha *gạ* 'pig'; B *nak*, Akha *nạ* 'black'. Akha further appears to have low-falling tone for the falling tone (×̀) of Burmese, as demonstrated by Shafer, and low-rising or high-rising tone for the level tone (×) of Burmese.

257 The 'creaky voice' tone (*auk-myit*) involves semi-closure of the glottis and a weak final glottal catch. Vowels affected by *auk-myit* are half-long, whereas vowels affected by low-level or high-falling (*she-pauk*) tone are long, and vowels before final stop consonants (glottal stop in Modern Burmese) are short. In the early inscriptions *auk-myit* was recorded with the 'vowel-support' sign (taken from Mon script), whence the modern symbol (subscribed dot). *She-pauk*, however, was usually left unmarked, although occasionally a final *-h* was added; the modern symbol (two dots) appears as early as A.D. 1219, in the Damayangyi pagoda inscription (see Tin, *JBRS* **19**, 1929).

258 Tones are marked as follows: ×̌ (high), ×̂ (low), ×́ (rising), ×̀ (falling), and ×̄ (mid-high). Mid-level tones are left unmarked. Glottal stops are clearly described for Lahu ($×^4$ and $×^5$ in Telford) and Lisu ($×^2$ and $×^6$ in Fraser). Liétard explains his tone symbols for Ahi and Lolopho only in terms of the conventional four tones of Mandarin Chinese, but the values to be assigned them must be those of the native dialect of Yünnan. In this dialect, as recorded by the writer (at K'unming, 1938), the *hsia p'ing shêng* is merged with *ju shêng* (glottal stop), and *shang shêng* and *ch'ü shêng* are reversed. Hence we write ×ʔ, ×̀, and ×́ for Liétard's $×^2$, $×^3$, and $×^4$, respectively. The falling-tone value (×̀) has also been assigned to Lahu ×, Lisu $×^4$, and Nyi ×̀.

	Burmese	Lahu	Lisu	Ahi	Lolopho	Nyi
six	*khrauk > thyauʔ*	*khɔ̀ʔ*	*tśhɔ̂ʔ*	*tśhuʔ*	*tśhoʔ*	*khú*
enough	*lauk > lauʔ*	*lɔ̀ʔ*	*lɔ̂ʔ*	*luʔ*	—	*lú*
eight	*hrats > hyiʔ*	*hí*	*hîʔ*	*ihʔ*	*hɛʔ*	*hè*
tree	*sats > θiʔ*	*šɨ̂ʔ*	*sǐʔ*	(*sə̏*)	(*sə̀* ~ *sə̏*)	*sə̀*
goat	*tshit > sheiʔ*	*áchèʔ*	*atśhîʔ*	*khiʔ*	*atśöʔ*	*tshɨ*
lie down, sleep	*ip > eiʔ*	*yɨ̂ʔ*	*yîʔ*	*yiʔ*	*yiʔ*	*í*
needle	*ap > aʔ*	*γòʔ*	*wɔ̂ʔ*	*woʔ ~ roʔ*	*vöʔ*	(*hŋə̂*)

Lahu and Lisu distinguish between low and high tones before glottal stop (the basis for this distinction has not been determined).[259] Ahi and Lolopho have only glottal stop, as in Burmese, and Nyi (if our interpretation is correct) lacks glottal stop and usually substitutes either falling tone (x̀) or rising tone (x́). Lahu often retains glottal stop in roots showing irregular treatment in Lolo; cf. B *phak* 'leaf', Lahu *ɔ̀-phàʔ*, but Lisu *phyǽ*, Ahi *phyè*, Lolopho *pǽ*, Nyi *phè*; B *nak* 'black', Lahu *nâʔ*, but Lisu *na*, Ahi *nyé*, Lolopho *nɛ̂*, Nyi *nè* (TB **nak*: T *nag-po*, Nung *naʔ*); B *krak* < *k-rak* 'fowl', Lahu *γâʔ*, but Lisu *aγuǎ*, Ahi *yé*, Lolopho *yí*, Nyi *yè*; B *myak*(*-tsí*) 'eye', Lahu *mɛ̂ʔ-šɨ̄*, but Lisu *myæ-sɨ̂*, Ahi *nye-sá*, Lolopho *mɛ̂-duʔ*, Nyi *ne-sə́*; B *ù-hnauk* 'brain', Lahu *ú-nɛ̂ʔ*, but Lisu *wǔ-nγų̌*, Ahi *ó-nǒ̈* (TB **s-nuk*). In rare instances glottal stop appears in Lolo in roots without final stop consonant, e.g. Ahi and Lolopho *liʔ* '4', B *lè*.

The 'creaky voice' tone (x́) of Burmese (where non-morphological) appears to be a relatively late variant of the level tone, and the tonal series in Lahu and Lolo is the same as that for level tone, e.g. B *lá* 'moon, month', Lahu *ha-pa*, Lisu *hą̀-bà*, Ahi *hlò-bò*, Lolopho *hyò*, Nyi *ślà-bà* (cf. T *zla-ba*). In Burmese morphology this tone often imparts a diminutive or otherwise specialized force, e.g. *lyà* 'thin', *lyá* 'flimsy'; *khà* 'bitter', *khá-khá* 'bitterish' (many forms of this type); B *lu* 'man', *lú* (pejorative), *ne* 'sun', *né* 'day', and also serves to subordinate pronouns and proper nouns, as in *ŋa* 'I', *ŋá* 'mine'. In addition, many doublet forms that do not readily yield to classification are found, e.g. *tu* 'hammer', *thú* 'pound, hammer'; *mań* 'to be named', *hmáń* 'to name'; *ńi* 'to be even', *hńí* 'make even'; *lań* 'revolve, turn around (intr.)', *hláń* 'turn around, make revolve (tr.)' (note the appearance

259 It now appears, at least as regards Lisu (Fraser), that this tonal distinction reflects an original (proto-TB level) distinction between voiced and unvoiced initials, of the same general type as that encountered in Karen, Chinese and elsewhere in S.E. Asia (Benedict, 1948); certain exceptional forms perhaps reflect lost prefixes, e.g. B-L **sat* 'kill' (low series = voiced initial) < TB **g-sat*; cf. JAM, 1970b.

of 'creaky voice' in these three transitive forms); *kwè* 'bend, curve', *khwe* 'curve, curl, coil', *kwé* 'bend round, be curved'. In some instances 'creaky voice' perhaps stands for an earlier stop consonant; cf. *mrá* 'very sharp, keen', *mrak* 'cut keenly'; *hlá* 'very, excessive' (verbal affix), T *hlag* 'more, beyond'; note also the correspondence to K suffixed *-t* and L *-k* in B *kyá*~*khyá*, K *khrat*, L *tla·k*~*thla·k* 'fall; let fall' (TB **kla*). In general, however, the problem is primarily one of morphology rather than phonology.[260] Shafer (*Sino-Tibetica* 4, 316) thus is not justified in writing *ă* for *á* and reconstructing TB final *-ə* on the basis of this supposed 'short vowel' in Burmese.

Lahu and the Lolo languages have two well-defined sets of tonal correspondences for the low-level and high-falling tones of Burmese (Lahu has two correspondences for low-level):

Burmese Low-level Tone[261]

	Burmese	Lahu	Lisu	Ahi	Lolopho	Nyi
house	*im*	*yɛ̀*	*hị̀*	*hæ̀*	*hì*	*hɛ̀*
rain	*rwa*	*mû-yè*	*hạ̀*	*hò*	*hò*	*hà*
ill	*na*	*nà*	*nà*	*nò*	*nò*	*nà*
buy	*wai*	*vɨ̀*	*wù*	*và*	*vɛ̀*	*vɛ̀*
I, me	*ŋa*	*ŋà*	*ŋwà*	(*gò*)	*ŋò*	*ŋà*
100	*ăra*	*ha*	*hạ̀*	*hò*	*hyò*	(*há*)
name	*mań*	*ɔ̀-mɛ*	(*mye*)	*mæ̀*	*mì*	*mɛ̀*
sun	*ne*	*mû-ni*	*nyì*	*nyì*	*nyì*	*nyì*
white; silver	*phru*	*phu*	*phù*	*thò*	*phì*	*ślù*
thick	*thu*	*thu*	*thù*	*thò*	*thù*	*thù*

260 Note also the use of 'creaky voice' with nominalizing *ă-* prefix: *nam* 'to smell (intr.)', *nàm* 'to smell (tr.)', *ănám* 'smell'; *thu* 'thick', *ăthú* (also *dú*) 'thickness'; these forms apparently were glottalized by the (non-phonemic) glottal onset of the prefix: *ʔa-thu* > *ă-thú*; also (with intervocalic voicing) > *ʔă-du* > *ʔdu* (the 'Tibetan stage' – see n. 339) > *dú*. Modern Burmese has 'creaky voice' as a suprasegmental morpheme of subordination, derived from the obsolete (literary) subordinating particle *-í*, which also has 'creaky voice' (see Benedict, review of W. Cornyn, *Outline of Burmese Grammar*, in *JAOS* (1945), 65–7, note 7). It would appear that the general subordinating suffix **-ki* of TB (see §17) was replaced in close juncture by *-ʔi*, the glottal stop then becoming the suprasegmental glottal accent (see n. 242 for a parallel development in Nungish).

261 See Burling and Matisoff, *opera citata*. The Lahu /\`/ tone, as in 'house', is from old plain initials; Lahu / / tone (mid, unmarked) is from old aspirated and glottalized initials (JAM).

Burmese High-falling Tone

	Burmese	Lahu	Lisu	Ahi	Lolopho	Nyi
child, son	*sà*	*yâ*	*râ*	*zó*	*zó*	*zá*
bee	*pyà*	*pɛ̂*	*byæ̂*	*dó*	*byó*	*dlá-mà*
eat	*tsà*	*câ*	*dzâ*	*dzó*	*dzó*	*dzá*
thin	*pà*	*pâ*	*bâ*	*bó*	—	*bá*
flesh, meat	*ăsà*	*ɔ̀-šā*[262]	*hwâ*	*hó~hú*	*hó*	*rá*
insect; silk	*puì*	*pû~pū*	*bü̂*	*bö́~bú*	*bö́*	(*bù*)
price	*ăphuì*	*phû*	*phü̂*	*phö́~phú*	*phö́*	(*phû*)
sky	*muì(gh)*	*mû*	*mû~mü̂*	*mú*	*amú*	*mú*
steal	*khuì*	*qhɔ̂*	*khû*	*khö́*	—	*khə́*
urine	*sè*	*jɨ̂*	*rzî*	*zö́*	—	*zə́*

The above tables yield the equations: B × = Lahu $\grave{\times}$ ~ × = Lisu, Ahi, Lolopho, Nyi $\grave{\times}$; and B $\grave{\times}$ = Lahu $\hat{\times}$ = Lisu $\hat{\times}$ = Ahi, Lolopho, Nyi $\acute{\times}$. Note that the Lolo languages tend to have falling tones for Burmese low-level tone, and rising tones for Burmese high-falling tone; also that Lahu has high-level, Lisu low-level, for Burmese high-falling. The original Burmese-Lolo values for these tonemes cannot be reconstructed. The fact that the distinction itself is of some antiquity is the important point here. The general picture is further complicated by the presence of an additional tonal series in Lolo, in which level tones (high or low in Ahi and Lolopho) play a predominant role. Burmese more often has low-level than high-falling in roots of this type, but the distinction is not clear-cut. Cf. the following (divided into two groups, Ahi having $\hat{\times}$ in the first group, $\check{\times}$ in the second group):

	Burmese	Lahu	Lisu	Ahi	Lolopho	Nyi
earth	*mre*	*mì-gɨ̀*	*mi-næ*	*mî*	*mî*	*mi*
short, low	*ním*	*nɛ̀*	*nyě*	*nê~nö̂*	(*nyiʔ*)	*nyī*
hair (body), feather	*ămwè*	*ɔ̀-mu*	*mü*	*nö̂*	—	*nū*
hear, listen	*na*	*na*	*na-năʔ*	*nô*	—	*na*
nose	*hna*	*nā-qhɔ̂*	*na-bè*	*nô-boʔ*	—	*na-bí*
know	*sí*	*ši̇̄*	*sγuě*	*sâ*	*sɛ̂*	*sā~sà*
sweat	*khrwè*	*kɨ̄*	*tśǐ*	*tśhâ*	—	*kiɛ̄*
left (hand)	*lak-waì* / *bhai*	*mɛ̄*	*læ̂ʔ-γǔ*	*vâ*	*vɛ̂*	*avɛ̄*

262 Lahu tone /^/ is the regular correspondence for the old B-L Tone 2 (high-falling in Burmese), but glottalized and sibilant-initial syllables on this tone have Lahu tone /¯/ (very low), as in 'flesh' (JAM).

	Burmese	Lahu	Lisu	Ahi	Lolopho	Nyi
much, many	*myà*	*mâ*	*myæ̂*	*nǒ*	*myô*	*nā*
iron	*sam*	*šo*	(*hɔ̀*)	*hǒ̌*	*hô*	(*rə̀*)
boat	*hle*	*hɔ-lòʔ-qō*[263,264]	*li*	*lǐ*	*lǐ*	*ślī*
tiger	*kyà*	*lâ*	*lâ-ma*	*lǒ*	*lǒ*	*lā*
red[265]	*ni*	*ni* ∼ *ní*	*ni*	*nyǐ* ∼ *nǐ*	*nyî*	*nyi*
ear	*nà*	*nā-pɔ*	*nǎ-pɔ*	*nǒ-pâ*	*nǒ-pâ*	*nā-po*

Two general types of explanation theoretically are available as regards the Burmese-Lolo tonal system: (*a*) the Burmese-Lolo system is an inherited TB feature; (*b*) it has been developed secondarily as the result of variation between surd and sonant initials (as in Tibetan), or through the loss of prefixed or suffixed elements, or through a combination of these factors. The fact that the Tibetan tonal system is unquestionably secondary constitutes a powerful argument against the first type of explanation. The Burmese-Lolo tonal system, however, seems to be quite independent of factors such as voicing of initial or affixed elements; at any rate, the writer has been unable to discover any relationship here. Tonal alternation between transitive and intransitive verb forms in Burmese is found in *nam* 'to stink', *ănam* 'unpleasant odor', *nàm* 'to smell (tr.)'; contrast *tshwai* 'attach to, connect with (tr.)', *tswaì* 'stick fast in, adhere (intr.)', and *phra* 'divide into several parts (tr.)', *prà* 'to be divided (intr.)'. Wolfenden[266] attempted to explain the high-falling tone of Burmese in terms of lost final consonants, but his analysis is altogether faulty. No general theory of TB tones can be attempted until the materials for a comprehensive comparative study of tones throughout the TB area are made available.[267]

263 Telford has *hɔn* 'boat', an odd shift paralleled by B *lè*, Lahu *hɔ̌n* 'heavy'; B *lè*, Lahu *ɔ̌n* '4'; B *lè*, Lahu *hɔ̌-mà* 'bow'; B *le*, Lahu *hɔ̀* 'wind' (all forms from Telford).

264 Telford's dialect of Lahu has more nasalization than Matisoff's, particularly after /ɔ/: *ɔ̂n* 'four', *ɔ́n* 'bend', *hɔn* 'elephant', *hɔ́n* 'under', etc. The nasalization is purely allophonic, of a type to be found throughout Southeast Asia (including Siamese and Lao), even in British English, in syllables beginning with *h-* or *ʔ-* (see Matisoff, *Lahu and PLB*; 'GD').

265 A root of restricted distribution can now be set up on the basis of Gyarung (Wolfenden) *əwurni* < **-rni*, Ch'iang (K. Chang) *n̊hi* 'red'; this root perhaps is the basis for a more widely distributed root, viz. **r-nil* ∼ **r-ni*(*y*) 'gums' (= its redness); TB **(r-)ni* 'red'.

266 'On the Ok Myit and She Pok, with a Proposed Revision of the Terminology of Burmese "Tones"', *JBRS* **19** (1929), 57–66.

267 See n. 494 for an over-view of tones throughout ST.

§13. Tibeto-Burman morphology (history)

Tibeto-Burman, as reconstructed, can be described in general terms as a relatively isolating language with roots of simple monosyllabic type, normally prefixing but occasionally suffixing. TB morphology has attracted the attention of a number of scholars, including Schiefner, Conrady, Von Koerber, Bonnerjea, Simon, and Wolfenden,[268] yet much analytical work remains to be done. Generally speaking, these students have attempted either to explain Tibetan in terms of itself, or to interpret all other TB languages in terms of Tibetan. This Tibetocentric bias is especially marked in the work of Conrady, and is clearly revealed even in the much more substantial analysis of Wolfenden. The lack of a sound phonological foundation further tends to vitiate many of the conclusions set forth in these pioneering efforts. In the present work we shall content ourselves with a review of the more salient features of TB morphology, in terms of the phonological framework already established.

§14. Tibeto-Burman morphology (categories)

At least four general categories of words (roots) can be set up for Tibeto-Burman, viz. verbs, nouns, pronouns, numerals. The derivation of nouns from verbs, through prefixation or suffixation, is a characteristic process of TB morphology, whereas the reverse type of derivation is exceedingly rare. The 'verb–adjective' and 'noun' categories are formally differentiated only to a minimal degree, as is shown below. Pronouns and numerals are formally of noun-type rather than verb-type as regards affixation patterns as well as syntactical relationships.

268 F. A. von Schiefner, 'Tibetische Studien', *Bull. de l'Académie des Sciences de St.-Pétersbourg* **8** (1851); A. Conrady, *Eine indochinesische Causativ-Denominativ Bildung und ihr Zusammenhang mit den Tonaccenten*, Leipzig, 1896; H. N. von Koerber, *Morphology of the Tibetan Language*, Los Angeles, 1935; B. Bonnerjea, 'Morphology of some Tibeto-Burman dialects of the Himalayan Region', *TP* **33** (1937), 301–60; W. Simon, 'Certain Tibetan Suffixes and their Combinations', *HJAS* **5** (1941), 372–91; 'Tibetan *dañ, ciñ, kyin, yin,* and *ḫam*', *BSOS* **10**, pt 4 (1942), 954–75; S. N. Wolfenden, *Outlines of Tibeto-Burman Linguistic Morphology*, London, 1929 (cited as *Outlines*). Note also the keen observations by Francke and Simon in H. A. Jäschke, *Tibetan Grammar* (with Addenda by A. H. Francke and W. Simon), Berlin, 1929.

§15. Tibeto-Burman pronouns

The 1st person and 2nd person independent personal pronouns are **ŋa* 'I' and **naŋ* 'thou':

(406) T *ŋa*, Kiranti *aŋ* (Rai, Rungchengbung) ~ *aŋ-ka* (Waling) ~ *ka-ŋa* (Rodong) ~ *əŋa* (Limbu), Nung *ŋa*, B *ŋa*, G *aŋ* 'I', with which must be grouped **ŋay* 'I; self', and perhaps Dhimal *ka*, L (and general Kuki) *ka* 'I'.

(407) Thami, Magari, Chepang *naŋ*, K *naŋ* ~ *na*, B *naŋ* 'thou', G *naʔa* 'thou', *naŋ-ni* 'thy' (cf. B *ńàń* < **nyìŋ* 'thou [female to female]'), L *naŋ*, also Dhimal and Nung *na* 'thou'.

Subordination is effected simply through anteposition or prefixation to the noun, often in abbreviated form, e.g. K *naŋ* ~ *na* 'thou', *nwa* (*n-wa*) 'thy father'. Pronominal inflection, clearly of secondary origin, is encountered in the Himalayish group and occasionally elsewhere; cf. B *ŋa* 'I', *ŋá* 'mine'; *naŋ* 'thou', *náŋ* 'thine' (see above); Dhimal *ka* 'I', *na* 'thou'; *kaŋ* 'my', *naŋ* 'thy'; *kyel* 'we', *nyel* 'you'; *kiŋ* 'our', *niŋ* 'your'. Various types of refinements, none of which can be regarded as inherited TB features, appear in random distribution. These include the distinction between exclusive and inclusive forms of the 1st person pronoun (notably in Himalayish, also in Tibetan and Mikir), the dual (Kanauri, Tibetan, Kachin),[269] and distinctions in sex of speaker (notably in Burmese). The concept of plurality is generally expressed through suffixation (as for nouns). No general TB 3rd person independent pronoun can be established.[270]

§16. Tibeto-Burman numerals

The TB numeral system is of decimal type, yet it seems to have included a vigesimal unit (see n. 23) along with the distinctive root *(*m*-)*kul* '20' (No. 397). As noted above, TB **s-nis* points to the use of a quinary basis ($5+2=7$), and it

269 The evidence for Tibetan is presented in A. H. Francke, 'Das tibetische Pronominalsystem', *ZDMG* **61** (1907), 439–40. Francke argues that T *ŋed* originally stood for 'we two'.

270 Kiranti and K-N have TB **a* in suffixed form as a 3rd person pronoun, while in Trung (Nungish) this same element occurs independently, but in nasalized form: *aŋ*.

is noteworthy that this root has been replaced in several TB groups (T *bdun*, L *səri*). No general TB root for '1' can be singled out, although several comparisons are available:

Lepcha *kat*, Kuki-Naga **khat* '1'; TB **kat*.

Kanauri *id*, B *ats* '1' (also 'unit' in Burmese); TB **it*.

Himalayish: Chingtang *thit(-ta)*, Rai *tik(-pu)*, Nung *thi*, B *tats* '1'; cf. also T *gtśig*; TB **t(y)ik*.[271]

The root **gip* '10' (No. 16) is poorly represented, and extreme variation obtains here (T *btśu*, L *śom*), yet a Kachin–Konyak–Bodo–Naga root can be established:

(408) K *tśi*~*śi*, Namsang *i-tśi*, Moshang *rok-śi*, G *tśi*, Dimasa *dźi* '10', also Miju *si* (in comp.), from TB **ts(y)i(y)*; B *ătshai* '10' appears to be related to this root through vowel gradation.[272]

The root **s-toŋ* '1,000' (No. 32) appears only in Tibetan and Burmese-Lolo,[273] but **r-gya* '100' (No. 164) is well represented, as are **g-nis* '2' (No. 4), **g-sum* '3' (No. 409), **b-liy* '4' (No. 410), **l-ŋa*~**b-ŋa* '5' (No. 78), **d-ruk* '6' (No. 411), **b-r-gyat* '8' (No. 163) and **d-kuw* '9' (No. 13). Note that all these widely distributed numerals are provided with prefixes. Prefixed **g-* in **g-nis* and **g-sum* is reflected in T *gnyis* and *gsum*, G *gni* and *githam*, as well as Digaro *kəyiŋ* and *kəsaŋ*, but replacement or loss of this element is common everywhere; cf. K *ni* '2', *məsum*<**b-sum* '3' (influenced by *məli*<**b-li* '4'); Nung *əni* '2', *ətsum* '3'; B *hnats* '2', *sùm* '3'; L *hniʔ* '2', *thum* '3'. Prefixed **b-* in **b-liy* '4' is well established; cf. T *bźi*<**bli* (this cluster lacking before *i* in Tibetan), Thulung *bli*, Kanauri *pö*<**pli* (see n. 126), Magari *buli*, Digaro *kəprei*, Miri *pi*, Nung *əbyi* (dial. *əbəli*), K *məli*<*b-li*, B *lè* (Maru *byit*<**b-liy*), Mikir *phli*. T *lŋa*, Old Kuki **r-ŋa* (e.g. Rangkhol *riŋa*) attest to TB **l-ŋa* '5', but prefixed **b-*, apparently through the influence exerted by **b-liy* '4', is much more generally represented (Thami *bəŋa*, Digaro *məŋa*, K *məŋa*<*b-ŋa*, Nung *pəŋa*, B *ŋà*, G *boŋa*, L *ŋa*). Prefixed **d-* is well attested in **d-ruk* '6' (T *drug*, Kanauri *ṭŭg*, Lepcha *tărăk*, Digaro *thərɔ*, G *dok*, Mikir *therok*) and **d-kuw* '9' (T *dgu*, Nung *təgö*, K *dźəkhu*,

271 We can now reconstruct TB **tyik* (to explain T *gtśig*), and can further set up a doublet in ST showing the medial *ya*~*i* alternation (n. 251), viz. **tyak*~**tyik*, the former represented by Ch. **t'i̯ăk/tśi̯äk*[a] 'single, one' (Ar. Ch. form not cited in *GSR*).

272 In view of the recognition of a separate palatal series for TB (n. 122), it is now possible to reconstruct this root as **tsyay*, yielding both B *ătshai* and the various palatalized forms with final *-i*.

273 Trung (Nungish) has *ti tuŋ ŋai* '1,000', *ti tuŋ gra* '10,000' (*ti* '1'), appearing to contain the **/toŋ* element, but analysis is uncertain (Trung has *ti śya* '100', *śyat* '8').

[a] 隻

G *sku*, Kuki-Naga **d-kua*), but note replacement of **d-* by *k-* before root-initial **r-* in Magari *kruk*, Nung *təru* (dial. *kru*), K *kru*, B *khrauk* '6'. The initials of **b-r-gyat* '8' and **r-gya* '100' tend to be absorbed in the prefixed elements; cf. K *mətsat* < *b-gyat* '8' (with loss of *r*) and *lətsa* < **r-gya* '100'; B *hrats* < (prefix +) *ryat* '8' and *ăra* (*rya* in inscriptions) '100'; L *riat* '8' and *za* < **ya* '100'. The general Kuki-Naga root **d-ryat* '8' (Khami *təya*, Lakher *tśəri*, Empeo *dəsat*, Sema Naga *tətśe*, Ao Naga *tezet*, also Meithei *təret* '7') shows replacement of **b-* under the influence of **d-kua* (TB **d-kuw*) '9'. Tibetan, on the other hand, has developed *brgya* '100' from **r-gya* through hybridization with *brgyad* '8', the general TB evidence (notably that of Kachin) unmistakably pointing to a distinction in the prefixes of these two roots.[274]

§17. Tibeto-Burman morphology and syntax (general)

The relationships that obtain among the several units of the TB sentence are indicated (*a*) through the relative positions of the units, and (*b*) through the employment of special relating morphemes, normally prefixes or suffixes. The syntactical factor tends to be the dominant one, however, hence one can describe Tibeto-Burman as 'relatively isolating'. Throughout the TB area the invariable syntactical rule is that the verb must be placed at the end of the sentence, followed only by suffixed elements or sentence-final particles. The object normally immediately precedes the verb and follows the subject, though no invariable rule can be stated here (in Burmese the object is somewhat emphasized when placed before the subject). The concepts of 'subject', 'object', 'indirect object', 'instrumentality', and the like are reinforced or expressed in modern TB languages by morphemes suffixed to nouns. The subject is often found standing alone, or construed as an instrumental, as in T *ŋa-s kho-la rduŋ* 'by-me to-him beat' = 'I beat him', *ŋa-s de śes* (or *ŋa-la* in modern dialects) 'by-me that know' = 'I know that'. Subordinated elements regularly precede rather than follow, although modifying elements are often suffixed; cf. Modern B *tyìdɛ́ khwè* 'big dog...' or 'dog (that is) big...' (*-dɛ́* with 'creaky tone', a morpheme of subordination), *khwè tyìdɛ* 'dog is-big', *khwèdyì* 'big-dog' (*t* > *d* in intervocalic position). It is a striking fact, however, that relating morphemes of the type in question seem to be of relatively recent origin in the several TB groups, strongly indicating that in the

274 See n. 148 for the present analysis of these two numerals.

parent language these elements were largely lacking. Only one correspondence of any significance has been uncovered here:

T *-kyi*~*-gyi*~*-yi*~*-i*, B *-í*, Meithei and Anal *-ki*, Dhimal *-ko* (Toto *-k*), Sho *-kheo*, a genitival (subordinating) suffix.[275]

§ 18. Tibeto-Burman affixes (special)

The study of TB morphology is in large measure simply the study of those prefixed and suffixed elements which can be shown to be of some antiquity. Certain of these prefixes (**g-*, **b-*, **l-*, **d-*)[276] have already been pointed out in connection with the numerals. In many instances, as here, no function can be assigned these elements, i.e. loss of morphological utility had already occurred in proto-TB times. A few suffixed elements can be readily analyzed. They include the 'gender' suffixes **-ma* (fem.) < **ma* 'mother', and **-pa* (masc.) < **pa* 'father', as well as **-la* (masc.), used with words for animals (in Tsangla, Digaro, Nung, Kachin, Burmese-Lolo, Konyak, Garo-Bodo, Mikir, and Meithei);[277] also the verbal noun (infinitive) suffix *-pa*~*-ba* 'that which is' (in Tibetan, Bahing, Meithei, Garo-Bodo, Burmese-Lolo); cf. T *khyi smyon-pa* 'mad dog', lit. 'a dog, one which (*-pa*) is mad' (see Wolfenden, *Outlines*, p. 75); Lahu *qai-pa̱ mâ-cɔ̀* 'there is no one to go', lit. 'one-to-go there-is-not'. This suffix is probably connected with the masculine noun suffix *-pa* mentioned above; note that Meithei sometimes distinguishes between *-ba* (masc.) and *-bi* (< Kuki-Naga **pwi*) (fem.) in adjectival forms, paralleling the distinction occasionally made in Tibetan, e.g. *dma-mo* 'low' but *mthon-po* 'high', *rgad-po* 'old man', *rgad-mo* 'old woman' (*rgad-pa*~*rgan-pa* 'old').

275 Simon (*BSOS* **10**, pt 4, 1942), on the basis of the Tibetan and Burmese evidence alone, reconstructs this suffix as *ʾyi* (a cluster distinctly alien to the TB system as a whole). The Meithei-Anal form, however, indicates that the velar element is archaic (TB **-ki* or **-gi*); cf. also n. 322.

276 The combination of prefixes *b-r-* in **b-r-gyat* '8' is unique, and prefixed **l-* can be reconstructed only for *l-ŋa* '5', although Tibetan has this prefix in a number of roots; cf. T *lba-ba* 'wen, goitre', Digaro *təba*, Moso *ba*~*mba* 'goitre'; T *lte-ba* 'navel', K *śədai*, G *ste* (TB **s-tay*).

277 Tibetan applies suffixes of this type (*-pa*~*-ba*~*-bo*, and *-ma*~*-mo*) to inanimates as well as animates, e.g. *khu-ba* 'liquid', *dri-ma* 'filth'. This usage is even commoner in the early texts, e.g. *gźu-mo* for *gźu* 'bow', *mda-mo* for *mda* 'arrow'. These suffixed forms are not otherwise differentiated, however, hence one cannot properly speak of grammatical gender here.

The negative elements **ma* and **ta* precede the verb in Tibeto-Burman (**ma* is often prefixed, as in Burmese). The simple negative is **ma*, with an almost universal TB distribution; Kachin has prefixed *n-*, an unstressed variant of *mə-* (cf. n. 327), while Kuki-Naga has suffixed *-mak*. The imperative negative is **ta*, which is almost equally well represented; it appears in Murmi, Himalayish (generally), Vayu, Kiranti (Rodong, Chintang), Burmese-Lolo (Lahu, Lisu, Ahi, Nyi, Manyak), and Bodo-Garo (generally).

§19. Tibeto-Burman affixes (general)

The prefixes and suffixes (apart from those used with numerals) of the reconstructed TB speech are listed below.[278] In modern TB languages the prefixes normally have reduced stress and the neutral *ə* type of vocalization. Thus, the form written **g-* is to be interpreted as **gə* (with *ə* as a separate phoneme) or as *gă* (with *ă* an allophone of the phoneme /*a*/ in syllables with reduced stress). The vowel of the prefix is affected by vocalic harmony in several groups, notably Bodo-Garo and Mikir; cf. Dimasa *gabaŋ* 'much', *gosoŋ* 'steep', *gusum* 'blue', *gepher* 'flat', *gimin* 'ripe'.

Suffixed **-s*: original function uncertain; often reflexive in verb roots.

Suffixed **-t* and **-n*: original function uncertain; sometimes used in deriving nouns from verb roots; also causative or directive.

Prefixed **s-*: causative, directive, or intensive with verb roots; often stands for TB **sya* 'flesh; animal' in noun roots.

Prefixed **r-*: both in verb and noun roots; function unknown.

Prefixed **b-*: perhaps pronominal in some roots, but function generally unknown.

Prefixed **g-*: rare; function unknown.

Prefixed **d-*: rare; function unknown.

Prefixed **m-*: pronominal in noun roots; intransitive in verb roots.

278 Nothing much has been written in the field of comparative TB morphology since 1940. The most important articles to appear on the subject are R. Shafer, 'Prefixes in Tibeto-Burmic', *HJAS*, 1945–7, and 'Phonétique comparée de quelques préfixes simples en sino-tibétain', *BSLP*, 1950; see also R. A. Miller, 'The Tibeto-Burman Infix System', *JAOS* **78**, 3, 1958 (JAM).

§20. Tibeto-Burman dental suffixes

The dental suffixes **-s*, **-t*, and **-n* are particularly troublesome. All three suffixes appear only in roots with vocalic or semivocalic ending, in accordance with the general TB phonemic rule that consonant clusters occur only in root-initial position.[279] In Tibetan, however, suffixed *-s* appears also after final *-g*, *-b* and *-ŋ*, *-m*, but not after dentals, hence *-s* is in many cases to be referred to **-ds* or **-ns*. Wolfenden, who has paid special attention to these suffixes,[280] makes this type of reconstruction for many Tibetan roots, even where there is ample TB evidence for a vocalic ending, e.g. T **zan* rather than **za* 'eat' (in the face of TB **dza*). As already shown above (n. 62), the West T data confirm the derivation of *-s* from **-ds* in *pus-mo* < **puds* 'knee' < TB **put*; cf. also the following root:

(412) T *mkhris-pa* < **mkhrids*, West T *ṭhigs-pa* 'bile', Nung *səhi* < **səkhri* 'gall-bladder' (cf. No. 38), B *sàñ-khre* 'gall' (*sàñ* 'liver'), G *kha-khit* 'bile' (*kha* 'bitter' = 'liver'), Dimasa *bikhlu* < **bikhlit*, *id.*, from TB **(m-)kri-t*.

The above root is a derivative of the following:

(413) Lepcha *kri* 'bitter', K *khri* 'acid, sour', Moshang *əhi* < **əkhri* 'acid' (cf. No. 416), Dimasa *khiri* 'sour', from TB **kri(y)*.

Suffixed *-ś(i)* ~ *-so* used to form a type of 'middle voice' is found in several languages; cf. Kanauri *krapśi* ~ *skrapśi* 'cry together', *toŋśi* 'strike oneself or one another', *sarśi* 'rise' (*sar* 'raise'), *zaśi* 'be eaten', *diśi* 'enter, lie down', *bŏśi* 'forget'; Nung *itśi* 'laugh', *ŋimśi* 'stoop', *narśi* 'stop (to rest)', *khuŋśi* 'awake', *məguśi* 'embrace, hug'; Bahing *riso* 'laugh', *khlöso* 'hide', *tśiso* 'bathe', *phiso* 'dress oneself', *gyerso* 'be glad', *biso* 'believe', *yoŋso* 'be melted'; Vayu *lita* ~ *lista* 'heavy', *liś(-tśe)* 'be heavy', *siśto* 'kill', *siś(-tśe)* 'kill thyself or for thyself' (< TB **siy* 'die').[281] Tibetan *-s* is regularly employed with verbs in the 'perfect root', but

279 In early Tibetan texts *-d* is found after *-n*, *-r*, and *-l*. This element, the *da drag* of Tibetan scholars, has been convincingly explained on phonological grounds by J. Przyluski and M. Lalou in their article, 'Le *da drag* tibétain', *BSOS* **7** (1933), 87–9. Both Wolfenden (*Outlines*, pp. 56 ff.) and Laufer, 'Bird Divination among the Tibetans', *TP* **15** (1914), 1–110, have unsuccessfully attempted to connect *da drag* with regular suffixed *-d*.

280 *Outlines*, pp. 56 ff.; 'On Certain Alternations between Dental Finals in Tibetan and Chinese', *JRAS* (1936), 401–16; 'Concerning the Variation of Final Consonants in the Word Families of Tibetan, Kachin, and Chinese', *JRAS* (1937), 625–55.

281 Suffixed *-s* ~ *-z* is also found in other Himalayish languages, e.g. Bunan *bris* ~ *briz* 'write' (T *'bri-ba*), *hoangs* 'come out' < TB **hwaŋ*; Manchati *braŋz* 'sit', Tinan *bragz* 'put together', *sams* 'think' (T *sem-pa*, pf. *sems* ~ *bsams*), *voas*

appears also in many 'present' roots, occasionally with extra-Tibetan correspondences, e.g. T *śes-pa*, Vayu *ses*(*-tśe*) 'know, understand' < TB **syey* (above); cf. also the following:

(414) T *gnas-pa* 'be, live, dwell, stay', Kanauri *na-śi* 'rest', Bahing *na-so* 'take rest' (TB **na*).

(415) T *thos-pa*, Vayu *thas*(*-tśe*), Tsangla *tha*, Lepcha *thyo* < **s-ta*, Nung *tha*, Miri *tat* 'hear' (TB **ta-s*).[282]

Kachin suffixed *-t* in verb roots is in most cases to be referred to TB **-t*, but perhaps stands for suffixed **-s* in intransitive forms such as *khrat* 'fall' < TB **kla* (above); cf. Kachin *-t* < **-s* in Nos. 5 and 6, also the following root:

(416) T *khri-le-ba* 'fear', Moshang *əhi* < **əkhri* 'fear' (cf. No. 413), L *ṭi* < **kri* 'fear, be nervous', K *khrit* 'fear, be afraid', *khrit gəriʔ* 'fear and tremble', perhaps also G *an-skit* 'quail, shudder', from TB **kri*(*y*).

Similarly, Lepcha suffixed *-t*, as in *zot* 'to graze' < *zo* 'eat' (T *za-ba*), can be assigned either to TB **-t* or **-s*.

TB suffixed **-t* and **-n* are best represented in Tibetan, Lepcha and Kachin, and most meagerly represented in Burmese-Lolo.[283] The original function of these suffixes (or variants of a single suffix) cannot be delimited from the available material. Both are ordinarily employed with verbal roots, but a few exceptional forms in **-n* from nominal roots have been noted;[284] cf. K *yu* ~ *yun* 'rat' < TB

'come out', as well as in Magari, e.g. *khus* 'steal' (T *rku-ba*), *ŋos* 'look, search', *khus* 'take up', connected with Bahing *ku-wo* 'ascend', *ku-to* 'bring up' (the transitive form), Yakha *khu* 'lift up, raise', B *khù* 'take out or up and put into a dish, pluck, gather'. Kanauri also has *-s* ~ *-ss* as an adjectival suffix, e.g. *tśis* 'rotten', *tshŏs* 'fat' < TB **tsow*, *kyŏs* 'drunk', *liss* 'cold', *thiss* 'wet' < TB **ti*(*y*).

282 Trung (Nungish) has *thaŋ* 'hear', with secondary final *-ŋ* (cf. n. 74); Newari has *ta-l*, with suffixed *-l* (see n. 294). This root has now been reconstructed **tâ-s* on the basis of T *thos-pa* (see n. 488).

283 Cf. B *thi* 'fear, stand in awe of', *thit* 'startle, be frightened'. Final *-n* ~ *-t* alternation is found in Burmese and elsewhere; cf. B *pwàn* 'to be rubbed off', *pwat* 'rub, grind; lathe'; *hmìn* 'to have the eyes shut', *hmit* 'shut (the eye), wink'; *pàn* 'go round', *pat* 'wind around, encircle' (note the intransitive vs. transitive distinction here); Nung *ph*(*y*)*it* ~ *ph*(*y*)*in* 'to loose, untie'; T *'phyen* ~ *phyen*, K *phyet* 'flatulence'; K *mot* ~ *mon* 'cut, slice, shave' (cf. T *rmo-ba* ~ *rmod-pa* 'plough').

284 TB final **-n* here can be identified as a special kind of 'collective' pluralizing suffix (possibly with dual force in K *-phan* 'palm, sole'), directly comparable with a similar suffix in Ch. (n. 428). K *śan* 'flesh, meat, deer' (text) has a direct cognate (the vocalism is regular) in Ch. *śi̯ĕn*[a] 'body' (AT has the identical semantic interchange; cf. IN **dagiŋ* 'body, flesh'). Kachin also has (*tśyə-*)*khan* 'crab' < TB **d-ka·y*. Burmese has this suffix in *yun* 'rabbit' (like rats, these come in large numbers) < TB **b-yəw* 'rat' (K *yu* ~ *yun* 'rat', T *byiu* 'alpine hare', L *sa-zu-pui* 'hare' = 'big rat'); cf. also B *ŋàn* 'goose' < **ŋa* (as shown by Ch. evidence; n. 428), whence T *ŋaŋ* (*-pa*, *-ma*) 'goose (wild)', from **ŋa*/*ŋa*; also B *kyì-kàn* 'crow' < TB

a 身

**b-yuw*, K *śan* 'flesh, meat, deer' < TB **sya*, also the following pair of roots:

(417) Chepang *ya*, Nung *ya*, Miri *yo* < **ya*, Mikir *dźo* < **ya*, but L *za·n* < **ya·n*, Thado *yan* 'night' (TB **ya*).[285]

(418) Nung *ur-pha* 'palm', Miri *lak-po* < **-pa* 'palm', *le-po* 'sole', B *bhăwà* (*phăwà*) 'palm, sole', G *dźak-pha* 'palm', *dźa-pha* 'sole', but K *ləphan* < **lak-phan* 'palm, sole' (all except Burmese in comp. with 'hand' and/or 'foot') (TB **pa*).[286, 287]

Suffixed **-t* is clearly causative or directive in some instances, e.g. T *'byed-pa* 'open, separate' (tr.) < *'bye-ba* (intr.), T *'gyed-pa* 'divide, disperse' (tr.) < *'gye-ba* (intr.), *nud-pa* (also *snun-pa*) 'suckle' < *nu-ba* 'suck', apparently related to the following root:

(419) T *nu-ma* 'breast', Tsangla *nu* 'milk', B *nuí*, L *hnu-te* 'breast, milk' (TB **nuw*).

**ka*: T *kha-tha* 'crow, raven', K *kha*, Nungish: Răwang *thaŋ-kha*, Trung *tak-ka* 'crow'. An additional important class of **-n* (and **-t*) suffixes for nominal roots is furnished by kinship terms, especially in Tibetan, which has a curious and complicated group of derivatives (typically with prefixed *s-*) from basic kinship roots (Benedict, 1941, 1942 bis), e.g. *pha* 'father', *pha-spad* 'father and children'; *phu* 'older brother' (< TB 'grandfather'), *spun* 'siblings, cousins'; (combining both roots) *span-spun* 'brothers, relatives'; *ʔa-khu* ~ *khu-bo* 'uncle (father's brother)' (< TB 'mother's brother'), *skud-po* 'brother-in-law, father-in-law' (Chinese has an *-n* derivative here; n. 428); *tsha* 'nephew/niece; grandchild' (< TB 'child'), *pha-tshan* 'cousins on the father's side', *khu-tshan* 'uncle and nephew', but this element also appears in the form *-tshan* 'termination of some collective nouns', e.g. *bźi-tshan* 'collection of four (*bźi*) things', also *gnyen-tshan* 'kindred, relations (*gnyen*)' (this directly cognate with similar form in Chinese; n. 428). This system is reflected elsewhere only sporadically, cf. B *khaŋ-pwàn* 'spouse' (B-L **khaŋ* 'grandfather', **bwa* 'grandmother'); Kanauri *mann* 'mother' < TB **ma* (cf. T *ma-smad* 'mother and children'); Lepcha *ă-fyăt* < **-sput* 'father-in-law, wife's older brother' < TB **pəw* 'grandfather' (cf. T *skud-po*, cited above), (*ă-*)*zon* < **-zan* 'grandchild' but (*ă-*)*zo* 'great-grandfather' (reciprocal terms), from TB **za* 'child'; Dhimal *tśan* 'son', from TB **tsa* 'child'. There is excellent evidence for similar suffixed *-t* as well as *-n* derivatives in Chinese (n. 428), hence this group of nominal suffixes must be assigned to ST itself.

285 Tiddim *za·n* 'night', as in Lushei, but Siyin (Stern, *Asia Major* **10**, 1963) has *za·n* 'to be evening', hence this apparently exceptional form in K-N belongs with the trio of roots cited below (pp. 102–3). Nungish has *dźia* (Răwang) and *yaʔ* (Mutwang) 'night'; for the latter, cf. B *ńá* 'night', from **n(é)-ya* (*ne* 'sun', *né* 'day'), which also belongs in this set. The appearance of 'creaky voice' here and in 'day' (*né*) and 'moon, month' (*lá*) hardly seems to be a matter of chance; see n. 487 for the glottalization of this root and for parallel features in the Chinese cognates.

286 L *kut-phaʔ* 'palm', *ke-phaʔ* 'sole' perhaps also belong here, but the glottal stop suggests a connection with Mikir *ri-pak* ~ *ri-pek* 'palm', *keŋ-pak* 'sole'.

287 This root now reconstructed **pwa* (n. 78), but **b-wa* is an alternative (and perhaps better) possibility.

Kachin also has causative suffixed *-t*, e.g. K *mədit* 'moisten, wet, dip' < *mədi* 'moist, wet'; K *mənit* 'laugh at' < *məni* 'laugh'. The Bahing-Vayu *-t(o)* suffix is exclusively of this type; cf. Bahing *ri-so* 'laugh', *ri-to* 'laugh at'; Vayu *khu* 'steal', *khut* 'cause to steal'; Vayu *muś(-tśe)* 'sit', *muś-to* 'seat' (also *mut* 'cause to seat'). In many instances, however, no function of precisely this sort can be traced; cf. T *'khru-ba* ~ *'khrud-pa*, K *khrut* 'wash, bathe' < TB **kruw*; T *gtśi-ba* ~ *gtśid-pa*, K *dźit dźi* ~ *dźit tśyi* 'urinate' < TB **ts(y)i*; T *stad-pa* 'put on' < TB **ta* 'place'; T *rnyed-pa* 'get, obtain' < TB **ney*; K *məsit* 'to comb' < TB **m-si(y)*; cf. also the following:

(420) T *rko-ba* ~ *rkod-pa* 'dig out, engrave', K *got* 'to be scooped out', *ləgot* ~ *ləkhot* (also *śəgot*) 'scoop up' (TB **r-ko-t*).

(421) T *'du-ba* 'assemble, meet, join', *dud-pa* 'to tie, knot', *mdud* 'knot, bow', *sdud-pa* 'put together, join, unite', *sdud* 'folds of a garment', *'thu-ba* 'gather, collect', K *tut* 'to be joined, bound or tied together', *mətut* ~ *kətut* 'join, connect', Nung *thu* 'join (as a stream)', *dəthut* 'join, unite', G *stit* < **stut* 'tangle', *ka-ani bistit* 'a knot' (*ka* 'tie') (TB **du-t* ~ **tu-t*).

(422) K *tsut* 'stop, plug, cork, as a bottle', *mətsut* 'to stop, cork; stopper', Nung *sü* 'to cork', *aŋsü* 'cork', B *tshuí* 'stop up', *ătshuí* 'stopper, plug' (TB **tsuw*).

(423) T *sud-pa*, Magari *su* 'to cough', from TB **su(w)*.[288]

(424) K *gəwa* ~ *kəwa* ~ *wa* 'bite', B *wà* 'chew', Bodo *wat* ~ *ot*, Dimasa *wai* < **wat* 'bite' (TB **wa*).

The Bodo-Garo evidence is complicated by the presence of a suffixed element **-wat* ('give, send') > G *-at*, as in the following:

(425) G *mat* 'to be spent', *gima-at* ~ *gimat* 'destroy, waste, obliterate', *gima-ani* 'loss, damage', Dimasa *gama* ~ *kama* 'lose, disappear, perish' *khama* 'injure, spoil, destroy', K *ma* 'to be exhausted, finished, spent', *mat* 'to be lost, to have disappeared', Gurung *hma*, Murmi *ma* 'to be lost', Magari *hma* ~ *hmat* 'to be lost; lose' (TB **ma-t*).

Alternation between final vowel and *-t* appears in a few badly recorded verb forms in Lushei (*na* ~ *nat* 'ill', *ba* ~ *bat* 'owe', *pu* ~ *put* 'carry'), but the true Kuki-Naga equivalent of TB **-t* in verb roots seems to be *-k* (alternating with glottal stop).[289] Haka (Central Kuki) is unique among TB languages in deriving verbs from

288 Garo and Dimasa *gusu* 'to cough' also appear to belong to this root of very limited distribution.

289 Cf. Kuki-Naga **dza(k)* 'eat' < TB **dza*, **ne(k)* 'drink', **pe(k)* 'give'; and L *tla·k* 'fall' < TB **kla*; Meithei *nok*, Mikir *iŋnek* < *m-nik* 'laugh' < TB **m-nwi(y)*; L *zuk* < *yuk* 'verbal affix indicating motion downwards' < TB **yu(w)*, as represented by Vayu *yu* 'descend' (*yut* tr.), Bahing *yu* 'descend', K *yu* 'descend', *śəyu* 'let down'.

nouns through suffixation of **-t* (>Haka *-θ*), as in *əfa* 'child' (<TB **za*), *fa·θ* 'to breed'; *əbu* 'nest' (L *bu*, Sho *əbü*, Khami *təbu*, Aimol *rəbu*), *bu·θ* 'build a nest'; *ərɔl* 'food', *rɔθ* 'grow food', *əva·r* 'husband', *va·θ* 'marry a husband'.

T suffixed *-d*<**-t* often appears in substantives derived from verbs, e.g. *ŋud-mo* 'a sob'<*ŋu-mo* 'weep', *lud-pa* 'phlegm'<*lu-ba* 'cough, throw up phlegm', *drod* 'heat'<*dro-ba* 'to be warm', sometimes paralleling forms in *-s*, as in *blud-pa*~*blus-ma* 'ransom'<*blu-ba* 'to ransom', *ltad-mo* 'sight, spectacle'~*ltas* 'miraculous sign, omen'<*lta-ba* 'to look'. As suggested above, many or all *-s* forms of this type may be derivatives of **-ds* forms:

(426) T *ʼthas-pa* 'hard, solid', Nung *that* 'thick', K *that* 'thick', *ləthat* 'coarse, rough', Mikir *arthat* 'fat, thick, callous', Meithei *ətha-ba* 'thick' (TB **r-ta-t*).[290,291]

TB **-t* also appears in this role in other languages, e.g. Kanauri *brad* 'branch'<*bra* 'forked' (cf. No. 327); K *lit* 'load'<*li* 'heavy'; K *wan-khut* 'smoke' (*wan-khut khu* 'to smoke'), Tangkhul *khut* 'smoke', TB **kuw*; TB **(m-)kri-t* 'bile'<**kri(y)* 'sour'.

Tibetan suffixed *-n* is often adjectival, as in *dron-mo* 'warm'<*dro-ba* 'to be warm', but is commonly found also in secondary noun forms, e.g. *rdzun* 'falsehood'<*rdzu-ba* 'deceive', *zan* 'food' (also *zas*)<*za-ba* 'to eat', *gtśin* 'urine'<*gtśi-ba* 'urinate'. Lepcha shows a similar pattern with suffixed *-n* and *-m*, the latter perhaps connected with the verbal-noun suffix *-m*~*-am*~*-im* of Kanauri; cf. Lepcha *ăzom* 'food'<*zo* 'eat', *ăhrum* 'hot'~*ăhrun* 'heat'<*hru* 'to be hot', *ăyam* 'knowledge'<*ya* 'know', *śim* 'being'<*śi* 'to be', *ăbun* 'vehicle'<*bu* 'carry' (note the use of prefixed *ă-*). Tibetan has suffixed *-n* by exception in the regular verb form in the following root:

(427) T *sbyin-pa* 'give', also 'gift', Kiranti **bi* (Dumi *bi*~*bi-ŋa*, Khaling and Rai *bi-ŋa*, Khambu *pi-*), Miri *bi*, Dhimal *pi*, B *pè*, Nyi Lolo *ve-bi*, Mikir *pi* 'give' (TB **biy*).[292]

Kanauri has *-n* as a transitive verb suffix in a few forms, e.g. *go-śi* 'commit adultery with', *gon* (tr.); *hu-śi* 'learn', *hun* 'teach'; cf. also *khun* 'steal', T *rku-ba* 'steal', *rkun-ma* 'thief; theft' (noun in *-n*), K *ləgu* 'steal', *ləgut* 'thief' (noun in *-t*), from TB **r-kuw* (above). Lushei has suffixed *-n* in the following trio of roots (note also T *-s*, K *-t*):[293]

290 T suffixed *-s* perhaps stands for *sa* 'place' in some forms, as suggested by Simon, *HJAS* **5**, 1941; cf. *nags* 'forest' and *nag-pa* 'black', *dbus* 'middle' and *dbu* 'head'.

291 L *tśhaʔ* 'thick' belongs with this set, which has now been reconstructed **r-tas* (n. 63), hence the analysis here in terms of suffixation must be considered faulty.

292 Trung (Nungish) has *biŋ* 'give', with secondary final *-ŋ* (n. 74).

293 Add K-N **ya·n* 'night; to be evening' (n. 285); also L *pan* 'thin', Tiddim *pa·*~*pa·t* 'to be thin', *pan* (same tone) 'to be very thin', from TB **ba* (No. 25).

(428) K *bu* 'wear (as a shirt or trousers)', Thado *bu* 'wear', Lakher *əbu* 'wear (as a cloth)', L *bun* 'put on or wear (as ring, boots), encircle', from TB **bu*(*w*).

(429) T *'bri-ba* 'draw, write', *bris* 'picture (drawn or painted)', *ris* 'figure, form, design', *ri-mo* 'figure, painting, drawing; markings', K *məriʔ* 'to mark, line, rule', *dumrit* 'mark with an edge-tool, as around a log', *rit* 'fix, as a boundary', *ərit* 'dividing line between two paddy fields', *dźərit* 'boundary, border', Nung *rəga dərit* 'boundary' (*rəga* 'country'), B *rè* 'write, paint, delineate', G *a-ri*, Dimasa *ha-ri* 'boundary' (*a-* ~ *ha-* 'earth'), L *ri* 'boundary', *ri·n* 'draw a line, scratch; line, scratch' (TB **riy*).

(430) Tsangla *yu*, Nung *əyü*, B *yui*, Meithei *yu* 'leak', Lakher *zu* < *yu* 'drip, leak; a drop', Haka *zuθ* < *yut* 'leak, drip, fall', K *yun* ~ *kəyun* 'leak', L and Haka *zun* < *yun* 'excrement, urine' (TB **yuw*).[294]

§21. Tibeto-Burman prefixes (general)

Two general points must be borne in mind as the prefixed elements (*s*-, *r*-, *b*-, *g*-, *d*-, *m*-) are reviewed: (*a*) these elements are peculiarly subject to replacement or loss, (*b*) they frequently, as unstressed units, exhibit phonetic shifts differing from those that obtain for phonemes within roots. Thus, Kachin has *r*- for TB **r*- in root-initial position, -*n* for TB *-*r* in root-final position, and either *lə*- or *n*- ~ *niŋ*- ~ *num*- for TB prefixed **r*-. The general TB root **r-pat* 'leech', however, is represented by K *wot* rather than **ləwot* or **nwot*; cf. also T *pad-ma* (with significant lack of aspiration, suggesting a lost prefix), Nung *dəphat* < **d-pat* ~ *phəphat* < **m-pat*, Miri *təpat* < **d-pat*, Digaro *kəpe* < **g-pat* (cf. B *krwat*), Mikir *iŋphat* < **m-pat*, Lakher *tśəva* < **d-wat* (the **d*- prefix here is of relatively late origin). Prefix variation of this kind has already been pointed out in connection with the numerals, and is characteristic of TB roots as a whole. This fact suggests that TB prefixes remained separable and largely functional well into the proto-TB period, and that the rigid schematicizations found in modern TB languages have been developed secondarily.

294 Newari has a verb conjugation in -*n*, as well as one in -*t* and three in -*l*; see H. Jörgensen, 'Linguistic remarks on the verb in Newari', *AO* **14** (1936), 280–5. These finals appear to be secondary for the most part; cf. *sit* 'die' < TB **siy* (but *syat* 'kill' < TB **g-sat*), *bil* 'give' < TB **biy*, *khul* 'steal' < TB **r-kuw*, *dźal* 'graze' < TB **dza* 'eat', *tal* 'hear' < TB **ta*.

The development of prefixes in the several TB nuclear groups has been as follows:

Tibetan-Kanauri: Prefixes well preserved in Tibetan, although sometimes treated as root-initials, as in *dom* < **d-wam* 'bear'. Gyarung likewise has a full set of prefixes, with significant differences from the Tibetan set (Wolfenden, *JRAS*, 1936). Prefixed **s*- is maintained in Himalayish, but other prefixes are ordinarily dropped. Lepcha has numerous prefixed forms, but these are largely of late origin. TB prefixed **s*- is reflected in Lepcha palatalized initials; TB **d*- is also maintained as **t*(*ă*)- (Nos. 51, 411, 461).

Bahing-Vayu: All TB prefixes regularly lost. Bhramu, an aberrant member of this nucleus, preserves prefixes in a number of roots.

Abor-Miri-Dafla: Prefixes occasionally preserved here, but replacement by *tə*- < **d*- is common. Aspiration or unvoicing of initial by prefixed **s*- is found both in Digaro and Dhimal. Digaro tends to preserve prefixes dropped elsewhere in this group.

Kachin: TB prefixes, with the exception of **b*-, are well preserved, although sometimes with pecular phonetic shifts. Replacement by or alternation with preformatives (full syllabic forms) is especially characteristic of Kachin. Jili differs significantly from Kachin, notably in the employment of *tə*- < **d*-. Kadu preserves prefixed **s*-.

Burmese-Lolo: Prefixed **s*- and **r*- reflected in aspiration or unvoicing of initials. Other prefixes normally dropped without trace,[295] but occasionally preserved before liquids or *w*-.[296] Nung, however, has a full set of prefixes comparable with that found in Kachin, which appears to have exerted some influence morphologically as well as lexically (the Nung are under the cultural and political domination of the Kachin).

Bodo-Garo: TB prefixes in general not so well maintained as in Tibetan or Kachin, partly because of replacement by the more recent pronominal elements **g*- and **b*-. Prefixes largely dropped in the Konyak group, which approximates to Burmese-Lolo in this respect.

Kuki-Naga: TB prefixes generally well preserved here, with the exception of the Central Kuki languages (excluding Lakher), although many unusual phonetic shifts are observed. Lushei, like Burmese, shows aspirated or unvoiced initials

295 JAM has now shown (n. 123) that TB prefixed **m*- was maintained in proto-BL, although only exceptionally in Burmese itself (except before liquids); we must also reconstruct B-L prefixed **b*- in 'four' (TB **b-ləy*) because of the Maru form (*byit* ~ *bit*).

296 Such is the case with the velar animal prefix, mentioned in STL and discussed in Matisoff, *Lahu and PLB* (JAM). Cf. also n. 301.

corresponding to TB prefixed **s-*. Mikir conforms to the general Kuki-Naga pattern of preserving prefixes, and is of especial value in reconstructing prefixed **b-*, **m-*, and **r-*, while Meithei tends to drop prefixes.

§22. Tibeto-Burman prefixed *s-

TB prefixed **s-* in verb roots is directive, causative, or intensive. It plays a prominent role in Tibetan (*s-*), Gyarung, Kachin (*śə-*~*dźə-*), and Nung (*śə-*), as well as in Lepcha (in the form of palatalization) and Burmese (in the form of aspiration or surdization of the initial);[297] cf. T *'khor-ba* 'turn round', *skor-ba* 'surround'; K *dam* 'stray', *śədam* 'lead astray'; *thum* 'to be ended', *dźəthum* 'to end' (*dźə-* for *śə-* before surd stops); Nung *ənem* 'to be low', *śənem* 'make low, lower'; Lepcha *thor* 'escape, get free', *thyor* 'let go, set free' (T *thar-ba* 'become free'); *rop* 'stick, adhere', *ryop* 'affix, attach'; *nak* 'to be straight', *nyak* 'make straight'; B *pyauk* 'disappear, be lost', *phyauk* 'cause to be lost, destroy'; *lwat* 'to be free', *hlwat* 'free, release' (cf. the discussion in §8). Maru *li* 'come', *śəli* 'bring' ('cause to come'), cited only by Abbey, lends support to our interpretation of the Burmese data, although it must be pointed out that Maru has come under direct Kachin influence.[298] Prefixed **s-* with verbs appears only sporadically elsewhere, e.g. Kanauri *stam* < *snam* 'give forth smell', an intransitive rather than transitive form (T *snam-pa* is tr.); G *stu* 'spit' (see n. 189).

As pointed out by Wolfenden (*Outlines*, pp. 46–7), T prefixed *s-* is also used to indicate 'general direction into the condition or state named by the verb root itself', as in *skraŋ-ba* 'become swollen, swell', *stor-ba* 'to be or become lost, go astray', *sŋo-ba* 'become green' (*sŋo* 'green'), *sgaŋ-ba* 'become full' (*'geŋs-pa*, Pf. *bkaŋ* 'fill'). This 'intensive' function of prefixed **s-* is reflected in TB **s-riŋ*~**s-raŋ* 'live, alive, green, raw', **s-kyur* 'sour', **s-lum* 'round', **s-liy* 'heavy' and the following pair of roots:[299]

297 There is every reason to believe that the marker of causativization was glottalization at the PLB stage; see *GD* (JAM).

298 Burmese perhaps retains prefixed **s-* before roots with initial *w-* or *hw-*; cf. *swàŋ* 'put into' and *waŋ* 'enter, go or come in' < TB **hwaŋ*; also *swà* 'go', Magari and Chepang *hwa* 'walk, move', Newari *wa* 'come', K *wa* 'to be in motion' (used as verbal affix), and the Kuki verbal affix **wa* used with verbs of movement (see Wolfenden, *Outlines*, p. 190).

299 This analysis in terms of an 'intensive' function can no longer be considered for three of these roots, which have now been reconstructed with initial clusters,

(431) Bunan *śrag* 'shame', Magari *kha-rak* 'to be ashamed', Nung *səra* 'shame', *śəra-śi* 'to be ashamed', B *hrak* 'to be ashamed, shy', Mikir *therak* 'shame, disgrace; to be ashamed, blush' (TB **s-rak*).[300]

(432) T *smin-pa* 'ripen; ripeness; ripe', Vayu *min*, Bahing *miŋ* 'to be ripe; to be cooked', Magari *min* 'ripe, ripen', Lepcha *ămăn* < **ămin* 'ripe, cooked', *myăn* < **s-min* 'to be ripe', Miri *min*, K *myin* 'ripe', Nung *min* 'to be cooked; to rot (as wood)', B *hmyáń* ~ *hmáń* 'to be ripe', G *min* 'fester, mature', *min-gipa* 'ripe', Dimasa *min* ~ *mun* 'ripen, cook' (intr.), *gimin* ~ *gumun* 'cooked, ripe, subdued' (*gumun di* 'pus'), L *hmin* 'ripen, ripe', Mikir *men* 'ripe' (TB **s-min*).

The following root shows a transfer of function from 'transitive' to 'intensive':

(433) T *riŋ-ba* 'long', *sriŋ-ba* 'extend, stretch, postpone', Lepcha (*ă-*)*hyrăn* < **/s-riŋ* 'long', K *ren* 'long', *śəren* 'lengthen', but Dhimal *hrin* < **srin*, B *hrań* < **sriŋ* 'long'.

TB prefixed **s-* is commonly found with noun roots, as in **s-la* 'moon', **s-kar* 'star', **s-nam* 'daughter-in-law', **s-m(y)ik* 'cane, sprout' and the following:

(434) L *ba-hra*, Meithei *ha*, Dimasa and G *tha* 'potato, yam' (TB **s-ra*).

(435) Miri *nam-duŋ*, Nung *sənam*, B *hnàm*, Mikir *nem-po* 'sesame' (TB **s-nam*).

(436) K *śiŋnat* ~ *sənat*, B *hnat*, Lakher *hna* < **hnat* 'heddles (of loom)', Ao Naga *ənet* < **ənat* 'weaver's stick' (TB **s-nat*).

With words for parts of the body and animals TB prefixed **s-* can be referred to TB **sya* 'flesh; animal'. It is seen as a separable element in Kiranti, as in Rungchengbung *yu-ba* ~ *sa-yu-ba* 'bone' but *pi-yu-ba* 'cow's bone' (*pi* 'cow'), *hö* ~ *sa-hö* 'blood', *hok-wa* ~ *sa-hok-wa* 'skin' but *siŋ-hok-wa* 'bark' (*siŋ* 'tree'), and occasionally appears as an added element in other languages, e.g. Nung *sərö*, Maru *səruk* 'bone' < **s-ruw*, corresponding to B *ărùi*, TB **rus*. TB roots of this type include **s-kra* 'hair', **s-lay* (also **m-lay*) 'tongue', **s-na* 'nose', **s-nap* 'snot', **s-niŋ* 'heart, brains', **s-nuŋ* 'back', **s-tay* 'navel, abdomen', **s-hwiy* 'blood' and the following (probably connected with TB **wa* 'bite, chew'):

(437) T *so* < **swa*, Murmi *swa*, Bhramu *swa*, Manchati *tshoa* (initial unexplained), Thebor *soa*, Lepcha *fo* < **swa*, Newari *wa*, K *wa*, Kadu *səwa*, Nung *sa*, B *swà*, Moshang *va*, G *wa*(*-gam*), Dimasa *ha*, L (and general Kuki) *ha* (initial unexplained), Mikir *so* < **s(w)a* 'tooth' (TB **s-wa*).

viz. TB **śriŋ* 'live' (n. 304), **zlum* 'round' (n. 136) and **śrak* 'shame' (n. 304). T *śags* < **śrag-s* 'joke, jest, fun' = 'a matter (*-s*) of shame (*śag*)' also belongs with this set; Gyarung (K. Chang) has *narsya* < **/syak* 'to be ashamed'.

300 Cf. TB **g-yak* 'ashamed, shy' (No. 452).

Lushei regularly prefixes *sa* 'animal' to words for animals, and other TB languages have closely parallel formations:[301]

Lushei *sa-kei* 'tiger', *sa-va* 'bird', *sa-vom* 'bear', *sa-hŋa* 'fish'.

Miri *si-tum* 'bear', *si-ram* 'otter', *si-be* 'monkey'.

Tibetan *sbal-pa* 'frog', *sdig-pa* 'scorpion', *srin-bu* 'insect', *stag* 'tiger', *spre* 'monkey'.

Kachin *səgu* 'sheep', *səwoi* 'pangolin', *śəkrep* 'bed-bug', *śəru* 'mole', *śəroŋ* 'tiger'.

Nung *səwi* 'bear', *sərɔ* 'ant', *səri* 'barking-deer'.

Most TB roots for animals can be reconstructed without this prefix, but the following are exceptional:

(438) T *sram*, Lepcha *săryom* < **săsram* (cf. Lushei!), Miri *si-ram*, Nung *səram*, K *śəram*, Burmese-Lolo **sram* (based on Maru *χrɛn*, Phunoi *sam*), G *matram*, Dimasa *matham*, L *sa-hram*, Mikir *serim* 'otter' (TB **s-ram*).[302]

(439) T *śig*, Bunan *śrig*, Kanauri *rik*, Lepcha *śak* < **śik*, K *tsiʔ*, Nung *śi*, Miri *təik* (Abor *tik*), G *tik*, Dimasa *thi-khu* ~ *thi-pu*, L *hrik*, Mikir *rek* 'louse' (TB **s-rik*).[303]

(440) T *ldźi-ba* ~ *'dźi-ba* < **sli*, Miri *i-po*, K *khələwi* ~ *khəlai* < **khwəli* (through

301 Bodo-Garo has prefixed *mi-* in this capacity; cf. G *matram*, Dimasa *matham* 'otter'; G *mattśa*, Dimasa *misi* 'tiger'; G *mattśok*, Dimasa *moso* 'deer'; G *moŋ*, Dimasa *miyuŋ* 'elephant' (*-yuŋ* is augmentative); G *mapil* ~ *mapbil*, Bodo *muphur* ~ *məfur*, Dimasa *misubur* 'bear' (note the vocalic harmony). This element is perhaps related to TB **r-mi(y)* 'man (homo)', as represented by T *mi*, Gyarung *tĕrmi*, Kanauri *mi*, Magari *bhərmi*, Kiranti **mi-na* ~ **yap-mi*, Digaro *nəme*, Lushei (and general K-N) *mi*. Burmese has prefixed *k-* in several roots, especially in relation to animal names; this prefix is exclusively a feature of Burmese and its dialects (incl. Phön) and does not appear in Maru or the Lolo languages; cf. the following:

B *krak* 'fowl'; cf. Maru *rɔ* < **rak*, Lahu *γâʔ*, also L *va-rak* 'duck', from TB **rak*.

B *krauŋ* 'cat'; cf. Maru *rauŋ* 'wild-cat', Lahu *γɔ̀*, also K *roŋ* ~ *śəroŋ* ~ *śəro* 'tiger, leopard', from TB **roŋ*.

B *krwak* 'rat'; cf. Maru *ruk*, Lahu *fâʔ* (known only from B-L).

B *kyà* < **klà* 'tiger'; cf. Samong *kəla*, Maru *lɔ* < **la* (known only from B-L, but related to Ch. *xo/xuo*[a] < **khlo* 'tiger').

B *krwat* 'leech', from TB **r-pat*.

B *krim* 'cane, rattan'; cf. Maru *wram* ~ *ram* < **rim*, also K *rim*, *id.*, Lepcha *rim* 'sp. of cane (Calamus flagellum)', from TB **ri·m*.

B *kyauk* < **klauk* 'stone'; cf. Samong *kəlauk*, Maru *lauk-*, from TB **r-luŋ*.

302 This root has been reconstructed **sram*, as clearly indicated by both the Lepcha and Lushei forms indicating **sa-sram* (**sa-* 'animal prefix'). Burmese has *phyam* 'otter', which can be analyzed as a derivative of **phram* < **p-sram*, with the *p-* element of undetermined origin.

303 This root now reconstructed **śrik* (n. 304).

a 虎

metathesis), Nung *səli*, B *khwè-hlè* (Maru *kəla*), L *ui-hli*, Mikir *tśikli* 'flea' (TB **s-liy*); note the appearance of this root in composition with TB **kwiy* 'dog' in Kachin, Burmese, and Lushei.

Cf. also **s-raŋ* 'horse', and **s-rik* ~ **s-ryak* 'pheasant', with prefixed **s-* much less in evidence. It is possible to reconstruct clusters (**sr-*, **sl-*) for roots of this type, but the reconstruction adopted above involves fewer phonetic difficulties. The combination **s-r-* has been treated as a cluster, however, in some languages; cf. T *śig* 'louse' < **s-rik*; K *tsi*, Nung *śi* 'louse' < **s-rik*, paralleling K *tsiŋ* ~ *kətsiŋ*, Nung *məśiŋ* 'green' < **s-riŋ*; G *tik*, Dimasa *thi-khu* 'louse' < **s-rik*, paralleling G *matram*, Dimasa *matham* 'otter' < **s-ram*; G and Dimasa *gathaŋ* 'green' < **s-raŋ*; G and Dimasa *tha* 'potato' < **s-ra*; Meithei *hik* 'louse' < **s-rik*, paralleling *hiŋ* 'to be alive' < **s-riŋ*, *ha* 'yam' < **s-ra*.[304]

304 Benedict (1948) has reconstructed **śr-* in TB **śriŋ* 'live' and **śrik* 'louse', and to these we must now add **śrak* 'ashamed', all three with excellent cognates in Chinese, which has **śr-/ṣ-* for TB (and ST) **śr-* (n. 457). The contrast with TB **sr-* is best shown in Tibetan, Kachin, Mikir and Garo; cf. the following:

	TB	Bunan	Tibetan	Kachin	Burmese	Mikir	Garo
otter	**sram*	—	*sram*	*śəram*	**phram*	*serim*	*matram*
live	**śriŋ*	—	—	*tsiŋ*	*hraŋ*	*reŋ*	*thaŋ*
louse	**śrik*	*śrig*	*śig*	*tsiʔ*	—	*rek*	*tik*
ashamed	**śrak*	*śrag*	*śags*	—	*hrak*	*therak*	—

The Garo distinction (not reflected in Dimasa, which uniformly has initial *th-*: *matham* 'otter', *thi-* 'louse', *gathaŋ* 'alive') enables us to reconstruct TB **śra* 'potato, yam' (No. 434) on the basis of Dimasa and G *tha*; cf. Ch. **d'i̯o/źi̯wo*[a] 'bulb, tuber; potato' (not in *GSR*), perhaps from a ST doublet form **źra* (see n. 457 for the initial, n. 487 for the final, correspondence). Lushei, like Burmese, has *hr-* for both clusters: *sa-hram* 'otter', *hrik* 'louse'. Kanauri has *śöŋ* 'live' but *rik* 'louse', the latter possibly through metanalysis: **s-rik* with TB **s-* 'animal prefix' (as in the text), the 'prefix' then dropping in customary manner for Kanauri. Kanauri regularly has *r-* for TB **sr-*, as in the following interesting pair of kinship terms: T *sriŋ-mo* 'sister (man sp.)', Kanauri and Kanashi *riŋz*, Bunan *śriŋs* (TB **śr-* and **sr-* fall together here), Thebor *śiŋ*, Manchati *hriŋ*, Chamba Lahuli *hrĩ* 'sister', Byangsi (state of Almora) *riŋ-śa* 'younger sister', Dhimal *ri-ma* 'sister', from TB **sriŋ*; T *sru* 'mother's sister', Kanauri and Chamba Lahuli *ru* 'father-in-law' (irregular in the latter language, perhaps a loan from Kanauri), Pyu *sru* 'relatives' (for the semantics, see Benedict, 1942bis); both roots have highly significant cognates in Chinese (n. 457). Finally, B-L apparently retained a three-way distinction here (later lost in Burmese itself); Lahu has *há* 'night'; 'pass the night' < ST **s-ryak* (n. 48); *šo* 'otter' (in *γɨ-šo-lo* 'gray otter' = 'water-otter-big', as analyzed by JAM) < ST **sram*; *yàʔ* (in *yaʔ-tɔ*) 'ashamed' (cited in JAM, 1970*a*) < ST **śrak*.

[a] 薯

§23. Tibeto-Burman prefixed *r-

Prefixed **r-*, of uncertain function, appears in a number of noun roots, and must also be reconstructed for a few verb roots. It is preserved in Tibetan, Kachin, Bodo-Garo, Mikir (*ar-*), and occasionally elsewhere; note especially Magari *ar-*, as in *arghan* 'wasp', *arkin* 'fingernail', *armin* 'name', but *ləwat* 'leech' < **r-pat*. Kachin usually has *lə-* for **r-* in verb roots (and in *lətsa* < **r-gya* '100'), but *n-* ~ *niŋ-* ~ *num-* in noun roots. Noun roots with prefixed **r-* include the following:

TB **r-ka* 'earth': Nung *rəga*, K *nga* (*n-ga*).

TB **r-saŋ* 'lizard': T *rtsaŋs-pa*, K *nsaŋ*.

TB **r-ka·m* 'edge, precipice': K *ngam* (*n-gam*) ~ *niŋgam*, G *rikam*.

TB **r-gu·ŋ* 'edge; shin': K *nguŋ* (*n-guŋ*), G *rikiŋ*, Dimasa *ruguŋ*, Mikir *arkoŋ*.

TB **r-luŋ* 'stone': K *nluŋ*, Mikir *arloŋ*.

TB **r-miŋ* 'name': Magari *armin*, Gyarung *-rmi*, Rangkhol *ermiŋ*.

TB **r-may* 'tail': Digaro *ləmi* ~ *ləmiŋ*, Aka *ərim* < **ərmi*, K *nmai*, Dimasa *khermai* ~ *bermai*, Aimol *rəmai*, Mikir *arme*.

TB **r-nil* ~ **r-ni(y)* 'gums': T *rnil*, Dimasa *ha-rni*, G *wa-riŋ* < **wa-rni* (in comp. with 'tooth').

TB **r-pat* 'leech': Magari *ləwat*, B *krwat* < **k-rwat*, G *ruat*, Rangkhol *ervot*, Angari Naga *reva*.

(441) K *nwa* ~ *niŋwa*, G *rua*, Dimasa *roa* 'ax' (TB **r-wa*).[305]

(442) T *rtsa(-ba)* 'vein; root', Lepcha *so* < **sa* 'veins, fibres of wood', K *ləsa* 'tendon, sinew, vein', Bodo *roda* ~ *rota* 'root; sinew, tendon', Dimasa *rada* 'vein', Chang (Konyak) *hau* < **sa* 'nerve, tendon, vein', L *tha* 'sinew', *tha-za·m* 'veins, arteries, nerves', Ao Naga *teza* 'vein', Mikir *artho* 'nerve, sinew, vein, muscle' (TB **r-sa*).

(443) B *rwa* 'to rain', L *ruaʔ* 'rain', Bahing *rya-wa* 'rain' (cf. Khambu *kəwa*, Waling *tśəwa*, Rodong *wa* 'water'), Digaro *kəra* 'rain', G *mikka wa*, Dimasa *ha* 'to rain' (with loss of prefix) (TB **r-wa*); perhaps also Lepcha *so*, from **/wa*.

(444) B *rwa* < **r-wa* (Maru *vɔ*, Lashi *wo*, Atsi *wa*), Horpa (Hsi-fan group) *hrəva*, but Phön (Samong dial.) *kəwa*, agreeing with L (and general Kuki) *khua* 'village' (TB **r-wa* ~ **g-wa*).[306]

305 This root has now been reconstructed **r-pwa* (n. 78). Chang Naga (Konyak group) has *wo* < **wa* 'ax', another item in the group of roots linking this group with Kachin and Bodo-Garo (pp. 6–7).

306 Nungish also has the **r-* prefix here: Mutwang (Morse) *rəwa* 'village, town'.

TB prefixed **r-* with verbs, analyzed as a 'directive' element by Wolfenden, plays a prominent role both in Tibetan and Mikir but is rare elsewhere.[307] Only one significant Tibetan-Mikir correspondence has been uncovered here, viz. T *rŋod-pa* ~ *rŋo-len-pa*, Mikir *arnu* < **arŋu* 'roast, fry' < TB **r-ŋaw* (above). Nung has prefixed *rə-* in the following:

Nung *rədul* 'roll, wrap, enwrap', but *hi-dul* 'legging' (= 'leg-wrapping'), *hi-dul dul* 'wear gaiters'; cf. West T (Ladakhi) *thul-ba* 'roll or wind up', T *thul-pa* 'dress made of the skins of animals' (= 'something rolled or wound up'), from TB **(r-)tul*.

Kachin has prefixed *lə-* for TB **r-* in *ləgu* 'steal', T *rku-ba* < TB **r-kuw*; *ləkhot* 'scoop up', T *rkod-pa* 'dig out' < TB **r-ko-t*; *ləthat* 'coarse' < TB **r-ta-t* (above); *ləmu* 'sky', T *rmu-ba* 'fog' < TB **r-muw*; also the following:[308]

(445) T *rga-ba*, K *ləga* 'old' (TB **r-ga*).

The Kachin prefix, however, unlike T *r-* or Mikir *ar-*, is extensively employed in deriving nouns from verbs, e.g. *bu* 'to wear', *ləbu* 'trousers, skirt'; *tśyen* 'to do', *lətśyen* 'work'; *śot* 'to scrape', *ləśot* 'chisel, gouge'. Bodo-Garo preserves TB prefixed **r-* in G *rittśeŋ*, Dimasa *redźeŋ*, Mikir *ardźaŋ* 'light' < TB **r-ya·ŋ* (above), also the following root:

(446) T *rma* 'wound', *rma-ba* 'to wound', K *nma* ~ *numma* 'wound, scar', G *mat* 'to wound', Dimasa *bumai* < **bumat* 'wound', also K *mat* ~ *tsəmat*, Nung *rəmat*, G *gilmat*, Dimasa *germa* 'nettle' (= 'the wounder'), with suffixed **-t* (TB **r-ma* and **r-ma-t*).[309]

§24. Tibeto-Burman prefixed *b-

T prefixed *b-* is characteristically found with the 'perfect' root of verbs, as in *gsod-pa*, Pf. *bsad* 'kill', yet occurs also with the 'present' root, as in *'bri-ba* 'draw,

307 Angami Naga (Burling) has *rətuu* < **rətul* 'roll', showing correspondence to Nungish; also *rəṅə* < **rəna* 'listen' < TB **r-na*, with correspondence to T *rna-ba* 'ear'; cf. also *rəlu* 'bathe' < TB **(r-)lu(w)* ~ **(m-)lu(w)*.

308 K *ləmu* 'sky' stands for *ləmuʔ* (n. 236) and belongs with T *rmugs-pa* 'dense fog', from TB **r-mu·k*; Gyarung (K. Chang) *termu* < **r-mu* or **r-muk* is indeterminate, as are Gurung and Thakali *mu* 'sky', but Chang Naga *müγ* < **məw* 'sky' belongs with TB **r-muw* = **r-məw*. Kachin has prefixed *lə-* corresponding to T *l-*, perhaps through coincidence, in TB **(l-)tak* (n. 338); JAM notes that there is a secondary Kachin prefixed *lə-* < **lak* 'hand', used in words pertaining to action with the hands and feet; see Hanson (1906), pp. 358–85, also Matisoff, *Lahu and PLB*.

309 This root is also represented in K-N: Tiddim *ma* 'sharp edge of a knife; wound'.

write' < **riy*. Wolfenden (*Outlines*, pp. 33 ff.) suggests that this prefix represents an 'acting subject'. Bodo-Garo has a 3rd person pronominal element *b-* occurring independently (Bodo *bi*, Dimasa *bo*) and as a prefix, e.g. Dimasa *bugur* 'skin', as contrasted with *sao-gur* 'human skin', *mi-gur* 'animal skin, hide' (cf. n. 301). Confusion between prefixed **b-* and **m-* (a pronominal element) is widespread in Tibeto-Burman, e.g. Kachin and Meithei have *mə-*, Nung has *phə-* (rarely *bə-*), and many Kuki-Naga languages have either *p-* (Lakher, Northern Khami) or *m-* (Rangkhol, Southern Khami) for both prefixes. Mikir and Ao and Sema Naga, however, regularly maintain the distinction between **b-* (Mikir *ph-*) and **m-* (Mikir *iŋ-*), thus permitting the exact reconstruction of Kuki-Naga roots such as the following:

**b-la* 'cotton': Mikir *phelo*, Lakher *pəla*, N. Khami *phəlo*, S. Khami *məhla*, L *la*.

Burmese has shifted **b-* to **m-* before **r-* or **l-* in three of the roots cited below (cf. *mrup* 'submerged' < TB **brup*), yet has simply *lè* '4' for TB **b-liy* (but Maru *byit* < **bliy*).

TB prefixed **b-* has been reconstructed for several roots:

TB **b-liŋ* 'forest': K *məliŋ*, G *buruŋ* ~ *briŋ*, Dimasa *ha-bliŋ*.

TB **b-yuw* 'rat': West T *byu-a*, T *byiu*, Kanauri *pĭu* (cf. *pö* '4' < TB **b-liy*), Mikir *phidźu*, Rangkhol *midźu*, Lakher *pəzu*, Sho *pəyü*, S. Khami *məyu*.[310]

(447) T *sbrul*, Thebor *brul*, Magari *bul*, B *mrwe* < **mrul*, Mikir *phurul* (early form) ~ *phurui*, Ao Naga *per*, Sema Naga *əpeγü* ~ *əpeγi*, Tangkhul *phərə*, N. Khami *pəwi*, S. Khami *məgui*, L *ru·l* 'snake' (TB **b-ru·l*).

(448) Nung *phəli*, B *mrè* (*mliy* in inscriptions), Lolo *li* 'grandchild', Mikir *phili-po* 'nephew', *phili-pi* 'niece', K *məli* 'young man', G (*aŋ-*)*ri* < **li*, Chang (Konyak) *li* 'nephew' (TB **b-liy*).[311, 312]

(449) Bahing *bla*, Vayu *blo* < **bla*, Newari *bala*, Magari *mya*, Nung *thəma*, K *pəla*, Jili *məla*, B *hmrà*, Phön (Samong dial.) *bya*, Kha Li (Southern Lolo) *ka-mla* (cf. *kha* 'bow') (Lefèvre-Pontalis), G *bra*, Dimasa *bala*, Tangkhul *məla* 'arrow' (TB **b-la*); note that Kachin has prefixed *pə-* rather than the anticipated *mə-*, the latter obtaining in Jili.[313]

310 Add Gyarung *peźiu* < **b-yu*; also B *yun* 'rabbit', with suffixed *-n* (n. 284); the **b-* prefix in this root perhaps stands for TB **bəw* (No. 27).

311 For the semantics, see Benedict, 1942bis; cf. T *tsha-bo*, L *tu* 'grandchild, nephew'.

312 K *məli* 'young man', originally 'nephew', as shown by the other meaning for this term, viz. 'father-in-law' (also *niŋli* in this sense) = 'uncle (mother's brother)' under a pattern of cross-cousin marriage (Benedict, 1941), i.e. the term is self-reciprocal: 'nephew' ~ 'uncle'. Gyarung (K. Chang) has *təphrer* 'grandchild', from **/phrəy*.

313 This root has now been reconstructed **bla*, agreeing with Karen (**bla*), but **mla* is also a possibility; T *mda* might be regarded as a derivative of the latter but

No function can be assigned prefixed **b-* in these roots, nor in the numerals **b-liy* '4' and **b-ŋa* '5'.[314] Similarly, the few verbal roots for which this prefix has been reconstructed shed little light on its nature:[315]

TB **b-rey* 'buy': K *məri*, G *bre*, Dimasa *barai.*[316]

TB **b-la·p* 'forget': K *məlap*, Dimasa *balau.*

(450) T *bred-pa* (with suffixed *-d*), Digaro *re*, Aka *rie*, Nung *phərɛ* 'to fear, be afraid', Mikir *phere* 'fear, doubt, dread' (TB **b-ray*).[317]

A causative *p-* prefix appears in Bodo-Garo and Mikir, e.g. Dimasa *nu* 'see', *phunu* 'show, point out'; Mikir *me* 'good, well', *peme* 'heal' (contrast K *mai* 'good', *śəmai* 'heal'). As already suggested by Wolfenden (*Outlines*, p. 166), this prefix can be referred to Mikir *pi* 'give' (TB **biy*) (but origin in Bodo-Garo is uncertain).

§25. Tibeto-Burman prefixed *g-

T prefixed *g-* has been interpreted by Wolfenden (*Outlines*, pp. 40–3) as 'directive' (*gtug-pa* 'reach, touch', *gtum-pa* 'wrap up', *gśo-ba* 'pour out'). Kachin has prefixed *gə-* ~ *kə-* ~ *khə-* with verb roots, in intransitives (e.g. *kəgat* 'run, flee', *khəra* 'to be indifferent') as well as transitives. Elsewhere, however, this prefix is virtually unknown in this role, although Tangkhul (Kuki-Naga) has an otiose prefix of the same form (*kəkap* 'shoot' < **ga·p*, *kəyap* 'fan' < **ya·p*, *kətśap* 'weep' < **krap*). Prefixed **g-* has been reconstructed in **g-ryap* 'stand' (K *tsap* < *g-yap*), **g-sat* 'kill; fight, strike' (T *gsod-pa*, Pf. *bsad* 'kill'; K *sat* 'kill', *gəsat* ~ *kəsat* 'to

Kachin (Khauri dial.) has an apparent cognate here (*niŋda*), hence it seems simpler to set up a distinct root **m-da* (n. 327).

314 It will be noted that prefixed **b-*, like prefixed **s-*, is commonly found before liquids and semi-vowels, suggesting initial clusters rather than prefixes as alternative types of reconstruction for some of these roots. The distinction cannot be drawn with any assurance in some instances, e.g. B *hmrà*, Bhramu *pəra*, Chepang *la* 'arrow', and B *myauk* (Intha dial. *mrok* ~ *mlok*), Bhramu *pəyuk*, Chepang *yuk* 'monkey' are parallel formations, yet the latter root has been reconstructed **mruk* rather than **m-ruk* or **b-ruk* on the strength of Bahing *moro*, Digaro *təmyu*, Gurung *timyu*, while the former has been reconstructed **b-la* rather than **bla.*

315 Add TB **b-riŋ* 'bark' (n. 245).

316 This has been identified (n. 242) as an old loan from AT, with initial **b-* handled as a prefixed element.

317 T *źed-pa* < **ryed-* 'fear, be afraid' (cited on p. 175) apparently also belongs here (secondary palatalization before the *e*); Angami Naga (Burling) has *prəi* 'fear', as if from **bray.*

fight; a fight'; general TB sense is 'kill by striking'); _*g-lwat_ 'free, release' (T _glod-pa_, B _lwat ~ kywat_ < _*klwat_), also the following pair of roots:

(451) T _g-ya-ba_, K _kəya_, B _yà_ 'to itch' (TB _*g-ya_).

(452) K _kəyaʔ_, L _zak_ < _*yak_ 'to be ashamed, shy', Tangkhul _khəyak khəvai_ 'venerable, shameful', _kəkhəyak_ 'pay respect, venerate; shame, veneration' (TB _*g-yak_).

Prefixed _g- ~ k-_ as an adjectival (or verbal-noun) prefix is found in Gyarung, Kachin, Bodo-Garo, and Mikir, e.g. Gyarung _kĕšĭk_ 'new', K _gəlu_, Dimasa _galau_ 'long', Mikir _kethe_ 'great, large'. Wolfenden rightly identifies this as an old pronominal element (cf. K _khan_ < _kha-ni_ 'they two'), which appears as a prefix with kinship terms in Kachin (_śi-a kəwa_ 'his father', as opposed to _na nwa_ 'thy father'). This element also is found as an inseparable prefix with words for parts of the body in Konyak (cf. Moshang _kəmul_ 'body hair') and in Kuki-Naga, e.g. all such words in the 'Chin' (Southern Kuki) vocabulary recorded by Hughes (1881) are provided with this prefix. In Bodo-Garo prefixed _*g-_ has in some roots coalesced with the initial and thus been preserved, while the more recent pronominal _*b-_ prefix has been added at a later date, e.g. G _groŋ_, Bodo _goŋ_ 'horn', Dimasa _groŋ_ 'horn', _goroŋ_ 'side, angle', _bogroŋ_ 'corner, horn', all from TB _*ruŋ_. The same type of development can be seen in T _grwa ~ gru_ 'angle, corner', _rwa ~ ru_ 'horn'; cf. Gyarung _təru ~ tere_, Kanauri _rud_, Digaro _ru ~ ro_ 'horn', also TB _*kruw_ 'horn'.[318] Pronominal prefixed _*g-_ perhaps plays a role in the following root:

(453) T _rna-ba_, Nung _əna_ 'ear', K _na_ 'ear', _na_ (diff. tone) 'hear'; B _nà_ 'ear', _na_ 'listen'; Rengma Naga _əkhəna_ 'ear', _na_ 'hear'; Bhramu _kəna_, Kadu _kənà_, Tangkhul _khəna_, Lamgang _əkəna_, Anal _kəna_ 'ear'; G _khna_, Dimasa _khana_ 'hear', G _na-tśil_ 'ear' (TB _*g-na_).[319]

Prefixed _*g-_, apparently of non-pronominal origin, has been recognized for _*g-ya ~ *g-ra_ 'right (hand)' (probably from the final velar of TB _*lak_ 'arm, hand'); also _*g-la_ 'moon' (L _thla_), _*g-ryum_ 'salt' (K _dźum_ < _*g-yum_), _*g-wa_ 'village'

318 For the semantics, cf. Ch. _chiao_[a] 'horn, angle'. Prefixed _*g-_ before _r-_ is regularly treated as an initial in Tibetan; cf. T _ʼgrib-pa_ 'decrease; grown dim', _sgrib-pa_ 'darken; darkened', _grib_ 'shade, shadow', _srib-pa_ 'grow dark', _srib(s)_ 'darkness; shady side', _rab-rib ~ hrab-hrib_ 'mist, dimness', B _rip_ 'throw a shadow', _ărip_ 'shadow, shade'; T _ʼgran-pa_ 'fight, contend with', B _ran_ 'quarrel'. A distinction is drawn in Tibetan script, however, between the cluster _gy-_ and the combination _g-y-_, e.g. _gyad_ 'champion' but _g-yas-pa_ 'right (hand)' < TB _*g-ya ~ *g-ra_. This would indicate that Tibetan formerly distinguished between [_gyad_] and [_gəyas_], and presumably between other pairs of this type, thus making _ə_ a phonemic element.

_319_ Angami Naga (Burling) has _rəńə_ < _*r-na_ 'listen', corresponding to T _rna-ba_ 'ear', hence a doublet must be recognized for TB: _*r-na ~ *g-na_.

[a] 角

(Samong *kəwa*, L *khua*), **g-pa* 'bamboo' (K *kəwa*, Mikir *kepho*); also the following pair of roots:

(454) K *buŋ-li* 'breeze' (*buŋ* 'blow'), Gyarung *khəle* < **khəli*, B *le*, Samong *kəli*, L *thli* < **khli* 'wind' (TB **g-liy*).

(455) K *kəmu*, B *hmui*, G *me-gumu*, Dimasa *mu-khmu*, Mikir *kimu* 'mushroom, fungus' (TB **g-muw*).

The derivation of L **thl-* < **khl-* from **g-l-* is questionable, however, and it is possible that here, as in Burmese (see n. 301), a distinct element *k-* is involved. Samong (Phön), which is archaic with respect to Burmese (cf. Samong *kəlauk* 'stone' = B *kyauk*; Samong *kəla* 'tiger' = B *kyà*), sometimes agrees with Lushei (as in *kəwa* 'village', *kəli* 'wind'), yet has *səla* 'moon' < TB **s-la* whereas Lushei has *thla* < TB **g-la*.

§26. Tibeto-Burman prefixed *d-

Prefixed *d-* in Tibetan parallels prefixed *g-* as a 'directive' prefix with verbs (Wolfenden, *Outlines*, pp. 40–3). Kachin *də-* (*tə-*, *thə-*) is nominalizing as well as directive, e.g. *bu* 'to be stubby', *dəbu* 'hump on cattle'; *dźu* 'converge at a central point', *dədźu* 'center', while Nung *də-* vies with *śə-* as a causative prefix, as in *suŋ* 'to be dry', *dəsuŋ* 'to dry or cause to dry'. Ao Naga *te-* forms verbal noun derivatives (substantival or adjectival), e.g. *tśak-ma* 'to crack', *tetśak-ma* 'crack'; *metśi* 'to bud', *temetśi* 'bud'; *əmaŋ* 'to believe', *təmaŋ* < **teəmaŋ* 'faith' (the Ao prefix, unlike its Kachin equivalent, appears before prefixed *me-* and *ə-* as well as the simple verb root). This prefix has been reconstructed with verbal roots only in the following pair:

(456) T *'drub-pa*, Lepcha *hrap*, Gyarung *tup*, Magari *rup*, B *khyup* 'sew' (TB **d-rup*).[320]

(457) T *drum-pa* 'long, languish, pine for', B *khyùm* < **khrùm* 'pine away' (T **d-rum*).

320 It has been suggested (Benedict, 1967 bis) that this represents an old loan from an AT root for 'needle' (see n. 82; this derivation is strongly supported by Thakali *hrup* 'needle', contrasting with *'tu* '6'); it has now been reconstructed **drub* as opposed to **d-ruk* '6', accounting for the following contrasts:

	TB	Lepcha	Trung	Lahu
sew	**drub*	*hrap*	*krap*	*tɔ́*
six	**d-ruk*	*tărăk*	*khlu*	*khɔ̀ʔ*

These roots closely parallel T *drug*, Gyarung *kutŏk*, B *khrauk* '6' < TB **d-ruk* (above).[321] Tibetan prefixed *d-*, like prefixed *b-* and *g-*, coalesces with TB initial **r-*; cf. the following:

(458) T *dra-ba* 'cut, clip, lop, dress, prune, pare', Lepcha *hra* 'cut', Nung *rat* 'sever', B *hrá* 'wound by a slight cut', G *ra~rat*, Dimasa *ra* 'cut, reap' (TB **ra*).

(459) T *dri(-ma)* 'dirt, filth, ordure; odor', Bahing *ri~əri* 'odor', *ri-ku* 'filth, dirt', Lepcha *məri* 'dirt', from TB **ri(y)*.

The above root is to be distinguished from the following:

(460) Kanauri and Thebor *kri* 'dirt, dirty', K *khəgrəwi* 'dirt, filth' (possibly from **khwəgəri* by methathesis; cf. No. 440), B *krè* 'to be dirty, filthy', *ăkrè* 'dirt, filth' (TB **kriy*).

Prefixed *d-~t-* with noun roots is characteristic of several scattered TB languages, viz. Gyarung, Abor-Miri, Nung, Jili, Phön (Samong dial.) and Ao Naga. In Abor-Miri, Nung, Jili and Samong this element appears as an inseparable prefix with TB roots normally showing either no prefix or another prefix:

Nung *thəmi*, Samong *təmi* (also Gyarung *timi*) 'fire' < TB **mey*.

Nung *təgi*, Jili *təkwi*, Samong *təkhwi* 'dog' < TB **kwiy*.

Nung *dəphat*, Miri *təpat* 'leech' < TB **r-pat*.

The Nung series is particularly rich: *dəgoŋ* 'tusk', *dəri* 'horn', *thəmö* 'eagle', *thəwa* 'bamboo', *thəri* 'cane', *thəma* 'arrow', *thəwan* 'snow, ice'. Gyarung prefixed *tĕ-~tə-*, as described by Wolfenden (*JRAS*, 1936), is a separable element employed when the substantive is used independently, as in *tĕrnä* 'ear' (T *rna-ba*) but *ŋo-ŋi rnä* 'my ear', *no-ni rnä* 'thy ear', *ni-ni rnä* 'his ear'; *təyăk* < **tĕ-əyăk* 'hand' but *ŋo-ŋəyăk* 'my hand', *no-nəyăk* 'thy hand', *ni-nəyăk* 'his hand'.[322] Ao Naga *te-~to-* is of similar type and, like the Gyarung prefix, is sometimes employed before other (older) prefixes, e.g. *tena-roŋ* 'ear', *tepok* 'belly', *toko* 'chest', *temeli* 'tongue' < TB **m-lay*.

The nominal prefix outlined above undoubtedly belongs to a relatively late morphological stratum, as suggested by Wolfenden (*Outlines*, p. 133), who attempts to connect it with T *de* 'that' < TB **day*. To the earliest level, however,

321 See the discussion of Tibetan dental (*d*): Loloish *k* in *Lahu and PLB*, for 'sew', 'six', etc. Lahu *tɔ́*, Akha *tɔ̀ʔ* fit with T *'drub-pa* 'sew' (JAM). Burmese has *khr-* < **d-r-*, *khy-* < **dr-*, but these medials are unstable in Burmese and the distinction is not reliable. On the basis of the Lahu and Akha evidence, however, we must set up a distinction here for proto-BL, unless it can be shown that the root for 'sew', a possible loan-word, is phonologically irregular.

322 The Gyarung genitival suffix here is composed of *-i* preceded by the consonant of the pronoun. It appears to have been derived from TB **-ki* or **-gi* (see n. 275) through assimilation, e.g. *ŋo-ŋi* < *ŋo-gi* < TB **ŋa-ki* or **ŋa-gi*.

must be assigned prefixed **d-* in TB **d-ruk* '6', **d-kuw* '9' (above) and the following root:

(461) T *dom* < **dwam*, Gyarung *twŏm*, Kanauri and Thebor *hom* (apparently from **s-wam*, with TB animal prefix **s-* for **d-*; cf. Lushei), Digaro *təham* ~ *təhum* (as above), Bahing *wam*, Miri *si-tum* < *-*twam* (with *si-* for the animal prefix) 'bear', Lepcha *sətum* 'wolf' (with analysis as for Miri), B *wak-wam* 'bear' (*wak* 'pig'), *wam-púlwe* 'wolf' (possibly related to *púlwe* 'flute'), Lahu *yɛ̀-mí-tɔ̄*, L *sa-vom* (Kuki-Naga **d-wam*), Mikir (*thok-*) *wam* 'bear', perhaps also K *ləwap* (couplet form) 'bear' (TB **d-wam*).

Kuki-Naga prefixed **d-* appears in **d-key* 'tiger', **d-yuk* 'deer' and **d-ka·y* 'crab' as well as in **d-wam* 'bear'; cf. the following table:

		TB	Khami	Mikir	Lakher	Khoirao	Poeron	Bete
411	six	**d-ruk*	*təru*	*therok*	*tśəru*	*səruk*	*kəruk*	*iruk*
13	nine	**d-kuw*	*təkɔ*	—	*tśəki*	*tśəku*	*kəkwa*	*ikok*
461	bear	**d-wam*	*təwun*	*-vam*	*tśəveu*	*tśəwom*	*kəbom*	*ivom*
462	tiger	**d-key*	*təkei*	*teke*	*tśəkei*	—	—	*ikei*
386	deer	**d-yuk*	*təzuk*	*thidźok*	*tśəsu*	—	—	—
51	crab[323]	**d-ka·y*	*təai*	*tśehe*	*tśəia*	*tśəγai*	*ai*	*iai*

(462) Kiranti **key-ba* 'tiger' (Sangpang *ki-pa*, Lohorong *ki-ba*, Limbu *keh-va*, Balali *kö-ba*), Miri *si-ke* 'species of civet cat'.[324]

The **d-* > *tś-* ~ *ś-* shift, found in Lakher and Western Kuki (e.g. Khoirao), is paralleled by K *dźəkhu*, G *sku* '9' < **d-kuw*; K *dźərit*, Nung *dərit* 'boundary'; cf. also Poeron **d-* > *k-* and K *kru*, B *khrauk* < **d-ruk* '6'. Bete *i-* must be regarded as a replacement rather than a phonetic equivalent of **d-*. Central Kuki (excluding Lakher) and Northern Kuki simply drop the prefix or replace it with *sa-* 'animal', e.g. L *ruk* '6', *kua* '9', *sa-vom* 'bear', *sa-kei* 'tiger', *sa-zuk* 'deer', *ai* 'crab'. Extra-Kuki support for prefixed **d-* is supplied in K *khyi* ~ *tśyəkhyi*, Kuki-Naga **d-khi* 'barking-deer'. Replacement by an 'animal prefix' is found in Miri *si-ke* 'civet cat' < **d-key*, and G *mattśok*, Dimasa *moso* 'deer' < **d-yuk* (see n. 301). Bodo-Garo supplies evidence for prefixed **d-*, however, in the following:

323 The prefix in the 'crab' root shows a distinctive treatment both in Mikir (*tśe-* rather than *te-*) and in Poeron (dropped rather than replaced by *kə-*); cf. also the distinctive treatment in Karen **shγai*; prefixed **dź-* for TB (and TK) is a possibility but seems unlikely.

324 B *khye-sats* 'leopard cat' (local) (*-sats* < TB **zig*) points to a variant TB **kəy*. Mikir *teke* 'tiger' contrasts with *tśehe* 'crab' (n. 323), pointing to a variant or doublet root with initial **g-* (this might also account for the distinction in form of the prefix).

(463) Bahing *li*, Lepcha *săli*, Vayu *li-wo*, Tsangla *li*, K *ləli*~*kuŋ-li* (Assamese dialect *kəli ndan*), B *lè* 'bow', Mikir *li* 'fiddle-bow', Miju *təli*, Nung *thəli*, G *tśri*, Dimasa *dźili* 'bow' (TB **d-liy*).[325]

§27. Tibeto-Burman prefixed *m-

TB prefixed **m-* is more readily interpreted than the stop prefixes analyzed above. With verb roots this prefix has a 'middle voice' force, often durative, intransitive, or reflexive. Tibetan *m-*, as brilliantly interpreted by Wolfenden, represents a 'neuter' subject, as opposed to *b-* and *'-* representing an 'acting' subject; cf. *mgu-ba* 'rejoice', *mŋa-ba* 'to be, exist', *mnal-ba* 'to sleep', *mtśhi-ba* 'appear, show oneself', *mnab-pa* 'dress oneself'. Prefixed **m-* in this role is retained also in Kachin, Bodo-Garo and Kuki-Naga, while Nung replaces this prefix with *phə-*<**bə-*: *phəsin* 'liver'<TB **m-sin*, *phəlɛ* 'tongue'<TB **m-lay*. The contrast with TB prefixed **s-* is especially clear in the following root; note that the unprefixed root may be either transitive or intransitive, whereas the prefixed **m-* form is always intransitive:

(464) T *mnam-pa* 'to smell, stink' (intr.), *snam-pa*~*snom-pa*~*snum-pa* 'to smell' (tr.), Lepcha *nom*<**nam* 'to smell' (intr.), *nyom*<**s-nam* (tr.); Vayu *nam* 'to smell' (tr.), *nam-saŋ* 'odor'; Bahing *nam* 'to smell' (tr.), *nam-ba* 'having odor'; Miri *nam* 'to smell' (tr.); K *nam* 'to taste or smell, as of spices', *mənam* 'to smell; smell, scent' (*mənam nam* 'to smell offensively'); Nung *phənam* 'to smell' (use uncertain);[326] B *nam* 'smell offensively, stink' (intr.), *nàm* 'smell, receive scent' (tr.), *ănám* 'odor'; Bodo *manam* 'to smell' (intr.); Dimasa *maram* 'to stink' (*n*<**r* through dissimilation); L *nam*, Ao Naga *menem* 'to smell' (intr.); Tangkhul *ŋənam* 'odor', *khəŋənam* 'to smell' (intr.); Mikir *iŋnim* 'to smell, be odorous' (intr.), *aŋnim* 'odor', *nem-so* 'slight smell, stink' (*-so* is diminutive), from TB **m-nam*.

325 Prefixed **d-* might also be reconstructed for T *dbu*, B *ù*, Anong (Nungish) *u* 'head'; T *dbaŋ*, B *aŋ* 'strength, power', the indicated Burmese phonetic shift being precisely that found in modern Central Tibetan dialects.

326 Trung (Nungish) has *pənam*<**mənam*, defined both as 'smell' (tr.) and 'stink', indicating that this language is exceptional in having the basic **m-* prefixed form in a transitive role. In addition to the medial *a*~*o*~*u* alternation in this root (Tibetan) we must also recognize medial *i*; cf. L *hni·m* 'smell', from **s-ni·m* (but Mikir *nim-*~*nem-* can be derived from **nam*; see discussion on p. 70); note that Karen has **num* rather than **nam* (the root apparently is not represented in Chinese).

TB prefixed *m- also appears in the following roots:

TB **m-nwi(y)* 'laugh' (above): K *məni*, Bodo and Dimasa *mini*, Khami *mənui*, Lakher *pəhnei*, Poeron *mənoi*, Ao Naga *mənə*, Tangkhul *khəmənə*, Mikir *iŋnek* (for the final *-k*, see n. 289).

TB **m-tok* 'spit' (above): Mikir *iŋthok*; cf. K *mətho*.

TB **m-sow* 'arise, awake' (above): Dimasa *masau*, Khami *ənthau*, Lakher *pətheu*, Ao Naga *meso*.

(465) K *məsaʔ* 'to be sharp, biting to the taste, causing an itching sensation', L *thak* < **sak*, Lakher *pətha*, Ao Naga *mesak*, Mikir *iŋthak* 'to itch' (TB **m-sak*); cf. also Lepcha *jak* 'to itch, tickle'.

(466) K *pəsi* 'comb, rake', *məsit* 'to comb, rake; rake' (the *pə-* form is highly exceptional for Kachin), Nung *əsi* 'comb; to comb' (TB **m-* replaced by **a-*), Ao Naga *məsə* 'to comb', Mikir *iŋthi* 'comb', from TB **m-si(y)*.

Tibetan-Kachin correspondences are found in TB **m-to* 'high' and **m-dza* 'love' (above), the latter showing K *n-* for **m-*.[327, 328] TB prefixed **m-* alternates with **s-* in the following:

TB **(m-)lyak* (Kuki-Naga) and **(s-)lyak* (Bodo-Garo) 'lick' (above): Sho *mli*, Lakher *pəli* < **pəliak* (cf. Lakher *hni*, L *hniak* 'footprint'; Lakher *bi*, L *biak* 'speak'), Ao Naga *məzak*, Lhota *myak* (*m-yak*), Sema *minya* ~ *minye*, Tangkhul *khəməlek*, Mikir *iŋlek*, but G *srak*, Dimasa *salau* < **salak*.

Wolfenden draws a sharp distinction between prefixed **m-* with verbs and prefixed **m-* with nouns (*Outlines*, p. 139), yet it is highly probable that a single element is involved. The clue to the origin of this prefix is offered by Meithei, which has *mə-* as a 3rd person pronominal prefix as well as an inseparable prefix with kinship terms, words for parts of the body, and the like; cf. *məpa* 'father' or 'his father', *məya-ma-gi san mətśin-na* 'by (*-na*) the mouth (*tśin*) of the cattle (*san*) of (*-gi*) his older brother (*ya-ma*)', *na-ton məkhul* 'nostril' ('nose its-hole'), *məhei* 'fruit', *məna* 'leaf', *məsa* 'branch', *məra* 'root', *mətu* 'feather', *məmei* 'teil', *məko* 'head', *məhau* 'fat', and *ya* 'tooth' but *məya* 'tusk', *tśin* 'mouth' but *mətśin*

327 K prefixed *n-* ~ *num-* ~ *niŋ-* appears to be a phonetic variant of **m-* as well as of **r-* (see above), although the conditioning factors involved are not clear. Interchange between *m-* and *n-* is fairly common; cf. *məbuŋ* ~ *nbuŋ* 'wind' < *buŋ* 'to blow'; *mədźo* ~ *ndźo* 'topknot' < *dźo* 'to be made into a topknot', yet the two types are often differentiated, as in *ba* 'to be big', *məba* 'chief, ruler', but *nba* 'great, big, ferocious'; *dup* 'pound', *mədup* 'sledge', but *ndup* 'blacksmith'. K *n-* ~ *niŋ-* stands for **m-* in *nkha* ~ *niŋkha*, Nung *məkha* 'chin, jaw'; *niŋda* (Khauri dialect), T *mda* 'arrow'; *nduŋ* ~ *niŋduŋ* 'sword', T *mduŋ* 'lance, spear, pike'. Lhota Naga has *n-* for **m-* before dentals, velars, and palatals (excluding *y*); cf. *nli* ~ *nni* 'tongue', Ao *temeli*, Sema *əmili*; *ntę* 'liver', Ao *temesen*; *ntśa* 'spittle', Ao *metsə*, Sema *əmthi*; *nkho* 'knee', Ao *temokok*; but *myak* 'lick', Ao *mezak*.

328 K *ndźaʔ* 'show love' may be unrelated (n. 89).

'beak', *na-ton*~*na-tol* 'nose' but *məna-tol* 'trunk'. In the light of this Meithei evidence, TB prefixed **m-* is to be regarded as an old pronominal element, with TB **m-nam* 'smell' < '(its) smelling' (as in Kachin) paralleling **m-kri-t* 'bile' < '(its) sourness (**kri*)'; cf. TB **m-sin* 'liver', from an old root **sin* still preserved in Meithei (*əsin* 'sour'), and Bodo-Garo *kha* 'bitter', *bikha*~*bakha* 'liver' (with the distinct pronominal prefix *b-*), Haka *hni·t-ka* 'bile' (*hni·t* 'gall bladder', *ka* 'bitter'). Prefixed **m-* in this role is much in evidence in Tibetan (e.g. *mgo* 'head', *mtśhi-ma* 'tear', *mtśhu* 'lip'), and occasionally is susceptible of analysis, as in *mtśhe-ba* 'canine tooth' (*tśhe-ba* 'large'), *mthe-bo* 'thumb' < TB **tay* 'large'.[329] In the Kuki-Naga nucleus, however, this prefix reaches the peak of development, being well attested in Sho, Khami (*mə-* in S. Khami, *pə-* in N. Khami), Lakher (*pə-*), Old Kuki (generally *mə-*, but *bə-*~*pə-* in Anal and Lamgang), Western Kuki (Khoirao *mə-*~*n-*, Empeo *bə-*), Tangkhul and Maring (*mə-*),[330] the several Naga languages (*mə-*), and Mikir (*iŋ-*); cf. the following table:

		TB	S. Khami	Lakher	Tangkhul	Ao Naga	Mikir
191	laugh	**m-nwi(y)*	*mənui*	*pəhnei*	*khəmənə*	*mənə*	*iŋnek*
281	tongue	**m-lay*	*əməlai*	*əlei*	*məle*	*temeli*	*de*
234	liver	**m-sin*	—	*pəthi*	*əməthin*	*temesen*	*iŋthin*
231	spittle	**m-ts(y)il*	*mətśe*	*pətśi*	—	*metsə*	(*iŋthe*)
397	twenty	**(m-)kul*	*kui*	—	*məgə*	*metsə*	*iŋkoi*

Notes: Standard Lakher *əlei* 'tongue' (replacement of **m-* by **a-*), but *pəlei* in the Tlongsai dialect. Mikir *de* 'tongue' is best explained as a contraction of **nle* < **iŋle*, yet Mikir has *iŋlit* 'leech' corresponding to Ao Naga *melet*. Mikir *iŋthe* 'spittle' is distinct from the Kuki-Naga root but shows the same prefix; cf. also K *məyen* 'spittle', perhaps from yet another root (but cf. No. 74). Mikir *iŋkoi* (early form *iŋkol*) '20' can be derived from *koi* 'all', i.e. 'all the fingers and toes'. S. Khami *kui* is frankly irregular. The connection of the Ao Naga form *mətsə* '20' is indicated by Sema Naga *muku*, with the initial stop preserved. For Tangkhul *məgə* < **m-kul*, cf. *phərə* < **b-ru·l* 'snake'.

329 Cf. S. N. Wolfenden, 'The Prefix *m-* with Certain Substantives in Tibetan', *Language* 4 (1928), 277–80; R. Shafer, 'Prefixed *m-* in Tibetan', *Sino-Tibetica* 3 (Berkeley, 1938). Wolfenden interprets T prefixed *m-* in this role as a nominalizing element, e.g. *mgal* 'jaw' < *'gal-ba* 'to be in opposition', paralleling K *məpyen* 'wings' < *pyen* 'to fly'. Shafer favors the view that **m-* with words for parts of the body goes back to TB **mi(y)* 'man (homo)', on the basis of compositions of this type in Magari and Empeo. The latter view must definitely be rejected, despite the parallelism presented by prefixed **s-* (< **sya* 'flesh').

330 Tangkhul occasionally has *ŋə-* rather than *mə-* in verb forms; cf. *khəŋənam*, Mikir *iŋnim* < **m-nam* 'smell'; *khəŋərum*, Mikir *paŋrum* < *paiŋrum* 'add' (Mikir *iŋrum* 'come together'); see Wolfenden, *Outlines*, p. 157. Nung has a curious nominalizing prefix *əŋ-*, which may even precede another prefix; cf. *əŋsü* 'stopper' < *sü* 'close up, cork'; *əŋwam* 'cover' < *wam* 'to cover'; *əŋməthip* 'fold' < *məthip* 'to

TB prefixed **m-* is tentatively reconstructed for roots in which it appears only in Tibetan or Kuki-Naga:[331]

TB **(m-)kri-t* 'bile': T *mkhris-pa.*

TB **(m-)kul* '20' (see above).

TB **(m-)yuŋ* 'finger, toe': Khami *məyuŋ~məzuŋ*, Lakher *pəzau* < **pəzuŋ*, Ao Naga *temeyoŋ.*

TB **(m-)li·t* 'leech': Ao Naga *melet*, Mikir *iŋlit.*

(467) TB **(m-)loŋ*: B *laùŋ* 'canoe', L *loŋ*, Haka *lauŋ*, S. Khami *mlauŋ*, N. Khami *phlauŋ*, Kyaw *mlauŋ*, Lakher *bəleu* 'boat'.

Where outside correspondences are available, the reconstruction is simply **m-*:

TB **m-lay* 'tongue': Kuki-Naga **m-lay* (see above); also Nung *phəlɛ* < **bəlay* (for **m-lay*).

TB **m-(t)sin* 'nail, claw': Khami *msiŋ~mseŋ*, Lakher *pətaŋ* < **pətiŋ*, Siyin *tśiŋ*, Khoirao *mətin*, Ao Naga *temezəŋ*; also Digaro *mśi*, Miju *msen* 'claw'.

Prefixed **m-* with words for parts of the body appears also in **m-kal* 'kidney' (Tangkhul *əməkei*) and in several Kuki-Naga roots:

**m-ku·k* 'knee': Lakher *pəkhu*, Aog Naga *temokok*, Lhota *nkho*, Tangkhul *khuk-sau*, Haka *kuk*, Thado *kug-bu*, but Siyin *kup*, L *khu·p* through assimilation; probably connected with T *khug(s)* 'corner, concave angle'.

**m-luŋ* 'heart': S. Khami *məluŋ*, N. Khami *pəlun*, Sho *mlüŋ*, Lakher *pəlau* < **pəluŋ*, Tangkhul *məluŋ*, Ao Naga *temuluŋ*, Haka and L *luŋ.*

**m-lyaŋ* 'shoulder': N. Khami *pəlain*, Sho *əhmleŋ*, Thado *leŋ*, Haka *liaŋ*, Meithei *leŋ-bal~leŋ-ban.*

Of special interest is the following series of roots (apparently all related):

(468) T *kha* 'mouth, opening', K *məkha* 'to open, as the mouth; to be open, as a door; an opening, the mouth, as of a cave', *tśyiŋkha* 'door', Nung *phəŋ-kha* 'door, gate', B *tam-khà*, *id.* (perhaps from **ta-mkha*), Haka and L *ka*, Banjogi *məka*, S. Khami *əmkha*, Lakher *pəka*, Mikir *iŋho* < **iŋkha* 'mouth', from TB **m-ka.*

(469) K *sumkha* 'to be wide open; spread, extend', B *kà* 'divaricate, be stretched apart, expanded, widened', L *ka* 'to open (as the legs)', from TB **ka.*

fold'. This prefix, like Mikir *iŋ-* and Tangkhul *aŋ-*, is of secondary origin, and hardly furnishes support for reconstructing TB prefixed **ŋ-* or **n-*. Shafer, 'Prefixed *n-*, *ng-* in Tibetan', *Sino-Tibetica* 1 (Berkeley, 1938), argues that T prefixed ʾ- stands for earlier *ŋ-* and *n-*, largely on the assumption that these elements 'must' have been present at an earlier period. T ʾ-, however, can with some assurance be derived from TB **a-*, as shown below, while the TB evidence in general makes it abundantly clear that neither **ŋ-* nor *n-* is to be included in the group of inherited prefixed elements.

331 Add TB **m-lyak* 'grass' (n. 142).

(470) K *niŋkha*∼*nkha*, Nung *məkha* 'chin, jaw', Dimasa *khu-sga* 'chin' (*khu* 'mouth'), Bodo *khu-ga* 'mouth', L *kha* 'lower jaw', Thado *kha* 'chin', from TB *(*m-*)*ka*∼*(*s-*)*ka*.[332,333]

§28. Tibeto-Burman prefixed *a-

Prefixed **m-* as a pronominal element can profitably be compared with TB **a-*, of almost universal distribution in the family. This element occurs as an independent 3rd person pronoun in Kiranti and Kuki-Naga (*a-ma, a-ni*), and as a pronominal prefix (*ə-*) in these same groups;[334] cf. Aimol *rəmai* 'tail', *rul ərmai* 'snake's tail'; Bahing *biŋ əta-mi* 'calf' ('cow its-child'), *byar əpwaku* 'sugar-cane' ('cane its-juice'). Throughout the TB area in general, however, a lapsing of function can be observed, and the prefix is retained only in forms (normally kinship terms or words for parts of the body) used independently, i.e. without the customary pronominal prefixes, e.g. K *wa* or *əwa* 'father' (*nwa* 'thy father', *kəwa* 'his father'), *mun*∼*əmun* 'body hair', *myi*∼*əmyi* 'eye'; Nung *əkhö* 'uncle', *əna* 'ear'; B *ăbhá* (*ăphá*) 'father', *ămí* 'mother' (but *mí-bá* 'parents'), *ăsà* 'flesh' (but *nwà-sà* 'beef' = 'cattle-flesh');[335] G *apa* 'father', *ama* 'mother';[336] Mikir *ari*∼*ri*

332 Note that Kuki-Naga prefixed **m-* is occasionally found with roots other than those for parts of the body; cf. **m-loŋ* 'boat' (this might also be reconstructed **b-loŋ*), **m-tow* 'fly' (S. Khami *məthaut*, N. Khami *pəthau*, Lakher *mətheu-pa*, L and Thado *thou*, Sema Naga *əmuthu*), **m-tsyi* 'salt' (L and Thado *tśi*, Banjogi *mitśi*, Rangkhol *midźi*, Tangkhul *mətsi*, Ao Naga *metsə*, Sema *əmti*, Mikir *iŋti*); also Mikir *iŋphat* 'leech' < TB **r-pat*, Lakher *pəhmo* 'eagle' < **muw*, and Haka *wi*, Sho *əmui*, Yawdwin *mwi*, Tangkhul *məhvü* < **m-*(*h*)*wi*, K *məgwi* (*gwi* in comp.) 'elephant', to be compared with Kuki **wi*, K *gwi* < TB **kwiy* 'dog'.

333 These forms appear to be directly related to No. 469 rather than No. 468, the basic concept being that of the jaws as divaricating or forking: Tiddim Chin has *ka* (rising tone) 'fork; to be fork-shaped'; cf. TB **ka·k* 'fork' (No. 327).

334 Cf. the discussion in S. Konow, 'Pronominal Prefixes in the Lai Dialect', *JRAS* (1904), 365–6.

335 Lahu has three vowel-initial noun prefixes: (1) *a-*, vocative prefix for kinship terms: *a-pa* 'father', *a-vi-a-ni* 'brothers (older and younger)', *a-pi* 'grandmother' (vocative or not); (2) *ɔ̀-*, the most common, used like Burmese *ă-*, from **aŋ-* (Bisu *aŋ-*); (3) *á-*, not productive but frequent, probably from the stopped variant of No. 2 (**ak-*), as in *á-lὲʔ* 'salt', *á-chὲʔ* 'goat', *á-phὲʔ* 'pepper' (JAM).

336 The Bodo-Garo evidence is complicated by the presence of a 1st person pronominal prefix *a-*, as in Bodo *aŋ-ni afa* 'my father', *naŋ-ni naŋfa* 'thy father', *bi-ni bifa* 'his father' (*a-* < *aŋ-*). TB prefixed **a-* is almost entirely unrepresented in this nucleus, where replacement by pronominal **g-* or **b-* is the general rule.

'hand', *aso~so* 'child'; Lhota Naga *okhe* 'hand', *eŋu* 'neck', *oka* 'daughter', *eŋü* 'wife' (**a- > o- ~ e-*), Sho *əho* 'tooth', *ətü* 'grandson'.[337] Semantic specialization is sometimes encountered; cf. B *swà* 'tooth', *ăswà* 'cutting edge'; *im* 'house', *ăim* 'sheath'; *myak* 'eye', *ămyak* 'knot in timber'; Lepcha *uŋ* 'water', *ăuŋ* 'water in which meat has been boiled'; *vi* 'blood', *ăvi* 'menses'; *vyeŋ* 'door', *ăvyeŋ* 'pass'; *kuŋ* 'tree', *ăkuŋ* 'bush'; *rip* 'flower', *ărip* 'flower of cloth'.

Prefixed **a-* with transitive or intransitive verbs appears in a number of languages, including Kachin, Nung, and Ao and Lhota Naga; cf. K *ətok* 'cut', *ədep* 'rap'; Nung *əpha* 'adhere' (intr.), contrasting with *pha* 'sew' (B *pha* 'patch') and *dəpha* 'adhere, patch, affix, transplant' (TB **pa*); *ətśuŋ* 'sag', as opposed to *tśuŋ* 'hang, suspend' (intr.) and *dətśuŋ* (tr.); Ao *əsam*, Lhota *eszan* 'run'; Ao *ənak*, Lhota *enak* 'scratch'. The same prefix appears in a nominalizing role in Burmese and occasionally elsewhere; cf. B *wak* 'halve', *ăwak* 'half'; *thùm* 'tie in a knot', *ăthùm* 'knot'; Lepcha *ŋan* 'sit', *ăŋan* 'dwelling'; *kut* 'rule a line', *ăkut* 'strake'; Mikir *ĭŋnim* 'smell', *aŋnim* 'odor'. The intermediate role of prefix in adjectival or verbal noun forms is characteristic of the Kuki-Naga languages but can also be observed elsewhere; cf. Lepcha *ăhrum* 'hot', as opposed to *ăhrun* 'heat' (*hru* 'to be hot'); K *əthat* 'thick', *əkha* 'bitter'; Mikir *ăthik* 'just', *ăkĕve* 'green, unripe' (*ă-* preceding prefixed *kĕ-*); Thado *əsa* 'thick' (contrast Sho *əso* 'thickness' < *so* 'to be thick', as in Burmese); Lhota Naga *ehme* 'ripe' (*hmen* 'ripen'), Ao Naga *təmen* < *te-əmen* 'ripe'.

Wolfenden (*Outlines*, pp. 177 ff.) attempts to draw a line between 'pronominal' and 'non-pronominal' prefixed **a-*, largely on the basis of the Tibetan evidence. Tibetan *ʔa-* with kinship terms (*ʔapha* 'father', *ʔakhu* 'uncle', *ʔaphyi* 'grandmother') is described as 'non-pronominal', and prefixed *a-* in a similar role elsewhere is united with the Tibetan element, while the typical pronominal prefix of Kuki-Naga is said to be wholly distinct. Tibetan prefixed '-, on the other hand, is written *ạ-* and explained as a phonetic variant of prefixed *b-* < **bạ-*, and the Kachin and Ao Naga *a-* prefix with verbs is referred to this hypothetical element. T '- appears as an initial before vowels (see §**8**), and as a prefix before sonant or aspirated surd stops or affricates, the latter replacing sibilants in this position (see n. 90).[338] This prefix is commonly found with the 'present' roots of Tibetan

337 TB prefixed **a-* in this role is curiously paralleled in two remote languages; cf. Navaho 'neutral prefix' *a-* in *ana* 'eye' (*bina* 'its eye'), *agud* 'knee' (*bogud* 'its knee'), *ak'wos* 'neck' (*bok'wos* 'its neck'), *amá* 'mother', *bamá* 'her mother' (*bi* is 3rd person pronoun) (see Fr Bernard Haile, *A Manual of Navaho Grammar*, St Michael's, Arizona, 1926); Abchas (Caucasic family) *abla* 'eye' (*səbla* 'my eye', *ubla* 'thy eye'), with *a-* apparently the same as the 3rd person neuter element (see A. Dirr, *Einführung in die kaukasischen Sprachen*, Leipzig, 1928).

338 TB prefixed **a-* is not represented in Tibetan before nasals, but may have

verbs, and often interchanges with prefixed *m-* or *b-*; cf. *ʼthol-ba*∼*mthol-ba* 'confess', *ʼkhyud-pa*∼*mkhyud-pa* 'embrace', *ʼgraŋ-ba*∼*bgraŋ-ba* 'count', *ʼdźo-ba* (<**ʼźo-ba*)∼*bźo-ba* 'to milk' (*źo* 'milk'). Prefixed ʼ- with non-verbal roots is much less in evidence but does occur, as in *ʼgul* 'neck' (=*mgul-pa*), *ʼdoms* 'pudenda' (sometimes *mdoms*), *ʼdre* 'demon', *ʼdab-ma* 'wing', *ʼbu* 'insect', *ʼbroŋ* 'wild yak', *ʼbras* 'rice', *ʼbrug* 'thunder', *ʼbru* 'grain, seed'. There can be little doubt that this prefix is the pure 'zero vocalization' representative of TB prefixed **a-*, regularly actualized in Tibetan as a kind of 'pause' phoneme before stops and affricates in verbal forms. T prefixed *ʔa-* with kinship terms, on the other hand, appears to be a stressed variant of the same element, phonetically [ʔa] as opposed to [ə].[339] Gyarung, as recorded by Wolfenden (*JRAS*, 1936), makes a similar distinction between *a-*, as in *atata* 'father', *ama* 'mother' and *ə-*∼*ä-*∼*ö-*, as in *əkĕsu* 'goat', *əphak* 'half' (cf. B *ăwak*), *älapo* 'donkey', *äśïä* 'flesh', *äśnäs* 'lip, beak', *öbŏrŏ* 'horse'. In general, then, all the prefixes described above, including T *ʔa-* as well as ʼ-, are to be referred to a single TB pronominal element **a-* found both with nominal and verbal roots, just as the several types of occurrence of prefixed **m-* can be brought under a single heading. It can be further stated that **a* was the TB 3rd person pronoun corresponding to **ŋa* (1st person) and **naŋ* (2nd person), whereas in proto-TB times prefixed **m-* had already become an old 3rd person pronominal element on the road to disappearance as an independent entity.

occurred before liquids, the suggested developments being **ar-*>*ʼdr-* and **al-*> **dl-*>*ld-*; cf. *ʼdre-ba* 'to be mixed with', *sre-ba* 'to mix' (tr.), from a root **re*, and *ldog-pa*, Pf. *log* 'return', *zlog-pa* 'cause to return', from a root **log*; *ldug(s)-pa*, Pf. *blugs* 'pour, cast', *lugs* 'casting, founding', *lugs-ma* 'cast', from a root **lug*. T *d-*∼*t-* after prefixed *l-* is sometimes original, however, as in *ltag-ma* 'upper part of place', Mikir *thak* 'surface, on, up, fore', K *ləthaʔ* 'upper, above', *kəthaʔ* 'above, overhead', Nung *tha-kha*∼*tha-lam* 'up, above', B *tak* 'ascend', *ăthak* 'upper part, space above', from TB **(l-)tak*; cf. Garo *dak* 'go, advance'.

339 This analysis now requires restatement. Tibetan (written or classical language) has a phoneme /ʼ/ actualized in three quite different ways: (1) before *y*, as *ə*: /*gʼyas*/ 'right (hand)'=*gəyas*, contrasting with *gyad* 'champion' (see n. 318); (2) before stops/affricates, as glottalization or as *ʔə* (optional), through rule that syllable-initial vowels are pre-glottalized: /*ʼbu*/ 'insect'=*ʔbu* or *ʔəbu*; (3) before vowels, as (zero): /*ʼog*/ 'below'=*og*, contrasting with /*og*/-*ma* 'throat'=*ʔog* (the latter, because of pre-glottalization rule).

The (zero) actualization of /ʼ/ results from the following:

ʔəʔog=*og*, with parallels elsewhere in Lahu, where this rule: ʔ+ʔ=ϕ leads to high-rising tone (Matisoff, *Lahu and PLB*), and in Highland Yao (H. C. Purnell, *Phonology of a Yao Dialect*, Hartford Studies in Linguistics, No. 15, 1965).

This analysis is in harmony both with the history of the element (TB prefixed **a-*) and with the script (the old inherent vowel sign). It yields a paradoxical assignment of phonetic values, of a type that could not have been reached on a purely phonological basis. As a result of this analysis, moreover, Tibetan ʔ before initial vowel is seen as non-phonemic (conditioned), as elsewhere in TB.

§29. Tibeto-Burman alternation (consonantal, vocalic)

Apart from prefixation and suffixation, only one general morphological process can be assigned to the parent TB speech, viz. alternation of root initial.[340] This feature is present in a number of TB roots reconstructed above, viz. **bar*∼**par* 'burn', **be*∼**pe* 'broken, break', **bleŋ*∼**pleŋ* 'straight, straighten', **bliŋ*∼**pliŋ* 'full, fill', **brup*∼**prup* 'overflow, gush', **byar*∼**pyar* 'affix, plait, sew', **dup*∼**dip*, **tup*∼**tip* 'beat', **dyam*∼**tyam* 'full', **gwa-n*∼**kwa-n* 'put on clothes', **du-t*∼**tu-t* 'join, tie, knot', **bip*∼**pip* 'conceal, bury'. In Tibetan, Kiranti, Bahing, Vayu, and Bodo-Garo the fundamental contrast is that between intransitives with sonant initials and transitives with surd initials, and this contrast surely is to be regarded as an inherited TB feature. No invariable relation existed between root initial and verbal function, as shown by transitive roots such as **dza* 'eat' with sonant initial; we can state simply that certain roots show the alternation, while others do not.

The alternation of initial sonant and surd in Tibetan itself is obscured by extensive prefixation and the specialization of verb forms as 'present', 'perfect', 'future', or 'imperative', e.g. *ʼbud-pa*, Pf. and Imp. *phud*, Fut. *dbud* 'put off, pull off', also *ʼphud-pa*. As noted by Francke and Simon (in Jäschke, *Tibetan Grammar*), the main line of cleavage in Tibetan roots is that between presents and futures (sonant initial, intransitive or durative) and perfects and imperatives (surd initial, transitive or active). This fact suggests that Tibetan has secondarily made use of initial alternation as a time-index; thus (from the forms cited above) *ʼbud* and *dbud* are derivatives of an intransitive stem **bud*, while *phud* and *ʼphud* are from a transitive stem **pud*.[341] In the following roots Tibetan has a verb of transitive form in the role of an intransitive:

340 For a view to the contrary, see R. A. Miller, 'The Tibeto-Burman Infix System', *JAOS* **78**, 3 (1958) (JAM). The 'infixes' described by Miller appear to be the product either of chance similarities, e.g. TB **krəw* 'bathe, wash' and T *khu-ba* 'fluid, liquid' (Miller finds an infixed *-r-* here) or of a misunderstanding of TB phonology, e.g. the *-y-* of T *khyi* 'dog' is not an infix (Miller) but represents the normal palatalization in Tibetan before the front vowel *i*; T *nya* 'fish' does not include an infixed *-y-* (Miller) but represents a normal shift (*ny-* < **ŋy-*) for Tibetan (long ago noted in Benedict, 1939), the medial appearing even in Ch. *ŋi̯o*/*ŋi̯wo*[a], from ST **ŋya*.

341 Conrady (*Eine indochinesische Causativ-Denominativ Bildung und ihr Zusammenhang mit den Tonaccenten*) failed to grasp the central fact of initial alternation, and hence was led to interpret all the variations of the Tibetan verb in

[a] 魚

(471) T *'pham-pa* 'to be beaten, conquered', but Kanauri *bam* 'to be defeated, lose', *pham* 'defeat, win', G *bam* 'submit', also 'sit', *bam-at* 'subdue', *bam-gop* 'crouch, bow, stoop', *bam-gipa* 'obedient', Lepcha *bam* 'remain', Tangkhul *pam*, Meithei *pham* 'sit', from TB **bam~*pam*.

T *'don-pa*, Pf. *bton*, Fut. *gdon*, Imp. *thon* 'cause to go out, go out', but Kanauri *dŏn* 'go or come out', *tŏn* 'put out', perhaps also Magari *don* 'pull' (='cause to come out'), from a root **don~*ton* (restricted occurrence).

In many roots, however, Tibetan presents a clear contrast:

'gril-ba 'to be twisted or wrapped round', *'khril-ba* 'wind or coil round, embrace'.

'du-ba 'come together, assemble, unite', *'thu-ba* 'gather, collect' (No. 421).

'bri-ba 'lessen, diminish' (intr.), *'phri-ba* (tr.).

'dzag-pa 'drop, drip, trickle', *'tshag-pa* 'cause to trickle, strain, filter'.

Kanauri shows initial alternation much more regularly than does Tibetan itself; cf. *byaŋ* 'to fear', *(s)pyaŋ* 'frighten', *bar* 'burst, split, tear' (intr.), *phar* (tr.); *bar* 'burn (wood)' (intr.), *par* (tr.); *boŋ* 'burn' (intr.), *poŋ* (tr.); *böŋ* 'to be filled', *pöŋ* 'to fill' (TB **bliŋ~*pliŋ*); *bi* 'go, flow, climb', *phi* 'take away, remove'; *blus* 'fall (house)', *phlus* 'knock down (house)'. In Bahing and Vayu the contrast is equally clear; cf. Bahing *guk* 'to be bent', *kuk* 'make bent'; cf. T *'gug(s)-pa*, Pf. *bgug*, Fut. *dgug*, Imper. *khug* 'bend, make crooked', *kug(-kug)* 'crooked; a crook', B *kauk* 'crooked', *ăkauk* 'a curve, bend' (TB **guk~*kuk*); *gik* 'to be born', *kik* 'give birth to'; Vayu *bok* 'to be born', *pok* 'give birth to'. Note especially Vayu *im* 'sleep', *hem* 'make sleep' (TB **ip*); *ram* 'fear', *χam* 'frighten'. Initial alternation is relatively rare in Bodo-Garo and is perhaps altogether lacking in Garo itself; cf. Bodo *geŋ* 'come loose', *kheŋ* 'loosen'; *beŋ* < **bleŋ* 'to be straight', *pheŋ* < **phleŋ* 'make straight'; Dimasa *beleŋ* 'to be erect, straight', *gibleŋ* 'erect, straight', *si-phleŋ* 'straighten out (crease, knot, kink)', *ga-phliŋ* 'straighten out, go straight' (*-phleŋ~-phliŋ* is verbal auxiliary) < TB **bleŋ~*pleŋ*. The Burmese-Lolo alternation between unaspirated initial (intr.) and aspirated initial (tr.) has been explained in terms of TB causative prefixed **s-* (see §**22**), yet the alternative explanation in terms of sonant vs. surd alternation cannot be excluded.[342] Thus, B *práń* 'full' < **bliŋ*, as shown by Lahu, Lisu, Lolopho *bi*, Ahi *dɛ*, Nyi *dlɛ*, but B *phráń* 'fill' < **s-bliŋ* (corresponding to K *dźəphriŋ*) or **pliŋ*. B *hŋ-*, *hń-*, *hn-*, *hm-*, *hl-*, and *hr-* (*hy-*) in transitive forms must be derived from prefixed **s-* forms, but

terms of prefixes (real and unreal). A thoroughly modern linguistic approach to this problem is found in Li Fang-kuei, 'Certain Phonetic Influences of the Tibetan Prefixes upon the Root Initials', *CYYY* **4** (1933), 135–57, in which the weakness of Conrady's position is exposed.

342 B-L does not appear to have the sonant vs. surd alternation (JAM).

pairs such as *tsut* 'to be torn', *tshut* 'to tear' indicate initial alternation (*tsut* < **dzut*, *tshut* < **tsut*). Siyin (Northern Kuki) has an initial alternation identical with that found in Burmese; cf. *kiem* 'grow less', *khiem* 'make less'; *kom* 'come together', *khom* 'bring together, collect',[343] but nothing comparable has been noted elsewhere in Kuki-Naga. Lepcha, which ordinarily forms its transitives through palatalization of the initial (see §22), has the interesting pair *dyuk* 'spittle', *tyuk* 'to spit' (cf. Mikir *iŋtok* 'to spit; spittle'); this should be compared with the following root:

(472) T *dug* 'poison', B *tauk* 'to be poisoned' < **tuk* rather than **duk*, on the basis of Lahu *ɔ̀tɔ̀ʔ* 'poisonous' (in comp.), Lisu *tɔ* 'poisonous', Nyi *tu* 'to be poisoned', Lolopho *tho* 'to poison (fish)', but Moso *ndu* 'poisoned (arrow)' (Rock) (TB **duk* ~ **tuk*).

Vocalic alternation, although encountered in several TB languages, appears to have played no role in proto-TB morphology. Conditioning phonological factors, often of an obscure nature, are involved in most or all cases; cf. G *tśha* 'eating', *antśhi* 'eat', *antśhe-oaŋa* 'have eaten' (Chuckerbutty); Bodo *za* 'eat', *fĭsi* 'feed' (*LSI*) < TB **dza*. Tibetan, however, shows a puzzling type of vocalic alternation in its verbs, in which stems in *a* regularly take *o* in the imperative and often either *o* or *e* in the present:[344]

T *'bab-pa*, Pf. *bab(s)*, Imp. *'bob* ~ *bobs* 'descend'.
T *'geŋs-pa*, Pf. *bkaŋ*, Fut. *dgaŋ*, Imp. *khoŋ* 'fill'.
T *'debs-pa*, Pf. *btab*, Fut. *gtab*, Imp. *thob* 'throw'.
T *gsod-pa*, Pf. *bsad*, Fut. *bsad* ~ *gsad*, Imp. *sod* 'kill'.
T *'dźog-pa*, Pf. *bźag*, Fut. *gźag*, Imp. *źog* 'put, place'.

The *e* of the present stem is possibly to be interpreted as an effect of the prefixed element *'*- < **a*- [ə-]. Similarly, the *o* of the imperative stem has perhaps been

343 Tiddim (Henderson, *Tiddim Chin*, 1965), another Northern Kuki speech, has several pairs of this type, including *kia* 'fall', *xia* < **khia* 'drop' < TB **gla* ~ **kla* or **kla* ~ **s-kla* (the situation is ambiguous, as in B-L).

344 The writers on TB ablaut, especially Miller and Pulleyblank (n. 217), have made much of this feature in Tibetan, but the origin of this alternation appears to lie in phonology rather than morphology. The Chinese vowels cannot be explained without setting up a 7-vowel system for ST (see §46) and Tibetan verb forms reflect this early system, as follows:
ST/TB **a* = T *a* ~ *a* (no alternation, except in the imperative)
ST/TB **â* = T *a* ~ *o*
ST/TB **ə* = T *a* ~ *e*
We can now, by way of illustration, reconstruct TB **g-sât* (T *gsod-pa*, Pf. *bsad*), the back vowel serving to explain the seemingly irregular Garo form: *soʔot* (n. 85); also TB **səm* 'breath, voice, spirit': T *sem(s)-pa*, Pf. *sems* ~ *bsams* 'think', *sem(s)* 'soul, spirit', *bsam-pa* 'thought'. Reconstruction along these lines also serves nicely to explain the cognate Ch. forms in these and other roots (nn. 482, 488).

conditioned by an archaic imperative suffix *-o*, found in Kanauri (e.g. *bih* ~ *bioh* ~ *biuh* 'go!' < *bi-mig* 'to go'), Manchati and Tinan (*-u*), Gurung, Bhramu, Magari and Bahing (cf. Trombetti, *Elementi di Glottologia*, pp. 601–2). In at least two roots, however, the original TB vowel appears to have been *o* rather than *a*:

T *skyoŋ-ba*, Pf. *bskyaŋs*, Fut. *bskyaŋ*, Imp. *bskyoŋ(s)* 'to guard', B *kyaùŋ* < TB **kyoŋ* (above).

(473) T *dkrog-pa* ~ *skrog-pa* 'rouse, scare up', *ʼgrog-tśe* (Ladakhi) 'take fright' (Wolfenden, *Outlines*, p. 49, note 1), a doublet of *skrag-pa* 'to be terrified, afraid', B *krauk* 'to fear' < **grok* (Lahu *kɔ̂ʔ*, Lisu *dzɔ*, Ahi *dźo* ~ *dźu*, Lolopho *dźo*, Nyi *gu*), *khrauk* 'frighten', from TB **grok* ~ **krok*.

§30. Karen (general)

The Karen languages are spoken by relatively primitive tribes in Lower Burma, the Shan States and northern and western regions of Thailand. The literary languages, recorded by European missionaries in Burmese script, are Pwo (Pgho), spoken primarily in coastal districts, and Sgaw, spoken throughout the Irrawaddy delta area. The remaining Karen languages, spoken in the Karenni Subdivision and other mountainous inland areas, are sometimes grouped together under the general term 'Bwe', but several distinct dialectal groups are included. Taungthu, the most highly individualized of all Karen languages, stands by itself. The best available classification of the remaining languages, none of which has been fully recorded, is that given by Taylor,[345] who recognizes five groups: Mopwa (or Mogpha); Karenbyu (White Karen), Bwe (or Bghai), and Brek; Karenni (Red Karen); Padaung, Yinbaw, and Gheko; Zayein.

Our analysis of Karen must be based in large part on the data from Pwo and Sgaw, the only two languages which have been fully recorded.[346,347] The sources on these literary languages, however, are far from satisfactory as linguistic tools,

345 L. F. Taylor, 'Indigenous Languages and Races', in *Census of India*, 1921, Vol. **10** (Burma), Appendix B.

346 C. H. Duffin, *Manual of the Pwo-Karen Dialect*, Rangoon, 1913; D. C. Gilmore, *A Grammar of the Sgaw Karen*, Rangoon, 1898; W. C. B. Purser and S. T. Aung, *A Comparative Dictionary of the Pwo-Karen Dialect*, Pt I (*Pwo-Karen-English*), Rangoon, 1922; Pt II (*English-Pwo-Karen*), Rangoon, 1920; J. Wade, *A Dictionary of the Sgau Karen Language* (recompiled and revised by E. B. Cross), Rangoon, 1896.

347 R. B. Jones' *Karen Linguistic Studies* (Univ. of California Publications in Linguistics, Vol. **25**, Univ. of Calif. Press, Berkeley, 1961) now provides us with excellent descriptions of Sgaw, Pwo, Taungthu (Pa-o) and Palaychi (not previously described; most closely related to Sgaw) as well as an etymological glossary of 859

especially on the phonetic side, where the recording has been done in modified Burmese script rather than a phonetic alphabet. The non-literary languages have been too scantily recorded to be of much value, although Taylor has given us a phonetic record of most of them.[348] On the comparative side, only the pioneer study by Mason and the more recent analysis by Gilmore can be cited.[349]

As has already been noted (§ **1**), Karen stands on the same taxonomic level as Tibeto-Burman, both having been derived from a common ancestral stock (Tibeto-Karen).[350] Lexically, Karen has a considerable proportion of important TB roots, but shows more affinity for the eastern TB languages (Kachin, Burmese-Lolo) than the western, suggesting that some borrowing has taken place. Recent Burmese loan-words, which constitute much of the 'learned' vocabulary, are in

items. Robbins Burling has recently published a valuable re-working of the Jones material: *Proto-Karen: A Reanalysis,* Occasional Papers of the Wolfenden Society on Tibeto-Burman Linguistics, Univ. of Michigan, 1969, greatly simplifying the complex reconstructions offered by Jones. Both these scholars unfortunately neglected the fundamental work by A. Haudricourt, 'Restitution du karen commun', *BSLP* **42** (1942–5), 103–11; 'À propos de la restitution du karen commun', *BSLP* **49** (1953), 129–32. This linguist, with the acknowledged aid of G. H. Luce, brilliantly solved the key problems in the reconstruction of Karen despite having only the limited, older Pwo and Sgaw sources at hand (see especially n. 367). The more recent Jones material is of special value as regards Taungthu, since this aberrant Karen speech preserves most nasal finals and shows various other archaic features (n. 384). We are now in a position to make generally satisfactory reconstructions of most Karen roots, although numerous problems of detail remain to be solved.

348 See the *Comparative Vocabulary* of the *LSI* (Grierson, 1928); also the comparative word-lists in Scott (1900), and B. Houghton, 'Short Vocabulary of Red Karen', *JRAS* (1894), 28–49; E. J. Walton, 'The Yang Kalo' (Karieng) or White Karens', *Journal of the Siam Society* **16** (1922), 39–46; 'The Red Karens', *ibid.* **17** (1923), 74–99.

349 F. Mason, 'Notes of the Karen Language', *JASB* **27** (1858), 129–68; D. C. Gilmore, 'Phonetic Changes in the Karen Language', *JBRS* **8** (1918), 113–19. In addition, Taungthu texts of the four gospels have been published by the British and Foreign Bible Society (Rangoon, 1917–29), but no analysis of this material has been attempted.

350 The tonal data (n. 494) furnish additional support for this concept of a Tibeto-Karen supergrouping, with indications of influences exerted by Thai (cf. also n. 367 for further Thai influence). The Karen lexical material has not yet been studied intensively, yet several important roots with Chinese (not TB) cognates have come to light, notably **tsü* 'arm/hand', **hyam* 'salty' and **hńa* 'flesh, meat', while another pair of roots shows a strange alignment with Chinese and Bodo-Garo, viz. **tho* 'bird' and **may* 'rice' (Benedict, 1967bis, note 7). Karen also has **mɛʔ* < **myak* 'eye' rather than **mik*, in agreement with B-L and Nungish (possibly also Gyarung), and this appears to reflect the archaic ST form (n. 251). An alternative possibility is that Karen split off at an early date from the BL/Nungish division of TB and was subsequently altered as a result of Thai influence.

general readily distinguished, as are the occasional Thai and Mon-Khmer borrowings. Morphologically, Karen diverges from Tibeto-Burman almost as widely as does Chinese, especially as regards syntax. Phonetically, Karen has undergone reduction of finals comparable with that found in Lolo, and has preserved initials only in part.

§31. Karen morphology (categories) and syntax

Karen represents a relatively pure type of monosyllabic, isolating language. Categories of noun, pronoun, numeral, and verb-adjective can be distinguished, as in Tibeto-Burman. The object follows rather than precedes the verb, although in disjunction the object is placed at the head of the sentence. Modifying words follow verbs as well as nouns. Relating elements, some of which precede rather than follow, make for flexibility in word-order, e.g. the most important such element in Pwo is *lö*, as in *ya le lö wį takhǫ* 'I go to Rangoon (city)'; *ya phe sabwa lö liʔ la bį* (or *ya phe liʔ la bį lö sabwa*) 'I give Sabwa a book'. Numerals are employed with numeral adjuncts or 'classifiers' (quantifiers), and the whole phrase is placed after the noun, much as in Burmese; cf. Pwo *liʔ la bį* 'book one flat-thing (*bį*)' = 'one book'; *γį ni phlǫ* 'house two round-things (*phlǫ*)' = 'two houses'; *γį a phlǫ* 'many houses'. Karen syntax in general, however, with the object placed at or near the end of the sentence and with relating elements preceding as well as following, stands close to Chinese and even closer to unrelated Thai, which has perhaps exerted some influence here.

§32. Karen pronouns

The Karen personal pronouns are *ya* (1st), *na* (2nd), and *awe* (3rd). Pwo has a special 1st person plural pronoun (*pa*), but ordinarily a plural suffix is employed with pronouns (Pwo -*θi*). Pwo also has special forms used in disjunction and after the verb *mwai* 'to be': *yö* 'as for me', *nö* 'as for thee'.[351] Karen *ya* is directly

351 White Karen exhibits vocalic harmony in its personal pronouns; cf. *ya la* 'I fall', *yo po* 'I awake', *yɔ ɔ* 'I awake', *yu pu* 'I carry', *yi śi-sa* 'I fear', *ye le* 'I go', *yä bä-bo* 'I am carried'; see G. A. Grierson, 'Vocal Harmony in Karen', *JRAS* (1920), 347–8.

cognate with TB *ŋa* 'I' (see below), while *na* can be compared, although not directly, with TB **naŋ* 'thou'. The 3rd person pronoun, *awe* (Sgaw *awɛ*), has been compounded from two distinct pronominal elements *a* and *we*. The latter is employed in Pwo after verbs in the 3rd person in a curious relative clause construction in which the principal noun is governed by *lö*, e.g. *γį lö sabwa θų̈ we nau* 'the (*nau* lit. 'that') house which Sabwa built'. The former is a pronominal prefix in constructions such as *sabwa aγį* 'Sabwa's house', *γį ado* 'big house', lit. 'house its-bigness'.[352] Purser and Aung (*Comparative Dictionary of the Pwo-Karen Dialect*) cite numerous forms with this prefix, e.g. *akhǫ* 'breadth', *athau* 'length, height', *alai* 'breadth, width', *alaų* 'length'; *aphiʔ* 'skin, bark', *amą* 'spleen',[353] *ale* 'kidney', and even *adi* 'bile' (a Thai loan-word). There can be no doubt that Karen *a* is directly connected with the TB 3rd person pronoun **a*. It is interesting to note that this element has undergone parallel development in both stocks.[354] The older TB pronominal element **m-* appears to be lacking in Karen.

§33. Karen numerals

The numeral system is decimal, as in Tibeto-Burman, but composite numerals (3+3=6, 3+3+1=7, etc.) are in use in some dialects, viz. White Karen, Bwe, Brek, Red Karen, Yintale, and Manö. The numerals are as follows:[355]

352 It is probable that prefixed *a-* is phonetically [ə-], and that *ə* must be set up either as an independent phoneme in weakly stressed syllables (as in Modern Burmese), or as an allophone of the phoneme *a* in syllables with phonemic weak stress. The pronouns *ya* and *na* are perhaps [*yə*] and [*nə*], with weak stress, as opposed to the disjunctive forms *yö* and *nö*, with strong stress. Our defective sources, however, enable us to draw only limited conclusions as regards Karen morphophonemics.

353 This also is a Thai loan: **maam* 'spleen'.

354 Palaychi has prefixed **a-* in *ʔa-m* 'name' and *ʔa-xi* 'bone', while Taungthu has this prefix in one root which is definitely verbal, showing that Karen has retained at least a trace of this nominalizing function of the prefix (see §**28**); cf. Pwo, Sgaw and Palaychi *sha* 'food' but Taungthu *ʔətśa*, from Karen *(*ă-*)*tsha* (tone B); the tonal agreement with the TB verbal root **dza* 'eat' indicates that this is not a loan from B *ătsha* 'food', which shows a shift to tone A.

355 The Karen numerals present many difficult problems, as noted in the text. Karen **hni* ~ **khi* '2' can be derived from **g-ni* (nn. 356, 369). The root for '7' is **hnət* or **hnwi-t*, to be compared with TB **s-nis*, but it is unclear whether the final *-t* is a Karen innovation (as in '9') or represents an original *-*s* (cf. n. 401

	TB	Taungthu	Pwo	Sgaw
one	—	ta	ka	ta
two	*g-nis	ni	ni	khi
three	*g-sum	θoum	θǫ̈	θö
four	*b-liy	lit	li	lwi
five	*l-ŋa	ŋat	yai	yɛ
six	*d-ruk	θu	χu	χü
seven	*s-nis	nöt	nwe	nwi
eight	*b-r-gyat	θɔt	χoʔ	χoʔ
nine	*d-kuw	kut	khwi	khwi
ten	*tsi(y)	tśi	shi	shi
hundred	*r-gya	rea	ya	ya

The intimate connection with the TB numeral system is sufficiently clear, especially in view of the fact that prefixes are regularly lost in Karen. The shift *s- > θ- in '3' is standard, as are Pwo and Sgaw *ŋ- > y- in '5' and *ts- > s(h)- in '10'. Pwo and Sgaw χ-, Taungthu θ- in '6' and '8' appear to be reflexes of stop + r clusters (see below); cf. TB *d-ruk '6' and *b-r-gyat (> *b-ryat) '8'. Our reconstruction *r-gya '100' (rather than *b-r-gya) for Tibeto-Burman is supported by the distinct treatment accorded this root in Karen: *r-gya > *rya > rea (Taungthu) ~ya (Pwo and Sgaw). Taungthu final -t in '4', '5', '7', '8', and '9' is clearly secondary, since final stops are not preserved as such in Karen. Pwo yai, Sgaw yɛ '5', and Pwo and Sgaw khwi '9', can be explained on the basis of vocalization of the final stop element: *ŋa-t > *ŋai > yai ~ yɛ; *k(h)u-t > *khui > khwi; also Sgaw lwi '4' < *lu-t < *li-t (possible influence of original prefixed *b-).

§34. Karen prefixes

Karen prefixation is in large part of late origin, as shown by the general lack of correspondences between Karen and TB prefixes.[356] Pwo θwa < *swa 'tooth', TB

for possible parallel with root for 'bone'). It is also unclear whether the suffixed -t must be reconstructed in the Proto-Karen root for 'four', since Pwo has simply li; it appears preferable to derive Sgaw (and Palaychi) lwi directly from *b-li (TB *b-ləy); cf. the parallel development in Taungtha (a transitional Central-Southern Kuki language) lwi 'nephew/niece' < TB *b-ləy (Benedict, 1941).

356 Prefixes are occasionally preserved in other Karen roots: Taungthu and Pwo ni (high tone) < *hni, Sgaw khi, Palaychi tśhi '2'; cf. TB *g-ni.

**s-wa*; Pwo and Sgaw *θwi* < **swi* 'blood', TB **s-hwiy*; are isolated instances of agreement. Sgaw has a fairly extensive set of prefixes, sometimes alternating with initial consonant clusters, as in *lɛ* 'exchange', *kəlɛ* ~ *klɛ* 'change, mix, combine', Pwo *lai* 'exchange, mix' (in comp.), TB **lay*;[357] Sgaw *wɔ* 'surround, encircle', *kəwɔ* 'circle; surround; to be circular', *kwɔ* (*k-wɔ*) 'encircle, bend into a circle or curve; circle, curve', Pwo *wą* 'encompass; to be circular', *khwą* (*kh-wą*) 'to be circular', TB **hwaŋ*.[358] Prefixed *k-* is especially common before *l-*, as shown by the following series:

		TB	Pwo	Sgaw
463	bow	**d-liy*	*khli*	*khəli* ~ *khli*
454	wind, n.	**g-liy*	*li*	*kəli*
440	flea	**s-liy*	*khli*	*kli*
448	grandchild	**b-liy*	*li*	*li*
474	boat	*(*m-*)*liy*	*khli*	*khli*

(474) K *li*, B *hle*, Kuki-Naga **m-liy* (or **b-liy*) 'boat' < TB *(*m-*)*liy*.[359]

It is probable that the correspondence in prefixes in TB **g-liy*, Sgaw *kəli* 'wind' is coincidental,[360] but a possible parallel (with Kuki-Naga) is presented by the following root, which shows a puzzling variety of prefixed elements in TB: Sgaw *kəla* 'spirit, soul; reflected image' (cf. *la* 'beauty') and the following:

(475) T *hla* 'the gods', Burmese-Lolo **s-la* 'soul' (Lahu *ɔ̀-ha-ku*, Ahi *i-hlo-zo*, Lolopho *vi-hyo-mo*, Nyi *i-śla*) (cf. B *hlá* 'beautiful'), K *minla* ~ *numla* 'ghost, spirit', *sumla* 'picture, image, idol', Nung *phəla* < **b-la* (probably for **m-la*) 'demon; soul', L *thla* < **khla* 'spirit, one's double', Tangkhul *maŋ-la* 'life, ghost, soul, spirit', from TB *(*m-*)*hla*.[361]

Taungthu *təwaʔ*, Pwo *waʔ* ~ *θəwaʔ*, Sgaw *θuʔ* < **θwoʔ*, Palaychi *ləro* < */*rwa*[ʔ] 'land leech'; cf. TB **r-pat* 'leech' (Garo *ruat*).

Taungthu *pəthoʔ* < **b-thoʔ* 'spittle', from **m-thok*; cf. TB *(*m-*)*tuk*.

The curious Karen root **khlo* 'snail' (Pwo, Sgaw and Palaychi all *khlo*) should be cited here; it fits with B *kharú*, *id.*, and Ch **klwa*/*kwa* ~ *glwâ*/*luâ*,[a] *id.* (n. 487).

357 The *k-* prefix in this root is matched in TB; cf. K *gəlai* 'change, exchange' (JAM).

358 Cf. also Karen **gwaŋ* 'circle, ring': Taungthu *kwaŋ*, Pwo *khwą*, Sgaw and Palaychi *kwɔ* (all low tones), with secondary voicing of the prefixed element. Karen also has this prefix in **wa* 'husband', **khwa* 'male (human)'.

359 Taungthu has *phri* 'boat', from **p*(*h*)*li*, indicating a possible correspondence with the prefix of the TB root.

360 Karen **khli* 'bow' has a possible correspondence in TB; cf. K *kuŋ-li* (Assam dial. *kəli ndan*), *id.*

361 TB **hl-* merges with **sl-* everywhere except in Tibetan; it may be a morpheme boundary that makes the difference: **sla* 'soul', **s-la* 'moon' (JAM).

This reconstruction is most uncertain; Lushei has *khla* here, identical in form with *khla* 'moon' < TB **s-gla*; perhaps **s-hla* or **s-kla* is to be preferred.

[a] 蝸

Karen also has discordant (with TB) prefixed *k-* in certain other roots:

Pwo and Sgaw *kwa* (*k-wa*) 'ax'; TB **r-wa*.

Sgaw *kəhaʔ* 'phlegm'; TB **ha·k* 'hawk, gag, choke'.

Pwo *kəshą*, Sgaw *kəshɔ* 'elephant'; B *tshaŋ*.[362]

Karen has prefixed *p-* for TB **b-* and **m-* in the following pair of roots:[363]

Pwo *phla*, Sgaw *pəla*~*pla* 'arrow'; TB **b-la*.

Pwo *phle*, Taungthu *pre*, Padaung *ble*, Sgaw *pəle*~*ple* 'tongue'; TB **m-lay*~**s-lay*.

The former root might be submitted as evidence for the reconstruction of TB **bla* rather than **b-la* 'arrow' (cf. n. 314). Similarly, Karen *khla* 'ashes' suggests that the TB root might be **b-la* (cf. Mikir *phelo* < **b-la*) rather than **pla* (cf. B *pra* < **pla*).[364] Karen *thwi* 'dog' in the face of TB **kwiy* is puzzling, but can be explained as follows: **kwiy* > **k-wiy* [*kəwiy*], with the initial interpreted as a prefix, whence **t-wiy* > *thwi* through the typically Karen process of alternating prefixes, e.g. Sgaw *kəθi*~*təθi* 'medicine, tobacco'.[365]

§35. Karen initial consonants and clusters

The phonemic system of Karen is a somewhat complicated version of that reconstructed for Tibeto-Burman. Extensive phonetic reduction, often paralleling shifts found within Tibeto-Burman, has taken place, but the historical connection of the two systems can be established. Pwo has the following phonemes: *k*, *χ*, *γ*, *t*, *d*, *s*, *ś*, *z*, *p*, *b*, *n*, *m*, ʿ, *θ*, *ϕ*, *r*, *l*, *y*, *w*, *h* and ʔ; *i*, *e*, *ü*, *ö*, *ə*, *a*, *u* and *o*. The consonant clusters, in initial position only, include *kh*, *th*, *ph*, *sh* (these might be regarded as unit phonemes); *k* or *p*~*b*+*y*, *w*, *r*, or *l* (the *w* and *l* clusters are typical); *my*, *ml*

362 This root appears to be an early loan from Burmese, since it has the same aberrant tone A as compared with Thai and Chinese, both with tone B (probably from an original AT source; see Benedict, 1967 bis); the prefix, which perhaps is related to the **k-* 'animal prefix' of TB (n. 301), is not found in Palaychi (*shɔ*) nor Taungthu (*tshaŋ*).

363 We now reconstruct Karen **bla*~**pla* (Taungthu) 'arrow' and **ble* 'tongue' (n. 367).

364 Taungthu has *pha* (same tone) 'ashes', perhaps from **phla*; the irregularities in this root are in keeping with the suggestion (Benedict, 1967 bis) that this is an old loan from AT.

365 Karen **thɔʔ* 'pig' has perhaps been derived from **thwak* < **phwak* (TB **pwak*) through a process closely analogous to that proposed for the root for 'dog', with the initial **p-* interpreted as a prefix: **p-wak*.

and *mw*; *tw, dw, nw, sw, χw, θw, yw, lw*. The only vowel clusters are *ai* and *au*. The phonemic systems of Sgaw and (insofar as can be inferred from our meagre data) of other Karen languages are of the same general type as that of Pwo, with differences in detail rather than in outline.[366]

Initial stops: Surd stops are maintained in Karen, usually in aspirated form (*kh, th, ph*):

Sgaw *ka* 'open, diverge, dilate'; TB **ka*.
Pwo *kha-laʔ*, Sgaw *kha* 'chin'; TB *(*m-*)*ka*~*(*s-*)*ka*.
Pwo and Sgaw *kha* 'bitter'; TB **ka*.
Pwo *khu*, Sgaw *khü* 'smoke, vapor'; TB **kuw*.
Pwo and Sgaw *khe* 'tiger'; TB **d-key*.
Pwo and Sgaw *khwi* < **khu-t* '9'; TB **d-kuw*.

Pwo *thaʔ tha*, Sgaw *tha tha* 'weave'; TB **tak*.
Pwo and Sgaw *thi* 'water'; TB **ti*(*y*).

Pwo *pha*, Sgaw *pa* 'father'; TB **pa*.
Pwo and Sgaw *pha* 'male' (gender suffix); TB *-*pa*.
Pwo and Sgaw *phi* 'grandmother'; TB **piy*.
Pwo *phu*, Sgaw *phü* 'grandfather'; TB **puw*.

In its treatment of initial sonant stops Karen resembles Lushei, in the Kuki (TB) group, i.e. initial **g*- has become *k*(*h*)-, while **d*- and **b*- are maintained only in part.[367] Initial **d*- is preserved in Pwo *dą*, Sgaw *dɔ* 'cut (with dah)', TB **dan*;

366 Excellent descriptions of the phonologies of the various Karen languages are now available in Jones' monograph (n. 347). Jones describes a symmetrical 9-vowel scheme for Pwo, but the vowels ɛ, ɔ and ə are all described as rare. Taungthu has a skewed arrangement, with a tenth vowel (high back unrounded).

367 Haudricourt (n. 347) has shown that a series of voiced stops must be reconstructed for Karen on the basis of tonal correspondences (two low series) as well as the equation of initials: Pwo aspirated stop = Sgaw plain stop (Taungthu agrees with Pwo, Palaychi with Sgaw), e.g. Pwo *pha*, Sgaw and Palaychi *pa* 'father', from Karen **ba* (but Taungthu has an irregular **pha* here). Initial **b*- as thus reconstructed appears in this root (cf. Ch. *b'i̯wo*/*b'i̯u*[a] < **bwa*) and in **bü* 'younger sibling', possibly cognate with T *bu* 'child, son' (cf. Benedict, 1941: the Old Kuki languages commonly replace TB **za* 'child' with forms derived from TB **na·w* 'younger sibling'), also in the cluster **bl*- (n. 363), but no Karen roots with initial **g*- or **d*- appear to have TB correspondences. Haudricourt has also shown that present Karen forms with initial *b*- and *d*- fit with a mid (high) tonal series and are to be reconstructed with initial *ʔ*b*- and *ʔ*d*-, precisely as in Thai. Historically, they stand for **p*- and **t*-, which are conspicuously rare or lacking in the system (n. 368 has one of the exceptional forms in **p*-) and they appear also in loan-words; cf. Karen *ʔ*dwaʔ* 'reckon', B *twak*; also *ʔ*dɔ* 'knife', Ch. *tog*/*tâu*[b].

[a] 父　　[b] 刀

cf. also Pwo and Sgaw *di* 'egg', K *di*, Moshang *wu-di*, which we have referred to TB **ti(y)* 'water' on the strength of the TB evidence as a whole (see n. 149). Inasmuch as Karen *thi* 'water' is unquestionably a derivative of this root, we may infer (*a*) that Karen *di* 'egg' has been borrowed from Kachin, (*b*) that TB had a root **di(y)* 'egg' distinct from **ti(y)* 'water', or (*c*) that Karen *di* 'egg' was originally the second part of a compound ('bird-water'), as in Tibeto-Burman, and that **t* became *d* in intervocalic position (Karen **tho-thi* > **tho-di* > *di*). Initial *b-* appears in Pwo and Sgaw *bü* 'rice (paddy)', Kuki **bu* (L *buʔ*, Thado *bu*). Karen has a number of important roots with these initials, e.g. *diʔ* 'wing', *de* 'frog', *düʔ* 'fight', *do* 'large', *dɔ* 'knife'; *bą* ~ *bɔ* 'yellow', *biʔ* 'squeeze', *be* ~ *khəbɛ* 'goat' (a Mon-Khmer loan-word), *bę* ~ *bu* 'thin', *buʔ* 'near', *bwa* ~ *wa* 'white' (cf. B *wa* 'yellow'), but TB cognates are exceedingly rare. The shift from sonant to surd stop is observed in Pwo and Sgaw *khaʔ* 'shoot', TB **ga·p*; Pwo (Tennasserim dialect) and Sgaw *phü* 'carry (child on back)', TB **buw*.[368]

Initial affricates and sibilants: Karen closely resembles Modern Burmese in the developments **ts* > *s(h)*, **s-* > *θ-*. Initial **dz-* and **z-* were unvoiced and fell together with their corresponding surd elements; cf. Pwo and Sgaw *sha* 'food', TB **dza* 'eat' (B *ătsa* 'food'); Pwo and Sgaw *pho-θa* 'child', *θa* 'fruit', TB **za* 'child'. Pwo has initial *z-* in loan-words, e.g. *ze* 'market', B *zè* < *dzhè*. Taungthu has *ts-* (*tś-* before *i*) corresponding to Pwo and Sgaw *sh-*; cf. *tśi* '10', Pwo and Sgaw *shi*, TB **tsi(y)*. The Karenni dialects (including Yintale and Manö) retain initial *s-*; cf. Yintale *sun*, Manö *su* '3'; Yintale *sai*, Manö *si* 'die'; also Yintale *təsi*, Manö

Karen **ʔdi* 'egg' (for *di*, text), for an earlier **ti*, agrees with **thi* 'water' (with tone change) but with unaspirated initial because of close juncture: **tho-ti* 'bird-water'. The corresponding unaspirated velar stop (**k-*) appears in Karen, as would be anticipated; cf. Karen **kauʔ* 'to call out, be called out' (Taungthu *kauʔ*, Pwo *koʔ*, Sgaw *kɔ̀ʔ*), T *'gug(s)-pa*, Pf. *bgug*, Imp. *khug* 'call, summon'. Bwe preserves the archaic stop series in detail (E. J. A. Henderson, *Vestiges of Morphology in some Tibeto-Burman Languages*, paper read at 4th Sino-Tibetan Conference, Indiana Univ., 1971).

368 It is now evident from the material cited by Jones that this is a complex root in Karen with several forms; Pwo has *phü* (tone B) 'carry (baby) on back' but Palaychi and Sgaw have **pü* (tone A), *id.*, with rare initial **p-* (n. 367); in the general meaning 'carry on back', a suffixed **-n* form must be reconstructed for Karen: **phün* (tone B) < **phü-n*: Pwo *phün* ~ *phən*, Palaychi and Sgaw *phü*; Taungthu has *bü* (same tone) < **ʔbü*. The suffixed **-n* here is strikingly similar to that found in TB (§**20**); cf. also Taungthu *təkhun* 'steal' (low tone A) < **gu-n*; T **r-kəw*, *id.* (T *rku-ba* 'steal', *rkun-ma* 'thief; theft'; Kanauri *khun* 'steal'); also Karen **kwan* < **kwa-n* 'put on (sarong), clothe (lower part of body)': Taungthu *kən*, Pwo *kę̈*, Palaychi *fvu*, Sgaw *ku*; TB **gwa-n* ~ **kwa-n* 'wear; dress'; also Karen **khon* < **kho-n* 'dig': Taungthu *khu* (with loss of *-n* after the mid vowel *o*, as described by Jones), Pwo *khən*, Palaychi *fo* < **kho*, Sgaw *khu*; TB **r-go-t* ~ **r-ko-t* 'dig up, scoop out' (T *rko-ba* ~ *rkod-pa*, K *ləgot* ~ *ləkhot*; no suffixed *-n* forms known from TB).

tisi 'horse', corresponding to Pwo *θe*~*kəθe*, Sgaw *kəθe*, Taungthu *θe* (an old Mon-Khmer loan; cf. Khmer *seh*). The regular Karen correspondences are illustrated below:

Pwo *sha* 'pain', Sgaw *sha* 'disease, pain, painful; hot'; TB **tsa*.

Pwo and Sgaw *shi* '10'; TB **tsi*(*y*).

Pwo and Sgaw *shi* 'urine'; TB **ts*(*y*)*i*.

Pwo *shə̨*, Sgaw *shə* 'mortar'; TB **tsum*.

Pwo and Sgaw *θi* 'die'; TB **siy*.

Pwo *θə̨*, Sgaw *θə* '3'; TB **g-sum*.

Pwo *θi* 'to comb' (comp.), Sgaw *θi* 'a comb'; TB **m-si*(*y*).

Pwo and Sgaw *θaʔ* 'itch'; TB **m-sak*.

Pwo *θį*, Sgaw *θe* 'tree, wood'; TB **siŋ*.

Pwo and Sgaw *θo* 'oil, fat'; TB **sa·w*.

Initial nasals: Initial **n*- and **m*- are preserved in Karen:[369]

Pwo *na*(*-phu*), Sgaw *na*(*-de*) 'nose'; TB **s-na*.

Pwo and Sgaw *na* 'ear' (also 'hear' in Sgaw); TB **g-na*.

Pwo and Sgaw *ni* 'petticoat, skirt'; cf. the following root:

(476) K *ni*~*əni*~*bəni* 'drawers, menstruation cloth', Mikir *pini* 'petticoat, skirt, apron', from TB **b-ni*(*y*).

Pwo *nį*, Sgaw *ni* 'year'; TB **niŋ*.

Pwo and Sgaw *ni* 'day (24 hours)'; TB **niy* 'sun, day'.

Pwo *nu*, Sgaw *nü* 'breasts'; TB **nuw*.

Pwo and Sgaw *ne* 'get, obtain'; TB **ney*.

Pwo and Sgaw *maʔ* 'son-in-law'; TB **ma·k*.

Pwo *mį*, Sgaw *mi* 'ripe, cooked'; TB **s-min*.

369 Following Haudricourt (n. 347) we reconstruct aspirated nasals (Luce notes that these are preserved in some Karen speeches) where the tonal series is high: Karen ***hna*** 'nose', ***hni*** 'petticoat, skirt', ***hneŋ*** 'year', ***hmin*** 'ripe/cooked', ***hme*** 'fire' (see text for these); also ***hni*** '2', ***hmai*** 'mole (on skin)', ***hna*** 'witch, spirit', ***hna*[*m*]** 'sesame', ***hma*** 'wife', ***hmi*** 'sleep', ***hnum*** 'smell', ***hńa*** 'fish' and 'flesh, meat' (see n. 494 for the tonal correspondences for these forms). These Karen clusters appear to have been derived from prefixed initials, especially **s*-prefix; cf. TB **s-na* 'nose'; **s-niŋ* 'year'; **s-min* 'ripe/cooked'; **s-nam* 'sesame'; also L *sa-hŋa* 'fish' (*sa* 'animal'), agreeing with Karen **hńa* < **hŋya*. Karen **hni* 'petticoat, skirt' is perhaps from **s-ni*; cf. B *hnì* 'spread out, for purpose of supporting', *ăhnì* 'anything spread out; diaper'; cf. also **hna* 'witch, spirit', B *nat* 'spirit', probably from TB **na* 'ill; pain' (see discussion in Benedict, 1939), pointing to a TK causative form **s-na* 'to bewitch' (='cause illness or pain').

Pwo *mį*, Sgaw *mi* 'name'; TB **r-miŋ.*

Pwo and Sgaw *me* 'fire'; TB **mey.*

Pwo *me*, Sgaw *mɛ* 'tail'; TB **r-may.*

Initial **ŋ-* is preserved in Taungthu and Zayein, but regularly becomes *z-* in Mopwa, *y-* in Pwo and Sgaw:

		TB	Taungthu	Zayein	Mopwa	Pwo	Sgaw
78	five	**l-ŋa*	*ŋat*	*ŋä~nyä*	*zä*	*yai*	*yɛ*
406	I, me	**ŋa*	—	*ŋa~nya*	*za*	*ya*	*ya*
477	plantain	**ŋak*	*ŋa*	—	—	*yaʔ*	*yaʔ*

(477) TB **ŋak* 'plantain', as represented by Kiranti **ŋak*, K *ŋa~ləŋa~ləŋu* (cf. Khaling *le-ŋak-si*, Nachereng *li-ŋak-si*), B *hŋak.*

Sgaw has initial *ŋ-* in *ŋa* 'borrow, hire, lend', a borrowing from B *hŋà.* Taungthu has retained initial **ŋ-* also in *təŋa* 'tooth', Ch. *ŋå>ŋa*[a] 'tooth', Thai **ŋa* 'tusk, ivory'.

Pwo and Sgaw Karen has *l-* for TB **l-* (initial), but the Karenni dialects show an unusual **l->t-* shift; cf. Manö *ta* 'moon'<**la*, *ta* 'leaf'<**la*, *ti* '4'<**li*, *pti* 'tongue'<**ple.* The regular Karen correspondence is observed in the following:[370]

Pwo and Sgaw *la* 'moon, month'; TB **s-la~*g-la.*

Pwo *lǫ*, Sgaw *lə* 'stone'; TB **r-luŋ.*

Pwo *lə̨*, Sgaw *lə* 'warm'; TB **lum.*

Initial **r-* in TB roots is represented by Pwo and Sgaw *γ-*:

Pwo and Sgaw *tho-γiʔ* 'pheasant' (*tho* 'bird'); TB **s-rik~*s-ryak.*

Pwo *γe*, Sgaw *γi~γe* 'rattan, cane'; cf. the following:

(478) Magari *ri* 'cane', K *ri* 'rattan, cane, cord, string, thread', *śiŋri~sumri* 'rope, cord', *ginri* 'fine thread, string, or cord', Nung *thəri* 'cane', *ban-ri* 'rope, string', *səri* 'thread', G *re*, Dimasa *rai* 'rattan, cane', from TB **rey.*

Pwo *γu*, Sgaw *γü* 'snake'; TB **b-ru·l.*

Pwo *γaį*, Sgaw, *γe* 'row'; TB **ren.*

Taungthu is distinctive in its retention of initial **r-*, as in *rea* '100' (TB **r-gya*), *rön* 'silver' (a Mon-Khmer loan-word), and note *pre* 'tongue' for **ple.* Pwo has initial *r-* in Mon, Burmese and English borrowings, e.g. *rǫ* 'courthouse'<B *rùm* (Modern *yoų̀*), *riphauʔ*<English *report.*

370 Karen occasionally has initial *l-* in a high tonal series, from **hl-*, paralleling the aspirated nasals (n. 369); the best examples are Karen **hla* 'moon', TB **s-gla*; Karen **hla* 'leaf', TB **(s-)la.*

[a] 牙

Sgaw has initial *h*- corresponding to Pwo *γ*- in a number of roots, including the following:

Sgaw *haʔ*, Pwo *γaʔ* 'walk'.

Sgaw *hɔ*, Pwo *γą* 'cry'.

Sgaw *hɛ*, Pwo *γai* 'pungent', also 'come'.

Sgaw *hɔ*, Pwo *γaṳ* 'gaping'.

The extra-Karen comparisons uncovered for this series do not suffice to clear up the problem:

Sgaw *ha*, Pwo *γa* 'evening'; TB **ya*.

Sgaw *hi*, Pwo *γį~yį* 'house'; TB **kim*.

Sgaw *hü* (*əhü*), Pwo *ąγu* 'steal'; TB **kuw*.

Sgaw *hɔ*, Pwo *γą* 'salty'; Ch. *g'am* > *γam*.[a]

The last three comparisons suggest that Tibeto-Karen **k*- ~ **g*- have yielded Sgaw *h*-, Pwo *γ*- under undetermined conditions (note that the TB root for 'house' shows irregular loss of the initial within TB itself).[371]

Initial semi-vowels: initial **w*- and **y*- appear to be maintained in Karen, but very few comparisons are available:

Pwo and Sgaw *wa* 'husband'; TB **wa*.

Taungthu *wa* 'bird'; TB **wa*.

Pwo *yu*, Sgaw *yü* 'rat'; TB **b-yuw*.

Sgaw *ya* 'roll up a cud of betel'; cf. B *ya*, *id*.[372]

Pwo and Sgaw *yu* 'to swallow' (usually in comp. with *ą~ɔ* 'eat'); cf. TB **mlyuw*, *id*. (K *məyu*).

Initial **w*- is preserved also in Pwo *θwa* 'tooth', TB **s-wa*, and Pwo and Sgaw *θwi* 'blood', TB **s-hwiy*. Initial *w*- would appear to be secondary in Pwo and Sgaw *wa* 'bamboo', TB **g-pa*, and Pwo *waʔ* ~ *θəwaʔ*, Sgaw *waʔ* 'small black land-

371 This cluster is best reconstructed **hy*- (Karen *y*- in high tonal series appears in loans from Burmese and is probably late; n. 372). The original was probably a palatalized aspirated velar stop, from whatever source:

**g-ya* 'evening' > **khya* (unvoiced) > **hya*

**kyim* 'house' > **khyim* (aspirated) > **hyi*[*m*]

**r-kəw* 'steal' > **khyəw* (aspirated; palatalized by **r*- prefix) > **hyü*

**-gam* 'salty' > **khyam* (unvoiced; palatalized by prefix) > **hyam*

Taungthu has *tśhom* 'salty', apparently from **khyam*.

372 Jones (*Karen Linguistic Studies*) cites Pwo, Palaychi and Sgaw *ya* 'betel cud' (high tone), an apparent loan from B *ya*. An excellent comparison for ST **y*- is furnished by Karen **ya* 'sail' (usu. in comp.) but Sgaw also 'expand to a great extent (as branches); to hoist (=spread) sail'; cf. TB **ya·r* ~ **yâr*, as represented by K *yan* 'to be unrolled and spread out, be extended, drawn out in a line', *əyan* 'extended, continuous', L *za·r* 'hang up (cloth), spread (sail)', Tiddim *za·k* 'spread a blanket', but T *g-yor-mo* 'sail'.

[a] 鹹

leech', TB **r-pat*. The **p-* > *w-* shift has been operative in both these roots within Tibeto-Burman, hence one must infer that the factors determining the development of this initial were present in Tibeto-Karen itself.[373,374]

Initial *h-* is found in many Sgaw words, but only one TB comparison has come to light, viz. *kəhaʔ* 'phlegm', TB **ha·k*. Pwo has *h-* in the loan-word *hau* (Sgaw *hɔ̀*) 'preach', B *haù* (> *hɔ̀*), and has voiced *ḥ-* (perhaps simply an allophone of *h*) in particles.

Initial clusters: Karen is fairly rich in initial consonant clusters, as described above. Many of these are to be interpreted as combinations of prefix + initial, as in **khli* 'boat', **p(h)le* 'tongue' (see above). Clusters with *r* and *y* appear to be of late origin, and often appear in loan-words, e.g. Pwo *mya-mya* 'many in company', B *myà* 'many'. Medial *l* is sometimes substituted for *r*, as in Pwo and Sgaw *mloʔ* 'cannon', B *ămrauk*. The most typical of all Karen initial clusters are with *-l-*: *k(h)l-* and *p(h)l-*. The only extra-Karen comparisons for the latter cluster are with TB roots reconstructed with labial prefix + *l-* initial; cf. Karen **p(h)la* 'arrow', TB **b-la*; Karen **p(h)le* 'tongue', TB **m-lay* (see above).[375] Three TB comparisons are available for Karen forms with velar + *-l-* initial clusters, but the material here is very limited:

Pwo and Sgaw *khliʔ* 'fold up'; cf. L *thlep* < **khlep*, *id.*

Pwo *khlaị* 'speak'; cf. T *gleŋ-ba*, *id.*

Pwo *khlüʔ* 'put on (hat), shut down (lid)', *khlüʔ biʔ* 'screen with a cover, hide from sight';[376] cf. the following:

(479) T *klub-pa* 'cover (e.g. the body with ornaments)', K *grup* 'cover (as with

373 The Karen data here might be used as an argument for recognizing doublet roots for Tibeto-Burman, e.g. **r-wat* and **pat* 'leech'. Borrowing might also play a part here, although the evidence as a whole does not favor this view.

374 See n. 78 for these roots: TB **pwa* 'bamboo' but **r-pat* 'leech'. The initial **p-* of the former appears to be reflected in Karen **hwa* 'bamboo' (high tonal series), with the cluster **hw-* paralleling **hl-* and the aspirated nasals (nn. 369, 370), indicating a development **phw-* > **hw-* very similar to that posited for Chinese (n. 463). This cluster (**hw-*) is rare in Karen, however, since TS **s-w-* and **s-hyw-* are represented by Karen **sw-* (preserved in Taungthu), as shown by Karen **swa* 'tooth' and **swi* 'blood' (Taungthu *swi*).

375 These roots have been reconstructed Karen **bla* 'arrow' and **ble* 'tongue' (n. 367). A true initial cluster is represented by Karen **p(h)le* (Taungthu *ple*, Pwo *phle*) ~ **ʔble* (Sgaw *ble*, Palaychi *bli*) 'slippery, smooth, clean'; TB **ble* 'slip, slippery'.

376 Jones cites Pwo *khlauʔ/khlüʔ*, Sgaw *kləʔ* (all on low tones) 'to cover', from **glüʔ*; also the apparent doublet root: Pwo *lauʔ* ~ *lüʔ*, Sgaw *lüʔ* (note vowel distinction) (all on high tones) 'cover (e.g. with blanket)', from **[k]hlüʔ*; perhaps an original **glup* (intr.) yielded Karen **glüʔ* while **klup* (tr.) yielded Karen **hlüʔ*, but both forms are now transitive in Karen.

a blanket), wrap (as a child in a blanket)', Bodo *dźokhlop* 'cover, shut', Dimasa *phukhlub* 'tuck in', *sukhlub* 'drown, immerse', *phun-khlub* 'wrap around' (*phun* 'wrap'), from TB **klup*.

Karen also has initial clusters with *-γ-*, best preserved in Sgaw (but with some alternation with *-w-*), but dropped or replaced by *-w-* in Pwo:

Sgaw *pγa*, Pwo *φa* (*pa* or *ha* in some districts) 'man'.

Sgaw *pγi*, Pwo *χwe* 'how many'.

Sgaw *pγε*, Pwo *χwe* 'full', from **pγay* (see below), a possible loan from B *práń*, phonemically */prain/*, *id.* (TB **bliŋ*).[377]

Sgaw also has the initial cluster *shγ-*, notably in the following pair of roots:

Sgaw *shγɔ* 'otter', from **shγą* (see below); cf. TB **s-ram*.[378]

Sgaw *shγε*~*shwε*, Pwo *shwai*~*shwe* 'crab'; cf. TB **d-ka·y*.

The former suggests Tibeto-Karen initial **sr-* (rather than **s-r-*) in this root, whence Sgaw *shγ-*. The latter is to be interpreted in the light of the above discussion of the Sgaw *h-* = Pwo *γ-* series, apparently corresponding to TB **k-* and Ch. *g'-* > *γ-*; note that Ch. also has *g'-* > *γ-* here (*γăi*).[a]

Clusters with *w* are common in Karen but many are secondary (see above). The comparative data indicate that Tibeto-Karen medial **-w-* is retained after velars, dropped after dentals and labials:

Pwo *kwe*, Sgaw *kwä* 'bee'; cf. TB **kwa·y*.

Pwo and Sgaw *khwi* 'comb (hair), brush (thread)'; cf. the following:

(480) Digaro *se-kwi* 'comb' (*se* 'to comb'), L *khuiʔ* 'comb', from TB **kwi(y)*.

Pwo and Sgaw *tha* 'span (1st to 3rd fingers); measure with a span'; cf. TB **twa*.

Pwo *phü-thą*~*phu-thą*, Sgaw *thɔ* 'bear'; cf. TB **d-wam* (here **d-* has been treated as an initial, as in T *dom* < **dwam*).

Pwo and Sgaw *ni* 'laugh'; cf. TB **m-nwi(y)*.

Pwo and Sgaw *phe* 'chaff, husks'; cf. TB **pwa·y*.

Pwo and Sgaw *mi* 'sleep'; cf. TB **mwiy*.

377 This root must be reconstructed **bγai* because of the low tonal series, hence it probably is cognate with TB **bliŋ* 'full' via **breŋ* although the loss of final nasal, is anomalous. Karen has the similar root **bγe* 'buy': Taungthu *phre*, Pwo *χwe*, Sgaw *pγe* (low tonal series), corresponding to TB **b-rey*, *id.*, but this is an old loan from AT in which the initial has perhaps been treated like an initial cluster **bl-* (n. 207).

378 This root has now been reconstructed TB **sram* on the basis of the TB data alone (n. 302) so that the Karen evidence merely serves to support this.

a 蟹

Medial *y has simply been dropped in Pwo and Sgaw *θe* 'to be skilled, able' ('know' in comp.), TB **syey*, but has exerted some effect in the following:[379]

Pwo *ya*, Sgaw *nya* 'fish'; TB **ŋya*.

Pwo *meʔ*, Sgaw *mɛʔ* 'eye'; TB **myak*.[380,381]

Note Sgaw *ny*- < **ŋy*-, as contrasted with *y*- < **ŋ*-. The Sgaw-Pwo correspondence reappears in Sgaw *nyɔ*, Pwo *yau* 'easy'; Sgaw *nya*, Pwo *ya* (in comp.), Taungthu *səŋa* 'before, in front of'; cf. T *sŋa* 'before (in time)', *ŋar* (West T *nyar*) 'fore- or front-side, forepart'. The vowels of *meʔ* ~ *mäʔ* 'eye' < **myak* can be explained on the basis of palatalization (final *-*ak* regularly yields Karen -*aʔ*), but only one possible parallel can be cited here, viz. Pwo *weʔ*, Sgaw *wäʔ* 'throw with a scooping motion, bale (water)' (Pwo 'sweep' in comp.), TB **pyak* 'sweep; broom'.

As suggested above, Pwo and Sgaw *χ*- appears to be the representative of stop + *r* clusters, as in *χu* ~ *χü* '6', TB **d-ruk*; *χoʔ* '8', TB **b-rgyat*. This is the surd velar fricative corresponding to the sonant *γ*, hence *χ*- < **hr*-, paralleling *γ*- < **r*-. Cf. Pwo *χi*, Sgaw *shγi* 'clean'; Pwo *χeʔ*, Sgaw *shγɛʔ* 'avoid, shun'; Pwo *χa*, Sgaw *tra* 'cage for fowls'; and Pwo *χai* alongside *thərai* 'deer', from B *darai̇* (*dəyɛ̀*). The TB comparisons, however, are few in number and of uncertain significance:[382]

379 This series also includes Karen **hlɛ*[*m*] 'lick': Pwo *lɛ̧*, Sgaw *le*, Palaychi -*li* (high tonal series); cf. TB *(*s*-)*lyam* 'tongue; flame'. Taungthu, however, has the remarkable form *lyak* 'lick' (high tone), from **hlyak*, corresponding exactly to the TB root *(*s*-)*lyak*; Burmese has only *lyak*, hence cannot be the source (via loan) of the Taungthu form; the latter is altogether irregular, since there is no other example of retention of final *-*k* in Taungthu or Karen, and Taungthu has *mɛʔ* < **myak* 'eye (face)'; we appear to have no alternative to regarding this form (**hlyak*) as a loan from some TB language other than Burmese.

380 The agreement with TB **myak* rather than **mik* is surprising, inasmuch as the latter is much better represented in Tibeto-Burman as a whole. The possibility of influence from Burmese-Lolo, in which **myak* is preserved, cannot be excluded here. Note Karen -*γiʔ* < *-*rik* 'pheasant' for TB **s-rik* ~ **s-ryak*.

381 See n. 251 for present view of significance of **myak* 'eye'.

382 Taungthu has *su* '6', *sɔt* '8' but Palaychi has *hu* '6' contrasting with *xo* '8', suggesting an original distinction in prefixes. Both these languages retain velar stop + *r* clusters in some instances:

	TB	Taungthu	Pwo	Palaychi	Sgaw
winnow	*krap*	—	*χaʔ*	*kra*	*χa*
body dirt	*krəy*	-*khri*	*χi*	*kri*	*χi*
grind	*krit*	*khrüt*	{ *γaiʔ* / *γɛʔ* }	(*ləwi*)	*χi*

T '*khrab-pa* 'strike, beat; winnow, fan'; Chepang *krap* 'winnow', *hrap* < **khrap* 'thresh'; Nungish: Răwang *rap* < **k*(*h*)*rap* 'winnow, thresh; paddle, row' (cf. Răwang *rip* 'flying ant' < TB **krep*).

Two of the above roots are in low tonal series, hence must be reconstructed with

Pwo *χaʔ*, Sgaw *χa* 'winnow'; cf. T *'khrab-pa* 'strike, beat; winnow, fan'.

Pwo *χį* 'set on edge, as the teeth'; TB **krim.*

§36. Karen final consonants and medial vowels

Final consonants are greatly reduced in Karen. Pwo parallels Modern Burmese in replacing final nasals by nasalization, and final stops by glottal stop. Sgaw lacks even nasalized vowels, but has glottal stop as in Pwo. Taungthu appears to retain distinctions in final nasals at least in part, but final glottal stops have not been recorded for this language.[383] Several of the Taungthu words with final nasal are isolated in Karen; cf. *prŏŋ* 'mouth', *hau poŋ* 'good', *lɔn* 'come', *lam* 'house', *kam* 'gold' (a Thai loan-word). The regular correspondences for TB final nasals are illustrated below:[384]

Pwo *khą*, Sgaw *khɔ*, Taungthu *kaŋ-ya* 'foot, leg'; cf. T *rkaŋ-pa.*

Pwo *kəshą*, Sgaw *kəshɔ* 'elephant'; cf. B *tshaŋ.*

initial **gr-*: **grap* 'winnow' (note complete loss of final stop in Palaychi and Sgaw); **gr[e]t* 'grind' (the Palaychi form is anomalous); cf. Pwo *χi* (low tone) 'set on teeth' (text), from **gri[m]*; TB **krim*; the voicing of the velar stop in these clusters is probably secondary in Karen.

383 The Taungthu dialect recorded by Jones (n. 347) regularly has final glottal stop corresponding to the same feature in Pwo and Sgaw.

384 Taungthu (Jones, *Karen Linguistic Studies*) uniformly preserves final **-ŋ* and **-m* but drops final **-n* before *a* and the mid-high vowels, *o, ə, e* (see example in n. 368); cf. also Karen **men* 'name': Taungthu and Sgaw *mi*, Pwo *mę* (n. 442). Other Taungthu forms with final *-aŋ* or *-am* are now available (Jones): *tśhaŋ* 'elephant', *biŋ-maŋ* 'dream', *tham* 'bear'; cf. also Karen **lam* 'place, track': Taungthu *lam*, Pwo *lą*, Sgaw *lɔ*; TB **lam* 'road; direction'. Taungthu (and Karen in general) does not distinguish between medial **a* + nasal and medial **ə* + nasal; cf. Karen **am* 'eat' (Jones cites Taungthu *ʔam*); TB **əm* 'eat; drink' (for **am*); to the forms cited in text, add Lepcha *am* 'food'; Răwang (Nungish): Mutwang dial. *əm* 'eat', also Lushei (and general Kuki) *in* 'drink' via **yəm* (cf. L *in* 'house' < TB **kyim*); also Karen **tha[ŋ]* 'up, go up': Pwo *thą*, Sgaw *thɔ*; TB: Bodish **s-təŋ* 'upper part'. Taungthu also has *rɛn* 'row' and *min* 'ripe'; *neŋ* 'year' and *seŋ* 'tree', confirming the reconstructed nasal finals in these roots. This Taungthu dialect (Jones) typically has medial *o* for **u* before nasal finals: *tśhom* 'mortar', *som* '3', *lom* 'warm', *loŋ* 'stone', *noŋ* 'horn', but *num* 'smell' (possibly reflecting an original distinction in vowel length); add Taungthu *ʔom* 'betel cud'; TB **(m-)u·m* 'hold in the mouth; mouthful'.

Pwo *mi mą*, Sgaw *mi mɔ* 'dream' (in comp. with 'sleep'); cf. TB *maŋ.
Pwo *wą*, Sgaw *wɔ* 'surround; circular'; TB *hwaŋ.

Pwo *ą*, Sgaw *ɔ*, Taungthu *am* 'eat'; cf. the following root:
(481) Nung *am* 'eat', Dhimal *am* 'drink' (TB *am).
Pwo *phü-thą~phu-thą*, Sgaw *thɔ* 'bear'; TB *d-wam.

Pwo *γɛ̨*, Sgaw *γe* 'row'; TB *ren.

Pwo *khlɛ̨* 'speak'; cf. T *gleŋ-ba* 'say, talk, converse'.[385]
Pwo *khɛ̨*, Sgaw *ki* 'tie around, gird, bind'; cf. B *khyań* 'bind, fasten'.[386]

Pwo *nǫ*, Sgaw *nə*, Taungthu *nuŋ* 'horn'; cf. TB *ruŋ (K *nruŋ*).
Pwo *lǫ*, Sgaw *lə*, Taungthu *luŋ* 'stone'; TB *r-luŋ.

Pwo *shə̨*, Sgaw *shə* 'mortar'; TB *tsum.
Pwo *θə̨*, Sgaw *θə*, Taungthu *θoum* '3'; TB *g-sum.
Pwo *lə̨*, Sgaw *lə* 'warm', TB *lum.
Pwo *nə̨*, Sgaw *nə* 'smell' (intr.); cf. T *snum-pa~snom-pa~snam-pa* 'smell' (tr.) and TB *m-nam.
Pwo *khə̨* 'block on which meat etc. is chopped'; cf. the following root:
(482) Lepcha *kam* 'block', *thyak-kam* 'pillow' (*thyak* 'head'), also *tăkám* 'seat', *kuŋ-kám* 'block of wood used as a seat', K *buŋ-khum* 'pillow' (*buŋ* 'head'), *ləkhum~puŋ-khum* 'chair, stool, bench, cushion', Nung *əgɔ məkhim* 'pillow' (*əgɔ* 'head'), B *khum* 'block, bench, table', L *khum* 'bedstead' (TB *kum).[387]

Pwo *nį*, Sgaw *ni* 'year'; TB *niŋ.
Pwo *θį*, Sgaw *θe* 'tree, wood'; TB *siŋ.
Pwo *mį*, Sgaw *mi* 'ripe'; TB *s-min.
Pwo *γį~yį*, Sgaw *hi* 'house'; cf. TB *kim.
Pwo regularly nasalizes vowels before (original) nasal consonants, but two or three possible exceptions have been found:
Pwo and Sgaw *na* 'thou'; TB *naŋ.
Pwo *mai*, Sgaw *mä* 'mole'; TB *r-men 'wen, mole': B *hmáń>hmɛ́*.
Pwo and Sgaw *phi* 'pus'; TB *pren: Lepcha *fren~frăn*<*phren 'boil, ulcer', B *prań>pyi* 'pus' (poss. direct influ. upon Karen).

385 Pwo *khlɛ̨* (low tone)<*glɛ[ŋ], agreeing closely with T *gleŋ-*.
386 Pwo *khɛ̨*, Sgaw *ki* (both low tone)<*gɛ[ŋ], probably a secondary voicing of the initial (B *khyań*).
387 Lahu *gɛ̂* 'pillow', Lolomaa *ŋk'ṿ*, from *məkhum (n. 123) (JAM).

Vocalic shifts before (original) final nasals are characteristic of Karen. Pwo retains *ą*, but Sgaw shifts to *ɔ*, whereas both retain **a* as a final or before stop consonants (see below). The high-front vowel **i* is maintained in most roots (Sgaw *θe* 'tree' < **siŋ* is altogether exceptional),[388] but in one instance this vowel has been replaced by *ü* before final *-n*:

Pwo *θų̈*, Sgaw *θu* 'liver'; TB **m-sin*.

Pwo, which lacks nasalized *u* and *e*, has shifted **u* to *o* before **-ŋ*, and to *ə̨* or *ų̈* before **-n* and **-m*.[389] In Burmese loan-words, however, the original vowel is simply approximated, e.g. *pǫ* 'story', B *pum* (> *poų*), *pǫ̈* 'own, possess', B *puiŋ* (> *pâį*). The vowels **o* and **e* have been diphthongized to *aų* and *aį*, respectively.

Pwo and Sgaw final glottal stop represents original final stop consonants. In loan-words from Burmese, both glottal stop and *auk-myit* (with final glottal catch) are represented by glottal stop; cf. *dwaʔ* 'reckon', B *twak* (> *twɛʔ*); *lwaʔ* 'saw', B *hlwá*. Replacement of final stop consonants by glottal stop is observed in the following:

Sgaw *kəhaʔ* 'phlegm'; TB **ha·k* 'hawk, gag, choke'.

Pwo *thaʔ tha*, Sgaw *tha tha* 'weave'; TB **tak*.

Pwo and Sgaw *maʔ* 'son-in-law'; TB **ma·k*.

Pwo and Sgaw *yaʔ* 'plantain'; TB **ŋak*.

Pwo and Sgaw *θaʔ* 'itch'; TB **m-sak*.

Pwo *waʔ* ~ *θəwaʔ*, Sgaw *waʔ* 'leech'; TB **r-pat*.

Pwo and Sgaw *khaʔ* 'shoot'; TB **ga·p*.

Pwo and Sgaw *χoʔ* '8'; TB **b-r-gyat*.

Pwo and Sgaw *noʔ* 'mouth'; cf. B *hnut*.

Pwo and Sgaw *nuʔ* 'brain' (generally in comp. with *kho* 'head'); cf. TB **nuk* (483), as represented by K *nu* ~ *ənu*, B *ù-hnauk* (*ù* 'head').

Pwo *ą γuʔ*, Sgaw *ə γüʔ* 'rob'; cf. L *ru·k*, Haka *ruk*, Lakher *pəru* (Kuki **m-ru·k*) 'steal'.

Pwo *khlüʔ* 'put on (hat), shut down (lid)'; TB **klup*.[390]

Pwo *khliʔ* 'fold up'; cf. L *thlep* < **khlep*.

Pwo and Sgaw *khliʔ* 'turtle'; cf. B *lip*.

Pwo and Sgaw *tho-γiʔ* 'pheasant'; cf. TB **s-rik* ~ **s-ryak*.

388 The Sgaw distinction between *ni* 'year' and *θe* 'tree' corresponds to a similar distinction both in TB (Mikir) and Chinese, apparently reflecting an archaic ST distinction in vowel length (n. 476).

389 Karenni, as recorded by Mason (*JASB* **27**, 1858), distinguishes between *θö* '3' and *nau* 'horn', *lau* 'stone'; cf. also Pwo *thų̈*, Sgaw and Karenni *tö*, Taungthu *thuŋ* 'ant' < **tum* (the Taungthu form is from Mason, who cites *θuŋ* '3' for *θoum*).

390 This root has a doublet: **hlüʔ* < **[k]hlup* (n. 376).

Sgaw _kiʔ_ (low tone) 'tie ligatures at intervals, gird the loins', _kiʔ_ (high tone) 'constrict, compress by twisting, screwing';[391] cf. the following:

(484) T _'khyig-pa_ 'bind', B _kyats_ 'twist hard and tight', Kuki _*d-khik_: Rangkhol _kit_, Kom, Aimol, Hallam _khit_ 'bind', Lakher _tśəkhi_ 'tie, knot', from TB _*kik_; K _kyit_ 'to gird, girdle', _śiŋkyit_ 'girdle', _gyit_ 'to tie, bind', Nung _śiŋkit_ 'band (waist), girdle, belt' (prob. loan from Kachin), are apparently distinct (cf. Ch. _kiet_).[a]

Pwo and Sgaw _phiʔ_ 'skin, bark'; cf. K _phyiʔ_ < _*phik, id._[392, 393]

Pwo _meʔ_, Sgaw _mɛʔ_ 'eye'; TB _*myak._

Vocalic shifts are less prominent before final stop consonants than before final nasals; cf. the following:

Sgaw _-aʔ_ < _*-ak_ but _-ɔ_ < _*-aŋ._

Pwo _-uʔ_ < _*-uk_ but _-ǫ_ < _*-uŋ._

Pwo and Sgaw _noʔ_ 'mouth', B _hnut_ 'mouth; womb' (above) also suggests the shift _*oʔ_ < _*-ut_, but cf. T _snod_ 'vessel', _bu-snod_ 'uterus', as if from TB _*s-not._ Pwo has final _-au̯_ and _-ai̯_ (above) but significantly lacks final _*-auʔ_ and _*-aiʔ_ (Pwo _kyaiʔ_ 'God' is exceptional), showing that diphthongization has not occurred before final stops.[394]

There is some evidence for complete loss of final stop in Karen, although the conditions governing this phenomenon remain obscure. Pwo and Sgaw vary in the following roots:

Pwo _tha_ 'weaving' (defined as a noun) but _thaʔ tha_ 'to weave', Sgaw _tha_ 'warp', _tha tha_ (tonally differentiated) 'to weave'; cf. TB _*tak._[395]

_391_ The Sgaw forms (Jones, _Karen Linguistic Studies_) point to an earlier doublet: _*giʔ_ ~ _*kiʔ_, the initial voicing probably being secondary.

392 The reconstruction _*phik_ is based on Jili _məphik_, with final velar stop preserved. Needham (1889) observes that the Kachin word is 'uttered sharply' (cf. n. 50).

_393_ Pwo and Sgaw _phiʔ_ but Taungthu _pi_, with complete loss of final stop (perhaps because root was prefixed, as shown by the unaspirated stop).

_394_ Moulmein Pwo has final _-auʔ_ corresponding to Bassein Pwo _-üʔ_ (Sgaw alternates with _-əʔ_) in two roots having TB cognates with final _*-up_ or _*-u·p_:

	TB	Taungthu	M. Pwo	B. Pwo	Sgaw
to cover	(_glup_)	—	_khlauʔ_	_khlüʔ_	_kləʔ_
	klup	—	_lauʔ_	_lüʔ_	_lüʔ_
to enter	_nu·p_	_nɨʔ_	_nauʔ_	_nüʔ_	_nüʔ_

For 'cover', see n. 376. For 'enter' Taungthu has _nɨʔ_ (high tone) < _*hnüʔ_, as if from _*s-nu·p_ (cf. the B-G initial _*hn-_ cluster in this root; n. 250).

_395_ Karen _*tha_ (tone B) 'weaving; warp', a nominalized form, as distinct from _*thaʔ_ 'to weave'. Sgaw and Palaychi have lost the glottal stop in the latter as

[a] 結

Pwo *tho phliʔ*, Sgaw *thuʔ pleʔ* ~ *thuʔ pγε* 'to spit'; cf. TB **(m-)tuk.*[396]

Pwo and Sgaw *θa* 'breathe' but *θaʔ* 'heart', the earlier meaning being reflected in certain compounds: Pwo *θaʔ-kaʔ* 'to have a sense of tightness in the chest so as to breathe with difficulty' (*kaʔ* 'tight');[397] cf. the following:

(485) K *saʔ* 'breathe', *niŋsaʔ* ~ *nsaʔ* 'breath, life', Nung *sa* 'breath of life', B *ăsak* (*sak* in comp.) 'breath, life', Chang (Konyak) *hak* < **sak* 'life, breath' (TB **sak*).

The following roots show complete loss of final stop both in Pwo and Sgaw:

Pwo *χu*, Sgaw *χü* 'six'; cf. TB **d-ruk.*

Pwo and Sgaw *θəli* 'leech' (cf. Pwo *θəwaʔ*, *id.*);[398] cf. TB **(m-)li·t.*

Pwo and Sgaw *e* 'feces'; cf. Kuki-Naga **e·k*: L *e·k* 'excrement; defecate', Haka, Rangkhol, Sho *ek*, Lakher *i* < **ek* 'dung, excrement'.[399]

There is no certain example of loss of final **-p*[400] but note the following, in which TB shows an unusual doublet:

Pwo and Sgaw *la* 'leaf'; cf. TB **lap* (above) and the following:

(486) Magari *hla*, Vayu and Chepang *lo* < **la*, Kiranti **la* (Kulung *la*, Rodong *la-bo*, Lambichong *lă-phak*, Limbu *pella*), Dhimal *hla-ba*, Mikir *lo* < **la* (TB **la*); cf. also B *lak-phak* ~ *lăbhak* 'tea' and the Lambichong form (see No. 40).

Final **-r*, **-l* and **-s* all appear to have been dropped in Karen, which lacks these consonants in final position. The following comparisons with TB are available:[401]

have both Pwo dialects cited in the Jones glossary, but earlier (1920–2) Pwo dictionaries (Purser and Aung, 1920 and 1922) cite *thaʔ tha* 'weave' (as in the text); Taungthu also preserves the glottal stop: *thaʔ* 'weave'.

396 The Jones glossary cites Sgaw *tho-* 'spittle' (in comp.), indicating recent loss of the glottal stop (cf. n. 395 for similar recent loss in Pwo), since the older Sgaw dictionaries (Wade, 1896; Blackwell, 1937) give *thuʔ* (as in the text). Taungthu has *pəthoʔ* (low tone, high tone) 'spittle', from **b-thoʔ* < **m-thok*, a rare example of preservation of a prefix in Karen (n. 356).

397 Taungthu follows the general Karen pattern here: *sa* 'breath; to breathe', *saʔ* 'heart'.

398 Taungthu has *lyɔʔ* 'leech', with final glottal stop preserved, but the vocalism appears to be irregular, possibly reflecting an archaic ST doublet: **(m-)lyat* ~ **(m-)li·t* (n. 251).

399 Taungthu also shows apparent loss of the final stop here: *ʔe* 'dung'. The K-N root (**e·k*) is a possible derivative (with loss of initial velar) of a TB root represented by T *rkyag(-pa)* ~ *skyag(-pa)* 'dirt, excrement', perhaps also B *kyaŋ* 'dung'.

400 The most likely example of complete loss of final **-p* in Karen is furnished by Pwo *χi* (low tone A), Sgaw *χi* (high tone B) 'ant', perhaps from **gri(p)* ~ **kri(p)*; TB **krep* (see n. 382 for the correspondence of initials).

401 Final **-r* is perhaps dropped only after a long vowel: cf. also Karen **ya* 'expand; sail'; TB **ya·r* ~ **yâr* (n. 372). There are two good examples of replace-

Pwo *phau*, Sgaw *phə* 'flower'; cf. TB **ba·r* (the Karen forms point to an intermediate **bor* ∼ **por*).

Pwo and Sgaw *thu* 'roll up (mat, cigar)'; cf. TB *(*r-*)*tul* 'roll up, wrap'.

Pwo *γu*, Sgaw *γü* 'snake'; cf. TB **b-ru·l*.

Pwo and Taungthu *ni* (Sgaw has *khi*) '2'; cf. TB **g-nis*.

§37. Karen final vowels and semi-vowels

Final vowels and semi-vowels undergo relatively little change in Karen, apart from levelling off of the latter. As in almost all TB languages, no distinction is made between *-*i* and *-*iy*, or between *-*u* and *-*uw*. Sgaw regularly has -*ü* for *-*u*, but -*u* appears in loan-words, e.g. Pwo and Sgaw *tu* 'hammer' < B *tu*. In Pwo, on the other hand, -*ü* is relatively rare (cf. *phü* 'carry', also 'younger brother', *bü* 'rice') and tends to alternate with -*u*, as in *khü* ∼ *khu* 'trap'. The following pair of roots are exceptional:[402]

Pwo and Sgaw *lu* 'pour'; cf. the following:

G *ru*, Dimasa *lu* 'pour', Mikir *iŋlu* 'bathe'; cf. TB *(*m-*)*lu*(*w*).

Pwo *yü lą* 'swallow down' but *ą yu* 'swallow' (*ą* 'eat'), Sgaw *yu* 'swallow';

ment of final *-*r* by -*n* after short vowels, viz. Karen **san* 'new'; TB **sar*: T *gsar-ba* 'new, fresh', Nungish: Răwang *aŋsar* 'new', Trung *aksal* 'fresh'; Kuki: L *thar* 'new, anew', Thado *ătha*, Tiddim *thak* 'new'; Karen **sən* 'louse'; TB **sar* ∼ **śar* (n. 179); the Karen vocalism suggests influence from an initial *ś*-, indicating correspondence with TB **śar* rather than **sar*.

Final *-*s* is probably replaced by -*t* rather than dropped; cf. the Karen forms for 'bone': Taungthu *tśhut*, Pwo *χwi*, Palaychi *ʔa-χi*, Sgaw *χi*, suggesting an original **k*(*h*)*rut* (see n. 382 for the initials), from **g-rus* (TB **rus*), the prefixed **g*- also being represented in Chinese (n. 419). The Karen example cited in the text, viz. *ni* '2', is not applicable in this connection, since the TB root has now been reconstructed without the final *-*s*, which is a separable element (n. 61); Karen may have -*t* for *-*s* also in **hnət* or **hnwi·t* '7' (n. 355).

402 Palaychi resembles Pwo rather than Sgaw in this series, but with -*ü* only in *mü* 'sun' and -*mü* 'female (human)' (Pwo *mü*), perhaps conditioned by the initial **m*-; it has an irregular -*lɔ* for 'pour'. Taungthu agrees with Pwo in general, with -*u* in most forms but *bü*- 'rice plant', *mü* 'sun', *bü* 'carry on back', *təʔü* 'rotten', and add *ŋü* 'cry (weep)', TB **ŋəw*; Taungthu has *phu* 'younger sibling' (Pwo *phü*) and *mu* 'female (human)' (Pwo *mü*), also the irregular *myɔ* 'to swallow' (n. 403). Final -*u* is found in all four Karen languages only in **ʔu* 'to blow': Taungthu, Pwo and Sgaw *ʔu*, Palaychi *vu*.

cf. TB **mlyuw* (the Karen forms point to an intermediate **myu* < **m-yu*, with the initial interpreted as a prefix; cf. K *məyu*).[403]

The regular Karen correspondences for TB *-*a*, *-*u*(*w*) and *-*i*(*y*) are illustrated below:

Pwo and Sgaw *kha* 'bitter'; cf. TB **ka*.

Pwo and Sgaw *na* 'ear'; cf. TB **g-na*.

Pwo and Sgaw *ma* 'wife'; cf. the following:

(487) T *ʔama*, Kanauri *ama*, Bahing *əmo* (but *wəma* 'my mother'), Vayu *umu* < **ama*, Chepang *ma*, Newari *ma*, Lepcha *amo* < **ama*, Digaro (*na-*)*ma*, Dhimal *ama*, Burmese-Lolo **ma* (B *má* is used only as fem. suffix), Bodo (*bi-*)*ma*, G *ama* 'mother' (TB **ma*).[404]

Pwo *khu*, Sgaw *khü* 'smoke, vapor'; cf. TB **kuw*.

Pwo *phu*, Sgaw *phü* 'grandfather'; cf. TB **puw*.

Pwo and Sgaw *mü* 'sun'; cf. the following:

(488) T *rmu-ba* 'fog', K *mu* 'to be cloudy; sky; thunder and lightning', *ləmu* (Khauri dial. *məmu*) 'sky', Nung *mu* 'sky' (*mu ru* 'to be struck by lightning'), B *muì*(*gh*) 'sky; clouds, rain' (the *-gh* is a product of etymologizing); cf. also B *muì* 'to cover, spread overhead (as an umbrella)', *ămuì* 'roof' (TB **r-muw*).[405,406]

Pwo *ü* ~ *o*, Sgaw *ü* 'putrid, rotten'; cf. the following:

(489) K *wuʔ* 'unclean, polluted', B *u* 'to be stale, tainted, begin to putrefy', Thado *vu* 'stink' (TB **u*).

Pwo and Sgaw *thi* 'water'; cf. TB **ti*(*y*).

Pwo and Sgaw *θi* 'die'; cf. TB **siy*.

Pwo *li*, Sgaw *kəli* 'wind'; cf. TB **g-liy*.

Pwo and Sgaw *shi* 'urine'; cf. TB **ts*(*y*)*i*.

Only two Karen comparisons are available for TB final *-*o* and *-*e*, which are rare elements:[407]

Pwo *thau*, Sgaw *thɔ*, Taungthu *əto* 'high'; cf. TB **m-to*.

403 Taungthu *myɔ* 'to swallow', with irregular final, supports the suggested development, but it is possible that this form has been derived from **ʔam-yu* or **ʔam-yəw* (**ʔam* 'eat'), corresponding to Pwo *ą yu* (text).

404 The semantic shift here is to be explained through teknonymy, i.e. the wife is addressed as 'mother' (as often in English).

405 For the semantics of this root, cf. T *gnam* 'heaven, sky', *nam* 'night' (*nam-mkha* 'sky'), Magari *nam-khan* ~ *nyam-khan* 'sun', *nam-sin* ~ *nyam-sin* 'day', *nam-bik* 'night', *nam-məra* 'evening', Chepang *nyam* 'sun', Vayu *nomo* < *nama* 'sun, sky', Bahing (and general Kiranti) *nam* 'sun' (also 'sky' in Balali), Nung *nam* 'sun' (dial. 'sky'), and perhaps Mikir *arnam* 'god' ('wind' in comp.).

406 The Kachin and Nung forms here belong with TB **r-mu·k* (n. 236).

407 An excellent comparison is available for final *-*e*, viz. Karen **p*(*h*)*le* ~ **ʔble* 'slippery', TB **ble* 'slip, slippery' (n. 375).

Pwo *phe*, Sgaw *he* (the initial is anomalous), Taungthu *pye*, Yeinbaw *phi* 'give'; cf. Kuki-Naga **pe(k)* (see n. 289), apparently distinct from TB **biy*.

The combinations **-aw* and **-ow*, **-ay* and **-ey* have generally been levelled off in Karen. In the single TB comparison that has come to light for Pwo *-au* (Sgaw *-ɔ*), the TB final is *-o* rather than *-aw* (see above). In four comparisons, furthermore, Pwo and Sgaw *-o* corresponds to TB **-aw*∼**-a·w* and **-ow*:

Pwo and Sgaw *θo* 'oil, fat'; TB **sa·w*.

Pwo and Sgaw *kho* 'head'; cf. the following:

(490) T *mgo*, Digaro *ku-ru*∼*mku-ra*, *mkau*, Nung *gɔ*∼*əgɔ*, G *sko*, Dimasa *sagau* (in comp.), Meithei *məko* 'head', from TB **m-gaw*∼**(s-)gaw*.

Pwo and Sgaw *tho* 'bird'; cf. Bodo-Garo **daw* (G *do*, Dimasa *dau*).

Pwo and Sgaw *mo* 'mother; female'; TB **mow*.

TB **-ey* regularly yields Pwo and Sgaw *-e* (*-i* in some Karen dialects; cf. Taungthu *mi* 'fire'):[408]

Pwo and Sgaw *me* 'fire': TB **mey*.

Pwo and Sgaw *ne* 'get, obtain'; TB **ney*.

Pwo and Sgaw *khe* 'tiger'; TB **d-key*.

Pwo and Sgaw *θe* 'to be skilled, able'; TB **syey* 'know'.

Pwo *γe*, Sgaw *γi*∼*γe* 'rattan, cane'; TB **rey*.

Pwo and Sgaw *me* 'boiled rice'; cf. Bodo-Garo **mey* or **may* 'rice, paddy' (see n. 206).

TB **-ay*∼**-a·y* are perhaps retained in Karen (Pwo *-ai*, Sgaw *-ε*) under certain circumstances, but in general tend to fall together with **-ey*.[409] Both *-ai* and *-e* are found in Pwo loan-words from Burmese; cf. Pwo *phai* 'playing card' and 'satin' (B *phaì* > *phὲ*), but Pwo *pwe*, Sgaw *pwε* 'festival' (B *pwaì* > *pwὲ*). Pwo also shows *-ai*∼*-e* interchange, as in *shwai*∼*shwe* (Sgaw *shγε*∼*shwε*) 'crab'; cf. TB **d-ka·y*. Sgaw sometimes preserves the distinction between **-ay* (> *-ε*) and **-ey* (> *-e*) in

408 The Taungthu dialect cited by Jones (*Karen Linguistic Studies*) has *me* 'fire' and *re* 'rattan', as in Karen generally. Palaychi has final *-i* here: *mi* 'fire', *γi* 'rattan', *ni*∼*ne* 'get, obtain'. For 'rice (cooked)', however, Palaychi has *mə* (cf. n. 409), indicating an original **may* for Karen (and by inference also for TB); this root appears to be an early loan from AT (cf. IN **imay* 'rice') and is represented also in Bodo-Garo (where the final could be either **-ey* or **-ay*) and in Chinese (n. 491); see discussion of terms for 'rice' in Benedict, 1967bis.

409 Taungthu uniformly has final *-e* in this series: *tshwe* 'crab', *me* 'tail', *nwe* 'yam (white)', *ʔe* 'to love', *phre* 'tongue', *pəde* 'navel', *phe* 'chaff, husks'. Palaychi has no fewer than four different reflexes here: *shwε* 'crab' and *nwε* 'yam'; *mə* 'tail' and *ʔə* 'love'; *ple* 'tongue'; *di-* 'navel'. The evidence in general suggests that Karen retains some distinction between original **-ay* and **-a·y* (contrast 'tail' and 'crab') but the evidence is not consistent (cf. 'husks, chaff', unfortunately not represented in Palaychi).

roots which are not differentiated in Pwo; cf. Sgaw *mɛ* 'tail', TB **r-may*, but *me* 'fire', TB **mey* (both *me* in Pwo). Sgaw *kwɛ*, Pwo *kwe* 'bee', TB **kwa·y*, fits into the same pattern, but this root has perhaps been borrowed from Burmese (*kwaì* > *kwɛ̀*). Pwo has *-ai* in *lai*, Sgaw *lɛ* 'exchange', TB **lay*; *nai* 'yam', Sgaw *nwɛ*; cf. K *nai*; also *ai* 'love', Sgaw *ɛ*; cf. Ch. *·əd* > *·ậi*,[a] *id.* In three reliable comparisons, however, both Pwo and Sgaw have *-e* in the face of TB **-ay* or **-a·y*, indicating that these finals had fallen together with **-ey* in proto-Karen times:

Pwo *phle*, Sgaw *pəle*~*ple* 'tongue'; TB **m-lay*~**s-lay*.

Pwo and Sgaw *de* 'umbilicus'; TB **s-tay*.

Pwo and Sgaw *phe* 'chaff, husks'; TB **pwa·y*.

§38. Karen tones

Pwo and Sgaw, and presumably other Karen languages as well, have complex tonal systems akin to those found in Tibeto-Burman.[410,411] Before final glottal stop, a distinction is made between high (×̌) and mid (×) tones, with Pwo having high tone for Sgaw mid and vice versa: Pwo *nǔʔ*, Sgaw *nuʔ* 'brain'; Pwo *noʔ*, Sgaw *nǒʔ* 'mouth'. Four tonemes are found with non-glottalized finals, as follows:

I Pwo ×̂ (low level), Sgaw × (mid level).

II Pwo ×́ (rising), Sgaw ×̌ (slightly high and level).

III Pwo ×̀ (mid level in Delta, abruptly falling in Tennasserim), Sgaw ×̀ (falling).

IV Pwo × (mid or low level), Sgaw ×̂ (low and falling).

The Karen tones show correlation with the Burmese-Lolo tonal system, with tonemes I and II correlating with Burmese level tone (including *auk-myit*), and III and IV with Burmese falling tone. As in Burmese-Lolo, it does not appear possible to interpret the distinction between I–II and III–IV in terms of lost

410 Tones are indicated in Karen script, but are poorly described in the standard Karen sources. The only adequate description of Karen tones is that found in Grierson, 1928, 'Introduction', pp. 14–18, based on the work of L. F. Taylor. This account is of especial value in giving separate descriptions of the tones in the Delta and Tennasserim dialects of Pwo Karen. For the tonal notation employed here, see n. 258.

411 See n. 494 for a full discussion of Karen tones in relation to those of TB and Chinese.

a 愛

prefixes or the like, but the first member of each Karen pair (Tonemes I and III) usually corresponds to unvoiced initials in Burmese, while the second member (Tonemes II and IV) corresponds to voiced initials. One of the apparent exceptions: B *hmrà* 'arrow', Pwo *phla*, Sgaw *pla*, is readily explained by reference to the TB root **b-la*, indicating a similar reconstruction for Karen. This would require reconstructions for other Karen roots, e.g. **hna-* 'nose' (Toneme I) and even **hŋa* 'fish' (Toneme 3); cf. L *sa-hŋa*, with a redundant *sa-* 'animal prefix' (*hŋa* < **sŋa*), but initials of this type do not appear in any known Karen languages of the present day. The following are representative of the main tonal correlations between Burmese and Karen:

	Burmese	Pwo	Sgaw
boat	*hle*	*khlî*	*khli*
pain	*tsha*	*shâ*	*sha*
bear, n.	*-wam*	*-thą̂*	*thɔ*
span	*thwa*	*thâ*	*tha*
nose	*hna*	*nâ-*	*na-*
smell (intr.)	*nam*	*nǫ̈̂*	*nö*
sleep	*mwé*	*mî*	*mi*
ripe	*hmáń*	*mį̂*	*mi*
die	*se*	*θî*	*θi*
elephant	*tshaŋ*	*kəshą̂*	*kəshɔ*
wind, n.	*le*	*lí*	*kəlǐ*
day	*né*	*ní*	*nǐ*
moon	*lá*	*lá*	(*la*)
name	*mań*	*mį́*	*mǐ*
warm	*lum*	*lǫ̈́*	*lö̌*
hundred	*ăra*	*yá*	*yǎ*
bow	*lè*	*khlì*	*khlì*
bitter	*khà*	*khà*	*khà*
smoke	*ăkhuì*	*khù*	*khǜ*
fish	*ŋà*	*yà*	*nyà*
dog	*khwè*	*thwì*	*thwì*
carry	*puì*	*phǜ*	*phǜ*
fire	*mì*	*mè*	*mè*
bamboo	*wà*	*wà*	*wà*
liver	*asàń*	*θų̈̀*	*θù*
blood	*swè*	*θwì*	*θwì*

[*cont. on p.* 152

	Burmese	Pwo	Sgaw
arrow	*hmrà*	*phla*	*plâ*
sun	*mui̇̀(gh)*	*mü*	*mü̂*
tail	*ămrì*	*me*	*mɛ̂*
five	*ŋà*	*yai*	*yɛ̂*
four	*lè*	*li*	*lwî*
ear	*nà*	*na*	*nâ*

The tonally irregular Sgaw form *la* 'moon' is matched by Sgaw *kwɛ* 'bee' corresponding to Pwo *kwé*, but Burmese has *kwai̇̀* (with falling rather than level tone). The tonal correlation between Karen and Burmese is not perfect, i.e. a number of exceptions have been found, but it can safely be regarded as 'statistically valid'. The most significant exceptions are as follows: B *kui̇̀*, Pwo *khwî*, Sgaw *khwi* '9'; B *sùm*, Pwo *θö̩̂*, Sgaw *θö* '3';[412, 413] B *khwè-hlè*, Pwo *khlî*, Sgaw *kli* 'flea'; B *aphui̇̀*, Pwo *phû*, Sgaw *phü* 'grandfather'; B *phwai̇̀*, Pwo *phê*, Sgaw *phe* 'husks'; B *mrè*, Pwo *lí*, Sgaw *lǐ*, 'grandchild' (all with falling rather than level tone in Burmese); B *tshum*, Pwo *shṳ̂*, Sgaw *shö̀* 'mortar'; B *im*, Pwo *γì̤~yì̤*, Sgaw *hì* 'house'; B *nuí*, Pwo *nu*, Sgaw *nü̂* 'breasts' (all with level rather than falling tone in Burmese); also B *ŋa*, Pwo and Sgaw *ya* 'I' (with Pwo mid rather than low tone).

§39. Chinese (general, history)

Chinese is the third and last major division of Sino-Tibetan to be considered in this review. Three stages of the language are conveniently recognized: (*a*) Archaic Chinese (Ar. Ch.), *ca.* 1200–800 B.C., (*b*) Ancient Chinese (Anc. Ch.), *ca.* A.D. 600, and (*c*) the modern dialects. Ancient Chinese has been reconstructed from the modern dialects together with the material found in the Ch'ieh Yün and other

412 Tonal irregularity in these two numerals is found also in Burmese-Lolo. Lahu *sèh*, Ahi *sö̀*, Lolopho *sò*, and Lisu *sa*, Nyi *sȫ* '3' all point to B **sum* rather than *sùm*. Lahu *kɔ̌* '9' agrees with B *kui̇̀*, but Ahi and Lolopho *kö̀*, Lisu *kǔ* and Nyi *kȫ* point rather to **kui*. Note that the Karen tones of these numerals agree with Burmese-Lolo as a whole.

413 'Three' is also irregular in Lahu: *šɛ̄* would be expected (it does occur before certain specific classifiers) but the usual form is *šɛ̄ʔ*, with final -ʔ. This arose from metanalysis with an automatic [ʔ-] before the vowel-initial in 'four' /ɔ̌/ ([ʔɔ̌]): i.e. in counting a [-ʔ-] demarcated 'three' from 'four' to prevent the two vowels from fusing (JAM). Lahu *gɔ̂* 'nine' is regular with respect to B *kui̇̀* (< **kuw* Tone 2), but cf. Lisu *ku*, from **ʔk*-, also with an intrusive glottal element (JAM).

lexicographical works of the first millennium A.D. Archaic Chinese represents a still farther projection into the past, achieved through the analysis of the Shih Ching rhymes and the phonetic elements of Chinese characters. A number of scholars, including Maspéro, Simon and Li Fang-kuei, have contributed to the brilliant results attained in this field,[414,415] but we are indebted above all to the monumental studies by Karlgren.[416] Our purpose here is not to review the developments within Chinese itself, but rather to study the earliest known stage of the language (Ar. Ch.) in the light of our reconstruction of Tibeto-Burman and Tibeto-Karen. The forms cited below accordingly are those of Ar. Ch., often along with the later Anc. Ch. forms, all as given in the *Grammata Serica* of Karlgren.

414 H. Maspéro, 'Le dialecte de Tch'ang-ngan sous les T'ang', *BEFEO* **20** (1920), 1–124; W. Simon, 'Zur Rekonstruktion der altchinesischen Endkonsonanten', *MSOS* **30** (1927), 147–67; **31** (1928), 175–204; 'The Reconstruction of Archaic Chinese', *BSOS* **9** (1938), 267–88; Li Fang-kuei,[a] 'Ch'ieh Yün â-ti lai-yüan'[b] ('Sources of Ch'ieh Yün *â*'), *CYYY* **3** (1931), 1–38; 'Ancient Chinese *-ung, -uk, -uong, -uok* etc. in Archaic Chinese', *CYYY* **3** (1932), 375–414; 'Archaic Chinese **-i̯wəng*, **-i̯wək* and **-i̯wəg*', *CYYY* **5** (1935), 65–74.

415 See Wang's article in *Current Trends in Linguistics* II for recent Chinese bibliography (JAM). Karlgren's reconstruction schema is conveniently presented in his *Compendium of Phonetics in Ancient and Archaic Chinese* (*BMFEA*, No. 26, Stockholm, 1954); Karlgren's *Grammata Serica Recensa* (cited as *GSR*) (*BMFEA*, No. 29, 1947) has superseded the earlier *Grammata Serica* (cited as *GS*) and is especially helpful in noting tones (omitted in the earlier work); some forms are glossed differently in these two works (see n. 488 for one instance). There have been numerous attempts to improve or even radically reshape Karlgren's reconstruction schema, notably E. G. Pulleyblank, 'The Consonantal System of Old Chinese', *Asia Major* **9** (1962), 58–144; 206–65, and 'An Interpretation of the Vowel System of Old Chinese and of Written Burmese', *Asia Major* **10** (1963), 200–21. The writer in general has not been impressed by the proposals offered, and steps such as interpreting B *sùm* '3' as *swìm* (Pulleyblank) certainly lead us nowhere. The weight of the comparative ST evidence in fact strongly favors the bulk of the Ar. Ch. reconstructions proposed by Karlgren, including his brilliant reconstruction of final **-r* (n. 460); the same evidence practically precludes most of the elaborate reconstructions suggested by writers like Pulleyblank. The most serious defects in the Ar. Ch. reconstructions by Karlgren lie in the initial consonant clusters (see n. 469 for one instance), which that scholar has recognized as the most uncertain area of his great work.

416 B. Karlgren, 'Études sur la Phonologie Chinoise', *Archives d'Études Orientales* **15**, 1–4, Upsala, 1915–26; 'The reconstruction of Ancient Chinese', *TP* **21** (1922), 1–42 (a critique of Maspero, *BEFEO* **20**, 1920); *Analytic Dictionary of Chinese and Sino-Japanese*, Paris, 1923; 'Problems in Archaic Chinese', *JRAS* (1928), 769–813; 'Shï King Researches', *BMFEA* **4** (1932), 117–85; 'Word Families in Chinese', *BMFEA* **5** (1934), 1–112 (reviewed in detail by S. Yoshitake in *BSOS* **7**, 931–41); *Grammata Serica, Script and Phonetics in Chinese and Sino-Japanese, BMFEA* **12** (1940), 1–471.

[a] 李方桂 [b] 切韻 *â* 的來源

§40. Chinese morphology (prefixes, suffixes, alternation)

The relationship between Tibeto-Burman and Chinese, as noted above (§**2**), is a remote one.[417] Indeed, on the basis of morphology alone, we should be quite unjustified in positing any direct genetic link between the two stocks. Chinese does, to be sure, resemble Tibeto-Burman in its use of monosyllabic roots, its system of tones, and its isolating characteristics, yet Thai, Kadai, Annamite, and Miao-Yao, all unrelated to Sino-Tibetan, also share in these features. Chinese actually approaches these languages rather than Tibeto-Burman in being a relatively 'pure' isolating language, lacking any but the most rudimentary system of affixes. As regards syntax, Chinese agrees with these languages and Karen in placing the object after rather than before the verb (there are occasional transpositions, as in Karen), in violation of the cardinal principle of Tibeto-Burman word-order.

Prefixes: Chinese has numerous initial consonantal groups, some of which can be interpreted in terms of prefixation,[418,419] but only sporadic examples can be

417 This is hardly an accurate statement; the term 'remote' should be applied to our state of knowledge at that time (early 1940s) rather than to the relationship between TB and Chinese. It is now quite clear that the great bulk of the core ST vocabulary is shared by these two language groups, e.g. whereas in his earlier study (Benedict, 1941) the writer was hard put to find more than one basic kinship term (ST **kəw* ~ **gəw* 'maternal uncle') shared by the two groups, he now recognizes a relationship for over half these basic terms; note also that certain Chinese roots lacking TB cognates do have Karen cognates (n. 350).

418 The view that these clusters consist of prefix + initial has been developed by Maspéro in his article, 'Préfixes et dérivation en chinois archaïque', *Mém. Soc. Ling. de Paris* **23** (1930), 313–27. The opposite view (that these are true clusters) is expressed in Wên Yu, 'The Influence of Liquids upon the Dissolution of Initial Consonant Groups in the Indo-Sinic Family', *JNChBRAS* **69** (1938), 83–91. Maspero reconstructs clusters freely, e.g.[a] 'order, to order' is reconstructed *löng* and regarded as phonetic in[b] 'confer a charge', reconstructed *m-löng*.

419 We have both indirect and direct evidence for prefixation in Chinese. Unaspirated surd stops/affricates point to an earlier prefixed form: *ki̯ŭg/ki̯əw*[c] '9' < ST **d-kəw*; *kân*[d] 'liver' < ST **b-ka-n*; *tsi̯əg/tsi*[e] 'child' < ST **b-tsa* (the prefixes cited are illustrative; the actual forms can only be inferred on the basis of TB models). This indirect evidence can be more subtle; note especially **b/li̯ôk/li̯uk*[f] '6', since graph is phonetic in *mli̯ôk/mi̯uk*[g] 'concord' (n. 474); also *si̯əd/si*[h] '4', from **p-səy* (n. 436), the prefix representing an inference required to explain the unvoicing of the initial; also *xiwet*[i] 'blood', TB **s-hywəy* (n. 441), but the graph is used as a phonetic or loan in forms with initial *si̯w-* and *sw-* (GSR- 410), indicating a doublet **siwet* which incorporates the **s-* prefix in the root (cf. B *swè*). More direct evidence of prefixation is supplied by very early loans from Chinese, notably

a 令 b 命 c 九 d 肝 e 子 f 六 g 睦 h 四 i 血

cited, e.g. *ńi̯ăr*[a] 'near', *sni̯ăr*[b] 'seal' ('something affixed'); *ni̯ôk*[c] 'ashamed', *sni̯ôg*[d] 'ashamed; to shame' (cf. TB **s-rak*); *mək*[e] 'ink', *χmək*[f] 'black' (cf. T *nag-po* 'black', *snag* 'ink', and B *maŋ*~*hmaŋ* 'ink'). Certainly no system of prefixes existed even in Ar. Ch., i.e. no general morphological role can be assigned to elements such as *s*- and *χ*-. The comparison *gli̯əp*>*li̯əp*[g] 'stand', TB **g-ryap* indicates that prefixed **g*- is an inherited ST element, preserved in Chinese in this root through its treatment as an initial (cf. K *tsap*<*g-yap*<*g-ryap*). The following pair, phonetically irregular, suggest that prefixed **s*- might be preserved in Chinese in the same manner: *ṣi̯ɛt*[h] 'flea, louse', TB **s-rik*; *sĕng*[i] 'live; bear, be born; fresh (as greens)', TB **s-riŋ*~**s-raŋ*. The addition of a prefix in Ar. Ch. can be demonstrated for *glâm*>*lâm*[j] 'indigo', T *rams*.[420,421]

in the numerals (n. 435). Prefixed **s*- is not represented by the forms in the text, which are from initial **śr*- clusters: TB **śrak* 'shamed', **śrik* 'louse', **śriŋ* 'live' (nn. 304, 457), but it is represented in **sri̯ôk*/*si̯uk*[k] 'pass the night', TB **s-ryak* (n. 457) and in a strange series developed from ST **s-n*- (n. 471); before initial **m*-, this prefix aspirated the initial (*χm*-) as indicated in the text; cf. also *mwən*/*muən*[l] 'sad, dull, stupid', *mwən*/*muən*~*χmwən*/*χuən*[m] 'blinded, confused', *χmwən*/*χuən*[n] 'dusk, evening, darkness; blinded', from ST **mun*~**s-mun*; T *mun-pa* 'dark', *dmun-pa* 'darkened'; also **s-ŋ*- yielded **χŋ*-; cf. < *ŋan*[o] 'goose', also **s-ŋan* (phonetic is *xân*[p] < **χŋân* 'cliff', and Thai loan is **haan* < **hŋaan*, with **s*- 'animal prefix' (p. 107) (**s-ŋâ-n*; n. 428). Prefixed **b*- is maintained before **r*/*l*- (n. 474). Prefixed **g*- is preserved in verbal roots before **r*- in *gli̯əp*[q] 'stand' (text) = **g-li̯əp* (n. 472) and *t'i̯an*<**kran*[r] 'battle' (n. 461); it is also maintained as an old pronominal element with words for body parts (see §25) before **r*/*l*- in three roots: *li̯ĕŋ*/*li̯äŋ*[s] 'neck, collar', *ki̯ĕŋ*/*ki̯äŋ*~*g'i̯ĕŋ*/*g'i̯äŋ*[t] 'neck', from **g-li̯ĕŋ*; TB **liŋ* 'neck'; *g'i̯ak*[u] 'tongue', from **g-li̯ak*, a doublet of *d''i̯at*/*dź'i̯ät*[v] (n. 472), *id.*; TB *(*m*-)*lyak*~*(*s*-)*lyak* 'lick; tongue'; *kwət*/*kuət*[w] 'bone', from **g-rus* (TB **rus*) via **k-rwət* (n. 479) with unvoicing of prefix (cf. n. 436); cf. Karen **k*(*h*)*rut*< **g-rus*; for other examples of retention of velar prefix, cf. 'right (hand)' (n. 449) and 'eagle' (n. 225). There is direct evidence of a special kind for prefixed **b*- in the numeral '100' (n. 435), also for prefixed **d*- in 'head' (n. 443). Finally, Chinese appears to have retained prefixed **r*- at times in metathesized form; cf. *mi̯ĕŋ*/*mi̯äŋ*[x] 'name'<**miŋ*; also *mi̯ăŋ*/*mi̯wăŋ*~*mi̯ĕn*[y] 'order, command; name', from **mli̯ĕŋ*~**mliăŋ*, as shown by the phonetic (and cognate) *li̯ĕŋ*/*li̯äŋ*[z] 'command', all from an original **mliŋ*<**mriŋ* (see n. 442 for alternation of finals); TB **r-miŋ* 'name' (also B *mín* 'order, command'); Karen **men* 'name'; cf. also the complicated development in 'tail' (n. 491).

420 Ch. *glâm*<*grâm*, as shown by Thai (Siamese and Lao) **graam*. The Thai borrowing can thus be dated as posterior to the prefixation of *g*-, but anterior to the *grâm*>*glâm* shift in Chinese. Borrowing must also be postulated for the Tibetan and Chinese forms, but the direction of transfer cannot be ascertained here.

421 This Ch. form has been interpreted (Benedict, 1967bis) as an early loan from AT (IN **taγum*, Thai **throom*), with *gr*- for *γ*-, a non-Chinese sound at that

a 邇 b 璽 c 忸 d 羞 e 墨 f 黑 g 立 h 蝨 i 生
j 藍 k 宿 l 悶 m 殙 n 昏 o 鴈 p 厂 q 立 r 戰
s 領 t 頸 u 臄 v 舌 w 骨 x 名 y 命 z 令

The modern dialects of Chinese employ a true prefix (*a-*) with kinship terms and certain forms of address; cf. the following examples from Cantonese:[422] *a-ma*[a] 'mother!', *a-yi*[b] 'aunt!', *a-wong*[c] 'Wong!', *a-yi*[d] 'No. 2 (servant)!' (reference to servant's order of birth). Maspéro[423] has shown that this usage extends back to the early T'ang and Six Dynasties period (*ca.* A.D. 600), but we do not meet with it in the early texts. Laufer[424] attempted to connect this Chinese element with the *a-* prefix found in Tibeto-Burman, which we have sought to show is of pronominal origin (§**28**). It is much more likely, however, that Chinese *a-* is an independent development, especially in view of the fact that it appears only at a relatively late stage of the language (Anc. Ch.).

Suffixes: Ar. Ch. lacks suffixes as well as prefixes, yet does show what appear to be remnants of a system of suffixes.[425] Alternation between final stop and nasal is of fairly frequent occurrence, as first pointed out by Courant.[426]

sât[e] and *sân*[f] 'scatter'.
ngi̯at∼*ngi̯an*[g] 'deliver a judicial decision'.
gi̯wăt[h] and *gi̯wən*[i] 'say, speak'.
·iwət∼*·iwăn*[j] 'luxuriant'.
k'wâk[k] and *k'wâng*[l] 'wide'.
gli̯ak∼*gli̯ang*[m] 'plunder, rob'.
·i̯ap∼*·i̯am*[n] 'grasp'.

We are justified in assuming that alternations of this type were the result of assimilation to verbal suffixes which had later been dropped (note the parallelism

time, yielding Thai **graam*, N. Thai **γraam* as back-loans; Tibetan has *rams*, with added *-s* as in other AT loans (*ltśags* 'iron', *zaŋs* 'copper', *phyugs* 'cattle') while Lepcha has *ryom* < **/ram*.

422 The Cantonese data are based on the writer's study of the language from a native (Canton city) informant at Yale University, 1942. These vocative terms are further set off by distinctive tonal treatment, which sometimes produces interesting contrasts, e.g. *a-ma* (high tone) 'mother!' but *a-ma* (low tone) 'grandmother!' (father's mother); *a-yi* (high tone) 'aunt!' (mother's younger sister), but *a-yi* (low tone) 'wife's sister' (descriptive term).

423 H. Maspéro, 'Sur quelques textes anciens du chinois parlé', *BEFEO* **14** (1914), 1–36.

424 B. Laufer, 'The Prefix a- in the Indo-Chinese Languages', *JRAS* (1915), 757–80.

425 Our present analysis of the tonal system (n. 494) provides excellent evidence for verbal and nominal suffixes, also sex modifiers of **-pa* and **-ma* type, yielding a general morphological picture very much like that of Tibetan.

426 M. Courant, 'Note sur l'existence, pour certains caractères chinois, de deux lectures distinguées par les finales k-ṅ, t-n, p-m', *Mém. Soc. Ling. de Paris* **12** (1903), 67–72.

a 阿媽 b 阿姨 c 阿黃 d 阿二 e 散 f 撒 g 讞 h 曰
i 云 j 菀 k 廓 l 廣 m 掠 n 擪

with verb paradigms in Bahing and many other TB languages). Boodberg[427] attempts to distinguish between an intransitive aspect in *-n* and a transitive aspect in *-t*, but his data are insufficient to establish this point. Alternation between surd and sonant stop finals is also encountered in Ar. Ch., e.g. *ni̯ôk*[a] and *sni̯ôg*[b] 'ashamed' (see above); *·âk* 'bad, evil' and *·âg* 'hate', both written;[c] *gʿộk*[d] 'learn' and *gʿộg*[e] 'teach'. The last example is most suggestive, allowing us to postulate the existence of a causative suffix (*-x*): **gʿộk-x > *gʿộg-x > gʿộg* (*k > g* in intervocalic position). A nominalizing suffix of similar type can be postulated for the following:

{*tʿwât ~ dʿwât*[f] 'peel off, take off (as clothes)'.
tʿwâd[g] 'exuviae of insects or reptiles'.

{*kiet*[h] 'to tie, knot'.
kied[i] 'hair-knot, chignon'.

{*d̂ʿi̯ək > dźʿi̯ək*[j] 'eat'.
dzi̯əg[k] 'food; feed'.

{*nəp*[l] 'bring in'.
nwəb[m] 'interior'; cf. *gʿəp*[n] and *gʿwəb*[o] 'join'; *təp*[p] and *twəb*[q] 'answer'.

Alternations in final consonants indicate that Chinese originally possessed suffixes, yet do not supply evidence for suffixes in Ar. Ch. itself. It is undoubtedly significant that in a few roots Chinese does have the 'added elements' *-n* or *-t*, apparently related to the widespread dental suffixes of Tibeto-Burman:

kʿiwən[r] 'dog'; TB **kwiy*.
χiwet[s] 'blood'; TB **s-hwiy*.
ńi̯ĕt[t] 'sun, day'; TB **niy*.
tsʿi̯ĕt[u] 'varnish'; TB **tsiy* 'juice, paint'.[428]

427 P. A. Boodberg, *Notes on Chinese Morphology and Syntax*; III: *The Morphology of Final -n and -t*, Berkeley, 1934.

428 A 'collective' suffixed **-n* must be recognized for Chinese (Benedict, 1968), directly related to that found in TB (n. 284). This suffix must be set up morphophonemically as */n/*, with **-a/n* yielding *-i̯ĕn ~ -ien* (root final **-a* treated as a short medial *a* before dental final; n. 488), as distinguished from the nominalizing suffix */·n/*, with **-a/·n* yielding *-ân* (root final **-a* preserved as long medial *a·*, yielding the anticipated vowel *â* before dental final; n. 488). In the single most interesting example of this suffix, however, there is unmistakable evidence that Chinese vacillated (perhaps dialectically) between these two morphophonemic processes; cf. *tʿien*[v] (A) and *χien*[w] (A) (not in *GSR*) 'heaven' (an oft-cited doublet), from **khien* (n. 464), from **kha/n* 'the heavens'; cf. T *mkha* 'heaven, the heavens' (cf. T *nam-mkha* 'heaven, sky', Magari *nam-khan* 'sun'); also the complex doublet *gʿi̯an/gʿi̯än*[x] 'heaven, heavenly', from **gen* (n. 481) < **ga/n*, showing voicing of the initial (after prefix) and intermediate palatalization of the vowel; also read *kân*,

a 忸　b 羞　c 惡　d 學　e 斆　f 脫　g 蛻　h 結　i 髻
j 食　k 食　l 納　m 內　n 合　o 會　p 荅　q 對　r 犬
s 血　t 日　u 漆　v 天　w 祆　x 乾

The most significant occurrence of suffixed *-n*, however, is in *kân*[a] 'liver' < (prefix) + **ka-n*, TB **ka* 'bitter', the root form being represented by *kʿo*[b] 'bitter' (with regular **-a* > *-o* shift after velar initial). The unaspirated initial of *kân* indicates that the word was originally prefixed (see below). The construction as a whole thus closely parallels TB **m-sin* 'liver' from an old root **sin* 'sour', as well as Bodo-Garo **b-ka* 'liver' from TB **ka* 'bitter' (see §27). Suffixed *-n*

from **ka/·n* (this character then applied to the homophone *kân* 'dry'; n. 444). The 'collective' suffixed **-n* has been noted in several Chinese forms (two with direct TB comparisons), and it is suspected that many others remain undiscovered; cf. *śi̯ĕn*[c] 'body', TB **śa* 'flesh' (K *śan*); *mi̯ĕn* ~ *mi̯ən/mi̯ĕn*[d] 'people', TB **r-mi*(*y*) 'man (homo)'; *tsi̯wən/tsiuĕn* ~ *tsʿi̯wən/tsʿi̯uĕn*[e] 'hare', TB **yəw* 'rat, rabbit' (B *yun* 'rabbit'); *dzʿwən/dzʿuən*[f] 'grass, herb', T *rtswa* 'grass' (n. 455). Alternation between suffixed and unsuffixed forms is reflected in the following pair: *bʿi̯ən/bʿi̯ĕn* ~ *bʿi̯ər/bʿyi*[g] 'female of animals', TB **pwi*(*y*) 'female' (see n. 463 for loss of medial **w*); *śi̯wər/św*i[h] 'water', *t'ʿi̯wən/tśʿi̯wän*[i] (irreg. for *tśʿi̯uĕn*) 'stream, river', TB **twəy* (see n. 452 for initials); cf. also *kʿiwən/kʿiwɛn*[j] < **kʿ*(*i*)*u-n* and *ku/kə̯u*[k] (both tone B) 'dog', TB **kwəy* (both forms show the **kwəy* > **ku* shift; the latter with unaspirated initial was prefixed); *ŋâ*[l] (tone A) 'domestic goose', *ŋan*[m] (tone C) < **ŋâ-n* (n. 488) 'wild goose' (= 'geese in flocks'), B *ŋàn* 'goose' with a similar suffixed *-n* (n. 284). Chinese also has two forms suggesting the function of a 'dual' (cf. K *-phan* 'palm, sole'), viz. *śi̯ôg/śi̯əu*[n] 'hand', *tsʿwən/tsʿuən*[o] 'thumb' (but used for 'hand' in graphs), Karen *tsü* 'hand/arm; *d'ʿi̯wən/dźʿi̯uĕn*[p] 'lips', T *mtśhu*, *id.* The appearance of suffixed **-n* in kinship terms in TB is paralleled in Chinese; cf. *swən/suən*[q] 'grandchild'; TB **śu*(*w*), *id.*: K *śu*, Mikir, Meithei, Anu (S. Kuki) *su*, Bodo *sou*, Dimasa *su*; *kwən/kuən* ~ **kʿwən/kʿuən*[r] (based on Mand. *kʿun*) 'older brother, descendant'; ST **kəw* ~ **gəw* 'maternal uncle' (B *-kui* 'older brother'); *tsʿi̯ĕn*[s] 'relatives', from **tsa-n*, ultimately from ST **tsa* 'child'; cf. the exactly parallel form in Tibetan (n. 284). In two instances the lack of final *-n* in Chinese indicates that the TB root is an old suffixed form; cf. *kwo/kuo*[t] 'net', from **kwa*; TB **kwan* ~ **gwan* 'casting net'; ST **kwa* ~ **gwa*; *tsâ*[u] 'left (hand)'; T *g-yon-pa*, *id.*, with suffixed *-n*, as shown also by T *g-yo* ~ *yo* 'craft, cunning, deceit' (cf. *sinister*); ST **yâ* (see n. 448 for the initial). As indicated by the text examples, Chinese appears to have *-t* as well as *-n* in this nominal suffix role, possibly conditioned by the high front vowel (add 'mud' from n. 474); it is also possible that this final *-t* represents a glottalization after the high front vowel, comparable to final *-g* after the vowel **a* (n. 487); cf. *ńi̯ĕt/ńźi̯ĕt*[v] 'sun/day'; TB **nəy*, but B *ne* 'sun', *né* 'day', the latter with 'creaky voice' (glottalization), probably from **a-nəy* = *ʔa-nəy*; Chinese has an apparent doublet here with suffixed *-n*, viz. *nien*[w] 'sunlight'. Two kinship terms, however, appear to have suffixed *-t* paralleling the Tibetan usage (n. 284); cf. *dʿiet* ~ *dʿi̯ĕt/d'ʿi̯ĕt*[x] 'nephew/niece'; TB **b-ləy* 'grandchild; nephew/niece' (see n. 458 for the initial); *t'ʿi̯wət/tśʿi̯uĕt*[y] 'nephew' (character borrowed in this meaning, which is not in *GSR*, but cited in *Erh ya*; see discussion in Benedict, 1942, where these terms are erroneously interpreted as forming a doublet); TB **tu* ~ **du* 'nephew'.

[a] 肝 [b] 苦 [c] 身 [d] 民 [e] 毚 [f] 荐 [g] 牝 [h] 水 [i] 川
[j] 犬 [k] 狗 [l] 鵝 [m] 鴈 [n] 手 [o] 寸 [p] 脣 [q] 孫 [r] 昆
[s] 親 [t] 罛 [u] 左 [v] 日 [w] 晛 [x] 姪 [y] 出

further appears in *nân*[a] 'difficulty, suffering', to be connected with TB **na* 'ill'; cf. also *tsʿân*[b] 'eat; food, meal', TB **dza*.[429]

The TB morphological alternation between initial surd and sonant stops (see §29) cannot be established for Chinese.[430] The surd vs. sonant alternation does occur in Ar. Ch., often with change in meaning, but no consistent pattern can be recognized. Cf. the following:

tʿwât ~ *dʿwât*[c] 'peel off, take off'.

təng[d] 'rise, ascend', *dʿəng*[e] 'mount, rise'.

429 The verbal suffix **-n* probably plays a much larger role in Chinese than hitherto suspected, although only rare correspondences with this element in TB have been uncovered; cf. *kwân*[f] (A) 'cap'; (C) 'put on cap'; TB **gwa-n* ~ **kwa-n* 'wear; dress'; Karen **kwan* 'put on (clothes)'; cf. also *tân*[g] 'red, vermilion; (KD) cinnabar' (='the red substance') and *tsi̯ĕn*,[h] also *tsʿiən/tsʿien*[i] 'red', from **ta-n* ~ *tya-n*; TB **tya-n*: B *tya* ~ *ta* 'very red, flaming red' (intensive), Tiddim Chin *tšhan* < **th(y)an* 'red'; *twən/tuən*[j] 'solid, thick; lie thick on', *ti̯wən/tʿi̯uĕn* ~ *dʿwən/dʿuən*[k] 'thick (*sc.* darkness)'; TB **tow* ~ **dow* 'thick' (but Chepang *dun*); *χi̯wən/χi̯uən*[l] 'to smoke' (intr.); TB **kəw* 'smoke' (but Sunwar *kun*, Newari *kɨn*). In other roots, Chinese suffixed *-n* has no parallel elsewhere or corresponds to suffixed *-t*; cf. *nan/ńan*[m] 'blush'; Karen (Taungthu) *ńa* 'red'; *dʿwən/dʿuən*[n] 'accumulate; bring together (soldiers as a garrison)', also *dʿwən/dʿuən*[o] 'tie together, envelop'; TB **du-t*: T *ʼdu-ba* 'assemble, meet, join', *sdud-pa* 'put together, join, unite', K *tut* 'to be joined, bound or tied together'. Suffixed *-t* appears to be much less common with verbal roots but there is one excellent correspondence with the same element in TB, with Karen showing suffixed *-n*, viz. *gʿi̯wət/gʿi̯uət*[p] 'dig out (earth)', also *kʿwət/kʿuət*[q] 'dig in the ground; underground'; TB **r-go-t* ~ **r-ko-t* (K *ləgot* ~ *ləkhot*, also *śəgot*, 'scoop up'); Karen **kho-n* 'dig' (n. 368); cf. also 'laugh' (n. 458) and perhaps also *dzʿi̯ət/dzʿi̯ĕt*[r] 'sickness, pain'; TB **tsa* 'hot; pain'. ST suffixed **-s* is probably represented by *-t* in Chinese (paralleling ST final **-s* > *-t*); cf. *si̯ĕt*[s] 'all, completely; (AD) thoroughly know, perfectly understand' (probably the more basic meaning; graph has 'heart' as signific); TB **syey* 'know' (T *śes-pa*).

430 The following root also shows an inconsistent pattern contrasting with that found in TB: *gʿi̯uk/gʿi̯wok*[t] 'compressed, bent, curved (body); curl, twist (hair)', *gʿi̯uk/gʿi̯wok*[u] 'bend the body', *kʿi̯uk/kʿi̯wok*[v] 'bend, bent; crooked, unjust'; TB **m-ku·k* 'angle; knee'; cf. also *ki̯ôk/ki̯uk*[w] 'bow, bend' and *ki̯ôk/ki̯uk*[x] 'convex side of river bend' (both characters loans in these senses); TB **guk* ~ **kuk* 'bend; crooked' (see n. 479 for the vocalic length distinction). There is, however, one possible example of direct correspondence, both phonologically and morphologically, within the same ST etymon; cf. *glâk/lâk*[y] 'to fear' (not in *GSR* in this meaning), *kʿlâk/kʿâk*[z] 'respect, reverent' = 'to inspire fear' (cf. *ki̯ĕŋ/ki̯ɒŋ*[a] 'reverent, respectful; careful', *ki̯ĕŋ/ki̯ɒŋ*[b] 'to be afraid; attentive; scare'), perhaps also *χi̯ăk/χi̯ɒk*[c] 'fear', from **khrăk* (n. 472); TB **grâk* ~ **krâk* 'fear; frighten'; cf. also Karen **xa* < **khra*[*k*] 'scare, frighten with outcries, use violent language in order to terrify'.

a 難　b 餐　c 脫　d 登　e 騰　f 冠　g 丹　h 經　i 綪
j 敦　k 窀　l 焄　m 赧　n 屯　o 純　p 掘　q 堀　r 疾
s 悉　t 局　u 跼　v 曲　w 鞠　x 鞫　y 雒　z 恪　a 敬
b 驚　c 覤

tsʿi̯ĕng[a] 'clear, pure, bright', *dzʿi̯ĕng*[b] 'clean, cleanse', *dzʿi̯ĕng*[c] 'quiet, pure'.
tʿâd[d] 'great, excessive', *dʿâd*[e] 'great'.
tʿiog[f] 'sell grain', *dʿiok*[g] 'buy grain' (note the alternation in finals).
kŏg[h] 'teach, instruct', *gʿŏg*[i] 'imitate, follow'.
tsi̯əg[j] 'son', *dzʿi̯əg*[k] 'beget'.
kian[l] 'see', *gʿian*[m] 'appear, be visible'. Here the sonant form is intransitive, the surd transitive, as in Tibeto-Burman; cf. *gʿŏg* 'imitate' and *dʿiok* 'buy grain', above.[431]

§41. Chinese pronouns

Chinese parallels Karen in having an exact cognate for TB **ŋa* 'I', viz. *ngo*[n] (with the regular *-*a* > -*o* shift after velar initial), but *ni̯o*[o] (cf. Karen *na*) corresponding to TB **naŋ* 'thou'.[432] As pointed out by Karlgren,[433] a type of pronominal inflection appears in certain early texts (Lun Yü, Mencius, Tso Chuan):

	1st person	2nd person
Subject position	*ngo*[p]	*ni̯o*[q]
Object position	*ngâ*[r]	*ni̯a*[s]

Both *ngâ* and *ni̯a* commonly appear also in subject (incl. genitive) position, whereas *ngo* and *ni̯o* are almost entirely restricted to this position, i.e. *ngâ* and *ni̯a* tend to usurp the nominative roles of *ngo* and *ni̯o* (cf. French *moi*, English *me*). In the older Shu Ching text, however, this distinction is not observed, and *di̯o*[t] or *di̯o*[u] is the dominant 1st person pronoun, with *ngo* entirely lacking and *ngâ* gradually

431 Karlgren's 'Word Families in Chinese' (*BMFEA* 5, 1934) comprises a systematic review of initial, final, and vocalic alternations. The discussion, however, is of limited value, inasmuch as no account is taken of the TB phenomena.

432 The **na* form for 'thou', found also in Nung, appears to be an unstressed form of ST **naŋ* ~ **na·ŋ* ~ **nəŋ*. TB has **naŋ* but a doublet **na·ŋ* can be reconstructed on the basis of Ch. *ńi̯ôŋ*/*ńźi̯uŋ*[v] (n. 488); cf. also *nəg*/*nậi* ~ **ńi̯əŋ*/*ńźi̯əŋ*[w] 'thou', the latter set up on the basis of the general use of the graph as phonetic in -*i̯əŋ* forms, including *ńi̯əŋ*/*ńźi̯əŋ*[x] 'repeat, as before; again and again; (AD) follow, imitate', TB *(*s*-)*naŋ* 'follow', from ST *(*s*-)*nəŋ*.

433 'Le proto-chinois, langue flexionelle', *JA* (1920), 205–32.

a 清 b 淨 c 靜 d 泰 e 大 f 糶 g 糴 h 教 i 效
j 子 k 字 l 見 m 現 n 吾 o 汝 p 吾 q 汝 r 我
s 爾 t 予 u 余 v 戎 w 乃 x 仍

increasing in usage. In the still earlier Shih Ching text, moreover, *ngâ* is the dominant form (exclusively used in songs from some districts), with *di̯o* as secondary form. Karlgren concludes that these differences reflect dialectical divergences, which are closely related to styles, and that the dialect of Lu,[a] reflected especially in the Lun Yü, retained a true inflection of the pronoun as an archaic feature. The fact that *ngo* rather than *ngâ* is the phonetically regular representative of TB **ŋa* strengthens the view that the Lu forms are archaic, yet the Tibeto-Burman and Karen evidence precludes the possibility of regarding pronominal inflection as an inherited ST trait. We must hold, rather, that Chinese, like some TB languages, has secondarily developed distinctions in pronominal forms.

§42. Chinese numerals

The Chinese numeral system, like that of Tibeto-Burman and Karen, is decimal. The numerals from '2' to '6', and '9' correspond to general Tibeto-Karen roots, and a Chinese-Kanauri correspondence has been found for '1'. It will be noted that here, as in other lexical fields, Chinese departs more widely from Tibeto-Burman than does Karen.[434, 435]

434 The Tibeto-Burman and Chinese numerals have attracted the attention of a number of writers, including T. C. Hodson, 'Note on the Numerical Systems of the Tibeto-Burman Dialects', *JRAS* (1913), 315–36; J. Przyluski and G. H. Luce, 'The Number "A Hundred" in Sino-Tibetan', *BSOS* **6** (1931), 667–8; S. N. Wolfenden, 'Concerning the Origins of Tibetan *brgi̯ad* and Chinese *pwat*[b] "eight"', *TP* **34** (1939), 165–73; Wang Ching-ju,[c] 'Chung t'ai tsang mien shu-ch'ieh-tzŭ chi jên-ch'êng tai-ming-tz'ŭ yü yüan shih ts'ai'[d] ('Comparative Study of the Numerals and Personal Pronouns in Chinese, Thai, Tibetan, and Burmese'), *CYYY* **3** (1931), 49–92. Wolfenden rightly keeps T *brgyad* and Ch. *pwat*[b] '8' apart, but fails to see that the seemingly discrepant TB forms for '8' can be derived from a single root (**b-r-gyat*). Wang, making no use of scientific methodology, arrives at roots such as **gret* '1', **gruk* '6', **bgrat* '8', and **(g)kiap* '10', while Przyluski and Luce surpass even these with **pargyak* '100', a kind of 'synthesis' of T *brgya* and Ch. *păk*.[e] The seeming parallelism presented by T *brgyad* and Ch. *pwat* '8', T *brgya* (< **r-gya*) and Ch. *păk* '100' has proved irresistible to most writers on the subject of ST numerals.

435 It now appears that all the Ch. numerals, including '100', are cognate with the TB set. Three of the numerals had substituted **b-* prefix (with unvoicing), on the basis of evidence from ancient loans in Thai and the related Ong-Be (Hainan island) language as well as from Chinese itself, paralleling a trend found also in

[a] 魯 [b] 八 [c] 王靜如 [d] 中台藏緬數目字及人稱代名詞語源試探 [e] 百

·i̯ĕt[a] '1'; cf. Kanauri *id.*
ńi̯ər > ńźi[b] '2'; TB *g-nis.
səm[c] '3'; TB *g-sum.
si̯əd > si[d] '4'; TB *b-liy.
ngo[e] '5'; TB *l-ŋa ~ *b-ŋa.
li̯ôk > li̯uk[f] '6'; TB *d-ruk.
ki̯ŭg > ki̯əu[g] '9'; TB *d-kuw.

The phonetic shifts illustrated in the above comparisons are regular for the most part (see below). Ar. Ch. *si̯əd* '4' for TB *b-liy, however, requires explanation, since initial *l- should yield Ar. Ch. *l-*, while *bl- should yield Ar. Ch. *bl-* (T *bźi* < *b-liy is a late development quite unrelated to the Chinese phenomenon in question). In view of the known tendency for one numeral to be 'contaminated' by another in Tibeto-Burman, e.g. K *məsum* '3' < *g-sum through the influence exerted by *məli* '4' < *b-liy and *məŋa* '5' < *b-ŋa (see § **16**), we must suppose that Ar. Ch. *si̯əd* '4' has been influenced by *səm* '3', with *s-* replacing initial *l-.[436]

TB; cf. *ŋo/ŋuo*[h] '5', from *ŋa (text), but Thai has *ha < *hŋa (Ong-Be *ŋa*), borrowed from a pre-Ar. Ch. form *hŋa < *ph(-)ŋa < *b-ŋa; TB *l-ŋa ~ *b-ŋa; *b-li̯ôk/li̯uk[i] '6' (cf. n. 474), reconstructed on basis of use of graph as phonetic in *mli̯ôk* (or *m-li̯ôk)/*mi̯uk*[j] 'accord', confirmed by the doublet *phrok reflected in Thai *hrok (but Tho has irreg. *sok*), Ong-Be *sok* < *phrok (a regular shift, e.g. Ong-be *sok* < *sak 'vegetable', Thai *phrak); TB *d-ruk; *pwăt*[k] '8', from *b-ryăt (n. 148) < *b-ryât (n. 488); TB *(b-)g-ryat, with simplification to *bwăt rather than *byăt, the latter also existing as a doublet which served as the basis for the early Min-chia (AT stock) loan: *pi̯at*, probably also Thai and Kam-Sui *peet (= *pe·t*), Ong-be *bɛt* = *pe·t*. For further details on these early loans from the Ch. numeral system, see Benedict, 1967bis; all these languages have *saam '3', agreeing with the irregular Anc. Ch. form *sâm* rather than with the regular Ar. Ch. form *səm*, TB *g-sum. The seemingly unrelated *ts'i̯ĕt*[l] '7' can be derived from ST *s-nis (n. 471). Finally, *păk/pɒk*[m] '100' can be analyzed as the product of a metathesized form: *b-grya, from *b-r-gya; TB *r-gya (T *brgya*), with typical unvoicing of the prefix, then vocalization of this element: *păk(-rya) < *băgrya; cf. T *brgyad* '8', metathesized from TB *(b-)g-ryat (n. 148); also, for '10' see n. 464.

436 This numeral can be derived from ST (and TB) *b-ləy via *b-źəy or *b-zəy (cf. T *bźi*) and *p-səy (regular unvoicing of the prefix, whence unvoicing of the initial through assimilation); there was a variant in final *-t* (the Tsi-yün mentions a dialectical reading *si̯ət* in Shensi), perhaps representing an old suffix (cf. Karen *lwi-t '4').

a 一　b 二　c 三　d 四　e 五　f 六　g 九　h 五　i 六　j 睦
k 八　l 七　m 白

§43. Chinese phonology (history)

The richly varied phonological system of Archaic Chinese offers many difficulties of comparison with the relatively simple scheme found in Tibeto-Burman.[437] The small number of roots which the two stocks have in common further contributes to this initial difficulty. Many of the problems have already been set forth in the few studies that have appeared in this field, notably Simon's comparison of Chinese with Tibetan[438] and Shafer's study of Sino-Tibetan vocalism (*JAOS* **60**, 1940; *JAOS* **61**, 1941). Simon's reconstruction of Tibetan, made almost wholly without reference to other TB languages, is faulty at many points, and his Archaic Chinese reconstitutions are less reliable than those of Karlgren. Shafer, on the other hand, has made valid TB reconstructions for the most part, but has compared these with Ancient Chinese rather than Archaic Chinese forms. Both writers make extensive use of questionable comparative material, including loan-words.[439] The present study is the first to attempt a comparison of properly reconstructed TB roots with Archaic Chinese forms.

437 Karlgren's phonetic notation has been adopted for this discussion of Archaic Chinese with a view to facilitating reference to the *Grammata Serica*. The following points should be noted: *ng* is the velar nasal *ŋ*; *j* is the palatal semivowel *y*; · is the glottal stop ʔ; *t̂* and *d̂* are palatal stops; *ṣ*, *tṣ*, and *dẓ* are supradental (cerebral); *â* is close (as opposed to open) *a*, and *ô* is close *o*; short vowels are indicated either by a micron or a subscribed dot, e.g. *ă* is short *a*, *ộ* is short *ô*; *å* is the low-back vowel ɔ; *ɛ* is the low-front vowel æ.

438 W. Simon, 'Tibetisch-Chinesische Wortgleichungen: ein Versuch', *MSOS* **32** (1929), 157–228. For a thoroughgoing critique of this study, see B. Karlgren, 'Tibetan and Chinese', *TP* **28** (1931), 25–70.

439 Many instances of this type can be cited from Shafer's paper, e.g. *d̂ʿa*[a] 'tea' and T *dźa*; *ṣi*[b] 'lion' and B *khraŋ-sé*; *dʿung*[c] 'copper' and T *doŋtse* (also *doŋtshe*) 'coin' (of Indic origin); *mi̯ŏu*[d] and T *mig-gi miu* 'pupil (of eye)', the latter to be analyzed (as in Jäschke) 'little man of the eye', with *miu* as diminutive of *mi* 'man', paralleling *rdeu* 'little stone' < *rdo* (cf. Ch. *dʿung*[e] 'pupil' and *dʿung*[f] 'boy').

[a] 茶　[b] 獅　[c] 銅　[d] 眸　[e] 瞳　[f] 僮

§44. Chinese consonants (initials, finals)

The consonants of Archaic Chinese are as follows:[440]

Laryngeal:	· (glottal stop)										
Velar:	*k*	*k*ʿ	*g*	*g*ʿ	*ng*	*χ*					
Palatal:	*t̂*	*t̂*ʿ	*d̂*	*d̂*ʿ	*ń*	[*y*]	*ś*				
Dental:	*t*	*t*ʿ	*d*	*d*ʿ	*n*	*l*	*s*	*z*	*ts*	*ts*ʿ	*dz*	*dz*ʿ
Cerebral:						[*r*]	*ṣ*		*tṣ*	*tṣ*ʿ		*dẓ*ʿ
Labial:	*p*	*p*ʿ	[*b*]	*b*ʿ	*m*	[*w*]					

Glottal stop occurs before (otherwise) initial vowels, as in Burmese and probably other TB languages. The phoneme *χ* can be derived from ST **h*-, inasmuch as Ar. Ch. lacks the free aspiration element. Only one cross-check with TB **h*- has been found, however, viz. *χiwet*[a] 'blood', TB **s-hwiy* (the TB prefix does not appear in Chinese).[441] The seeming lack of the palatal semivowel *j* can

440 The writer (Benedict, 1948) has made a systematic comparison of the TB and Ar. Ch. consonantal systems, pointing out that the main discrepancies in the two systems lie in the presence in Ar. Ch. of a second series of voiced stops and affricate (*b* is perhaps lacking except in initial clusters) and of an incomplete cerebral (retroflex) series; the suggested solutions to these two problems still appear to be sound (nn. 446 and 457). The recognition of a separate palatal series for TB (n. 122) brings this language stock into general agreement with Ar. Ch.

441 This still remains our only substantial comparison for TB **h*- = Ar. Ch. *χ*- (ST **h*-); the TB root is now (n. 169) reconstructed **s-hywəy* 'blood', with **hyw*- showing unit-for-unit correspondence with Ch. *χiw*- (for the suffixed -*t* see n. 428; for the 'lost' prefixed *s*- see n. 419). Another source for Ar. Ch. initial *χ*- is **khy*-, either from palatalized (by high vowel) **kh*- or from a **khl*- or **khr*- cluster (n. 472); cf. *χi̯wən*/*χi̯uən*[b] 'to smoke' (intr.), TB **kəw* 'smoke' (see n. 429 for suffixed -*n*); *g*ʿ*i̯ŭg*/*g*ʿ*i̯əu*[c] (C) 'owl' (only KD in this meaning; signific is horned owl), also *χi̯ôg*/*χiəu*[d] (A) 'owl' and *kiog*/*kieu*[e] (A) 'kind of bird (owl?)', TB **gu* ~ **ku* 'owl' (add Gyarung *pra-khu* 'owl' to forms cited in text); the Ch. forms are, respectively, from **gəw*, **khəw* (unprefixed) and **kow* (prefixed), all with vowel gradation; cf. also Anc. Ch. *xə̥u*[f] 'nutmeg, cardamon' (not in *GSR*) but all dialects point to Anc. Ch. **k*ʿ*ə̥u* (Karlgren); note that the phonetic remained unpalatalized: *k*ʿ*u*/*k*ʿ*əu*[g] 'rob', TB **r-kəw* 'steal'; cf. also 'heaven' (n. 464). Chinese has some interchange of velar stop with · (= ʔ) in several phonetic series, and there is one ST comparison; cf. ·*ien*[h] 'smoke', from *ʔi·n* < **ʔu·n* (n. 429), a complex doublet of the verbal form cited above; Nungish (Rawang) *məö* shows similar irregular loss of the velar stop, apparently via **m-ʔö* < **m-k*(*h*)*əw*, and it is possible that the Chinese doublet ·*ien* similarly reflects an earlier prefix or preposed element (ST **mey* 'fire').

a 血 b 熏 c 舊 d 鵂 e 梟 f 蔻 g 寇 h 烟

be attributed to Karlgren's non-phonemic notation; actually, as shown below, Ar. Ch. had the semivowels *j* and *w* as distinct from the vowels *i* and *u*. The absence of *ź* (palatal) as well as *ẓ* (cerebral) is noteworthy. Anc. Ch. had *ź*, but Karlgren has shown this to be the end-product of a development *d̂* > *dź* > *ź*. In the absence of *ẓ*, the affricate *dẓ* must be considered a unit phoneme rather than *d* + *ẓ*, and similarly (for the sake of pattern congruity) the other affricates. The aspirated stop consonants also are better regarded as unit phonemes than as stop + *χ* clusters. The number of consonant phonemes thus attained (35) is exceptionally high – over twice the number (16) reconstructed for Tibeto-Burman.

The surd, aspirated surd, and aspirated sonant stops occur freely in initial position, while only the unaspirated surd and sonant stops (excluding palatals) are found in final position. The final sonant stops, differing from anything found in Tibeto-Burman (as reconstructed), are best handled in connection with the vocalism of Archaic Chinese (see below). The final surd stops and nasals regularly correspond to those in Tibeto-Burman, but in a few roots an assimilative shift to dental after the high-front vowel **i* can be observed (cf. the Burmese and Lushei treatment of finals discussed in §7):[442]

tsiet[a] 'knot, joint'; TB **tsik*.
nien[b] 'harvest, year'; TB **niŋ*.
si̯ĕn[c] 'firewood'; TB **siŋ* 'tree, wood'.

The contrast between aspirated and unaspirated surd stops is to be explained on the basis already employed (§7) for Tibetan and other TB languages, viz., aspiration appears after unprefixed stops, but is lacking after stops originally affected by prefixes. It may have been that, as in Tibetan, not all prefixes exercised this effect on stops, but for this we have no good evidence. The contrast between the two types of initials is best shown in the example cited above, viz. *k'o*[d] 'bitter', TB **ka* (*kha* in most TB languages), but *kân*[e] 'liver', from a prefixed root such as **m-ka-n* or **b-ka-n*; cf. also *ki̯ŭg*[f] '9', TB **d-kuw*. The fact that very few prefixed roots have cognates in Ar. Ch. makes it difficult to establish this generalization, yet no other theory offers so many advantages. Doublets such as *pi̯ôk*[g]

442 Add **śri̯ɛt/ṣi̯ɛt*[h] 'louse', TB **śrik* (n. 457); also 'fear' (n. 466). The conditioning factors governing this shift have not been uncovered. A doublet form **r-miŋ* ~ **r-min* 'name; command' can be set up for ST itself: TB **r-miŋ* 'name', **min* 'command' (Burmese); Karen **men* < **min* 'name'; Ch. **mli̯ĕŋ* ~ **mli̯ĕn* 'name; command' (from **r-miŋ* ~ **r-min* (n. 419). A similar shift after medial **y* apparently has occurred in one root, viz. *d''i̯at/dź'iät* < **g'li̯at*[i] 'tongue', a doublet of *g'i̯ak* < **g'li̯ak*,[j] *id.* (n. 419), TB **(m-)lyak* ~ **(s-)lyak* 'lick; tongue'; Magari has *let* 'tongue' while Kachin has *śiŋlet* ~ *śiŋlep*, Maran dial. *śiŋriat*, *id.*, from this root, showing parallel shift.

[a] 節 [b] 年 [c] 薪 [d] 苦 [e] 肝 [f] 九 [g] 腹 [h] 蝨 [i] 舌 [j] 臄

'belly', *pʻi̯ôk* (also *bʻi̯ôk*)[a] 'cave' (TB **pu·k*), can readily be interpreted in terms of lost prefixes, pronominal or other, e.g. **m-pu·k* > *pi̯ôk*, **pu·k* > *pʻi̯ôk*. Similarly, a lost prefix must be postulated for forms such as *ti̯ək*[b] 'weave', TB **tak*. Actually, the problem of initial aspiration in Chinese is no greater than in many TB languages, in which prefixes play a similar dominant role.

The initial sonant stops of Tibeto-Burman are normally represented by aspirated sonants in Ar. Ch., to judge from the few good comparisons that can be made here:

gʻwo[c] 'fox'; TB **gwa*.

gʻog[d] 'call, cry out'; TB **gaw*.

gʻəm[e] 'hold in the mouth', also (tone C) 'put in the mouth'; TB **gam* (491), as represented by T *'gam-pa* 'put or throw into the mouth', Miri *gam* 'seize (with teeth, as a tiger)'.

bʻi̯ŭg[f] 'carry on the back'; TB **buw*.

dʻôk[g] 'poison, poisonous'; TB **duk* ~ **tuk*.

Ar. Ch. has surd for TB sonant stop in *pi̯əd*[h] 'give', TB **biy*[443] (but note also Kuki **pe-k*), while the inverse relationship obtains in *gʻi̯ôg*[i] 'uncle (mother's brother), father-in-law', TB **kuw*.[444] Morphology may sometimes play a role here, e.g. *gʻo*[j] 'door, opening' has perhaps been derived from an intransitive root with voiced initial (**ga*) corresponding to TB **ka* and **m-ka*.[445]

443 ST initial **b-* apparently was well maintained in Chinese in the cluster **bw-* (n. 463) but was often (perhaps usually) unvoiced elsewhere; cf. also *pi̯uk*[k] 'bat' (not in *GSR*), T **ba·k* (see n. 488 for the vocalism); *pwən/puən*[l] 'root, trunk', TB **bul* ~ **pul*: K *phun* 'tree, bush, stalk, wood', Moshang *pu·l* 'tree' (length probably secondary), G *bol* 'tree', L *bul* 'cause, beginning, the root, stump or foot (of tree), the lower end (as of stick, post, etc.)', Tiddim *bul* 'bottom, base, foot (of building)' (but this root used in compounds meaning 'tree' in Anal and other Kuki languages); *pʻi̯an/pʻi̯än*[m] 'fly about, flutter', TB **byer* 'fly'; also 'uncle/older brother' (n. 463). This parallels the surdization of prefixed **b-* in the numerals (nn. 435 and 436) and elsewhere (n. 474). Finally, ST **b* yielded (*w*)*u* after prefixed **d-* in *dʻu/dʻə̯u*[n] 'head', TB **(d-)bu*.

444 For this root Chinese also has a cognate with surd initial and suffixed *-n*, viz. *kwən/kuən* ~ **kʻwən/kʻuən*[o] 'older brother' (n. 428). Chinese also has *gʻĕg/γai*[p] 'crab', TB **d-ka·y*, but note Karen **tsγai* (a 'problem' root; see n. 323); cf. also *kân*[q] 'dry', *gʻân/γân*[r] 'drought, dry' (text); TB **kan*: K *kan* 'to be dried up (as a stream)', B *khàn*, Atsi (Burling) *kʔan* (BL **kan*) 'dry up'; also *gʻi̯ək*[s] 'ridge of house; the highest point; extreme limit, utmost', B-L **khak* 'reaching its peak; (in price) expensive' (this reconstruction by JAM), from ST **gək* ~ **kək*; also 'needle' (n. 464).

445 TB perhaps has a variant **ga* here; cf. Trung (Nungish) *saŋ ga* 'window' (= 'window-opening'), Rawang *sərim saŋ*, *id*. (*saŋ* possibly a loan from Ch. *chʻuang*).[t]

a 𥨍	b 織	c 狐	d 號	e 含	f 負	g 毒	h 畀	i 舅	j 戶
k 蝠	l 本	m 翩	n 頭	o 昆	p 蟹	q 乾	r 旱	s 極	t 窗

The unaspirated sonant stops *g* and *d* are found in initial position only before semivocalic *i̯* (=*j*), while initial *b*- is altogether lacking. Initial *gi̯*- yields *ji̯*, and *di̯*- yields *i̯*-, in Anc. Ch. Karlgren's reconstructions here are based on strong evidence from the analysis of phonetic elements in characters, and cannot successfully be attacked. Inasmuch as Ar. Ch. lacks both initial **w*- and **y*-, we might infer that these semivowels in Sino-Tibetan yielded weakly articulated voiced stops.[446] The only substantial comparisons available support this view; cf. *gi̯wo*[a] 'rain',[447] TB **r-wa*; *di̯əng*[b] 'fly', and TB **yaŋ* (No. 492), as represented by West T *bu-yaŋ* 'bumble-bee', Kanauri *yăŋ* 'fly, bee', B *yaŋ* 'fly, insect'.[448] In addition, *g*- shows interchange with the other velar initials, and *d*- with the other dental initials, hence we may infer that these initials in many instances have been derived from prefix + sonant stop clusters. Direct comparisons with TB initial **g*- or **d*-, however, cannot be cited.[449]

446 This analysis is developed in detail in Benedict, 1948, where it is pointed out that the shifts **y* > *d* and **w* > *g* occurred both in initial and final position as one aspect of a single dynamic generalization, i.e. the voiced fricatives (incl. semi-vowels) of ST received a stop element in the course of their evolution in Chinese; this 'law' serves to explain the parallel **z*- > *dz*- and *ź*- > *dʻ*- shifts (found only in initial position). Phonemically, these unaspirated stops (*d* and *g*) remained allo-phones of the phonemes /*y*/ and /*w*/, maintaining the contrast with the initial aspirated stops (*dʻ*- and *gʻ*-) but with some tendency to become transformed into the latter (n. 449).

447 Add (from Benedict, 1948) *gi̯wo/yi̯u*[c] 'proceed, go to', TB **s-wa*: Magari and Chepang *hwa* 'walk, move', Newari *wa* 'come', K *wa* 'to be in motion', B *swà* 'go', Kuki group *-*wa* (affix used with verbs of motion); cf. additional examples in n. 449.

448 This TB root has been reconstructed *(*s*-)*brəŋ* (n. 469). For ST **y*-, cf. *di̯an/i̯än*[d] (A) 'extend; continue; delay; stretch', *di̯an/i̯än*[e] (A) 'mat' (='something spread out'), *di̯an/i̯än*[f] (C) 'flow out, extend', perhaps also *di̯ĕn/i̯ĕn*[g] (C) 'draw the bow; pull, draw; extend; prolong'; TB **ya·r* ~ **yâr* 'spread, extend; sail'; Karen **ya* 'expand, hoist (sail); sail' (='something extended'), but note also Tiddim (Kuki) *zan* < **yan* 'stretch'. It is possible that ST initial **y*- yielded Ar. Ch. *di̯*- only in unprefixed roots, and that after (most or all) prefixes, this same initial yielded Ar. Ch. *zi̯*- (Benedict, 1948), with further evolution to *dz*- and even to *ts/tsʻ*-, the last with three excellent examples; cf. *zi̯ak/i̯äk*[h] 'armpit', TB *(*g*-)*yak* (text; cf. n. 108); *zi̯ăg/i̯a*[i] (C) 'night', *dzi̯ak/zi̯äk*[j] 'evening, night', TB **ya* 'night', Karen **hya* 'evening' (see n. 487 for final); *tsi̯ôg/tsi̯əu*[k] 'spirits, wine' (note phonetic is *zi̯ôg/i̯əu*,[l] defined in KD as 'wine must'; see text), TB **yu*(*w*) 'liquor'; *tsi̯wən/tsi̯uĕn* ~ *tsʻiwən/tsʻi̯uĕn*[m] 'hare' (with 'collective' -*n* suffix; see n. 428), TB **b-yəw* 'rat, rabbit' (B *yun* 'rabbit'); *tsâ*[n] 'left (hand)', T *g-yon-pa*, *id.* (with suffixed -*n*; see n. 428).

449 A direct comparison of this type is furnished by the following (Benedict, 1967bis): *gwia/jwie̯*,[o] an obsolete root for 'elephant', the graph showing a hand at the head of an elephant (recognized by P. Boodberg, *HJAS* **2**, 1937, 239–72,

[a] 雨 [b] 蠅 [c] 于 [d] 延 [e] 筵 [f] 演 [g] 引 [h] 腋 [i] 夜 [j] 夕
[k] 酒 [l] 酉 [m] 毚 [n] 左 [o] 爲

Ar. Ch. appears to be more archaic than Tibeto-Burman in possessing a series of palatal consonants distinct from the dental series.[450] Both types of consonants appear in initial position before semivocalic *i̯*, hence are phonemically as well as phonetically distinct. Palatal *ń-* corresponds to TB **n-* in *ńi̯ər*[a] '2', TB **g-nis*; *ńi̯ĕt*[b] 'sun, day', TB **niy*. It may be that original **n-* was palatalized before *i* in Ar. Ch. (cf. T *gnyis* '2', *nyi-ma* 'sun'), while Ar. Ch. dental *n-* belongs to a later level.[451] No significant comparisons have been found for *t̂*, *d̂*, or *ś*.[452]

note 68), TB **m-gwi*(*y*) 'elephant': K *gwi* ~ *məgwi*, Răwang (Nungish) *məgö* < **məgwi*, S. Kuki **m-wi*. It also seems certain, from the initial interchange shown in many phonetic series, that even an original surd stop could become first voiced in close juncture, then unaspirated; cf. the following: *di̯ər/i* (A) ~ *tʿi̯ər/tʿiei*[c] (C) 'mucus from the nose' (note the tones), TB *(*sna-*)*ti*(*y*) (A) 'nose-water' (Dhimal *hna-thi* 'snot'), ST **təy* 'water'; the aspirated (hence unprefixed) form has tone C, indicating an original suffix (n. 494). The phonetic in this series (*GSR*-551) is *di̯ər/i*[d] 'barbarian', the graph showing 'man' and 'arrow', the latter as the basic phonetic (not recognized by Karlgren), to be interpreted as a close-juncture form (e.g. 'bow' + 'arrow') of **tʿi̯ər* (TB **tal*), whence *śi̯ər/śi*[e] 'arrow' (n. 461); this series includes another close-juncture form of this type, viz. *di̯ər/i*[f] (A) 'the fat over the stomach', from *t'i̯ər/tśi*[g] (A) 'fat', TB **tsil* (n. 461). Prefixed **g-* is apparently represented by *g-* in *gi̯ŭg/ji̯ə̯u*[h] 'right (hand)', TB **g-ya* (see n. 487 for final). An aspirated voiced stop was developed in at least two roots, both from initial **w-*; cf. *gi̯um/jiuŋ* ~ *gʿium/γiuŋ*[i] (AD citation, based on irreg. Mand. *hiung*) 'bear', from **wum* < **wam* (n. 488), TB **d-wam*; *gi̯wan/ji̯wän*[j] (A) 'circle, circumference; round; return', *gi̯wan/ji̯wän*[k] (A) 'round', *gi̯wan/ji̯wän*[l] (C) 'wall round a courtyard'; also (aspirated and palatalized) *gʿiwan/γiwen*[m] (B) 'tie around, encircle', *gʿi̯wan/gʿi̯wän*[n] (B) 'enclosure for pigs' (also read *gʿi̯wăn/gʿi̯wɒn*); also (without palatalization) *gʿwan/γwan*[o] (A) 'turn round, return', *gʿwan/γwan*[p] (A) 'ring; encircle'; also (with **wa* > **u* > *wə* shift) *gʿwən/γuən*[q] (C) 'pig-sty', TB **wal* 'round, circular'. It appears that in parallel fashion ST (and TB) **hw-* yielded *k*(*w*)*-* in Chinese; cf. *kâm*[r] 'dare', perhaps by dissimilation from **kwâm* (lacking in Chinese), TB **hwam*, *id.*; Karlgren (*AD*) notes that there is a 'bear' in the graph for 'dare', and it now appears that this element was really a phonetic, pointing to an early alternate development (**wam* > **gwam*) in the root for 'bear' (above); the resemblance to Japanese *kuma*, Korean *kom* 'bear' appears to be due to convergence.

450 A palatal series has also now been recognized for TB (n. 122).

451 It must be borne in mind that only a relatively small segment of the Chinese lexical material is of ST origin, and that Chinese may have been reoriented phonemically several times before attaining what we know as the 'Archaic' stage. Our task is not so much to identify all the phonetic elements of Ar. Ch. in terms of Sino-Tibetan, as to establish the course of development of ST elements in Ar. Ch.

452 The palatal series is not prominent in TB, but there are two significant correspondences with Ch. palatals, sufficient to establish this series as a feature of ST, viz. *t'ʿi̯ăk/tśʿiäk*[s] 'red', TB **tśak*, *id.*; *śi̯ôg/śi̯ə̯u*[t] 'animal', TB **śa* 'flesh, meat, animal' (see n. 487 for final), also the forms with 'collective' *-n* suffix (n. 428):

a 二 b 日 c 洟 d 夷 e 矢 f 胰 g 脂 h 右 i 熊 j 員
k 圓 l 院 m 繯 n 圈 o 還 p 環 q 圂 r 敢 s 赤 t 獸

The dental sibilants and affricates probably correspond to TB **s*, **z*, **ts*, and **dz*, although no reliable comparisons have been found for the voiced members of this group.[453] Initial **s*- is particularly well represented, as in *səm*[a] '3', TB **g-sum*. Final *-*s*, a rare element even in Tibeto-Burman, has perhaps undergone rhotacism in Ar. Ch., as suggested by Karlgren (*BMFEA* 5, 1934); cf. *ńi̯ər*[b] '2', TB **g-nis*.[454] TB initial **ts*- is represented by *ts*- or *ts'*- in *tsiet*[c] 'knot, joint', TB **tsik*; *ts'i̯ĕt*[d] 'varnish', TB **tsiy*; *ts'ung*[e] 'onion', T *btsoŋ*, but simply by *s*- in *sam*[f] 'hair', TB **tsam*; cf. also *dz'â*[g] 'salt, salty', TB **tsa*.[455] Initial *z*-, like initial *śi̯ĕn*[h] 'body', K *śan* 'flesh, meat, deer'. The voiced stop in this series is represented only by *d'i̯wən/dź'i̯uĕn*[i] 'lips' (with -*n* suffix), T *mtśhu*, *id*. ST (and TB) initial **ś*- before the high back vowel *u* yielded Ch. *s*- in *swən/suən*[j] 'grandchild' (with -*n* suffix; n. 428), TB **śu(w)*, *id*.; perhaps also ST **tś*- > Ch. *ts*- before *u* (n. 455). The rare initial clusters of dental stop or affricate + *y* in ST yielded palatal stop in Chinese; cf. **t'i̯ăk/tśi̯äk*[k] 'single, one', ST **tyak* (n. 271); *t'i̯u/tśi̯u*[l] 'red', ST **tya* (n. 487); *t'i̯o/tśi̯wo*[m] 'boil, cook', TB **tsyow*. In the single comparison for the voiced stop in this series, however, Ar. Ch. has the dental + *y* (*i̯*) cluster, viz. *d'i̯ôŋ/d'i̯uŋ*[n] 'insect', Bodo-Garo **dyuŋ* (n. 109). Finally, there is substantial evidence in Chinese for the evolution of dental affricates and stops to palatal stops and spirants, especially before the high vowels *i* and *u* and/or after an aspirated (= non-prefixed) initial; cf. the following: *t'i̯ər/tśi*[o] 'fat', TB **tsil*; *d'i̯ək/dź'i̯ək*[p] 'eat', TB **dza* (but dental preserved in *dzi̯əg/zi*[q] 'food, give food to' (probably from a prefixed form); *t'i̯wət/tś'i̯uĕt*[r] 'nephew' (with suffixed -*t*; n. 428), TB **tu* ~ **du*; *śi̯wər/świ*[s] 'water', also (with suffixed -*n*) *t'i̯wən/tś'i̯wän*[t] (irreg. for *tś'i̯uĕn*) 'stream, river', TB **twəy* 'water'; *śi̯ər/śi*[u] 'arrow', TB **tal*: Mikir *thal* (Old) > *thai* (Modern) 'arrow', L *thal* 'arrow, dart', but Tiddim *thal* 'bow', perhaps also Deori Chutiya (B-G group) *thal* 'bough' (Benedict, 1940, No. 72); also (with initial alternation) *təŋ*[v] 'rise', *t'i̯əŋ/tś'i̯əŋ*[w] 'lift', TB **(s-)təŋ* (n. 482). In one root, however, Chinese appears to have dental affricate corresponding to palatal in TB; cf. *tsi̯ap/tsi̯äp*[x] 'connect, come in contact; close to', TB **tśap* 'join, connect; adhere' (G *tśap-tśap* 'adjacent'), possibly from ST **tsyap*.

453 ST (and TB) initial **z*- is represented in Chinese by the anticipated *dz-/z*- initial in *dzi̯əg/zi*[y] 'child', a doublet of *tsi̯əg/tsi* (n. 86), TB **za* ~ **tsa*, *id*.; cf. also Ch. *dz'i̯əg/dz'i*[z] 'beget', all pointing to a basic ST root **tsa* ~ **dza*, with **za* as a doublet of the latter (the initial **dz*- form is lacking in TB, which has only T *btsa-ba* 'to bear offspring'). The rare ST (and TB) **zy*- cluster is represented simply by *zi̯*- in the one Ar. Ch. comparison available, viz. *zi̯ôg/i̯ə̯u*[a] 'rot, decay', TB **zya·w* ~ **zyu(w)* 'rot, decay; digest'. ST (and TB) initial **dz*- is represented by *d'/dz'*-, with doublet *dz/z*-, in the basic root for 'eat' (n. 452). Finally, one excellent comparison is available for B-L (and by inference TB) initial **dzw*-, viz. *di̯wan/i̯wän*[b] 'hawk, kite', B-L **dzwan* (n. 162).

454 Ch. *ńi̯ər/ńźi*[c] '2' points to a basic ST root without final *-*s*, agreeing with the evidence from TB (n. 61) and Karen (n. 401). This ST final is represented by Ch. -*t* in 'bone' (n. 419) and '7' (n. 471), also (as suffix) by -*t* in 'know' (n. 429).

455 TB has initial alternation in the root for 'hair' (see n. 92 for interpretation); cf. the alternation (with differing vowel length) in Ch. *tsiet*[d] 'joint', TB **tsik* (text,

[a] 三 [b] 二 [c] 節 [d] 漆 [e] 蔥 [f] 彡 [g] 鹺 [h] 身 [i] 脣 [j] 孫
[k] 隻 [l] 朱 [m] 煮 [n] 蟲 [o] 脂 [p] 食 [q] 飤 [r] 出 [s] 水 [t] 川
[u] 矢 [v] 登 [w] 爯 [x] 接 [y] 子 [z] 字 [a] 庮 [b] 鳶 [c] 二 [d] 節

d-, appears only before semivocalic *i̯*. In the following comparisons, which are of dubious significance, it corresponds to TB **y-*; cf. *zi̯ak*[a] 'armpit', L *zak* < *yak*, *id.* (cf. n. 108); *zi̯ôg*[b] 'wine-must' (graph is drawing of wine vessel), TB **yu(w)* 'liquor'.[456]

The cerebral series *ṣ*, *tṣ*, *tṣ'*, and *dẓ* cannot be connected with anything to be found in Tibeto-Burman or Karen. It may be that Sino-Tibetan had cerebral, palatal, and dental series, simplified in various ways in Tibeto-Burman; cf. *tṣ'o*[c] 'thorny trees, thorns', TB **tsow*; and *t̂i̯o*[d] 'boil, cook', TB **tsyow*. The comparative data gathered to date, however, are far too meagre to support this view, yet do not militate against it.[457]

above); *si̯ĕt*[e] 'knee' (='leg-joint') (cf. G *dźa-tśik* 'leg-joint'='knee'); also *ts'wən/ts'uən*[f] 'thumb' (but used for 'hand' in graphs), from **tsu-n* (n. 428) but *śi̯ôg/śi̯əu*[g] 'hand' (note the palatalization), Karen **tsü* 'hand/arm'; here we might reconstruct ST **tśəw*, with palatal shifting to dental affricate before the high vowel *u*, as in *swən/suən*[h] 'grandchild', TB **śu(w)* (n. 452). Contrariwise, Chinese clearly has developed a secondary affricate in one root, viz. *ts'əm/ts'âm*[i] '3, a triad', a doublet of *səm/sâm*[j] '3', TB **g-sum* (possible effect of the prefix; cf. Nungish: Răwang *ətsum* '3') and at times has an affricate initial in the face of a spirant in TB; cf. *ts'i̯əm*[k] 'sweep', from **ts'im*; TB **śim*: Nungish: Răwang *śim*, Trung *śyəm* 'sweep', B *sim* 'strike with a motion towards one's self', Maru *śam* < **śim* 'sweep' (Benedict, 1940, No. 45); *ts'i̯əm*[l] 'to lie down to sleep', from **ts'im*; T *gzim-pa* (perhaps from **g-dzim*) 'to fall asleep, sleep' (*ibid.* No. 46); *ts'i̯əp* ~ *tsi̯əp*[m] 'whisper', from **ts'ip/tsip*; T *sib-pa* ~ *śub-pa*, *id.* (perhaps from **syip* ~ **syup*) (*ibid.* No. 39); *dz'i̯ĕn*[n] 'exhaust, entirely; (KD) use to the utmost; use up, finish', from **dz'in*; T *zin-pa* (perhaps from prefix + **dzin*) 'to draw near to an end, to be at an end, to be finished, exhausted, consumed'. TB and Chinese differ in voicing of the initial affricate in several instances; cf. *dz'wən/dz'uən*[o] 'grass, herb' (with 'collective' *-n* suffix; n. 428), T *rtswa* 'grass' (n. 161); *dz'i̯ət/dz'i̯ĕt*[p] 'sickness, pain' (with suffixed *-t*), TB *tsa* 'hot; pain', but *ts'ân*[q] 'eat; food, meal', from **ts'a-n*, TB **dza* 'eat' (text and n. 487); possibly also *tsi̯ər/tsi*[r] 'older sister', TB **dzar* 'sister (man sp.)'. It appears that initial affricates in general were highly unstable elements in ST, particularly so in Chinese.

456 See n. 448 for further analysis.

457 The Chinese retroflex (cerebral) series represents a secondary development from palatal + *r* clusters (Benedict, 1948). There are three excellent comparisons for Ch. **śr/ṣ-* = TB **śr-* (n. 304): **śri̯ɛt/ṣi̯ɛt*[s] 'louse', TB **śrik* (see n. 442 for final); **śrĕŋ/ṣɒŋ*[t] 'live; bear, be born; produce; fresh (as greens)', TB **śriŋ* 'live, alive; green; raw' (see n. 476 for vocalism); **śri̯ək/ṣi̯ək*[u] 'color (of face); looks, (womanly) beauty (also 'lust' in *AD*); to show off', TB **śrak* 'ashamed, shy' (='to show color of face'). The cluster **śr-* can be reconstructed for Ar. Ch. itself on the basis of graph connections not only with *l-* but also with *γ-*; cf. **śri̯əg/ṣi*[v] 'recorder; record' phonetic in *li̯əg/lyi*[w] 'officer'; **śriəm/ṣi̯əm*[x] and *gli̯əm/li̯əm*[y] 'forest'; *śri̯əm/ṣi̯əm*[z] and *gli̯əm/li̯əm*[a] 'drip' (these are both cognate pairs); **śri̯u/ṣi̯u*[b] (B) 'count';

a 腋　b 西　c 楚　d 煮　e 膝　f 寸　g 手　h 孫　i 參　j 三
k 㬰　l 寢　m 咠　n 盡　o 荐　p 疾　q 餐　r 姊　s 蝨　t 生
u 色　v 史　w 吏　x 森　y 林　z 滲　a 淋　b 數

Ar. Ch. has initial *l-* for both **r-* and **l-*, as in *li̯ôk* '6', TB **d-ruk*. Early Chinese loan-words in Thai retain original **r-*; cf. Thai **hrok* '6', and **graam* 'indigo', Ar. Ch. *glâm*,[a] T *rams*.[458] The fate of final **-r* and **-l* in Chinese is not so readily

(C) 'number' (cognate with TB **-tśrəy*, below) has *gli̯u/li̯u*[b] 'drag' as phonetic; also *gʿɔ/γa*[c] 'summer' phonetic in **ṣrɔ/ṣa*[d] 'side-room' and **śrɔ/ṣa*[e] 'hoarse' (only in *AD*); **śri̯o/ṣi̯wo*[f] '(place) where', with *gʿo/γuo*[g] 'door' as phonetic (JAM suggests a comparison with K *ra* ~ *śəra* 'place'). Another strong argument for reconstructing **śr-* (or **śl-*) is provided by an early loan from AT, viz. **śrĕŋ/ṣɒŋ*[h] 'reed organ' (note[i], above, as phonetic), from AT **kluḷiŋ* 'flute' (IN **t'uliŋ*, Thai **khlui* < **kluriŋ*) via **śu*[*r, l*]*iŋ* < **khlu*[*r, l*]*iŋ* (see n. 472 for *ś-* < **khl-*). The initial cluster **tśr-* (= **ćr-*) has been reconstructed for three TB roots (n. 95), one of which has a Ch. cognate with the anticipated cluster (voiced); cf. **dźrʿi̯ər/dẓʿi*[j] 'spittle (of dragon)' (Ar. Ch. form not cited in *GSR*), TB **m-tśril* 'spittle'; cf. also **śri̯u/ṣi̯u*[k] (B) 'count'; (C) 'number' (above), TB **(r-)tśrəy* 'count', via **śrəy*, with vowel shift after the retroflex initial similar to that found in 'foot' and 'son-in-law' (n. 472). Ar. Ch. apparently also had the initial cluster **sr-* (> Anc. Ch. *si̯-*) corresponding to TB **sr-*, since there are two comparisons in the above phonetic series[l] (*GSR*-812); cf. **sri̯ĕŋ/si̯äŋ*[m] 'clan, family, family name' (the original matrilineal lineage, as indicated also by the use of *ni̯o/ni̯wo*[n] 'woman' as signific in the graph), TB **sriŋ* 'sister': T *sriŋ(-mo)* 'sister (man sp.)' (= 'the one carrying the matri-clan name', paralleling T *miŋ-po* 'brother (woman sp.)' = 'the one carrying the patri-clan name', from TB **miŋ* 'name'); cf. also **sri̯ĕŋ/si̯äŋ*[o] and[p] 'weasel', TB **sre*[*ŋ*] 'weasel, squirrel'. The initial cluster **sr-* can also be inferred (and reconstructed) for the following: **sri̯u/si̯u*[q] 'older sister', TB **sru(w)* 'aunt' (T *sru*); cf. also 'bark' (n. 245). The prefixed combination ST **s-r-* also yielded Anc. Ch. *si̯-*, probably from Ar. Ch. **sr-*; cf. **sri̯ôk/si̯uk*[r] 'pass the night', TB **s-ryak* 'day (24 hours)' but Lahu *há* 'night; pass the night', L *riak* 'pass the night' (n. 154); also **sri̯am/si̯äm*[s] 'sharp' (graph has **dʿi̯am* < **li̯am*[t] 'tongue' as phonetic; n. 458), TB **(s-)ryam*, *id.* The dental stop + *r* cluster is represented only by *t'i̯ək/tśi̯ək*[u] 'weave', TB **trak*. The corresponding voiced palatal or dental + *r* clusters are rare; cf. *d'i̯aŋ/źi̯aŋ*[v] 'upwards; high, admirable; superior' (used as a title), TB **źraŋ* 'uncle' (see n. 155 for parallel Tibetan use of the term); ST **źr-* > *d'i̯/źi̯-* in Chinese, which lacks initial **ẓ-*; cf. also *d'i̯an/źi̯än*[w] (B) 'earthworm', also *di̯ĕn/i̯ĕn*[x] (B) and *di̯ən/i̯ĕn*[y] (B), *id.* (note that all three triplet forms have the same tone), TB **zril* 'worm' (B *ti*, Thado *til* 'earthworm'), showing ST **zr-* > **źr-* > *d'i/źi-*, varying with **zr-* > **zy-* > **y-* > *di̯/i-*.

458 See n. 421 for present analysis of 'indigo'. Under conditions of palatalization (not fully worked out) ST **l* tends to be replaced in Chinese by *i̯* or *di̯/i*; cf. 'neck' and 'tongue' (n. 419), 'eagle' (n. 225), also **di̯ək/i̯ək*[z] 'wing' (*GSR* cites Ar. Ch. *gi̯ək*, but *di̯ək* is indicated since the phonetic series includes *tʿi̯ək/t'ʿi̯ək*),[a] TB **g-lak* 'arm' (this semantic interchange also appears in AT; cf. Formosa: Paiwan dials. *valaŋa* 'wing', *valaŋa/laŋa/n* 'arm'); *di̯ap/i̯äp*[b] 'leaf', TB **lap*, *id.* There is evidence for further evolution of ST **l* to other dental stops (voiced or unvoiced), paralleling the Karenni **l* > *t* shift (p. 137), especially in the *GSR*-413 series (phonetic is *t'i̯ĕd/tśi*[c]); cf. *dʿiet* ~ *dʿi̯ĕt/d'ʿi̯ĕt*[d] 'nephew/niece' (with suffixed

a 藍 b 婁 c 夏 d 廈 e 嗄 f 所 g 戶 h 笙 i 生 j 漦
k 數 l 生 m 姓 n 女 o 狌 p 鼪 q 嫂 r 宿 s 銛 t 舌
u 織 v 尙 w 蟺 x 蚓 y 螾 z 翼 a 趩 b 葉 c 至 d 姪

determined. Karlgren (*BMFEA*, **5**, 1934) has ingeniously reconstructed final *-r* for Ar. Ch. on the basis of the Shih Ching rhymes, together with morphological contacts and doublets such as *dʻân* ~ *dʻâr*[a] 'alligator', *bʻi̯ən* ~ *bʻi̯ər*[b] 'female'. Karlgren's theory, although rejected by Simon and others, seems to explain the Ar. Ch. facts better than any alternative theory. On the comparative side, however, we can cite only *pi̯wər*[c] 'to fly', TB **pur* ~ **pir*, in support of a direct Ar. Ch.–TB correspondence for this final.[459, 460] As shown below, the final *-r* thus reconstructed

-t; n. 428), TB **b-ləy* 'grandchild; nephew/niece'; *t'i̯ĕt/tśi̯ĕt*[d] 'leech' (not in *GSR*), TB **(m-)li·t* 'water leech' (*contra* Benedict, 1967bis, where an AT origin is suggested); possibly also *ṭi̯ĕd/t'i*[e] (C) 'heavily weighted down', from **li̯ĕd* < **li̯ĕt* (note tone), TB **(s-)ləy* 'heavy' (Bodo *illit* ~ *gillit*, L *rit*); cf. also the following: **tʻiam/tʻiem*[f] 'lick, taste' (not in *GSR*), from **liam/*liem*, as shown by the Cantonese reading *li·m* (Karlgren calls this a 'synonymous word'), TB **(s-)lyam* 'tongue; flame'; this root is also represented in Chinese by the 'hidden' word for 'tongue' (**dʻiam* ~ **dʻi̯am* < **liam* ~ **li̯am*),[g] explaining the use of[h] as phonetic in *dʻiam/dʻiem*[i] 'calm' and **sri̯am/si̯äm*[j] 'sharp' (n. 457), also in **dʻiam/dʻiem*[k] 'sweet' (not in *GSR*), cognate with TB: Kiranti **lem*, *id.*: Waling, Nachereng, Chingtang, Rungchangbung *lem*, Rodong *lam-*, Limbu *ke-lim-ba*, Yakha *lim* (contrast Yakha *lem* 'tongue' < TB **lyam*). Chinese initial *zi̯-/i̯-* definitely represents an earlier **r-* in the cyclical term *zi̯ôg/i̯əu*[l] 'cock' (n. 487) and corresponds to TB (and ST) **ry-* in *zi̯ak/i̯äk*[m] 'fluid, moisture', TB **ryak* 'grease, oil, juice'. ST (and TB) **ry-* apparently shifted to **ly-* (perhaps because of the prefix) in *dʻiok/dʻiek*[n] 'pheasant', possibly also *dʻi̯ər/dʻi*,[o] *id.*, from **l[i]yak*; TB **s-rik* ~ **s-ryak*, *id.* Both types of correspondences are indicated in the following: *zi̯ôg/i̯əu*[p] 'laugh' (graph is a loan in this sense), TB **rya-t*, *id.* (see n. 488 for final), also *dʻiet*,[q] *id.* (from the phonetic series singled out above), from **lyat* < **ryat* (with typical palatalization of the vowel; n. 488).

459 Ar. Ch. *χwâr*[r] 'fire' might be compared with Nung *hwarr* 'burn, kindle', K *wan*, Moshang *varr*, G *waʔl* 'fire', but these forms appear to belong with TB **bar* ~ **par* 'burn' (see § **8**).

460 It now appears that ST final **-r* was generally replaced by *-n* in Chinese, with some *-r* ~ *-n* doublet formation; cf. *tsi̯ər/tsi*[s] 'older sister', TB **dzar* 'sister (man sp.)'; *pi̯wər/pywe̯i*[t] (A) 'fly', *pi̯wən/pi̯uən*[u] (A) 'fly, soar', *pi̯wən/pi̯uən*[v] (C) 'spread wings, fly up', TB **pur* ~ **pir* 'fly'; *χwâr/χwâ*[w] (A) 'fire', from **phwâr* (n. 463), *bʻi̯wăn/bʻi̯wɒn*[x] (B) 'burn, roast' (series includes final *-r* forms), TB **bwâr* ~ **pwâr* 'burn; fire'; *si̯ĕn*[y] (A) 'new, renew', *si̯an/si̯än*[z] (A) 'fresh (fish, meat); (KD) new, fine, clean', TB **sar* 'new, fresh'; **si̯ĕn*[a] 'louse' (phonetic is *si̯ĕn*[b]; graph later applied to synonymous **śri̯ɛt/si̯ɛt*; see n. 457), TB **sar* ~ **śar*, *id.*; *sian/sien*[c] 'sleet', T *ser-ba* 'hail'; *swân/suân*[d] 'sour' (series includes final *-r* forms), TB **swa·r*, *id.*; *bʻwâr/bʻuâ* ~ *pwâr/puâ*[e] 'white', L *va·r*, *id.*, from **pwa·r*; Karen **ʔ(b)wa*, *id.*, from **ʔbwar* < **pwar*; *pwâr/puâ*[f] (C) 'spread out, sow; distribute; banish, reject; winnow; shake' (Benedict, 1967bis, considers an AT loan), also (with apparent loss of final **-r*) *pwâ/puâ*[g] (B ~ C) 'to winnow'; TB

a 鼉　b 牝　c 飛　d 蛭　e 輊　f 舔　g 舌　h 舌　i 恬　j 銛
k 甜　l 酉　m 液　n 翟　o 雉　p 猶　q 咥　r 火　s 姊　t 飛
u 翂　v 奮　w 火　x 燔　y 新　z 鮮　a 蝨　b 卂　c 霰　d 酸
e 皤　f 播　g 簸

for Ar. Ch. in most cases stands for vocalic or semivocalic final in Tibeto-Burman. Final **-l* appears to have become *-n* in Ar. Ch.; cf. *ngi̯ɛn*[a] 'silver', TB **ŋul*; *miən*[b] 'close the eyes, sleep', TB **myel* 'sleepy'.[461] The following comparison suggests that roots in final **-l* sometimes gave rise to the final *-n* ~ *-r* doublets noted above: *si̯ən* ~ *si̯ər*[c] 'wash', TB **(m-)s(y)il* (493), as represented by T *bsil-ba* 'wash' (a' respectful' usage, apparently derived from a meaning 'to cool'), K *śin* ~ *kəśin* 'wash, bathe', L *sil*, Rangkhol *gerśil*, Thado *śil* ~ *kiśil*, Khami *məse* (cf. *mətśe* 'spittle' < **m-ts(y)il*), Lakher *pəśi*, Mikir *iŋthi* (Kuki-Naga **m-s(y)il*) 'wash, bathe'.[462]

**bwâr*: T *ʾbor-ba*, pf. *bor* 'throw, cast, fling; leave, forsake', Bahing *war* 'throw away, squander, abandon', Chepang *wa·r* 'sow', Mikir *var* 'throw, cast, fling', L *vorʔ* 'scatter, throw up, toss'; *di̯an/i̯än*[d] (A) 'extend; continue; stretch', *di̯an/i̯än*[e] (C) 'flow out, extend' (series includes final *-r* forms), TB **ya·r* ~ **yâr* 'spread, extend; sail' (but note Tiddim *zan* < **yan* 'stretch'; n. 448); **bʿi̯an/bʿi̯än*[f] (B) 'braid, plait' (not in *GSR*), *pian/pien* ~ *pi̯an/pi̯än*[g] (A) 'plait, weave', also read *bʿian/bʿien* (B) 'arrange in a series', TB **byâr* ~ **pyâr* 'affix; plait, sew' (but note Tiddim *phan* 'weave, plait'). It is probably significant that three of the above forms in *-n* are from phonetic series which include forms in final *-r*, suggesting that the **-r* > *-n* shift was of late date, at least in some instances.

461 ST final **-l* appears to have fallen together with final **-r* in Chinese, with general replacement by *-n* but with occasional retention of *-r*; again, some of the phonetic series yielding these cognates contain forms with final *-r*, suggesting a late shift; in addition to the text examples note the following: *t'i̯ər/tśi*[h] 'fat', TB **tsil*, *id.* (n. 452); *mi̯ər/mjwi* and *mi̯wər/mjwi̯i*[i] (this doublet form reflected in the loan use of the graph) 'eyebrow', from **mir* ~ **mur* (**mil* ~ **mul*), TB **(s-)mul* ~ **(s-)mil* ~ **(r-)mul* 'body hair' (T *smin-ma* 'eyebrow'; n. 56); *di̯ən/i̯ĕn*[j] (series includes final *-r* forms), also *di̯ĕn/i̯ĕn*[k] and *d'i̯an/źi̯än*[l] (all on tone B) 'earthworm', TB **zril* 'worm' (n. 457); *śi̯ən/śi̯ĕn*[m] 'base of tooth' (= 'gums') (phonetic of this series is *śi̯ər/śi*[n] 'arrow', below), TB **s-nil* 'gums' (nn. 452, 471); *mi̯an/mi̯än*[o] 'face', L *hmel*, *id.*; *bʿi̯ən/bʿi̯ĕn*[p] 'poor', from **bʿil*; T *dbul*, *id.*; *dʿi̯ĕn/d'ʿi̯ĕn*[q] 'dust', from **dʿil*; T *rdul*, *id.* (see n. 477 for the vocalism of these last two roots); *pwən/puən*[r] 'root, trunk', TB **bul* ~ **pul* 'root, stump, tree' (n. 443); *śi̯ər/śi*[s] 'arrow', TB **tal* 'arrow; bow' (n. 452); *d'i̯ĕn/źi̯ĕn*[t] 'kidney', TB **m-kal* (n. 463); *tʿân*[u] 'coal, charcoal; lime' (= ashes); T *thal-ba* 'dust, ashes and similar substances'; *t'i̯an/tśi̯än*[v] 'battle; to fight' (series includes final *-r* forms), from **kran* < **g-ran*; TB **(g-)ra·l* 'fight, quarrel; war' (see n. 472 for initial); *gi̯wan/ji̯wan*[u] 'round', etc., TB **wal* 'round, circular' (n. 449).

462 The Tibetan form is perhaps unrelated; the TB root has now been reconstructed **(m-)syil* ~ **(m-)syal*, the doublet being represented by T *bśal-ba* 'wash, wash out of, off, clean by washing, rise', Răwang (Nungish) *thi zal* 'bathe, wash' (*thi* 'water').

[a] 銀 [b] 眠 [c] 洗 [d] 延 [e] 演 [f] 辮 [g] 編 [h] 脂 [i] 眉 [j] 螾
[k] 蚓 [l] 蟺 [m] 矧 [n] 矢 [o] 面 [p] 貧 [q] 塵 [r] 本 [s] 矢 [t] 腎
[u] 炭 [v] 戰 [w] 圓

§45. Chinese consonant clusters

Original ST clusters with *w* and *y* are probably maintained in Ar. Ch. in the form *w* or *iw* and *i̯* (phonemically *j* in Karlgren's notation). The available comparisons, however, are not numerous; cf. the following:[463]

k'iwən[a] 'dog'; TB **kwiy.*

χiwet[b] 'blood'; TB **s-hwiy.*

g'wo[c] 'fox'; TB **gwa.*

swân[d] 'garlic'; cf. B *krak-swan* 'onion'.

ngi̯o[e] 'fish'; TB **ŋya.*

ki̯ang[f] 'ginger'; cf. B *khyàŋ, id.*[464]

g'i̯at[g] 'hero'; cf. T *gyad(-pa)* 'champion, athlete'.[464]

463 The ST labial stop + *w* cluster is especially well represented in Chinese; cf. *pi̯wo/pi̯u*[h] 'man; (KD) husband', TB **(p)wa* 'man, person, husband', Karen **wa* 'husband'; *pi̯wo/pi̯u*[i] (A) and *pi̯wo/pi̯u*[j] (B) 'ax', TB **r-pwa, id.* (n. 78); *pi̯wo/pi̯u*[k] 'breadth of four fingers', TB **pwa* 'palm (of hand)' (B *phăwa*); *b'i̯wo/b'i̯u*[l] 'father', TB **pwa*, Karen **ba* ~ **pha* (ST **bwa* ~ **pwa*); *b'wâ/b'uâ*[m] 'old woman' (not in *GSR*), also 'grandmother (vocative)' (Benedict, 1942), B *ăbhwà* ~ *ăphwà* 'grandmother'; *b'wâr/b'uâ* ~ *pwâr/puâ*[n] 'white', L *va·r* < **pwa·r*, Karen **ʔ(b)wa* < **pwar* (n. 460); *pwâr/puâ*[o] 'sow; winnow', *pwâ/puâ*[p] 'winnow', TB **bwâr* 'throw, scatter, sow' (n. 460); note the regular palatalization of the initial stop before the front low vowel *a* but not before the back low vowel *â*. The aspirated (= non-prefixed) surd stop + *w* yielded Ch. *χw-* (see n. 374 for the parallel shift in Karen); cf. *b'i̯wăn/b'i̯wɒn*[q] < **bwan* < **bwâr* 'burn, roast', *χwâr/χwâ*[r] < **phwâr* 'fire' (n. 460), with *â* > a shift in the former before the secondary *-n* (n. 488); *χi̯wăŋ/χi̯wɒŋ*[s] < **phwăŋ* 'elder brother', TB **bwaŋ* 'uncle (usu. father's brother)'; cf. also *păk/pɒk*[t] 'eldest brother, eldest' (later developed present meaning: 'father's elder brother'), perhaps from **pwăŋ* (see n. 443 for unvoicing of initial). The ST labial stop or nasal + *w* cluster, however, was apparently unstable in Chinese before high front vowels, tending to be lost; cf. *b'i̯ən/b'i̯ĕn* ~ *b'i̯ər/b'yi*[u] 'female of animals', TB **pwi(y)* 'female' (n. 428); *mi̯əd/myi*[v] 'sleep, lie down to sleep', TB **(r-)mwəy* ~ **(s-)mwəy* 'sleep'; the latter word perhaps lost the medial **w* at a relatively late stage, since the graph has the cyclical character *mi̯wəd/mywe̯i*[w] as phonetic, and the phonetic series (*GSR*-531) has otherwise only initial *mi̯w-* and *mw-* forms; cf. also *mi̯wər/mywe̯i*[x] 'minute, small', B *mwé, id.*, from **mwəy*, with retention of the medial **w*.

464 Initial velar stop + *y* clusters are rare in our comparative ST material generally, and the text examples are of limited significance (Benedict, 1967 bis, has identified 'ginger' as an old loan from AT). The best comparison for this cluster in TB shows a shift to dental initials before the mid-high front vowel **e*, viz.[y] and

a 犬 b 血 c 狐 d 蒜 e 魚 f 薑 g 傑 h 夫 i 鈇 j 斧
k 扶 l 父 m 婆 n 皤 o 播 p 簸 q 燔 r 火 s 兄 t 伯
u 妣 v 寐 w 未 x 微 y 經

In some cases it is difficult to determine whether medial *i̯* represents original medial **y* or is simply an index of palatalization;[465] cf. *gli̯əp*[a] 'stand', TB **g-ryap* (where *i̯* might be regarded as a representative of **y*), but *kʿli̯əp*[b] 'weep', TB **krap* (where *i̯* stands for palatalization); cf. also **niəp*[c] (based on Anc. Ch. *niep*) 'to pinch, nip with the fingers', TB **nyap* 'pinch, squeeze'; *niəm*[d] and *ńi̯əm*[e] 'think', T *snyam-pa* 'think, imagine; thought, mind', *nyam(s)* 'soul, mind; thought'; *ti̯ək*[f] 'mount, advance, promote', T *theg-pa* < **thyak* (as shown by West T dialects) 'lift, raise'; also *li̯ĕt*[g] 'fear', T *źed-pa* < **ryed* 'fear, be afraid'.[466]

tʿi̯ĕŋ/tʿi̯ăŋ[h] (A) 'red', *si̯ĕŋ/si̯ăŋ*[i] (A) 'red ox; red', from **khi̯ĕŋ*, TB **kyeŋ*. This shift explains the doublet: *tʿien*[j] (A) and *χien*[k] (A) 'heaven', from **khien* (n. 428) (see n. 441 for the **kh-* > *χ-* shift). The initial cluster appears to be preserved in *kian/kien*[l] 'see', *gʿian/γien*[m] 'appear' (text), TB **(m-)kyen* 'know' (for the semantics, cf. PN **kite* 'see, appear, know'), but the medial **y* is perhaps secondary in the TB root, with the likely ST reconstruction being **(m-)ke·n* ~ **(m-)ge·n* (contrast the equation in n. 481 for the short ST vowel: TB **e* = Ar. Ch. *i̯a*). Other ST roots show similar shifts in Chinese to palatal or dental initial from velar stops before the front vowels **ə* (primary or secondary) and **a* as well as **i*; cf. *d'i̯əp/źi̯əp*[n] '10', from **g(y)ip*, TB **gip, id.*; *t'i̯əm/tśi̯əm*[o] 'needle' (phonetic is *gʿεm/γăm*),[p] also written[q] (with above root as phonetic), from **k(y)əm* ~ **k(y)əp*, TB *kəp, id.* (n. 82); *d'i̯ĕn/źi̯ĕn*[r] 'kidney', from **g(y)al*, TB **m-kal, id.*; *ti̯əm/t'i̯əm*[s] (A) 'chopping-block' (phonetic series includes *kʿəm/kʿâm*[t] 'vanquish, kill'), also *t'i̯əm/tśi̯əm*[u] (B ~ C) 'pillow; to use as pillow', both from **k(y)im* (see n. 477 for vocalism), TB **kum* 'block; pillow', Karen **khu[m]* 'chopping-block'; note also *kʿəm/kʿâm*[v] 'vanquish, kill' (same word as above), in a series (*GSR*-658) with *ki̯əm*[w] 'now' as phonetic but including also *tʿi̯əm/t'ʿi̯əm*[x] 'walk hesitatingly' and even *tʿəm/tʿâm*[y] 'covet' (the last listed separately by Karlgren under *GSR*-645); cf. T *'gum-pa*, pf. *gum*, *'gums* 'die', pf. *bkum* 'kill, slaughter'; cf. also *kʿu/kʿə̯u*[z] (C) 'rob', *tʿu/tʿə̯u*[a] (A) 'steal', TB **r-kəw* (B) 'steal' but Karen **hyü, id.*, reveals an initial palatalizing element (n. 371), apparently leading to the dental shift in Chinese. The frequent interchange of velar and dental/palatal initials in the Chinese graphs points unmistakably to a relatively late date for the above shift, probably with much dialectical variation (note that Thai **sip* '10', considered a very early loan-word from Chinese, has initial **s-*, probably from **ź-*, which is lacking in Thai).

465 This difficulty is accentuated by the present recognition of the vowel *ə* as a basic ST unit (n. 482), requiring reconstructions such as ST **g-ryəp* 'stand', **krəp* 'weep', **ńəp* 'pinch' (with doublet **ńap*; n. 471); *ńəm* 'think', *tək* 'mount; raise'; note that Chinese tends to shift the palatal to a dental nasal in some cases (see n. 452 for the parallel **ś-* > *s-* shift) but the palatal form is maintained in *ńi̯əm/ńźi̯əm*[b] 'soft', B *ńám, id.* (L *nem, id.*, appears to be indirectly cognate), ST **ńəm*. Inasmuch as palatalization occurs in Chinese before most vowels (notably excluding *â*), medial **y* can be reconstructed for ST only in those roots for which it is attested in TB (**g-ryəp* 'stand').

466 A better comparison is provided by T *'dźigs-pa* 'to be afraid; fear, dread; fearful', from **ă-lig* (n. 104), ST **lik*, with shift of final **-k* to *-t* before **i* (n. 442).

a 立 b 泣 c 捻 d 念 e 恁 f 陟 g 慄 h 赬 i 騂 j 天
k 祆 l 見 m 現 n 十 o 鍼 p 咸 q 針 r 腎 s 椹 t 戡
u 枕 v 戓 w 今 x 趻 y 貪 z 寇 a 偷 b 荏

Initial clusters can be reconstructed for Ar. Ch. on the basis of the use of phonetic elements in characters.[467,468] Combinations of stop, nasal or sibilant + *l* are most in evidence, while *sn-*, *śń-*, *χm-* and perhaps *tʻn-* and *sng-* also appear; cf. the following:

gli̯ôg > *li̯ə̯u*[a] 'whistling of the wind', *kli̯ôg* > *ki̯ə̯u*[b] 'down-curving', *gʻli̯ôg* > *gʻi̯ə̯u*[c] 'kind of precious stone', *tʻli̯ôg* > *tʻi̯əu* ~ *li̯ôg* > *li̯ə̯u*[d] 'to get cured', *mli̯ôg* > *mi̯ə̯u*[e] 'bind around'.

tsʻi̯am[f] 'all', *kli̯am* > *ki̯äm*[g] 'measure, control', *gʻli̯am* > *gʻi̯äm*[h] 'restrict, frugal', *χli̯am* > *χi̯äm*[i] 'precipitous', *ngli̯am* > *ngi̯äm*[j] 'verify', *gli̯am* > *li̯äm*[k] 'gather, accumulate'.

blwân > *luân*[l] 'phoenix', *pli̯an* > *pi̯än*[m] 'change', *mlwan* > *mwan*[n] 'southern barbarian', *slwan* > *ṣwan*[o] 'twins'.[469]

467 Karlgren has freely reconstructed initial clusters in his *Grammata Serica*, while Simon (*BSOS* **9**, 1938) has paid especial attention to the *sn-* ~ *śń-* cluster. Boodberg has made extensive use of 'rhyming binoms' (*tieh yün*)[p] in reconstructing complex clusters; see his *KD Notes* 1–4 (Berkeley, 1934–5), and 'Some Proleptical Remarks on the Evolution of Archaic Chinese', *HJAS* **2** (1937), 329–72.

468 The problem of initial clusters in Chinese has received much attention; note especially R. A. D. Forrest, 'A Reconsideration of the Initials of Karlgren's Archaic Chinese', *TP* **51** (1964), 229–46. Much remains to be done here, and Karlgren's reconstructions (including some cited in the text) must be viewed with circumspection (cf. n. 415, also the following note).

469 For *pli̯an*/*pi̯än*[q] 'change', cf. Thai **plian*, *id.*, from **pliyan* (IN **liyan*); this appears to be an old loan-word in Chinese. The early loan-word material further indicates **pl-* > *t'*/*tś-* and **pʻl-* > *t'ʻ*/*tśʻ-* shifts in Chinese; cf. *t'i̯ôg*/*tśi̯ə̯u*[r] 'boat', from **pli̯ôg*/*pli̯ə̯u*; cf. IN **parau* (Gurung, in the Himalayas, has *plava*); **t'ʻi̯ôg*/*tśʻi̯ə̯u*[s] (*GSR* cites *tʼni̯ôg* for Ar. Ch.) 'ox' (calendrical term), from **pʻli̯ôg*/*pʻli̯ə̯u*; cf. Thai **plaw*; from this same (ultimate AT) source came T *phyugs* < **phlug-* 'cattle', with the suffixed *-s* characteristic of these loans from AT (Benedict, 1967 bis). Prefixed **b-* + *r*/*l-* gave rise to Ch. *bl*/*l-* (n. 474), while ST (and TB) **bl-* and **br-* (generally) merged in Chinese with loss of the stop element, yielding *di̯*/*i̯-*; cf. *di̯ək*/*i̯ək*[t] 'shoot with arrow with string attached; arrow [of this type]' (graph is picture of same), TB **bla* 'arrow' (see n. 487 for the final), perhaps also **t'i̯ak*/*tśi̯ak*[u] (Ar. Ch. form not cited in *GSR*) 'string attached to arrow', from **pli̯ak* (see discussion above); *di̯ĕŋ*/*i̯äŋ*[v] 'full, fill', TB **bliŋ* 'full' ~ **pliŋ* 'fill' (latter not represented in Ch.); *di̯əŋ*/*i̯əŋ*[w] 'fly', TB *(*s*-)*brəŋ* 'fly, bee' (text **yaŋ*; add T *sbraŋ* fly, bee', Lepcha *sum-bryoŋ* 'fly'). ST **br-* appears to parallel **y-* (n. 448) in yielding an affricate rather than *di̯*/*i̯-* when prefixed; Mand. *tsʻaŋ*[x] 'housefly' (listed in *AD*, but no Anc. Ch. or Ar. Ch. reading) thus is to be considered a doublet of the above word for 'fly'; also (from the same phonetic series) *d'ʻi̯əŋ*/*dźʻi̯əŋ*[y] 'string, cord', from prefix + **bliŋ*, Nungish: Metu *ambriŋ* = **a*(*m*)*briŋ* (typical Nungish nasalized **a-* prefix) 'cord' (Desgodins, *La Mission du Thibet*, 1872); this character is also read *di̯əŋ*/*i̯əŋ* 'full (*sc.* of grain)', apparently a doublet of the form cited above.

a 飂 b 樛 c 璆 d 瘳 e 繆 f 僉 g 檢 h 儉 i 險 j 驗
k 斂 l 鸞 m 變 n 蠻 o 孿 p 疊韻 q 變 r 舟 s 丑 t 弋
u 繳 v 盈 w 蠅 x [illegible] y 繩

sli̯əg > *ṣi*[a] 'recorder, record', *li̯əg* > *lji*[b] 'officer'.[470]

sngi̯ad > *ngi̯äi*[c] 'cultivate, agriculture', *śi̯ad* > *śi̯äi*[d] 'force, influence'.

ńi̯o > *ńźi̯wo*[e] 'like', *śńi̯o* > *śi̯wo*[f] 'indulgent', *sni̯o* > *si̯wo* 'coarse raw silk' and *tʿni̯o* > *t̂ʿi̯wo* 'season, flavor', both written[g].[471]

lât[h] 'wicked', *tʿlât* > *tʿât*[i] 'otter'.

li̯ər > *liei*[j] 'ritual vase', *tʿli̯ər* > *tʿiei*[k] 'body'.

mək[l] 'ink', *χmək* > *χək*[m] 'black'.

Note the loss of the medial element after surd initials, in contrast to the loss of sonant stop (but not nasal) initials before medial *l*, e.g. *klan* > *kan*[n] 'select, distinguish', but *glân* > *lân*[o] 'barrier'. This generalization, which underlies the reconstructions made by Karlgren, is supported by *glâm* > *lâm*[p] 'indigo', Thai **graam*, as well as by the following comparisons from Tibeto-Burman:[472]

470 See n. 457 for analysis of this cluster, now reconstructed **śr-*.

471 There is evidence that ST prefixed **s-* remained as a separable element in Chinese; cf. **ni̯ap*/*ni̯äp*[q] 'pincers, tweezers; to pinch, a pinch' (not in *GSR*), a doublet of **niəp*[r] (above), from ST **ńəp* ~ **ńap*, also (from same phonetic series) *śńi̯ap*/*śi̯äp*[s] 'pinch between'; *ni̯ôk*/*ńi̯uk*[t] 'ashamed', *sni̯ôg*/*si̯ə̯u*[u] 'shame' (loan use); perhaps we should reconstruct **s-ni̯ôk* contrasting with *sni̯ôg*. The latter would represent a fusion of prefix with initial at an Ar. Ch. level; a still earlier fusion, at a ST level, is represented by *śi̯ən*/*śi̯ĕn*[v] 'base of tooth' (= 'gums'), TB **s-nil* 'gums'. There is also evidence, however, that Chinese developed a stop element in this **s-n-* combination under undetermined conditions, comparable to Kanauri *st-* (n. 117; Kanauri *stil* 'gums'); cf. the phonetic element **tʿi̯ôg*/*t′ʿi̯ə̯u*[w] (cyclical character) (Karlgren cites Ar. Ch. *tʿni̯ôg*) for 'ashamed/shame' (above) and the text example (*ńi̯o*/*ńźi̯wo*[x] 'like' phonetic in **tʿi̯o*/*t′ʿi̯wo*[y] 'season'). There is also evidence for initial *n-* ~ *ts-* interchange in Chinese, including the classical Shuo Wên interpretation of the character *nien*[z] 'year' as including *tsʿien*[a] 'thousand' as a phonetic (cf. the discussion in P. Boodberg, 'Some Proleptical Remarks on the Evolution of Archaic Chinese', *HJAS* **2**, 1937), from ST **s-ni·ŋ*, with support for the prefix furnished by the Chinese tonal system (n. 494; S. China dialects also reflect an earlier initial **hn-* or the equivalent in this root). A pair of apparent Chinese–TB correspondences bear on this point: *tsʿi̯ĕt*[b] '7', TB **s-nis*; **dzʿi̯əg*/*dzʿi*[c] (Ar. Ch. form not cited in *GSR*) 'self', but graph is drawing of nose, and it is used as a signific in *bʿi̯əd*/*bʿyi*[d] 'nose', TB **s-na*; these roots imply **st-* > *tsʿ-* and **sd-* > **zd-* > *dzʿ-* (cf. N. Bodman, *BIHP*, *Academia Sinica*, 39, pt. 2, 1969).

472 Ar. Ch. apparently distinguished between *gli̯*/*i̯-*, as in *gli̯am*/*i̯äm*[e] 'salt' (Ar. Ch. form not cited in *GSR*, but phonetic is *klam*/*kam*[f] 'see'), TB **gryum*, *id.* (see n. 479 for vocalism), and prefixed *g-li̯*/*li̯-*, as in *g-li̯əp*/*li̯əp*[g] 'stand', TB **g-ryap*, paralleling a similar distinction between *bli̯*/*i̯-* and *b-li̯*/*li̯-* (n. 474). ST velar stop + *r*/*l* clusters also gave rise in Chinese to palatalized velars and palatal or dental stops/spirants under conditions which have not yet been determined. The Chinese correspondences for B-L *(*k-*)*la* 'tiger' (ultimately a loan from Austro-

a 史　b 吏　c 埶　d 勢　e 如　f 恕　g 絮　h 賴　i 獺　j 豊
k 體　l 墨　m 黑　n 柬　o 闌　p 藍　q 鑷　r 捻　s 攝　t 忸
u 羞　v 殀　w 丑　x 如　y 絮　z 年　a 千　b 七　c 自　d 鼻
e 鹽　f 監　g 立

gli̯ang > *li̯ang*[a] 'cool'; TB **graŋ* 'cold'.

glâk > *lâk*[b] 'kind of bird'; cf. T *glag* 'eagle, vulture'.

kʻli̯əp > *kʻi̯əp*[c] 'weep'; TB **krap*.

The first of the above comparisons parallels *gli̯əp* > *li̯əp*[d] 'stand', TB **g-ryap*, in which the prefix has been treated as an initial. We may infer that medial **r* and **l* after labial initials underwent similar shifts in Ar. Ch., but comparative material is lacking here.[473,474]

Asiatic **k*(*u*)*la*; n. 83) are especially enlightening; cf. *χo*[e] 'tiger', from **χlo* < **khlo* (prefix treated as first member of cluster), phonetic in several phonetic series: *kʻi̯o* ~ *χi̯o*,[f] from **khlo* ~ **χlo* (medial *i̯* for **l*); *lo*[g] (prefix dropped), phonetic in *li̯o*,[h] which again is phonetic in **tʻi̯o*/*t'ʻi̯wo*[i] (*GSR* cites Ar. Ch. *tʻli̯o*), from **khli̯o*; *t'ʻi̯o*/*tśʻi̯wo*,[j] also from **khli̯o* (possibly via **khri̯o*). Before the final *-*əy*, ST **kl*- (aspirated = non-prefixed) yielded Ch. *ś*- via **tśʻ*-; cf. *śi̯ər*/*śi*[k] 'dung', TB **kləy* 'excrement'. Chinese also has *ś*- for initial **k*(*h*)*l*- in early loans from AT; cf. 'reed organ/flute' (n. 457), also *śi̯uŋ*/*śi̯woŋ*[l] 'to hull grain with a pestle' (graph shows two hands with a mortar and pestle), Sui *tyuŋ* 'to hull (rice)', Thai **klooŋ*: Ahom *klɔŋ* 'to husk paddy', Siam. *khau klɔ·ŋ* 'rice (*khau*) partly shelled', IN *lət'uŋ* < */*kluŋ* 'mortar' (Benedict, 1967 bis). This article also presents loan-word (Thai) evidence that **gl*- ~ *gl*- yielded Ch. dental stop on occasion; cf. **dʻəg*/*dʻâi*[m] 'moss, lichen' (not in *GSR*), Thai **glay* 'moss'; *tieŋ*[n] 'cauldron; (*AD*) sacrificial tripod', Thai **gliaŋ*, Kam-Sui **gliaŋ* 'tripod'; cf. also *d'ʻi̯at*/*dźʻi̯ät*[o] 'tongue', from **gliat* < **g-lyak* (n. 419). ST prefixed **g*- + *r*- yielded Ch. *t'*/*tś*- (unvoiced) in *t'i̯an*/*tśi̯än*[p] 'battle; to fight', TB *(*g*-)*ra·l* (n. 461). Two sets of reflexes occur in the comparisons for ST initial **kr*-, the basis for the apparent distinction remaining unknown; cf. **χiər*/*χiei*[q] 'vinegar; (*AD*) sour' (Ar. Ch. form not cited in *GSR*), TR **kri*(*y*) 'acid, sour' (cf. also 'fear', n. 429), but **śri̯o*/*śi̯wo*[r] 'foot', TB **krəy*, *id.*; **sri̯o*/*si̯wo* ~ **sriər*/*siei*[s] (a doublet, one known from Ar. Ch., the other from Anc. Ch.) 'son-in-law', TB **krwəy*, *id.* (see n. 486 for the vocalism in this pair of roots).

473 Ar. Ch. *pli̯ət* > *pi̯et*[t] 'writing brush' has been compared with T *'bri-ba* 'write', but the Tibetan form has been derived through prefixation from **riy* 'write'; cf. also *pli̯əm* > *pi̯əm*[u] 'receive from superiors' (also read *bli̯əm* > *li̯əm* 'grain allowance from public granaries'), *bli̯əm* > *li̯əm*[v] 'government granary', and T *'brim-pa* 'distribute, deal out, hand out', Nung *ərim* 'cast away' (the Tibetan word is used in this meaning in the Ladakhi dialect).

474 See n. 469 for labial stop + *r*/*l* cluster. The two comparisons cited in n. 473 both indicate that ST prefixed **b*- + *r*/*l* yielded Ch. *bli̯*/*li̯*- and (through unvoicing; n. 443) *pli̯*/*pi̯*-; thus, ST (and TB) *(*b*-)*rim* 'distribute; cast away', Ch. *bli̯əm* (= *b-li̯əm*)/*li̯əm*[w] and *pli̯əm*/*pi̯əm* (n. 473); cf. also **bliwət*/*i̯uĕt*[x] (*GSR* suggests *bi̯wət* for Ar. Ch.) 'writing brush', from **blut*, a loan from AT **bulut* 'body hair, fur, fibre' (Benedict, 1972), with doublet **b-li̯wət*/*li̯uĕt*[y] 'pitch-pipe', from **b-lut* (cf. Eng. *quill* 'feather; pen; musical pipe'); as shown above (n. 469), ST **bl*- yielded Ch. *di̯*/*i̯*-, hence Ch. *bl*- here must be of more recent origin, confirming the loan status of this term in Chinese; **pli̯ĕt*/*pi̯ĕt*[z] (*GSR* cites Ar. Ch. *pli̯ət*) 'writing brush', with the same phonetic, from **plit*, is the doublet of **blut*, with

a 涼 b 雒 c 泣 d 立 e 虎 f 虚 g 盧 h 慮 i 攄 j 處
k 屎 l 舂 m 苔 n 鼎 o 舌 p 戰 q 醯 r 疋 s 壻 t 筆
u 稟 v 廩 w 稟 x 聿 y 律 z 筆

§46. Chinese vowels and diphthongs

The Arc. Ch. vowel system, as reconstructed by Karlgren, comprises some 10 vowel phonemes, half of which are distinguished quantitatively:

Front vowels: *i*; *ĕ*~*e*; *ε*

Back vowels: *ŭ*~*u*; *ộ*~*ô*; *ŏ*~*o*; *å*

Central vowel: *ə*

Low vowels: *â*; *ă*~*a*

It is apparent that this vowel system is far richer than anything to be found in Tibeto-Burman, and indeed serious difficulties arise in comparative analysis. In final position only the following vowels (all long) are found: *a*, *â*, *å*, *o*, and *u*. Final *i* appears only as the first member of a diphthong, while *e*, *ε*, *ô*, and *ə* appear only before final stop, nasal, or *-r*. The dissimilarity of the two systems, then, extends even into the features of distribution.[475]

Diphthongization, as already pointed out by the writer (Benedict, 1940), is the keynote of the development of vowels in Ar. Ch. This feature is best revealed in the Ar. Ch. treatment of original medial **i* before surd stops and nasals (**i* > *-i̯ĕ-*):[476]

characteristic unvoicing of the labial stop (n. 443) and substitution of medial *i* for *u* (n. 477); T *pir* '(writing) brush, pencil' shows the same vocalic shift and the unvoicing, but with the fore-stress (rather than end-stress) and the *l*>*r* shift which are typical features of these early AT loans in TB (Benedict, 1967bis). The rare ST **ml-* cluster possibly yielded Ch. *ni-*; cf. *niər/niei*[a] 'mud, mire', *niet*[b] 'black sediment in muddy water; (*AD*) clay, mud' (with suffixed *-t*; n. 428), TB **mləy* 'earth, country'. ST initial **mr-*, however, apparently yielded **mw-* at an early stage in Chinese; cf. 'horse' (n. 487) and 'tail' (n. 491), perhaps also *mi̯waŋ*[c] 'look from afar, look towards; admire; hope', TB **mraŋ* 'see'; cf. also *pwăt*[d] '8', from **b-ryât* (possible effect of the vowel *â*).

475 Despite this dissimilarity, regular correspondences can now be demonstrated for these two vowel systems, as shown below.

476 ST (and TB) medial **i* and **i·* are subject to various shifts in Chinese, as shown in the following table:

ST	TB	*-k/-ŋ*	*-t/-n/-r*	*-p/-m*
i	*i*	*i̯ĕ*	*i̯ĕ*~*ie*~*i̯ə*	*i̯ə*
i·	*i·*	*ie*	*i̯ĕ*~*ie*	[ ]

The ST high vowel **i* regularly shifts to *i̯ə* before final *-r* and final *-p/-m* (Ch. lacks medial *i̯ĕ* or *ie* in these positions) and shows alternation between *i̯ĕ* or *ie* and *i̯ə* before final *-n*, while *iə* appears in one doublet from an original final **-l* ('wash'; text and n. 462); before *-k/-ŋ*, *i̯ĕ* or *ie* is the regular reflex, with one instance each of alternation with *i̯ə* ('full', n. 469) and *i̯ă* ('name'; n. 419); after initial **śr-*, the

[a] 泥 [b] 涅 [c] 望 [d] 八

si̯ĕn[a] 'firewood'; TB **siŋ* 'tree, wood' (Trung also 'firewood').

si̯ĕn[b] 'bitter'; TB **m-sin* 'liver' < **sin* 'bitter, sour'.

mi̯ĕn[c] 'order, command' (this earlier reading for *mi̯ăng* is revealed in several Shih Ching rimes); cf. B *min*, *id.*

·i̯ĕt[d] '1'; cf. Kanauri *id.*

ńi̯ĕt[e] 'sun, day' (with suffixed *-t*); TB **niy*.

mi̯ĕng[f] 'name'; TB **r-miŋ*.

li̯ĕng[g] 'neck, collar'; TB **liŋ*.

In the above examples *i̯* represents the semivowel *j* (in Karlgren's notation), e.g. *si̯ĕn* phonemically is */syen/*. True diphthongs, with vocalic *i*, also appear in this position; cf. the following:

nien[h] 'year'; TB **niŋ*.

tsiet[i] 'joint'; TB **tsik*.

tieng[j] 'top of the head, summit'; cf. K *puŋdiŋ* 'zenith, top' (*puŋ-* is a preformative).

tiek[k] 'drop; to drop, drip'; cf. T *gtig(s)-pa* ~ *btig-pa* ~ *'thig-pa* 'drop, drip', *thigs-pa* 'a drop'.

kiet[l] 'to tie, knot'; cf. K *kyit* 'to gird, girdle', *gyit* 'to tie, bind' (apparently distinct from TB **kik*).

niek[m] 'sink, drown'; cf. B *nats* < **nik* 'sink into, be immersed', *hnats* < **s-nik* 'make to sink, immerse'.

·ieg[n] 'strangle' (note the sonant final); TB **ik*.

Ar. Ch. also draws a distinction between semivocalic *i̯* + *w* and vocalic *i* + *w*. Phonemically, medial *i̯w* can be interpreted as */jw/*, and *iw* as */u/*, the latter probably actualized as [*ü*]. Thus, we may write */sjwər/* for *si̯wər*[o] 'water'; */gʽuət/* for *gʽiwət*[p] 'dig out'. Considered thus phonemically, Ar. Ch. has the diphthongal pairs */ia/*

vowel is lowered to *ĕ* ('live') or *i̯ɛ* ('louse') (see n. 457). There is now some comparative support for the hypothesis (Benedict, 1948, note 6) that the Ch. medial *i̯ĕ* vs. *ie* distinction reflects an original ST length distinction (Mikir and Sgaw Karen show a similar lowering of the vowel when short):

	ST	Mikir	Sgaw	Chinese
tree/wood	**siŋ*	*theŋ*	*θe*	*si̯ĕn*[q]
year	**s-ni·ŋ*	*niŋ*	*ni*	*nien*[r]

ST long medial **i·* also appears to be reflected in *·ien*[s] 'smoke', from **ʔi·n* < **ʔu-n* (with suffixed *-n*; nn. 429, 441, 477); in the single comparison for TB final **-i·t*, Ch. has *-i̯ĕt* ('leech'; n. 458), but note *-iet* ~ *-i̯ĕt* for **-i-t* (suffixed **-t*) ('nephew/niece'; n. 428).

a 薪 b 辛 c 命 d 一 e 日 f 名 g 領 h 年 i 節 j 頂
k 滴 l 結 m 溺 n 縊 o 水 p 掘 q 薪 r 年 s 烟

and */ua/*, */ie/* and */ue/*, */iə/* and */uə/*, all found in medial position only. In the following pair of roots medial vocalic *u* stands for TB medial **w*:

kʿiwən/kʿuən[a] 'dog'; TB **kwiy*.

χiwet /χiuet/[b] 'blood'; TB **s-hwiy*.

The medial cluster *i̯w* (=*jw*) before *ə* corresponds to TB medial **u* in the following:

pi̯wər /pjwər/[c] 'fly'; TB **pur* ∼ **pir*.

pi̯wət /pjwət/[d] 'knee-cover'; TB **put* 'knee'.[477]

Ar. Ch. has simple medial *u* before velar finals, but the best available comparisons are with TB medial **o* rather than **u*; cf. *tsʿung*[e] 'onion', T *btsoŋ*; *khŭk* > *khåk*[f] 'shell, husk', TB **kok* 'bark, rind, skin';[478] perhaps also *kuk*[g] 'grain', B *kauk* 'rice plant'. Lowering of medial **u* to *ô* before final *-k* is indicated by the following, although it should be noted that Anc. Ch. usually has *u*:[479]

477 Chinese has a doublet here: *pi̯wət/pi̯uət*[h] and *pi̯ĕt*[i] 'knee-cover', from **put* ∼ **pit*, with evidence of similar doublets in other roots: 'eyebrow' (n. 461), paralleling similar doublet in TB; 'writing brush' (n. 474); 'enter' (n. 479). At times Chinese has medial **u* for TB **u* ∼ **i* doublets ('to fly', n. 460; 'house', n. 479) but at other times it has medial **i* for TB medial **u* ('poor' and 'dust', n. 461; 'block/pillow', n. 464; 'smoke', n. 476); this alternation, which is more common in association with labial initials or finals (assimilation or dissimilation), must be assigned to ST itself.

478 The TB root has now been reconstructed **(r-)kwâk* (n. 229) and has a Ch. correspondence in final *-wâk* (n. 488). The correspondence for 'onion' (text) indicates that ST medial **o* (rare) fell together in Chinese with **u*; cf. also 'dig' (n. 429), which has *-wət/uət* < **-ut* for TB **-ot* (original suffixed **-t*). A different correspondence is suggested by *bʿăk/bʿɒk*[j] 'white'; S. Kuki **bok*, *id.* (Sho and Chinbok *bok*, Yawdwin *pok*); G *gibok* ∼ *gipok*, Dimasa *guphu* < **g-phuk*, *id.*; perhaps also Lepcha (*ă-*)*bók* 'white and black, nearly half of each (of animals)', from TB **bok*(?).

479 The ST high back vowel **u* undergoes shifts in Chinese closely analogous to those shown by **i*; cf. the following table:

ST	TB	*-k/-ŋ*	*-t/-n/-r*	*-p/-m*
u	*u*	(*i̯*)*ô*	(*i̯*)*wə*	*ə*
u·	*u·*	(*i̯*)*ŭ* ∼ (*i̯*)*u*	*wə*	(*w*)*ə*

Short medial **u* before labials is represented by '3' (text); long medial **u·* by **·əm/·ậm*[k] 'put in mouth; hold in mouth' (not in *GSR*), TB **(m-)u·m*; also *nəp/nập*[l] 'bring in', *nwəb/nuậi*[m] (C) 'interior, inside, inner, in; enter (loan for following)', the latter from **nu·b* < **nu·p* (note tone); also the doublet *ńi̯əp/ńźi̯əp*[n] 'enter; bring in', from **n(y)ip*, TB **nu·p* ∼ **ni*[·]*p* 'sink', but Bodo-Garo also 'enter', with the same **u* ∼ **i* alternation (n. 477); cf. also **təp/tập*[o] 'ears long and hanging down' (not in *GSR*), also *ti̯ap/t'i̯äp*[p] 'hanging ears', apparently related (loan) to Thai (Siam.) **tu·p* 'hanging ears (of dog)'. ST (and TB) medial **-yu-* also yielded *-i̯a/i̯ä-* ('salt'; n. 472), as in the above doublet ('hanging ears'). Apart from forms

[a] 犬 [b] 血 [c] 飛 [d] 巿 [e] 葱 [f] 殼 [g] 穀 [h] 巿 [i] 韠 [j] 白
[k] 唵 [l] 納 [m] 內 [n] 入 [o] 耷 [p] 耴

li̯ôk > li̯uk[a] '6'; TB **d-ruk*.

pi̯ôk > pi̯uk[b] 'belly', *pʿi̯ôk ~ bʿi̯ôk*[c] 'cave'; TB **pu·k*.

dʿôk > dʿuôk[d] 'poison'; TB **duk ~ *tuk*.

mi̯ôk > mi̯uk[e] 'eye'; cf. TB **mik*. The **u ~ *i* alternation shown here is fairly common within Tibeto-Burman (see § **11**).

Comparative material for TB medial **u* before dentals and labials is extremely sparse (see Shafer, *JAOS*, **61**, 1941, p. 26). Dissimilation of this vowel before the final labial *-m* is observed in *səm*[f] '3', TB **g-sum* (the later Anc. Ch. form *sâm* is irregular), with **u* replaced by the 'neutral' (mid-central) vowel *ə*. Yet Ar. Ch. does have final *-um*, dissimilated to *-ung* in Anc. Ch., e.g. *pi̯um > pi̯ung*[g] 'wind', *gʿium > γi̯ung*[h] 'bear' (cf. Korean *kom*, Jap. *kuma*).[480]

derived from suffixed *-n* and *-t* (several cited in nn. 428 and 429) there is only one likely comparison for long medial *u·* before final dentals (rare in TB), viz. *mwən/muən*[i] 'gate, door', TB **mu·r* 'gills, beak, mouth, face'; cf. also *mi̯wən/mi̯uən*[j] 'corner of lips; shut the lips'. As in the case of medial **i·*, however, the ST length distinction is reflected in forms with velar finals, the short vowel being lowered to *ô* (the palatalization = *i̯* is variable, probably influenced by lost prefixes); cf. **b-li̯ôk/li̯uk*[k] '6', TB **d-ruk*; *dʿôk/dʿuok*[l] 'poison', TB **duk ~ *tuk*; *dʿi̯ôŋ/dʹʿi̯uŋ*[m] 'insect', Bodo-Garo **dyuŋ* (note G *dok* '6', *dźoŋ* 'insect'); *ki̯ôŋ/ki̯uŋ*[n] 'dwelling-house; palace; apartment; temple' (graph shows two rooms and a roof), from **kyum* (cf. 'bear'; n. 449), TB **kyim ~ *kyum* 'house'; *ki̯ôŋ/ki̯uŋ*[o] 'body, person', TB **guŋ*: Nungish: Răwang *guŋ* 'body, animal, self', Mutwang dial. *goŋ* 'body', B *ăkauŋ* 'body, animal body', Atsi *kuŋ*, Lisu *go-* 'body' (B-L **guŋ* or **goŋ*); contrast *ki̯ŭŋ/ki̯uŋ*[p] 'bow (weapon)', TB **ku·ŋ* 'tree; branch; stem': B *ăkhuiŋ* 'stalk, branch', also *ăkuìŋ* 'large branch, bough', apparently from *kuìŋ* 'hang over in a curve, bend downwards' (cf. Deori Chutiya *thal* 'bough', cognate with Tiddim *thal* 'bow' < TB **tal* 'arrow; bow'); *muŋ*[q] (A) 'darkened, blind' (this character also read *mi̯ŭŋ/mi̯uŋ* 'dream', below), *mi̯ŭŋ/mi̯uŋ* (A) ~ *mwaŋ*[r] (A) 'darkened; ashamed, despondent', TB **mu·ŋ* 'cloudy, dark; sullen'; *χmwəg/χuai*[s] (C) 'last day of moon; dark, obscure, darkness', from prefix + *mwək* + suffix (note tone), TB **r-mu·k* 'fog(gy); dark, dull' (an ST doublet of the foregoing root); *kʿuk*[t] 'lament, weep', L *ku·k* 'shriek'; *kʿi̯uk/kʿi̯wok*[u] 'bend, bend' (and related forms cited in n. 430), TB **m-ku·k* 'angle; knee', related to an ST doublet with short vowel represented by *ki̯ôk/ki̯uk*[v] 'bow, bend', *ki̯ôk/ki̯uk*[w] 'convex side of river bend' (both characters loaned in these senses), TB **guk ~ *kuk* 'bend; crooked'; cf. the similar ST doublet: *pi̯ôk/pi̯uk*[x] 'belly', *pʿi̯ôk/pʿi̯uk*[y] ~ *bʿi̯ôk/bʿi̯uk* 'cave' (text), TB **pu·k ~ *buk* 'cave; belly', from ST **puk ~ *buk* and **pu·k ~ *bu·k*; vowel length is discrepant in *ti̯ôŋ/tʹi̯uŋ*[z] 'middle; midway; interior, in', TB **tu·ŋ* 'inside; middle'. As indicated in two of the above comparisons, Ch. medial *-wə-* is an alternative reflex for ST long medial **u·* before velar finals.

480 Ar. Ch. final *-um* was derived from **-wam*; cf. the analysis of 'bear' (n. 449), also *pi̯um/pi̯uŋ*[a] 'wind', with phonetic *bʿi̯wăm/bʿi̯wɒm*[b] 'every, all' but also used in meaning 'wind'.

a 六	b 腹	c 復	d 毒	e 目	f 三	g 風	h 熊	i 門	j 吻
k 六	l 毒	m 蟲	n 宮	o 躬	p 弓	q 夢	r 瞢	s 晦	t 哭
u 曲	v 鞠	w 鞫	x 腹	y 復	z 中	a 風	b 凡		

Only scattered comparisons can be cited for the mid-back and mid-front vowels **o* and **e*, which are poorly represented in Tibeto-Burman itself.[481] Shafer (1941, *JAOS*, **61**, pp. 18 and 24–5) has tables for both vowels, but the material is of uncertain quality. The best single comparison for TB medial **e* is *miən*[a] 'close the eyes, sleep', TB **myel* 'sleepy' (see Benedict, 1940, p. 113). In the following pair, comparisons may be made with medial **a* as well as **e*:[482]

481 See n. 478 for ST medial **o*. The text example shows *-iən* for ST **-yel*, but Ar. Ch. has *-i̯an* in the one comparison for ST **-yer* ('to fly', n. 443) while *-ian* corresponds to ST **-er* ('sleet/hail', n. 460). The regular correspondence for ST medial **e* before dental or labial finals, however, is Ar. Ch. *i̯a*, which shows a similar lowering of the vowel, paralleling the medial **i* > *i̯ĕ* ~ *ie* shift (n. 476); cf. 'sweet' (n. 458), 'face' (n. 461), also *li̯an/li̯än*[b] (A) 'connect; unite; in a row, consecutively', *li̯an/li̯än*[c] (A) 'join, bring together', TB **ren* 'equal; place in a row; line, row'; also *mi̯at/mi̯ät*[d] 'drown; extinguish, destroy', T *med-pa* 'to be not, to exist not' (not from *mi yod-pa*, as Jäschke believed, if this form is cognate), a doublet of the general TB root **mit* 'extinguish' (but Dimasa 'destroy'), ST **met* ~ **mit*. The two examples of ST final **-eŋ* have Ch. *-i̯ĕŋ/i̯äŋ* ('weasel', n. 457; 'red', n. 464), suggesting that it fell together with ST **-iŋ* (short *i*).

482 The two TB roots cited have now been reconstructed **səm* 'breath, voice, spirit' and **təp* ~ **dəp* 'fold; repeat', on the basis of the medial *a* ~ *e* alternation in Tibetan (n. 344). It is difficult to reconstruct medial **ə* (as distinct from medial **a*) for TB roots lacking the Tibetan alternation, but we have done so (provisionally) in a few roots, and these all have Ch. cognates with the same medial vowel; cf. TB *(*s*-)*brəŋ* 'fly, bee' (to explain B *yaŋ*, from **ryaŋ* < **ryəŋ* < **bryəŋ*, palatalized before *ə*), Ch. *di̯əŋ/i̯əŋ*[e] (n. 469); TB **əm* 'eat, drink' (to explain Kuki **in*), Ch. *·i̯əm*[f] (text); TB **kəp* 'needle' (to explain B *ap*, from **kyəp*, with eventual loss of velar initial), Ch. *t'i̯əm/tśi̯əm*[g] and **t'i̯əp/tśi̯əp*[h] (n. 464); TB **gəm* 'jaw (molar teeth)' (to explain B *àm*, from **gyəm*, as in above root), Ch. *g'əm/γậm*[i] 'jaw'. The vowel is not palatalized in the latter, paralleling *gʿəm/γậm*[j] (A) 'hold in the mouth'; (C) 'put in the mouth', TB **gam* 'put into mouth, seize with mouth' (text), from ST **gəm*; also (with palatalized doublet) **kʿəm/kʿậm*[k] (C) 'cliff, bank; steep' (not in *GSR*), *kʿi̯əm*[l] (A) 'precipitous', TB **r-ka*[·]*m* (L *kam* 'bank, shore, mouth', *kha·m* 'precipice'), from ST *(*r*-)*kə*[·]*m*; cf. also 'cough' (below). Generally, however, the correspondence is Ch. medial *i̯ə* = TB medial **a*, with numerous examples in final velars and labials (but no certain comparisons for final dentals); cf. ST *tək* 'mount; raise' (text and n. 465); **trək* 'weave' (text); **sək* 'breathe, breath, life' (text), **gək* ~ **kək* 'ridge (of house); peak (highest point)' (n. 444), **śrək* 'color (face); shame' (n. 457); *(*g*-)*lək* 'arm; wing' (n. 458); **g-ləŋ* ~ **g-lək* 'eagle, falcon' (nn. 225, 458); *(*s*-)*təŋ* ~ **dəŋ*: *təŋ*[m] (A) 'rise, ascend; raise' (note lack of palatalization in this originally prefixed form), *t'ʿi̯əŋ/tśʿi̯əŋ*[n] (A) 'lift, hold', *d'ʿi̯əŋ/dźʿi̯əŋ*[o] (A) 'mount, ascend; ride, drive; be on top, above', *d'i̯əŋ/źi̯əŋ*[p] (A) 'lift, hold' (note same tone A in all four forms); TB: Bodish **s-təŋ* 'upper part'; Karen **tha*[*ŋ*] 'up, go up' (n. 384); **nəŋ* ~ **naŋ* 'thou' (n. 432); *(*s*-)*nəŋ* 'follow(ing)' (n. 432); cf. also **krəp* 'weep' (text); **ńəp* ~ **ńap* 'pinch' (text and n. 471); **səm* 'breath, spirit; heart' (text); **ńəm* 'think' (text and n. 465); **ńəm* 'soft' (n. 465); cf. also **təl* 'arrow; bow' (n. 452) and **dzər* ~ **tsər* 'sister' (n. 460). ST long medial

a 眠 b 連 c 聯 d 滅 e 蠅 f 飲 g 鍼 h 針 i 頷 j 含
k 墈 l 嶔 m 登 n 爯 o 乘 p 丞

si̯əm[a] 'heart'; cf. T *sem(s)* 'soul, mind, spirit', *sem(s)-pa* 'think'; also *bsams* (a Pf. form of *sem(s)-pa*) and *bsam-pa* 'thought'.

dʻi̯əp[b] 'pile on; duplicate, repeat; fold'; cf. T *ldeb-pa* 'bend round or back, double down', *lteb-pa* 'turn down, turn in', *thebs* 'series, order, succession'; also TB **tap* (No. 493), as represented by T *ltab-pa* 'fold or gather up, lay or put together', *ltab-ma* 'a fold', *ldab-pa* 'do again, repeat', K *thap* 'layer', *kəthap* 'add, place one upon another; again and again', B *thap* 'place one on another, add to; repeat, do again'.

Ar. Ch. has final *-u*, but this element is rare and only one good comparison has been found, viz. *kʻu*[c] 'rob', TB **r-kuw* 'steal'.[483] Final *-i*, as pointed out above, is altogether lacking in Ar. Ch. as reconstructed by Karlgren.[484] Ar. Ch. regularly has *-i̯ŭg* or *-i̯ŏg* for TB **-u* ~ **-uw*, and *-i̯əd* or *-i̯ər* for TB **-i* ~ **-iy*:

**ə·* can be reconstructed for the following: *ki̯əp*[d] 'draw (water)', TB **ka·p, id.*, from ST **kə·p*; cf. also *kʼəg/kʼậi*[e] (C) 'cough', from **khək-ma* or the like (n. 494); TB **ka·k* 'cough up; phlegm' (Mikir and Lushei), as if from ST **kə·k*, but T *khogs(-pa)* 'cough', v/n. points to a TB doublet **kâk*.

483 The reconstruction of TB **-u* as opposed to the more common **-əw* is based entirely on evidence supplied by B-L and Nungish, and the Chinese evidence is hardly sufficient to set up this distinction for ST itself. Chinese has many forms in final *-u/ə̯u* but the best comparisons are either with TB roots in final **-əw* (= *-uw* in text) or in final **-u(w)*, which can be either **-u* or **-əw* (in absence of B-L or Nungish cognates); cf. *kʻu/kʻəu*[f] 'rob', TB **r-kəw* 'steal' (but Dimasa has *khau*) (for the semantics, cf. TK **-ru·k*: K-N 'steal', Karen 'rob'); *kʻi̯u*[g] 'body, person', TB **(s-)kəw* 'body': T *sku*, B *kui(y)* (the *-y* is a product of etymologizing); *ńi̯u/ńźi̯u*[h] 'nipple; milk; suckle; (*AD*) breast', TB **nəw* 'breast; milk'; also **sri̯u/si̯u*[i] 'older sister', TB **sru(w)* 'aunt' (n. 457); *kʻu/kʻəu*[j] 'mouth', Bodo-Garo **k(h)u, id.*: G *ku* ~ *khu*, Dimasa *khu*, from TB **ku(w)*. The Dimasa ablaut form (*khau*) for 'steal' suggests that the first three ST roots, at any rate, are to be reconstructed with final **-ə·w* rather than **-əw*, paralleling the indicated distinction in ST between medial *ə·* and *ə* (n. 482). In one comparison, however, final **-u* can be reconstructed for ST on the basis of B-L data: *dʼu/dʻə̯u*[k] 'head', TB **(d-)bu* (B *ù*).

484 Chinese final *-ia/ię*, which is well represented in the language, apparently stands for ST final **-i* (= *-i·*), paralleling medial *-ie-* for ST long medial **i·* (n. 476). TB has both **-əy* and **-i*, but this distinction is maintained only in B-L, and comparative data are inadequate for setting this up as a feature of ST itself (cf. n. 483 as regards the similar situation for the ST high back vowel). A direct correspondence is supplied by *gʻia/gʻyię*[l] 'ride (horse)', B *tsì* (but *ki* in inscriptions), from **gi* (Lisu *dzi*, Ahi and Lolopho *dze*, Nyi *de*), but these forms appear to involve old loans from AT with typical loss of an original medial **w* (Thai **khwi* ~ **gwi*) (Benedict, 1967bis); the correspondence in final with Thai **-i* is found also in *kia/kyię*[m] 'odd (number)', Thai (Siam.) **gi, id.* There is one excellent comparison with TB, viz. *gwia/ywię*[n] 'elephant' (obsolete), TB **m-gwi(y)* (n. 449), but this TB root can be reconstructed in either **-i* or **-əy* (no B-L cognate). Other comparisons for Chinese final **-ia/ię* are of doubtful significance; cf. *pia/pyię*[o]

a 心 b 疊 c 寇 d 汲 e 咳 f 寇 g 軀 h 乳 i 嬃 j 口
k 頭 l 騎 m 奇 n 爲 o 羆

ki̯ŭg[a] '9'; TB **d-kuw*.

g'i̯ŭg[b] 'owl' (signific is picture of horned owl); TB **gu* (No. 494), as represented by K *u-khu* (*u* 'bird'), B *khu* (Tavoyan dialect, as recorded by Tin, 1933), Lisu *gu*,[485] Lakher *va-ku* (*va* 'bird'), Mikir *iŋhu* < **iŋkhu* 'owl', perhaps also Kanauri *kug* ~ *kuk* through reduplication.

sug[c] 'cough'; TB **su*(*w*). Note that the Ar. Ch. initial is not palatalized in this example.

b'i̯ŭg[d] 'carry on the back'; TB **buw*.

ki̯ôg[e] 'pigeon, turtle-dove'; TB **kuw* (No. 495), as represented by Miri *pəkü*, B *khui*, Meithei *khu-nu*, Khami *iŋməkhu* 'pigeon' (contrast B *khrui̇*, Khami *məkhru* 'dove').

g'i̯ôg[f] 'uncle, father-in-law'; TB **kuw*.

si̯əd[g] '4'; TB **b-liy*.

pi̯əd[h] 'give'; TB **biy*.

si̯ər[i] 'die'; TB **siy*.

The reconstruction of final *-g*, *-d*, and *-r* for Ar. Ch. in roots of this type will be questioned by many.[486] Simon (*MSOS*, **30**, 1927) showed the way here with his 'brown-and-white bear', Răwang (Nungish) *śəwi* 'bear', possibly from TB **pwi*(*y*) (plus **s-* 'animal prefix'), with regular loss of medial **w* in Chinese before the front vowel *i* (n. 463).

485 The word for 'owl' is not cited in the standard Lisu source (Fraser), but does appear in C. M. Enríquez, 'The Yawyins or Lisu', *JBRS* **11** (1921), 70–4, in the form 'owl or night-bird'. The Kachin and Burmese forms (with aspirated initial) suggest the reconstruction **ku* rather than **gu*.

486 This knotty problem was resolved in Benedict, 1948 bis in favor of the 'offglide' explanation of Ar. Ch. final *-g* and *-d* as derivatives of ST final *-w* and *-y*, respectively, this all tying into a general interpretation of the development of the voiced fricatives (including semi-vowels) in Chinese (n. 446); for Ar. Ch. final *-r* in roots of this type, however, the writer favored Karlgren's view that this element is essentially a rhotacism, and here he cited *ńi̯ər*/*ńźi*[j] (C) '2', TB **g-nis*. This is no longer tenable, however, since the ST root must be reconstructed without the final **-s*, and in any event Chinese has *-t* rather than *-r* for this final (see discussion in n. 454). We must therefore revert to our earlier view (text) of final *-r* as an offglide in roots of this type. It also now appears that final *-r* forms normally occurred in Ar. Ch. in open juncture (tones A and B), final *-d* forms in close juncture (tone C) (n. 494); cf. *si̯əd*/*si*[k] (C) '4', TB **b-ləy* (text); *pi̯əd*/*pyi*[l] (C) 'give', TB **bəy* (text); *mi̯əd*/*myi*[m] (C) 'sleep', TB **(r-)mwəy* ~ **(s-)mwəy* (n. 463); contrast *si̯ər*/*si*[n] (B) 'die', TB **səy* (text); *śi̯ər*/*śi*[o] (B) 'dung', TB **kləy* (n. 472); *b'i̯ər*/*b'yi*[p] (B) 'female of animals', TB *pwi*(*y*) (n. 428); *mi̯wər*/*mywəi*[q] (A) 'minute, small', TB **mwəy* (n. 463); note also *GSR*-519, with *li̯əd*/*lyi*[r] (C) 'sharp' as phonetic in a fairly large series exclusively with final *-r* forms all in tone A. Tonal alternation is found in *pi̯ər*/*pyi*[s] (B ~ C) 'deceased mother or ancestress', TB **pəy* 'grandmother', while both tonal and vocalic alternation are displayed by *di̯ər*/*i* (A) ~ *t'i̯ər*/*t'iei*[t] (C)

[a] 九 [b] 舊 [c] 嗽 [d] 負 [e] 鳩 [f] 舅 [g] 四 [h] 畀 [i] 死 [j] 二
[k] 四 [l] 畀 [m] 寐 [n] 死 [o] 屎 [p] 牝 [q] 微 [r] 利 [s] 妣 [t] 洟

reconstruction of final spirants (-*γ*, -*δ*), and Karlgren later (*BMFEA*, 5, 1934) suggested the forms adopted in this review. It might be argued that Ar. Ch. -*g* was developed secondarily after the back vowel *u*, and -*d* after the front vowel *i*, yet Ar. Ch. has -*g* after medial *i̯ə* as well as *i̯ŭ* and *i̯ô*. The assumption that all final sonant stops were dropped or replaced by -*w* or -*y* in Tibeto-Burman, on the other hand, involves no insuperable difficulty. Inasmuch as Tibeto-Burman retains final *-*r*, however, we must infer that Ar. Ch. -*r* in *si̯ər*[a] 'die' represents a type of consonantal offglide, i.e. ST *-*i* > Ar. Ch. -*i̯ər*, falling together with ST *-*ir* > Ar. Ch. -*i̯ər*.

TB final *-*a* after velars is represented by Ar. Ch. -*o*:

kʻo[b] 'bitter'; TB **ka*.
gʻwo[c] 'fox'; TB **gwa*.
ngo[d] 'I'; TB **ŋa*.
ngo[e] '5'; TB **l-ŋa* ~ **b-ŋa*.
ngi̯o[f] 'fish'; TB **ŋya*.

'mucus from the nose', TB **ti*(*y*) 'water' (n. 449). The root for '2' (above) also shows final -*r* with tone C (close juncture), so it could be argued that some other distinction should be reconstructed, e.g. ST *-*ə·y* > -*i̯ər* contrasting with ST *-*əy* > -*i̯əd* (paralleling the distinction suggested in n. 483 for the ST high back vowel); it is also possible that an original ST suffixed *-*s* (cf. TB **g-ni-s* '2') yielded Ar. Ch. -*i̯ər* rather than -*i̯əd*. Final -*iər* (rather than -*i̯ər*) also appears in *χiər*/*χiei*[g] (A) 'sour', TB **kri*(*y*) (n. 472); **sriər*/*siei*[h] (C) 'son-in-law', TB **krwəy*, and it is possible that this final is the derivative of ST *-*ə·y* (but note that two of the -*iər*/*iei* forms are in tone C). For 'son-in-law' (above), Chinese has the doublet **sri̯o*/*si̯wo*, paralleling *śri̯o*/*şi̯wo*[i] 'foot', TB **krəy* (n. 472) as well as *śri̯u*/*şi̯u*[j] 'count', TB *(*r*-)*tśrəy* (n. 457), all apparently through the effect of the retroflex (*r*) initial cluster; cf. the similar shift of final *-*a* after initial palatals (n. 487).

ST (and TB) final *-*əw* is usually represented by Ch. -*i̯ŭg*/*i̯ə̯u* ~ -*i̯ôg*/*i̯ə̯u*, with palatalization before the vowel, as shown by the text citations. The basis for the apparent distinction in Ar. Ch. (based on evidence from rhymes) is not known, but it is possible that it reflects an ST distinction in vocalic length: ST *-*ə·w* > -*i̯ŭg* contrasting with *-*əw* > -*i̯ôg*; cf. the ST medial **u·* ~ **u* shifts described in n. 479. It has also been suggested (n. 483) that Ch. -*u*/*ə̯u* and -*i̯u* might also be derivatives of ST *-*ə·w*, and certain phonetic series (notably *GSR*-131 and *GSR*-132) show interchange between the two types of finals. The correspondence for 'owl' (text) is irregular and shows vowel gradation, as do the two related forms (n. 441).

The above evidence suggests an essentially circular development for both ST *-*əy* and *-*əw* (and corresponding long vowel forms), e.g. ST *-*əw* > -*i̯ôg* (Ar. Ch.) > -*i̯ə̯u* (Anc. Ch.). This seems somewhat unlikely (although possible) and perhaps it is preferable to regard Ar. Ch. as a 'sister' (but older) dialect of Anc. Ch. rather than as directly ancestral to it, allowing ST *-*əw* > -*i̯ə̯u* (Anc. Ch.) directly. This view is of help in explaining the numerous irregularities noted by Karlgren in the development of Anc. Ch. forms, e.g. Anc. Ch. *sâm*[k] '3' (irregular), from ST *-*sum* directly rather than via *səm*, the Ar. Ch. form (which should have yielded Anc. Ch.

a 死 b 苦 c 狐 d 吾 e 五 f 魚 g 醯 h 婿 i 疋 j 數
k 三

The fate of original _*-a_ after other types of initials, however, cannot be determined with any assurance.[487] The available comparisons indicate that _-a_, _-â_, or _-å_

*sậm); the unusually large number of doublets, triplets and even more complex multiple forms in Chinese also lends itself to a general explanation along these lines.

_487_ Final _*-â_ must be reconstructed for a few ST roots (in TB and Karen it falls together with _*-a_); cf. _*tsâ_ ~ _*dzâ_ 'salt' (text and n. 161; the Tibetan '_wa-zur_' form: _tswa_ is perhaps significant here); _*ŋâ_ 'goose' (nn. 428, 488); _*nâ_ 'red' (n. 429); _*bwâ_ 'old woman, grandmother' (n. 463); _*(g-)yâ_ 'left' (n. 428), contrasting with _*g-ya_ 'right' (n. 449); also _kâ_[a] 'sing, song', TB _*ka_ 'word, speech' (JAM notes meaning 'sing' in Lahu), from ST _*kâ_; _ŋâ_ 'I' has a special grammatical function (p. 160) and cannot be set up as an ST form distinct from _*ŋa_ (text). The apparent alternation _-wâ_ ~ _-o_ appears in _tʻwâ_[b] (C) 'spit', _tʻo/tʻuo_[c] (B ~ C) 'eject from the mouth; (_AD_) vomit, spit out', TB _*(m-)twa_ ~ _*(s-)twa_ 'spit; spittle' (also 'vomit' in Nungish and Kachin); cf. also _*klwa/kwa_ ~ _glwâ/luâ_[d] 'snail', _*glwâ/luâ_[e] '_kuo-lo_ (a small wasp, a kind of mollusc)', Karen _*khlo_ 'snail', B _khărú_, _id_. The final _-wa_ of 'snail' (above) is a rare instance of this final in Chinese, since it generally has shifted to _-wo_ ('fox', text) or to _-å/-a_, especially after labial initials, as in the text citations (see n. 463 for an interpretation of these).

ST (and TB) final _*-a_ is subject to several different shifts in Chinese, with final _-o_ appearing not only after initial velars (text) but also after labials and (non-palatalized) dentals; cf. _*(r-)wa_ 'rain' (text); _*(s-)wa_ 'be in motion, go, come' (n. 447); _*pwa_ 'man, husband, person' (n. 463); _*pwa_ or _*b-wa_ 'palm (of hand)' (n. 463); _*r-pwa_ 'ax' (n. 463); _*pwa_ ~ _*bwa_ 'father' (n. 463); _*(k-)la_ 'tiger' (n. 472); also _*(s-)la_ 'salt': _lo/luo_[f] 'salty; (_AD_) rock-salt' (used in graphs as general signific for 'salt'), TB _*la_ 'salt' (Miri _əlo_ < _*a-la_), Karen _*hla_, _id_. (Pwo _la_, on high tone); _ni̯o_[g] 'thou', TB (Nungish) _*na_ (n. 432); _no/nuo_[h] 'crossbow', corresponding to Thai _*hna_, Vn. _na_, Răwang (Nungish) _thəna_, Moso (B-L) _tăna_ 'crossbow', Sui _hna_ 'bow' (Benedict, 1967bis, considers the Ch. form an early loan from an unknown source; cf. the Ch. forms for 'tiger', similarly attributed to borrowing; these must all date from a period antedating the _*-a_ > _-o_ shift in Chinese); _no/nuo_[i] (A) 'wife and children' (cf. T _ma-smad_ 'mother and children'), with the basic phonetic (and cognate) _ni̯o/ni̯wo_[j] (B) 'woman, lady, girl', TB _*(m-)na_: T _mna-ma_ 'daughter-in-law', Murmi _na-na_, Vayu _nu-nu_ < _*na-na_, K _na_, Chang Naga _a-no_ < _*-na_ 'older sister', Byangsi (Almora State) _na_ 'mother', _pu-na_ 'aunt', Miri _a-nă_ 'mother' (Abor 'grandmother'), Lakher (Kuki) _i-na_ 'mother'. The _*-a_ > _-o_ shift in Chinese apparently occurred not long before the Archaic period, since the original vowel is reflected in an early loan in the AT languages, viz. Thai _*ha_ < _*hŋa_, Ong-Be _ŋa_ '5' (n. 435).

The normal shift after the palatals _*ś-_ and _*y-_ was to _-i̯əu_ in Anc. Ch., with correspondences in Ar. Ch. as described in n. 486; cf. _śi̯ôg/śi̯əu_[k] 'animal', TB _*śa_ 'flesh, meat, animal' (n. 452); _gi̯ŭg/ji̯əu_[l] 'right (hand)', TB _*g-ya_ (n. 449); also _zi̯ôg/i̯əu_[m] 'laugh' (character borrowed in this meaning), TB _*rya-t_ (see n. 458 for the _-t_ suffixed form of this root); cf. also (from the same phonetic series) _zi̯ôg/i̯əu_[n] 'cock' (calendrical term), which has been identified (Benedict, 1967bis) as a probable loan from _*raka_, the equivalent term in the Cambodian calendar, apparently via _*rəw_ < _*ra(ka)_, showing fore-stress as in the TB loan (_*rak_ 'fowl')

[a] 歌 [b] 唾 [c] 吐 [d] 蝸 [e] 蠃 [f] 鹵 [g] 汝 [h] 弩 [i] 孥 [j] 女
[k] 獸 [l] 右 [m] 猶 [n] 酉

are the Ar. Ch. representatives of ST **-a*; cf. *sa*[a] 'sand', T *sa* 'earth'; *ngâ*[b] 'I', TB **ŋa*; *dz'â*[c] 'salt', TB **tsa*; *på*[d] 'kind of bamboo', TB **g-pa* 'bamboo'; *på*[e]

but with different syllabic division (**ra-ka* ~ **rak-a*); the corresponding term in the Thai calendar is **raw*, which now appears to have been influenced (possible 'back-loan') by Chinese, since Thai itself does not show the vocalic shift from **a*; cf. Thai **kaw* '9', a loan from Ch. *ki̯ŭg/ki̯əu*[f] (Benedict, 1967bis, indicates **raw* < **raga* < **raka*, a possible alternative explanation). A similar shift to the closely related final *-i̯u* is shown by *t'i̯u/tśi̯u*[g] 'red', TB **tya* (n. 452).

A third correspondence for ST (and TB) final **-a* is found after dental affricates and sibilants and palatalized **n* and **l* (at early level); cf. *ńi̯əg/ńźi̯*[h] 'ear', TB **r-na* (apparently palatalized early by the **r-* prefix); **dz'i̯əg/dz'i*[i] 'self' (=nose), TB **s-na* (n. 471); *tsi̯əg/tsi* ~ *dzi̯əg/zi*[j] 'child', TB **tsa* ~ **za* (n. 86); *d''i̯ək/dź'i̯ək*[k] 'eat' (note the final *-k*) and *dzi̯əg/zi*[l] 'food, give food to', TB **dza* (n. 452); perhaps also, with suffixed *-t*, *dz'i̯ət/dz'i̯ĕt*[m] 'sickness, pain', TB **tsa* 'hot; pain' (n. 429) (we would anticipate **dz'iet/dz'iet* here; n. 488). The final *-g* of these forms is to be interpreted as a secondary development after the vowel *ə*, which does not occur as a final; the forms for 'eat' (above) show that final *-k* is possible here as a doublet formation; cf. also *di̯ək/i̯ək*[n] 'arrow with string attached', TB **bla* 'arrow' (n. 469).

Finally, a fourth correspondence for ST (and TB) final **-a* is found under conditions of initial (non-phonemic) glottalization of the root (or of the prefix **a-*), with parallels in TB and Karen; cf. *·ăg/·a*[o] 'dumb (mute)', TB **a=ʔa*; Burmese has *á* with 'creaky voice' (glottal accent) and Karen has **-ʔaʔ*; cf. also *zi̯ăg/i̯a*[p] 'evening', *dzi̯ak/zi̯äk*[q] 'evening, night', TB **ya*; Burmese has *ńá* with 'creaky voice', from **né-ya* < **ne-ăya* 'day-its (*ă-*) evening', from **nəy ʔa-ya* while Răwang (Nungish), Mutwang dial. has *yaʔ*; Karen **hya* also points to an earlier prefixed element, perhaps *ʔ(a)-* rather than *k-* (n. 371).

As indicated in the text, Ar. Ch. also has *-å* (= *-ɔ*) appearing to correspond to TB final **-a* in some roots, especially after labial initials. This final, recognized by Karlgren as distinct from Ar. Ch. final *-a* (Anc. Ch. has *-a* for both) on the basis of rhyme evidence, apparently had been developed in many if not most instances from an earlier **-wa* (virtually absent in the Ar. Ch. system of finals); cf. **på/pa*[r] 'father (vocative)' (not in *GSR*), from **pwa*, a complex doublet of *b'i̯wo/b'i̯u*[s] (n. 463), from ST **pwa* ~ **bwa*; **på/pa*[t] (A) 'palm of hand' (not in *GSR* in this meaning), also **på/pa*[u] (B) 'grasp; handful', from **pwa*, a complex doublet of *b'i̯wo/b'i̯u*[v] (n. 463), from ST **pwa* ~ **bwa* or **b-wa*; **på/pa*[w] 'kind of bamboo' (not in *GSR*), from **pwa*; ST **(g-)pwa*; cf. also **må/ma*[x] (*AD* cites only Mand. and Cant. forms) 'mother, old woman', from **mwa*, a doublet of the old reading for this character: **mo/muo* 'mare'; ST **ma* (TB **ma* 'mother', also **-ma* 'fem. suffix'). It thus appears that Ar. Ch. generally maintained ST final **-wâ*, with a rare doublet in *-o* (n. 487), but shifted final **-wa* either to *-(i̯)wo* (add 'fox', from text, to the above examples) or to *-å*, with frequent doublet formation; cf. also *kå/ka*[y] (A) 'male pig, boar', from **kwa*, a doublet of *g'i̯wag/g'i̯wo*[z] (A ~ C) 'kind of boar', probably from **gwa-gwa* (note tone C doublet), apparently related also to

a 沙 b 我 c 鹾 d 芭 e 巴 f 九 g 朱 h 耳 i 自 j 子
k 食 l 飤 m 疾 n 弋 o 啞 p 夜 q 夕 r 爸 s 父 t 巴
u 把 v 扶 w 笆 x 媽 y 豭 z 豦

'palm of the hand', TB **på*; *på*[a] 'father' (Ar. Ch. form inferred), TB **pa*; *må*[b] 'mother' (Ar. Ch. form inferred), TB **ma*.

Medial **a* is sometimes retained in the form *a* or *â*, sometimes replaced by the palatalized combination *i̯ə*.[488] No equation can be made for the short vs. long

g'wân/g'uân[c] (A) 'kind of pig' (with 'collective' *-n* suffix). This last root is of unusual interest since it perhaps represents an archaic form of *på/pa*[d] 'sow, pig', from **pwa*; cf. TB **pwak* (both identified as loans from AT; n. 78). On the basis of this present interpretation of Chinese final *-å/a*, we can reconstruct **mwa* (rather than **mra*, as suggested by Pulleyblank) for *må/ma*[e] 'horse', from an earlier **mra*; cf. TB **s-raŋ* ~ **m-raŋ* (Gyarung has *öbŏrŏ*), but the finals do not correspond, hence there is presumptive evidence here of an early loan from a disyllabic (or longer) form: **m*[ ]*raŋ*[ ] (source unknown), with Chinese and TB showing the same distinction in syllabic division as in other early loans; cf. the following:

	(Source)	TB	Chinese
cock/fowl	**raka*	**rak*	*zi̯ôg/i̯ə̯u*[f] < **r(y)əw* < **ra*
pig	**mba(γ)-*	**pwak*	*på/pa*[g] < **pwa*
horse	**m*[ ]*raŋ*[ ]	**m-raŋ*	*må/ma*[h] < **mwa* < **mra*

We can confidently reconstruct **mwa* in the 'horse' phonetic series because of the following excellent comparison: *må/ma*[i] (C) 'revile, curse', from a form such as **mwa-pa* (note tone), T *dmod-pa* 'curse', from **-mwa-d* (with verbal suffixed *-d*), a regular shift in Tibetan (p. 49).

488 We must reconstruct both medial **a* and **â* for ST, along with medial **ə* (n. 482), but the correspondences are complex, as shown by the following set for ST (and TB) medial **a*:

**-(r, y)aŋ* > *-i̯aŋ*: **graŋ* 'cold' (text), **kyaŋ* 'ginger' (text and n. 464); **źraŋ* 'uncle; superior (title)' (n. 457).

*(palatal) + *-ak* > *-i̯ăk*: **tśak* 'red' (n. 452); **(g-)tyak* '1' (n. 271); **ryak* 'grease, oil; juice, fluid' (n. 458); **(g-)yak* 'armpit' (text and n. 448), but **-yak* > *-i̯ak* ~ *i̯at* in *(m-)lyak* ~ **(s-)lyak* ~ **(g-)lyak* 'lick; tongue' (n. 419).

**(y)ap* > *-i̯ap*: **tsyap* (or **tśap* ~ **tsap*) 'join, connect; close/adjacent' (n. 452); **lap* 'leaf' (n. 458).

**-yam* > *-i̯am*: **s-ryam* 'sharp' (n. 457); cf. also *g'ɛm/γăm*[j] 'salt; salty'; Karen **hyam* 'salty' (n. 371), from ST **gyam* (?).

**-a(r, l)* > *-i̯ĕn*: **sar* 'new, fresh' (n. 460) (note Ch. alternation: *si̯ĕn* 'new' ~ *si̯an* 'fresh'); *sar* ~ *śar* 'louse' (n. 460); **(m-)kal* ~ **(m-)gal* 'kidney' (n. 460).

**-a-n* (suffixed *-n*) > *-i̯ĕn* ~ *ien*: **śa-n* 'flesh/body' (n. 428); **tsa-n* 'child; relatives' (n. 428); **tya-n* 'red' (n. 429); **ka-n* 'heavens' (n. 428).

**a-t* (suffixed *-t*) > *-iet*: **rya-t* 'laugh' (n. 458).

**maŋ* > **măŋ*; cf. TB **maŋ*: Trung (Nungish) *dəmaŋ* 'big (of persons); (comp.) older (brother, uncle)', B *ù-màŋ* 'uncle' (*màŋ* 'ruler, governor, official'), Ch. *măŋ/mɒŋ*[k] 'eldest (of brothers); great, principal'.

**-waŋ* > *-wăŋ*: **bwaŋ* ~ **pwaŋ* 'uncle/older brother' (n. 463).

**(w)am* > *-um*: **(d-)wam* 'bear' (n. 449).

a 爸 b 媽 c 豲 d 豝 e 馬 f 酉 g 豝 h 馬 i 駡 j 鹹
k 孟

medial *a* distinction in Tibeto-Burman, inasmuch as no sure Ar. Ch. comparison has been found for TB long *a*. This fact is clearly borne out in the table arranged

*(*w*)*al* > -*wan* ~ -*wăn* ~ -*wən* (< *-*un*): **wal* 'round, circular; circle, enclosure; encircle' (n. 448).

*-*wan* > -*wan* ~ -*wən* (< *-*un*): **dzwan* 'hawk, kite' (n. 453); *(*r*-)*tswa* ~ *(*r*-)*dzwa-n* 'grass' (n. 161) (latter with *dzʻiən*/*dzʻien* doublet).

The corresponding long vowel, ST medial **a·*, shifted in Chinese before final velars to a mid or high back vowel: *o* ~ *ô* or *ŭ* ~ *u* (usually palatalized; medial **ya·* regularly yields medial *i̯ô*), paralleling similar shifts of final *-*a* = -*a·* (n. 487); cf. **ba·k* 'bat' (n. 443); *(*s*-)*naŋ* ~ *(*s*-)*na·ŋ*; cf. L *hna·ŋ* 'thick (fluid)', Ch. *ńi̯aŋ*/*ńźi̯aŋ* (A)[a] 'heavy with dew', *ńi̯aŋ*/*ńźi̯aŋ*[b] (A ~ B) 'rich growth of grain', also *nuŋ*[c] (A) ~ *ńi̯uŋ*/*ńźi̯uŋ* (A) 'thick, rich (*sc.* dew)', *ni̯uŋ*/*ńi̯woŋ*[d] (A) ~ *ńi̯uŋ*/*ńźi̯woŋ* (A) 'thick covering, luxuriant growth' (note same tone throughout); also **dwa·ŋ*: cf. T *dwa·ŋ* 'hole, cave, pit', Ch. *dʻuŋ*[e] (C) 'hole, cave, ravine' (meanings not attested in Ar. Ch.), probably also *dʻuŋ*[f] (A) 'tube' (the vocalism in this root could also be explained in terms of the medial **w*). As in the root for 'thick' (above), an ST doublet is indicated for the following: *(*r*-)*maŋ* ~ *(*r*-)*ma·ŋ* 'dream'; cf. TB *r-maŋ*, Ch. *mi̯ŭŋ*/*mi̯uŋ*[g] 'dream'; **naŋ* ~ **na·ŋ* (also *nəŋ*) 'thou' (n. 432); **s-ryak* ~ **s-rya·k* 'day (24 hours); pass the night' (n. 457). Vowel length is indeterminate in the following pair: **ka*[·]*ŋ*; cf. TB **kaŋ* (= **k*[*a*, *a·*]*ŋ*): Nungish: Trung *a-kaŋ*, Răwang *əkhaŋ* 'grandfather'; B *phá-khaŋ* 'father', *mí-khaŋ* 'mother' (*khaŋ-pwàn* 'spouse', *khaŋ-bhya* 'sir, madam'), Ch. *kuŋ*[h] 'father' > 'grandfather (vocative)' (honorific); *(*s*-)*ńa*[·]*k* 'meat/flesh'; cf. Karen **hńa* < **hńak* (loss of final -*k* perhaps conditioned by a long vowel), Ch. *ńi̯ôk*/*ńźi̯uk*.[i] Another pair of roots shows a final *-*yak* ~ *-*ik* doublet in TB, and here also length can only be reconstructed provisionally for ST; cf. *(*s*-)*rya*[·]*k* 'pheasant' (n. 458); **mya*[·]*k* 'eye' (n. 251), Ch. *mi̯ôk*/*mi̯uk*[j] (text); perhaps ST *(*s*-)*ryə·k* and **myə·k*.

ST long medial **a·* before dentals is represented by Ch. *â*, intrinsically a long vowel (in Anc. Ch. the short vowel 'gap' was filled by *ậ*, derived from Ar. Ch. *ə*). This shift is shown conclusively by several roots in final *-*a* (= *a·*) with the nominalizing -*n* suffix = /·*n*/, differing morphophonemically from the similar /*n*/ 'collective' and 'verbal' suffixes cited above, which yield Ch. final -*i̯ĕn* ~ -*ien* (n. 428). The basic *-*a-n* > -*ân* shift is shown by the following ST roots: **ka* 'bitter', *(*b*-)*ka-n* 'liver' (text); **na* 'ill, pain', **na-n* 'difficulty' (text); **ta* 'bright red', **ta-n* 'vermilion (cinnabar)' (n. 429); **gwa* ~ **kwa* 'wear, put on (clothes)', **gwa-n* ~ **kwa-n* 'clothes; cap' (n. 429) (note that Ch. *kwân*/*kuân*[k] is primarily nominal: tone A = 'cap'); **dza* 'eat', **dza-n* 'food' (text and n. 455). On the basis of this correspondence we can reconstruct ST long medial **a·* in several other roots, all with Ch. final -*ân*; cf. **ga·n* ~ **ka·n* 'dry' (n. 444); **swa·r* 'sour' (n. 460); **swa·n* 'onion/garlic' (text) (this ST root is a possible loan from AT); cf. also ST **ta·n*: TB **tan*: T *than-pa* 'dry weather, heat, drought', B *thán-thán* 'nearly dry', Ch. *tʻân*[l] (not *tʻnân*, as in *GSR*) 'to dry up (as a river)' (*GS* gloss; GSR glosses 'foreshore'); ST *(*m*-)*da·n*: K *ndan* 'crossbow' (dial. *kəli ndan* 'bow'), from TB **m-dan*, Ch. *dʻân*[m] 'shot pellets; pellet of crossbow; (*AD*) crossbow'. The distinction between medial **a·* and *â* before final *-*r* cannot be established with any certainty for ST, and there is interchange here within TB itself

a 瀼　b 穰　c 濃　d 穠　e 洞　f 筒　g 夢　h 公　i 肉　j 目
k 冠　l 灘　m 彈

by Shafer (*JAOS*, **61**, 1941, p. 28), yet he seems to conclude (p. 29) that a quantitative distinction can be established for Sino-Tibetan. Actually, we can simply point out that there are two types of correspondences in Ar. Ch. for TB medial *a*:

ngan[a] 'goose (wild)'; cf. B *ŋàn*, T *ŋaŋ*.

gʿân[b] 'drought', *kân*[c] 'to dry; dry'; cf. B *khàn* 'dried up'.

swân[d] 'garlic'; cf. B *krak-swan* 'onion'.

tâm[e] 'carry on the shoulder'; cf. B *thàm*, *id.*

sam[f] 'hair'; TB **tsam.*

sat[g] 'kill'; TB **g-sat.*

t'i̯ək[h] 'weave'; TB **tak.*

si̯ək[i] 'breathe'; TB **sak.*

kʿli̯əp[j] 'weep'; TB **krap.*

If sonant stop finals are reconstructed for Sino-Tibetan, we should expect the following developments in Tibeto-Burman:[489]

ST **-ag* (or *-ab*) > TB **-aw* (length not considered).

ST **-ad* > TB **-ay.*

('spread; sail', n. 448). In the best comparison for TB long medial **a·* before labial final ('draw water', n. 482), Ch. has final *-i̯əp*, apparently from ST final **-ə·p*.

ST medial **â* is reflected in the medial *a* ~ *o* alternation in Tibetan (n. 344). Several roots show a direct correspondence with Ch. *â* before final velars, labials or **-r*; cf. **grâk* ~ **krâk* 'fear; frighten' (n. 430); **(r-)kwâk* 'bark, skin, leather' (n. 229); **(g-)tâm* ~ **(g-)dâm* 'talk, speak' (Ch. also *dəm*) (n. 217); also **bwâr* ~ **pwâr* 'burn; fire' (n. 460); **bwâr* ~ **pwâr* 'toss, cast (away), sow, winnow' (n. 460), but **pwâr/bwâr* ~ **pwa·r* 'white' (n. 460). In other ST roots we can reconstruct medial **â* on the basis of the Ch. cognate: **hwâm* 'dare' (n. 448); **tâm* 'carry on shoulder' (text). Before dental finals, however, ST medial **â* was assimilated to the final, shifting to *a*, as shown conclusively by *ŋâ*[k] 'domestic goose', *ŋan*[l] 'wild goose', with 'collective' *-n* suffix (text and n. 428); cf. also *sat*[m] 'kill', TB **g-sât* (text and n. 344); *χwâr/χwâ*[n] 'fire' but *bʾi̯wăn/bʾi̯wɒn*[o] 'burn' (above), with **â* > *ă* before the secondary final *-n*; **nâ* 'red' (n. 429); **byâr* ~ **pyâr* 'plait' (n. 460); **yâr* (TB also **ya·r*) 'spread, extend; sail, mat' (n. 448); ST **yâr* yielded Ch. *-i̯an* in the last two roots; cf. also *pwăt*[p] '8', indicating ST final **-ryât* rather than **-ryat* (this perhaps explains the anomalous **-ɔ[t]* final in Karen). This secondary *a* vowel in Chinese is normally not palatalized (except where *i̯* stands for **y*), contrasting with the normally palatalized primary *a* (above), but *t'i̯at/tśi̯ät*[q] 'break; bend; destroy', TB **tśât* 'break, cut' is a possible exception here (note *t'i̯-* = **tś-*); cf. also *sam*[r] 'hair' (non-palatalized), TB **tsâm* ~ **sâm* 'head hair' (T *ʾag-tshom* 'beard'), indicating ST **tsâm* ~ **sâm* (with shift to *a* in Chinese perhaps conditioned by the initial); cf. also *t'i̯an/tśi̯än*[s] 'battle; to fight', TB **(g-)ra·l* (n. 472), with indicated final *-âl* for ST.

489 A reconstruction schema of this kind for ST finals still cannot be excluded but it seems much less likely than the proposals offered in the present notes.

a 鴈　b 旱　c 乾　d 蒜　e 擔　f 彡　g 殺　a 織　i 息　j 泣
k 鵝　l 鴈　m 殺　n 火　o 燔　p 八　q 折　r 彡　s 戰

ST *-og (or -ob) > TB *-ow.

ST *-od > TB *-oy.

ST *-eg (or -eb) > TB *-ew.

ST *-ed > TB *-ey.

The Ar. Ch. finals, if correctly reconstructed, point to an ST system of the type shown above. Anc. Ch., however, has diphthongs of TB type, and a few direct comparisons can be made:[490, 491]

490 It is possible that Tibeto-Burman simply dropped an original sonant stop after a short medial vowel; cf. ·ăg > ·a 'dumb',[a] TB *(m-)a (note B á in this root).

491 As presently reconstructed, ST lacks true diphthongs but numerous forms with final *-w or *-y are theoretically possible: ST *-aw and *-ay, *-âw and *-ây, *-ow and *-oy, *-ew and *-ey, as well as *-əw and *-əy (this pair covered in n. 486); a full set of ST finals of the above type with corresponding long vowels is also theoretically possible. Our comparative material on these finals is still scanty, more so than might be anticipated, and we have good evidence for only a few of the possible combinations. Chinese has final -og/âu corresponding to TB final *-aw as well as *-a·w (these also are the most likely ST reconstructions), as shown in three text examples ('call/cry out', 'fry/roast', 'fat'); cf. also mog/mâu[b] 'hair; fur, feathers', K nmun nmau 'beard' (couplet form), from TB *r-mul *r-m[a, a·]w. In two comparisons involving isolated TB forms, however, Chinese has final -u/ə̯u or -i̯u (palatalized), possibly from ST *-âw; cf. ·u/·ə̯u[c] 'vomit', B aú, id., from *[a, a·]w; ŋi̯u[d] 'monkey', K-N *ŋa·w 'ape/, monkey': Tiddim ŋa·u 'ape', L ŋau 'gray monkey'; cf. the ablaut in the root for 'steal' (n. 483). There are three different reflexes in the Chinese comparisons for TB final *-ow, perhaps because of influence exerted by the initials; contrast məg/mə̯u[e] 'mother', TB *mow 'woman' (text) (cf. Karen *mü 'female') and t'i̯o/tśi̯wo[f] 'boil, cook', TB *tsyow (n. 452); also the following pair, which show identical fronting (*o > e) after initial t-; cf. *tiog/tieu[g] 'deep, profound' (not in GSR), TB *tow ~ *dow 'thick' (also suffixed -n forms showing -wən/uən < *-un < *-o-n; n. 429); tiog/tieu[h] 'bird' (phonetic in above), Bodo-Garo *d[a, o]w, Karen *to < ST *tow ~ *dow (cf. K-N *m-tow 'fly', n.). Support for the indicated *-ow > -i̯o/i̯wo development after initial palatals ('boil/cook') is furnished by śi̯o/śi̯wo[i] 'rat', probably from *ś(y)ow < *ś(a)yəw < *śa-yəw; ST *yəw 'rat' + *śa 'animal' as prefixed element, precisely paralleling L sa-zu (see n. 428 for suffixed -n doublet from this root).

The material on final *-y forms is still skimpier, if anything, and in general is quite unsatisfactory. Chinese apparently retained distinctions among ST *tây 'big', *(d-)ka·y ~ *(d-)ga·y 'crab' and *r-may 'tail' (text), the last showing centralization of the short medial *a, along with metathesis of the prefix (cf. 'name'; n. 419) followed by *r > w after initial m- (cf. 'horse'; n. 487), as follows: *r-may > *r-məy > *mrəy > *mwəy > mi̯wər/mywə̯i (see n. 486 for last shift); an identical metathesis should probably now be recognized also for Burmese and Bahing (n. 204). A similar *a > ə or *a > e shift appears in the following pair: ·əd/·ə̯i[j] (C) 'love', Karen ʔai (text, p. 150); miər/miei[k] 'rice (paddy)' (text), B-G *m[a, e]y 'rice', Karen *may (n. 408); see n. 486 for effect of tone on final -d. Two comparisons for TB final *-oy indicate that palatalization also occurred here; cf. dʿiər/dʿiei[l]

[a] 啞 [b] 毛 [c] 嘔 [d] 禺 [e] 母 [f] 煮 [g] 窵 [h] 鳥 [i] 鼠 [j] 愛 [k] 米 [l] 弟

γâu < *g‘og*[a] ‘cry out, call’; TB **gaw*.

ngâu < *ngog*[b] ‘fry, roast’; TB **r-ŋaw*.

sâu < *sog*[c] ‘fat (of animal)’; TB **sa·w*.

mə̯u < *məg*[d] ‘mother’; TB **mow* ‘woman’, Karen **mo* ‘mother, female’.

t‘âi < *t‘âd*,[e] *d‘âi* < *d‘âd*[f] ‘great, big’; TB **tay*.

γăi[g] ‘crab’; TB **d-ka·y*.

mjwe̯i < *mi̯wər*[h] ‘tail’; TB **r-may*.

miei < *miər*[i] ‘rice (paddy)’; cf. Bodo-Garo **may* or **mey* (n. 206).

ńźie̯ < *ńi̯ăr*[j] ‘near’; TB **ney*. Cf. also *ńi* < *ni̯ər*[k] ‘near, close’, *ńi̯ĕt* < *ni̯ət*[l] ‘close-standing, familiar’, *ńi̯ək* < *ni̯ək*[m] ‘near, familiar’, and Kiranti **ne* ~ *nek* ~ *neŋ* ‘near’.

Here we may infer either (*a*) final sonant stops were replaced by semivowels both in Ar. Ch. and Tibeto-Burman, or (*b*) final sonant stops in Ar. Ch. (if actually present) simply represented consonantal off-glides. If the first alternative is chosen, we must still interpret final *-r* in the last three comparisons as an offglide, inasmuch as Tibeto-Burman maintains original final **-r*.

§47. Chinese tones

The Chinese tonal system can be interpreted in terms of three tonemes, viz. level (unmarked), rising (x́), and falling (x̀), or *p‘ing shêng*,[n] *shang shêng*,[o] and *ch‘ü shêng*,[p] respectively. The so-called *ju shêng*[q] of Chinese philologists is simply the level tone in syllables with final stop consonant (glottal stop in many modern dialects). The three tonemes are conditioned (in Ar. and Anc. Ch.) by the initial, being relatively high in words with surd initial, relatively low in words with sonant initial. With the general shift from sonant to surd initials shortly after the Anc. Ch. period (A.D. 600–900), the high and low varieties of each toneme tended to become phonemically distinct, so that all modern dialects have several separate

‘younger brother’, TB **doy* ~ **toy* ‘younger (youngest) sibling’ (cf. Anc. Ch. *-ieu* = TB **-ow*, above); *mi̯ər*/*myi*[r] ‘beautiful’, TB **moy*, *id.* (showing further palatalization of the vowel). The Ch. doublet for ‘near’ (text) shows typical replacement of **e* by *i̯ă* (= *i̯a* before most finals; n. 481) or by *i̯ə* (> *-i̯ər*/*i*; n. 486); cf. also *siər*/*siei*[s] ‘rhinoceros’, T *bse*, *id.*, probably from **b-sey* (this isolated comparison suggests basic retention of **-ey* in Chinese).

[a] 號 [b] 熬 [c] 臊 [d] 母 [e] 泰 [f] 大 [g] 蟹 [h] 尾 [i] 米
[j] 邇 [k] 尼 [l] 昵 [m] 暱 [n] 平聲 [o] 上聲 [p] 去聲 [q] 入聲 [r] 美
[s] 犀

tonemes.[492, 493] The falling toneme has generally been regarded as of late origin, by Chinese as well as Western scholars. It is undoubtedly significant that many Anc. Ch. words derived from Ar. Ch. forms in *-g* or *-d* should bear this toneme, but we find it also with words in final *-m*, *-n*, or *-ng*, in which loss of final cannot be postulated. We must infer, then, that all three tonemes existed in Ar. Ch.

A careful comparison of Chinese tones with the Tibeto-Karen system represented by Burmese-Lolo and Karen has yielded no positive results.[494] If any inference at all about Sino-Tibetan tones is justified, it must be the negative conclusion that tones were lacking in the parent speech, and that the TB and Ar. Ch. tonal systems were developed independently. Ar. Ch. tones occasionally play a morphological role, as in *maí*[a] 'buy', *maì*[b] 'sell' (Anc. Ch. forms); *·ịə́m*[c] 'drink', *·ịə̀m* (same character) 'give to drink', *ńịə̀g*[d] 'ear', *ńịə̀g*[e] 'cut off the ears'; *gịwắn*[f] 'distant', *gịwằn* (same character) 'keep away from, keep aloof from', but no constant function can be assigned any given toneme.[494]

492 Simon has shown that the widespread shift from *shang shêng* to *ch'ü shêng* in words with stop, affricate, or fricative initial is directly connected with surdization of these initials; see his article, 'Die Spaltung der chinesischen Tieftonreihe', *AM* **4** (1927), 612–18.

493 Certain Wu dialects have reduced to a pair of tonemes and apparently even to zero contrast (toneless language); cf. Benedict, 1948bis.

494 A two-tone system has now been reconstructed for ST; see Benedict, 'The Sino-Tibetan Tonal System' (mimeographed), read at *Second Conference on Sino-Tibetan*, Columbia University, October, 1969 (to appear in revised form in the Haudricourt commemorative volume, Paris, 1972). The Chinese *ch'ü shêng*, a late development in that language (text), now appears to have been a sandhi tone, replacing either of the two basic tones in close juncture. Downer ('Derivation by tone-change in Classical Chinese', *BSOAS* **22**, 1959, 258–90) has described eight different categories in which *ch'ü shêng* (C) is paired with either *p'ing shêng* (A) or *shang shêng* (B), with many different types of morphological relationships (hence no constant tonal function; see text). Category H (Derived Forms used as Compounds) yields the clue to the puzzle, e.g. *g'yię*[A][g] 'to ride' (citing only Anc. Ch. forms) < **gi*, *g'yię*[C]*-dz'ək*[h] 'mounted bandits'. The remaining categories can readily be accounted for by reconstructing a system of suffixes, resulting in a morphological picture much like that of Tibetan, e.g. with verbalizing function: *t'ịuŋ*[A][i] 'middle' < **tuŋ*, *t'ịuŋ*[C][j] 'hit the middle' < **tuŋ-ba* (or similar form); with nominalizing function: *g'yię*[A][k] 'to ride' (above), *g'yię*[C][l] 'rider' < **gi-bo* (or similar form); *b'ịwɒn*[B][m] 'eat' < **bwăn*, *b'ịwɒn*[C][n] 'food' < **bwăn-mo* (or similar form). The kinship terminology furnishes further striking examples of the sandhi shift; cf. *d'iei*[B][o] 'younger brother' < **doy* (n. 491), *d'iei*[C][p] 'to act as a y. bro.' < **doy-ba* (or the like), also *d'iei*[B] ~ *d'iei*[C][q] 'younger secondary wife', the latter from **doy-ma* (female suffix); *g'ịə̯u*[B][r] 'mother's brother' < **gəw* (n. 417), *g'ịəm*[C][s] 'mo.'s bro.'s wife' < **gəw-ma* (with female suffix) (this contraction recognized by H. Y. Fêng, 'The Chinese kinship system', *HJAS* **2**, 1937, No. 2); also *sịwo*[C] ~ *siei*[C][t] 'son-in-

a 買 b 賣 c 飲 d 耳 e 刵 f 遠 g 騎 h 騎賊 i 中 j 中
k 騎 l 騎 m 飯 n 飯 o 弟 p 弟 q 娣 r 舅 s 妗 t 壻

§48. Résumé (Chinese)

In conclusion, the following points *in re* Chinese and Tibeto-Burman (or Tibeto-Karen) should be resumed: (*a*) Chinese shows almost no trace of the fairly elaborate TB morphology, (*b*) the two stocks have only a small segment of roots in

law' < **k(h)rwəy-pa* (n. 472) (with male suffix); cf. B *khrwe-má* 'daughter-in-law' (with female suffix). The sandhi hypothesis also serves nicely to explain the well-known correlation between *ch'ü shêng* and Ar. Ch. final *-g* and *-d* (text), since it would be anticipated that secondary voicing would occur in close juncture (note also the correlation described in n. 486). Final support for this hypothesis comes from early Chinese loans from AT, which show tone C in penultimate syllable positions comparable to those that obtain in the sandhi situations described above; cf. the following: *d'u/d'ə̯u*^{C} [a] 'bean'; Thai **thua* but N. Thai **dua*, from AT **duba* (regular Thai shift via **duwa*), as confirmed by Miao-Yao **dop*, with Chinese showing the same kind of syllabic division (**du-ba*) as described above (n. 487) for other early loans; Chinese has a doublet here (N. Bodman; personal communication), viz. **təp/tâ̦p* [b] 'a kind of pulse' (not in *GSR*), also read in *Fang-yen* as **d'əp/d'â̦p*, with syllabic division (**dub-a*) of the kind characteristic of TB (n. 487); this doublet points to an earlier **tup* ~ **dup* (n. 479).

The remaining two (basic) tones of Chinese now appear to correlate with the two-tone system of TK as represented in B-L and Karen (text). The situation is not nearly so clear for TB in general, in part because of the continuing scarcity of tonal data for most of these languages; it should also be noted that some TB groups appear to lack tonal systems (secondarily), e.g. Tibetan (the modern tones are secondary) and Bodo-Garo (R. Burling; personal communication). The writer long ago noted a correlation of the TK tones with those of Trung (Nungish), essentially a two-tone system, as recorded by C. P. Lo (n. 27); we now also have information on the tones of a fairly large number of forms in the Mutwang dialect of Răwang (Morse; n. 27), which has three tones correlating with the two tones of Trung (details not all worked out). More recently the writer has had access to a considerable body of material on Kachin tones (L. Maran; personal communication). Kachin has three tones (reduced to two in syllables with final stop) appearing to show a bewildering complexity of relationships to the B-L tones (JAM has undertaken an analysis of this material) but with one basic underlying correlation (K high tone with our tone B; see below). Finally, the tones of several Kuki languages have now become available to a restricted degree, viz. Lushei (R. Burling, 'Lushai phonemics', *Indian Ling.*, XVII, 1957), Tiddim (Henderson; n. 46) and Siyin (Stern; n. 46); these show a systematic correlation with one another (three or four basic Kuki tones) as well as a basic correlation with the above TK system: Kuki Tone *1 (Lushei high-level, marked with superscript 1 in Burling) with our tone A (see below). As in the case of Kachin, only a beginning has been made towards the solution of the complex problems presented by this tonal system. Burling has also published a paper ('Angami Naga phonemics and word list', *Indian Ling.*, XXI, 1962) on the tones of Angami Naga; this material has not yet been studied in detail, and must be supplemented by tonal data on other Naga languages, but

[a] 豆 [b] 答

common, (*c*) the phonological systems of the two stocks differ in many respects, and can scarcely be reconciled at all at some points, (*d*) the tonal systems of the two stocks appear not to be correlated. Our belief that the two stocks are genetically

there appears to be a complex relationship of the five Angami tones to the basic two-tone system of B-L and Karen, with the two mid tones ('resonant' and 'normal') showing a general correlation with our tone A (see below). The fragments of information available on other TB languages suggest that they also will eventually be shown to correlate with this basic two-tone system; cf. the following contrast from Taman (R. G. Brown, 1911), a language with closest affinity for Kachin: 'egg' = 'fowl (its-) water' (n. 149); separate roots for 'water': TB **ti*(*y*)^{A} and **twəy*^{B}; cf. Dhimal *tui* < **twəy* 'egg' but *tśi* < **ti*(*y*) 'water' (no tonal data for this language); probably tone-sandhi in both roots is involved (T Tiddim, S Siyin):

	Karen	Kachin	Taman	Kuki	Angami
{ water	*thi*^{A}		*thi* (high)	**twi*^{3}	*dźə* (high)
{ wet		*mədi* (mid)			
egg	*ʔdi*^{B}	*di* (low)	*thi* (low)	{ **twi*^{4} (T) { *-*twi*^{1} (S)	*dźə* (low)

The two-tone system of TB can be traced back to the eleventh century and earlier in the Pyu inscriptions (Burma; capital city near modern Prome), a language most closely related to Nungish (n. 33). Pyu has two basic tones, one represented by: (visarga), the source of this tone mark (tone *B) in Burmese, and these two tones show a general correlation with the two basic tones of Burmese, as recognized by Shafer (*HJAS* 7, 1943). The divergences are interesting: *piŋa*^{A} '5' and *tkuo*^{A} '9' agreeing with Nungish as against Burmese, but *ho*^{B} '3' agreeing with the divergent Burmese tone (n. 413); *o*^{A} 'village' agreeing with Burmese as against Nungish; *pli*^{A} 'grandchild' agreeing with Karen as against both Burmese and Nungish; note also *sni*^{B} 'year' and *la*^{A} 'moon', serving to establish the basic tones of those two roots in which B-L and/or Nungish forms have undergone special development or tone change. Pyu has two-tone contrast also in stopped syllables (only final -ʔ), a point which eluded Shafer; contrast *plaʔ*^{A} '4' with *paʔ*^{B} 'give', both probably reflecting old suffixed forms (cf. Karen **lwi-t* '4').

The basic two-tone correlation involving TB (Karen, B-L and Trung) and Chinese is as follows (see text for details of Karen and B-L tones):

	Karen	Burmese	Trung	Chinese
Tone *A	I (high)	level	mid-falling	*p'ing* ('level')
	II (low)	(unmarked)		
Tone *B	III (high)	falling	high-level	*shang* ('rising')
	IV (low)	(')		

The Mutwang dialect of Răwang (Nungish) appears to have low tone for *A and high tone for *B, while the mid tone has some correspondences with each (insufficient data for analysis). The so-called 'third tone' of B-L (Tone No. 3 in the Burling–Matisoff system) is clearly peripheral although apparently of some antiquity in this group; it appears to be the product of glottalization (nn. 260, 487). TB **be* ~ **pe* 'broken; break' is exceptional in showing widespread glottalization: B *paí* ~ *phaí*, L *peʔ* (text) and add Răwang (Mutwang dial.) *peʔ rat* 'break', perhaps

related must rest, ultimately, on the fact that they have certain basic roots in common, and that phonological generalizations can be established for these roots. It might be argued that the ST elements constitute only a superstratum in Chinese, and that the substratum is of distinct origin. In historical terms, the Chou people might be regarded as the bearers of a ST language, which became fused with, or perhaps immersed in, a non-ST language spoken by the Shang people. In any event, it is certain that the ST hypothesis illuminates only one of the many dark recesses in the complex linguistic history of the Chinese.

also Karen **beʔ* 'chop (off)', yet one hesitates to reconstruct glottalization as a distinctive feature for TB or ST.

As might be anticipated, there are numerous exceptional forms, especially in the numerals, with Chinese perhaps having more than its share, yet the fact of the correlation itself seems clear enough. The writer had originally (1948) inclined to the view that no correlation between the TK and Chinese tonal systems could be established, partly because he had not hit upon the sandhi explanation for *chʻü shêng* (above). He had also been led astray by irregular tones appearing in several basic roots, especially with *pʻing* tone rather than the anticipated *shang* tone; cf. the following: *si̯ĕn*^{A} [a] 'firewood' but TK **siŋ*^{B} 'tree/wood'; *si̯ĕn*^{A} [b] 'bitter' but TK **sin*^{B}, as reflected in **m-sin*^{B} 'liver'; *śi̯ĕn*^{A} [c] 'body' but TK **śa*^{B} 'flesh/meat/animal', K *śan* (low tone) (Trung has *śya*^{A}); *swân/suân*^{A} [d] 'sour' but TK **swa·r/su·r*^{B} (Trung *sul*^{B} 'spoiled'); **sri̯u/si̯u* [e] 'older sister' but TK **sru(w)*^{B} (Pyu *sru*^{B} 'kinsmen'); cf. also *nien*^{A} [f] 'year' but TK **s-ni·ŋ*^{B} (Karen **hneŋ*^{B}); *ŋi̯o/ŋi̯wo*^{A} [g] 'fish' but TK **(s-)ŋya*^{B} (Karen **hńa*^{B}). These exceptional forms in Chinese reflect a consistent tone *B > *A shift after initial **s/h-*, paralleling a very similar situation uncovered in Lahu (JAM: 'GD'); this might also account for the irregularity in another basic root, viz. *si̯ər/si*^{B} [h] 'die' but TK **səy*^{A}.

[a] 薪　[b] 辛　[c] 身　[d] 酸　[e] 嬃　[f] 年　[g] 魚　[h] 死

APPENDIX I

Tibeto-Burman roots

Prefatory note: Numbers in parentheses refer to the series running through the text. Page references in bold type are for those numbered in the text.

a-

a (3rd pers. prn.) 93, 121, 123, 130
(m-)a dumb (mute) (105) **36**, 188, 192
ak crack; mouth (106) **36**
am = *əm* eat, drink (481) 142, **143**, 183, 194
a·w cry out (273) **63**

b-

ba thin (25) **19**, 22, 90, 102
ba carry (26) **19**
ba = *(l-)ba* ~ *(m-)ba* goitre 96
ba·k bat (animal) (325) **71**, 166, 190
bal tired (29) 15, **20**
s-bal frog 15, 21, 107
bam ~ *pam* be defeated, sit; defeat (471) **125**
(d-)baŋ strength 117
s-baŋ dung 21
bar ~ *par* = *bwár* ~ *pwár* burn; fire (220) 7, 23, **50**, 124, 125, 172, 174, 191
ba·r bloom; flower (1) **15**, 71, 147
bay = *bway* left (hand) (47) **24–5**, 65, 90
be peas, beans (253) **59**
be ~ *pe* broken; break (254) **59**, 196–7
bip ~ *pip* conceal; bury (376) **80**, 124
biy = *bəy* give (427) **99**, 112, 166, 185, 196
bla See *b-la*
ble slip, slippery (141) **40**, 59, 139, 148
bleŋ ~ *pleŋ* straight; straighten (352) **75**, 124, 125
bliŋ ~ *pliŋ* full; fill (142) **40**, 78–9, 80, 124, 125, 140, 176, 179
bok white 181
bop leg, calf of leg (30) **20**
boy cowlick (308) **67**
bra forked, scattered, divided (132) **40**, 91, 102
bra See *bya*
brak rock (134) **40**
bran convalesce (133) **40**, 70
braŋ give birth (135) 31, **40**
(s-)braŋ name 31
(s-)braŋ See *yaŋ*
bren See *pren*
broŋ wild yak; buffalo (136) **40**, 123
brup ~ *prup* overflow; gush, squirt (151) **44**, 81, 111, 124
br(w)ak ~ *(s-)br(w)aŋ* speak 42, 118
bu ~ *pu* open; bud (260) **62**
(d-)bu head 117
(r-)bu (K-N) nest 102
bul ~ *pul* root, stump, tree 166, 173
buw = *bəw* carry (on back or shoulders) (28) **20**, 22, 101, 102, 135, 147, 151, 166, 185
buw = *bəw* insect, snake (27) **19**, 22, 90, 111, 123
**bu(w)* (K-N) rice paddy 135
bu(w) wear (428) **103**, 110
bwa (B-L) grandmother 24, 100, 174, 187
bwam = *(s-)bwam* plump, swollen (172) 24, **46**
bwaŋ uncle 23, 174, 189
bwâr throw away, cast, sow, toss 172–3, 174, 191
bwâr See *bar*
bwat flower 24
bway See *bay*
bwiy = *bwəy* bamboo rat (173) 32, **46**
bya = *bya* ~ *bra* bird; bee (177) 29, **46**, 90
byar ~ *pyar* = *byâr* ~ *pyâr* affix; plait, sew (178) **46**, 124, 173, 191
byer fly, 83, 166
byon go; come (179) **46**

d-

m-da arrow 96, 111–2, 118
dap=*dəp* See *tap*
dan cut (22) **19**, 134
daw defy, interfere, be at enmity with (267) **63**
daw (B-G) bird 149, 192
day that, this (21) **19**, 115
di egg 45, 135, 196
(*s*-)*di·k* scorpion (56) 14, **26**, 79, 80, 107
do related (249) **59**
don ~ *ton* go out, come out, pull 125
doŋ=(*m*-)*doŋ* peacock (341) **73**
dow See *tow*
doy See *toy*
drup See *d-rup*
du knee; elbow 21
duk ~ *tuk* poison; poisonous, poisoned (472) 76, **126**, 166, 182
(*r*-)*dul* ~ *tul* dust 173, 181
duŋ=*duŋ* ~ *tu·ŋ* long; length (20) **19**, 75
du·ŋ See *tu·ŋ*
m-duŋ sword, spear 118
dup ~ *dip*, *tup* ~ *tip* beat (399) **83**, 124
du-t ~ *tu-t* join; tie, knot (421) **101**, 124, 159
dwaŋ=*dwa·ŋ* hole, cave, pit (169) 22, **45**, 74, 190
dyal ~ *tyal* village 52
dyam straight (227) 52
dyam ~ *tyam* full; fill (226) 52
dyuŋ (B-G) insect 34, 169, 182

dz-

dza eat (66) **28**, 30, 33, 58, 90, 98, 99, 101, 102, 126, 130, 135, 157, 159, 169, 188, 190
m-dza love (67) **28**, 118
dzar sister (of man) (68) **28**, 170, 172, 183
dzim green; raw 81
dzo·p suck; kiss (69) **28**, 73
dzu[·]*k* erect, plant (360) 76, **77-8**
dzwan (B-L) hawk, kite 49, 169, 190

dzy-=*dź*

dzya·l=*dźa·l* far (229) **54**, 71
dz(*y*)*im*=*dźim* sweet (71) **29**
dzyon=*dźon* ride (72) **29**
dźuk vulva **53**
dzywal=*dźwal* hang down, sag (242) **56**

e-

e·k (K-N) feces 26, 146
ew (K-N) lean back 68

g-

r-ga old (445) **110**
s-ga·l back, loins, groin 18
gam=*gəm* jaw (molar teeth) (50) **25**, 183
gam put into mouth, seize with mouth (491) **166**, 183
ga·p shoot (219) **50**, 73, 112, 135, 144
gar leave, abandon (15) **19**
ga·r dance, leap, stride (11) **18**, 71
gaw=*gaw* ~ *kaw* call (14) **19**, 63, 66, 166, 192, 193
m-gaw ~ (*s*-)*gaw* head (490) 119, **149**
gi (B-L) ride (horse) 184
gip ten (16) **19**, 21, 94, 175
gla See *kla*
s-gla See *s-la* ~ *g-la*
glak See *klak*
glaŋ cold; freeze 39
gle·k (K-N) thunderbolt 41
gliŋ ground, island (128) 34, **40**, 78
gliŋ tube; flute 41
gow cross over (318) **69**
grâk See *grok*
gram rough **51**
graŋ cold (weather) (120) **39**, 178, 189
s-graw bark; skin (121) **39**
griy=*grəy* copper (39) **22**, 61
grok ravine (122) **39**
grok ~ *krok*=*grâk* ~ *krâk*; *grok* ~ *krok* fear; frighten (473) 76, **127**, 159, 191
groy crow, howl, screech, scream (310) **67**
gryum See *g-ryum*
gu=*gu* ~ *ku* owl (494) 46, 164, **185**
guk ~ *kuk* bend; crooked 77, 125, 159, 182
guŋ body 182
r-guŋ edge, side; shin (395) **82**, 109
gwa fox 34, 166, 186
gwa-n kwa-n wear, dress (160) **44**, 124, 135, 159, 190
(*m*-)*gwi*(*y*) elephant 121, 167–8, 184

r-gya hundred (164) **45**, **54**, 57, 89, 94, 95, 109, 131, 137, 151, 161–2
b-r-gyat = *(b-)g-ryat* eight (163) 35, **45**, 54, 57, 74, 88, 95, 96, 131, 141, 144, 161–2, 179, 191

h-

ha·k hawk, gag, choke (323) **71**, 133, 139, 144
haŋ pant, gasp 33
hap bite, snap at, mouthful (89) **32**, 33
ha·w announce, bespeak 33
m-hew (K-N) spoiled, waste(d) 68
(m-)hla soul, demon, god (475) **132**
hla(k) more, beyond, excessive 89
hu breath 17
hus moisture; wet 2, 17
hwam dare (216) **50**, 168, 191
hwaŋ come (out); enter (218) **50**
hwaŋ encircle, circular; fence (217) **50**, 132, 143
hwa-t shine; light (221) **50–1**
s-hwiy = *s-hywəy* blood (222) **51**, 61, 106, 122, 132, 138, 139, 151, 154, 157, 164, 181
hyak scratch (230) **55**
s-hywəy See *s-hwiy*

i-

ik older brother (112) **36**, 79
ik strangle (113) **36**, 180
ip = *yip* sleep; conceal (114) **36–7**, 88, 125
it one 94, 162

k-

ka bitter (8) **18**, 21, 58, 88, 119, 122, 134, 148, 151, 154, 158, 165, 186, 190
ka crow, n. 99–100
ka I 93
ka open, divaricate, spread (469) **120**, 121, 134
ka word, speech (9) **18**, 21, 187
(m-)ka ~ *(s-)ka* jaw, chin (470) **121**, 134
m-ka open(ing); mouth; door (468) 38, **120**, 166
r-ka earth (97) **33**, 109
kak = *khak* (B-L) reaching its peak 166, 183
ka·k fork (327) **71**, 121
ka·k ~ *kâk* cough up; phlegm 71, 184
kal congeal 15
k(a)li See *g-li*
m-kal kidney (12) **18**, 120, 173, 175, 189
r-ka[·]*m* edge, bank, precipice; lips, mouth (329) **71**, 109, 183
kan dry up 158, 166, 190
kaŋ dry up (331) 71, **72**
kaŋ father, grandfather 100, 190
ka·ŋ roast, toast, burn (330) **71**, 72
(r-)kaŋ leg, foot 70, 142
ka·p draw (water) (336) **73**, 184, 191
kap = *kəp* needle (52) **25**, 26, 70, 88, 166, 175, 183
kap fork (of legs), groin (338) **73**
kar lead, bronze 15
s-kar = *s-kər* star (49) **25**, 106
kat one 94
kaw See *gaw*
kaw basket (266) **63**
kaw = *khaw* (K-N) grasshopper 66
d-ka·y crab (51) **25**, 99, 116, 140, 149, 166, 192, 193
ke = *(s-)ke(k)* neck(-shaped) (251) **59**
ke·l = *kye·l* ~ *kyi*[·]*l* goat (339) 15, **73**
d-kew = *d-k(h)ew* (K-N) pick, dig out, scratch 68
d-key = *d-key* ~ *d-kəy* tiger (462) 107, **116**, 134, 149
kik bind, twist, tie (484) **145**
ki·l bind, twist; roll; angle (373) 75, **80**
kim = *kyim* ~ *kyum* house (53) 25, **26**, 89, 122, 138, 143, 152, 182
ki·n weigh (369) **79**
d-kiy = *d-kəy* barking-deer (54) **26**, 116
s-kiy = *s-kəy* borrow (31) **21**
kla = *gla* ~ *kla* fall (123) **39**, 41, 89, 99, 101
klak = *glak* ~ *klak* cook (124) **39**, 41
klaw dig out, weed (269) **63**
kliŋ = *r-kliŋ* marrow (126) **39**, 41, 80, 85
kliy = *kləy* excrement (125) **39**, 41, 178, 185
klum sweet 75
klup cover, wrap (479 **139–40**, 144, 145
klu·ŋ valley, river (127) **127**, 78
kok = *(r-)kwâk* bark, rind, skin (342) 20, **74**, 76, 106, 191

kor valley; pit; cave (349) **74**
r-ko-t = *r-go-t* ~ *r-ko-t* dig up, scoop out (420) **101**, 110, 135, 159
koy bend (307) **67**, 89
(*s-*)*kra* hair (115) **38**, 106
kraŋ mosquito (322) **71**
krap beat, thrash, winnow 74, 141–2
krap weep (116) 13, **38**, 41, 73, 98, 112, 175, 178, 183, 191
krep bug; ant; lac (347) **74**, 107, 146
krim threaten; set teeth on edge (379) **81**, 142
krit grind (119) **38**, 141–2
(*m-*)*kri-t* bile (412) **98**, 102, 119, 120
kriy = *krəy* foot (38) **22**, 178, 186
kriy = *krəy* dirt, filth (460) **115**, 141
kri(*y*) acid, sour (413) **98**, 102, 119, 120, 178, 186
kri(*y*) fear (416) 99
krok = *k*(*h*)*rok* (K-N) sour, acid 41
krok See *grok*
kroy borrow, lend; debt (312) **68**
kroy shell(-fish) (311) **67**, 67–8
kroy surround (313) **68**
kruŋ to be born; live; green (382) **81**
kru·ŋ cage (389) **82**
kruw = *krəw* bathe, wash (117) **38**, 101, 124
kruw = *krəw* horn (37) **22**, 113
kruw = *m-krəw* dove (118) **38**, 68, 185
krwap rustle (243) **56**
krwiy = *krwəy* son-/daughter-in-law (244) **56**, 178, 186
krwiy = *khrwəy* (B-L) sweat 90
krwi(*y*) = *khrwi*(*y*) (K-N) sew 41
ku take up, lift 99
ku See *gu*
kuk bag, basket, receptacle (393) **82**
kuk See *guk*
ku·k shear, strip, pare (388) 75, **82**
(*m-*)*ku·k* angle; knee 120, 159, 182
(*m-*)*kul* all; twenty (397) 15, 18, **83**, 119, 120
kum block, pillow; bench; bedstead (482) 38, **143**, 175
ku[·]*m* concave, convex 75, 78
kun See (*m-*)*kul*
ku·ŋ tree; branch; stem (359) 75, **77**, 122, 182
kut scrape, rule (line), scratch, itch, cut, carve (383) **81**, 122
kuw = (*m-*)*kəw* pigeon (495) **185**
kuw = *kəw* smoke (256) **61**, 102, 134, 148, 151, 159, 164, 180
kuw = *kəw* uncle (maternal); father-in-law (255) **61**, 100, 121, 122, 154, 158, 166, 185, 194
ku(*w*) (B-G) mouth 184
d-kuw = *d-kəw* ~ *d-gew* nine (13) **19**, 23, 45, 61, 94–5, 116, 131, 134, 154, 162, 185, 188, 196
r-kuw = *r-kəw* steal (33) **21**, 60, 69, 90, 99, 101, 102, 110, 135, 138, 164, 175, 184
(*s-*)*kuw* = (*s-*)*kəw* body 184
kwan = *kwan* ~ *gwan* casting net (158) **44**, 49, 158
kwar hole (350) **74**
(*r-*)*kwâk* See *kok*
kway conceal, hide, shun (303) **67**
kwa·y bee (157) **44**, 67, 140, 150, 152
kwiy = *kwəy* dog (159) 26, **44**, 55, 61, 115, 124, 133, 151, 157, 158
kwi(*y*) comb (480) **140**
(*r-*)*kyak* ~ (*s-*)*kyak* excrement 26, 146
kyam cold; snow, ice (224) **51**
r-kyaŋ single (34) **21**
kye·l ~ *kyi*[·]*l* See *ke·l*
(*m-*)*kyen* know (223) **51**, 160, 175
kyeŋ red; ashamed (162) **45**, 174–5, 183
kyoŋ = *kyâŋ* ~ *kyoŋ* guard; tend cattle (161) **45**, 127
s-kyur = *s-kywa·r* sour (42) **23**, 75, 105
kyuw = *khyəw* (B-L) sweet 60
s-kywa·r See *skyur*
kywiy = *kywəy* yam (238) **56**

l-

-la (masc. suffix) 96
la = (*s-*)*la* leaf (486) 137, **146**
la salt 187
b-la = *bla* arrow (449) 43, **111**, 112, 133, 139, 151, 152, 176, 188
b-la (K-N) cotton 111
g-la foot 34
(*k-*)*la* (B-L) tiger 26, 41, 91, 107, 114, 177–8, 187
s-la ~ *g-la* = *s-gla* moon (144) 32, 34, **42**, 88, 106, 113, 114, 132, 196
lak = *g-lak* arm, hand (86) **32**, 34, 87, 110, 171, 183

lam road; direction (87) 14, **32**, 70, 142
la[·]*m* fathom (arm-spread) 71
laŋ falcon, vulture, eagle, kite, hawk (333) **72**, 155, 171, 183
lap leaf (321) **70**, 146, 171, 189
b-la·p forget (335) **73**, 112
lay change, exchange (283) **64**, 132
lay pass, exceed (301) **66**
m-lay~*s-lay* tongue (281) 33, **64**, 66, 106, 115, 117, 119, 120, 133, 137, 139, 149, 150
la·y center; navel (287) **65**
la·y dig, hoe (288) **65**
lep=(*s-*)*lep* slice, pare, cut off (351) **75**
(*r-*)*ley* barter, buy **64**
li=*li*~(*m-*)*ley* penis (262) **62**
g-li=*k*(*a*)*li* tickle; armpit (265) **265**, 265–6
liŋ=(*m-*)*liŋ* neck (96) **33**, 79, 155, 171
b-liŋ forest (378) **80**, 80–1, 111
lip dive, sink, drown (375) **80**
(*m-*)*li·t* water leech (396) 2, 75, **83**, 84, 120, 146, 172, 180
b-liy=*b-ləy* four (410) 33, 61, 88, 91, **94**, 104, 111, 112, 131, 152, 154, 162, 185, 196
b-liy=*b-ləy* grandchild, nephew/niece (448) 42, 43, 61, 111, 131, 132, 152, 158, 171–2, 180, 196
d-liy=*d-ləy* bow, n. (463) **117**, 132, 151
g-liy=*g-ləy* wind, n. (454) 61, 91, **114**, 132, 148, 151
(*m-*)*liy* = (*m-*)*ləy* boat (463) 61, 91, **132**, 139, 151
s-liy=*s-ləy* flea (440) 33, **107–8**, 132, 152
s-liy=(*s-*)*ləy* heavy (95) **33**, 61, 98, 102, 105, 172
(*m-*)*loŋ* boat (467 **120**, 121
low (K-N) field 66
low long, tall (279) **64**, 113
luk (B-L) enough 88
lum warm (381) 75, **81**, 84, 137, 142, 143, 151
s-lum=*zlum* round (143) **42**, 105, 106
m-luŋ (K-N) heart 120
r-luŋ stone (88) **32**, 41, 75, 77, 79, 82, 109, 114, 137, 142, 143, 144
(*m-*)*lu*(*w*)=(*r-*)*lu*(*w*)~(*m-*)*lu*(*w*) pour; bathe 110, 147
lwan bore, pierce 49
g-lwat free, release (209) 41, **48**, 105, 113
lway easy (302) **67**
lwa·y buffalo (208) **48**
lwi(*y*) flow; stream (210) **48**
lyak-s (Bod.) good 54
(*m-*)*lyak*~(*s-*)*lyak* lick; tongue (211) **48**, 118, 141, 155, 178, 189
m-lyak See *mrak*
(*s-*)*lyam* tongue; flame 48, 64, 141, 171, 172
m-lyaŋ (K-N) shoulder 120
lyap flat, thin (212) **48**
lyap=(*s-*)*lyap* flitter, flash; lightning (213) **49**
(*s-*)*lya·w* lick; tongue 48

m-

-ma (fem. suffix) 96
ma (negative) 96
ma mother (487 96, 121, 123, 136, **148**, 156, 188, 189
r-ma wound (446) **110**
ma·k son-in-law (324) **71**, 136, 144
maŋ big; older (brother, uncle) 189
maŋ=*r-məŋ* dream (82) **31**, 79, 142, 143, 182, 190
ma-t lose, disappear (425) **101**
r-ma-t nettle See *r-ma* (446)
may good (300) **66**, 112
may (B-G) rice, paddy 65, 128, 149, 192, 193
r-may tail (282) **64**, 66, 109, 118, 121, 137, 149, 150, 192, 193
r-men wen, mole (104) **36**, 74, 79, 136, 143
mey fire (290) 31, **65**, 66, 115, 136, 137, 149, 150, 151
mik~*myak* eye (402) 14, 29, 55, 56, 80, **84**, 88, 121, 122, 128, 141, 145, 182, 190
s-min ripe, cooked (432) 14, 55, 79, 80, **106**, 122, 136, 142, 143, 151
r-miŋ name (83) 29, **31**, 78, 79, 80, 88, 89, 109, 130, 137, 142, 151, 155, 165, 180
mit extinguish (374) **80**, 183
r-mi(*y*) man (homo) 107, 119, 158
mliy=*mləy* earth, country (152) 42, **44**, 90, 179
mlyuw=*mlyəw* swallow, v. (153) 42, **44**, 138, 147–8

mow, move, work, do (280) **64**
mow woman, bride (297) **66**, 149, 192, 193
moy beautiful (304) **67**, 193
(*r-*)*moy* bud, blossom (304) **67**
mra much, many (148) 29, **43**, 91, 139
mrak = *mrak* ~ *brak* cut, tear (147) **43**, 89
mrak = *m-lyak* grass (149) **43**
mraŋ see (146) **43**, 179
mruk monkey 43, 112
mruw = *mrəw* grain, seed; lineage **43**, 123
mu·k arm(-length), cubit (394) **82**
mu·k rubbish, refuse, dust, weeds (363) 75, **78**
r-mu·k fog(gy); dark, dull (357) 75, **77**, 110, 148, 182
mul = (*s-*)*mul* ~ (*s-*)*mil* ~ (*r-*)*mul* bodyhair **15–16**, 75, 83, 84, 90, 113, 121, 173, 181
mu·m bud (364) **78**
mu·ŋ cloudy, dark; sullen (362) 75, **78**, 182
mu·r gills, beak, mouth, face (366) **78**, 182
(*s-*)*mut* blow (mouth, wind) 75
muw = *məw* eagle, hawk (257) **61**, 77, 115, 121
g-muw = *g-məw* mushroom, fungus (455) **114**
(*r-*)*muw* = (*r-*)*məw* sky, clouds, fog (488) 77, 90, 110, 147, **148**, 152
mwiy = (*r-*)*mwəy* ~ (*s-*)*mwəy* sleep (196) 31, **47**, 136, 140, 174, 185
(*s-*)*mwiy* = (*s-*)*mwəy* twirl; spindle (195) **47**
myak See *mik*
myel sleepy (197) **47**, 78, 173, 183
s-m(*y*)*ik* cane; sprout (237) **56**, 79, 83, 106

n-

na dwell, rest (414) **99**
na ill; pain (80) **31**, 89, 101, 136, 158–9, 190
g-na = *r-na* ~ *g-na* ear; hear (453) 58, 91, 110, **113**, 121, 136, 148, 152, 188, 194
(*m-*)*na* mother, older sister, daughter-in-law 187
s-na ~ *s-na·r* nose (101) 16, **35**, 90, 106, 136, 151, 177, 188
nak black 88, 102, 155
nam sun, sky 148
m-nam smell (464) 35, 70, 89, 91, 105, **117**, 119, 122, 136, 142, 143, 151
s-nam daughter-in-law, wife, sister (103) **35**, 70, 84, 106
s-nam sesame (435) 70, **106**, 136
naŋ = (*s-*)*naŋ* follow (334) **72**, 160
naŋ thou (407) **93**, 123, 130, 143, 160, 190
s-nap snot (102) **35**, 106
s-nat heddles (436) **106**
na·w younger sibling (271) **63**, 66, 134
na·y twist, knead (286) **65**
nem ~ *nyam* = *ńam* low (348) **74**, 85, 105
s-nes lip 16, 123
ney near (291) **65**, 68, 155, 193
ney = (*r-*)*ney* hair (of head) (292) **65**
(*r-*)*ney* get, obtain (294) **66**, 101, 136, 149
(*r-*)*ni* red 46, 91
r-nil ~ *r-ni*(*y*) ~ **s-nil* gums (3) **16**, 35, 75, 91, 109, 173, 177
niŋ = *s-niŋ* year (368) **79**, 84, 136, 142, 143, 144, 165, 177, 180, 196, 197
s-niŋ heart, mind, brain (367) **79**, 106
nip crush, compress **84**
g-nis = *g-ni-s* two (4) **16**, 75, 94, 130, 131, 147, 162, 168, 169, 185, 186
s-nis seven (5) **16**, 79, 93–4, 130, 131, 147, 162, 169, 177
niy = *nəy* sun, day (81) **31**, 55, 88, 89, 136, 151, 157, 158, 168
ni(*y*) aunt, mother-in-law (316) **69**
b-ni(*y*) drawers, petticoat (476) **136**
s-not vessel; womb 144, 145, 150
now tender, soft (274) **274**
nuk = (*s-*)*nuk* brain (483) 88, **144**, 150
nu·l rub, rub against (365) **78**
s-nuŋ back; after (354) **76**, 106
nup ~ *nip* = *nu·p* ~ *ni*[·]*p* sink (400) 75, **83–4**, 145, 157, 181
nuw = *nəw* breast; milk (419) **100**, 136, 152, 184
m-nwi(*y*) laugh (191) **47**, 49, 101, 118, 119, 140

ny- = *ń-*

nyam = *ńam* See *nem*
nyap = *ńap* pinch, squeeze (192) **47**, 175, 177, 183

nye=*ńe* punish (252) **59**
nyen=(*s*-)*ńen* press(ed); oppress, coerce (193) **47**
n(*y*)*ik*=(*s*-)*ńik*~(*s*-)*ńek* filth, excrement (235) **55**
n(*y*)*it*=*ńit* nod; sleep (236) **56**
nyuŋ=(*s*-)*ńuŋ* sad; tired; ill (194) 47

ŋ-

ŋa I (406) 88, 89, **93**, 123, 129–30, 137, 152, 186, 187
l-*ŋa*~*b*-*ŋa* five (78) **31**, 54, 58, 94, 112, 131, 137, 152, 162, 186, 187, 196
s-*ŋa* (B) before 141
ŋak=(*s*-)*ŋak* plantain (477) **137**, 144
ŋa-*n* goose 99, 155, 158, 187, 191
r-*ŋaw* fry, roast (270) **63**, 110, 192, 193
ŋa·w (K-N) ape, monkey 192
ŋay I; self (285) **65**, 93
ŋow=(*s*-)*ŋow* white, green, yellow (296) **66**, 105
ŋoy gentle, quiet, moderate (315) **68**
ŋra meet (154) **44**
ŋray contradict, deny (155) **44**
ŋruw=*ŋrəw* dark; faded, withered (156) **44**
ŋul=(*d*-)*ŋul* silver 15, 173
ŋuw=*ŋəw* weep, cry (79) **31**, 60, 102, 147
ŋwa cattle (215) **50**
ŋwap cousin, in-law 50
ŋya fish (189) **47**, 54, 58, 107, 124, 136, 141, 151, 174, 186, 197
r-*ŋya* borrow (190) 35, **47**, 137

o-

ok below (110) **36**, 76, 123
o·l finish; relax (111) **36**, 73
on nauseated; vomit (343) **74**

p-

-*pa* (masc. suffix) 96, 134
pa=*pwa* father (24) **19**, 23, 58, 96, 100, 113, 118, 121, 122, 134, 174, 187, 188, 189
pa=*pwa* palm, sole (418) 24, **100**, 174, 187, 188–9
pa patch, sew 122
g-*pa*=*g*-*pwa* bamboo (44) **23–4**, 114, 115, 138, 139, 151, 188
pak=*pwak* hide, v. (46) **24**, 50
pak=(*r*-)*pak* leaf (40) **23**, 88
pak=*pwak* pig (43) 14, **23–4**, 87, 133, 189
pam See *bam*
paŋ=*pwaŋ* spindle (48) **25**
par trade, buy, sell 35
par See *bar*
r-*pat* leech (45) 2, 20, **23–4**, 103, 109, 115, 121, 132, 138–9, 144
pe See *be*
pe(*k*) (K-N) give 101, 149
pe·r flat, thin (340) **73**, 97
pik (bowels (35) **21**, 80
pip See *bip*
pir See *pur*
piy=*pəy* grandmother (36) **21**, 121, 122, 134, 185
pla ashes (137) **40**, 133
pleŋ flat surface, plank, slab (138) **40**, 79
pleŋ See *bleŋ*
pliŋ See *bliŋ*
ploŋ burn (139) **40**
ploŋ run, flee (140) **40**
plu white 41, 46, 60–1, 89
d-*po*=*d*-*pho* (K-N) shield 58
pop aperture, crack (345) **74**
pra good (129)
pral=*phral* (K-N) cold (dry) season 42
praŋ dawn, morning (332) **72**
pren=*pren*~*bren* pus; boil 143
priŋ=*b*-*riŋ* bark, v. (377) **80**, 112
pro delight, enjoy (130) **40**, 58
pro=*pro*(*k*) come out, bring out (248) **59**
u-*prok*=-*phrok* (K-N) toad 41
pruk scratch (391) **82**
prup See *brup*
prut boil, v. (131) **40**
pryo soft, boiled; boil (250) **59**
pu See *bu*
pu·k=*pu·k*~*buk* cave; belly (358) 75, **77**, 83, 115, 165–6, 182
pun wrap, cover; wear (385) **81**
pur~*pir* fly, v. (398) **83**, 172, 181
put knee (7) **16–17**, 20, 75, 83, 98, 181
puw=*pəw* grandfather; older brother (23) **19**, 21, 100, 134, 148, 152
puw=*pəw* valuable; value, price (41) **23**, 90

pwa See *pa*
(*p*)*wa* See *wa*
g-pwa See *g-pa*
pwak half 24, 122
pwak See *pak*
pwa See *pa*
pwâr See *bar* ~ *par*
pwa·y husks; shavings (170) **46**, 140 149, 150, 152
pwi(*y*) female (171) **46**, 96, 158, 174, 185
pyak = *pywak* sweep broom (174) 14, **46**, 141
pyam fly, v. 29, 51
pyaŋ hang (175) 20, **46**
pyar See *byar*
pyaw fly, swim (176) **46**
pywak See *pyak*

r-

ra = *ra-t* cut (458) **115**
g-ra See *g-ya*
s-ra = *śra* potato, yam (434) **106**, 108
rak fowl 88, 107, 187–8, 189
s-rak = *śrak* ashamed, shy (431) 34, **106**, 108, 155, 170, 183
(*g-*)*ra·l* See *ran*
s-ram = *sram* otter (438) 70, **107**, 108, 140
ran = (*g-*)*ra·l* fight, quarrel; war 15, 71, 113, 155, 173, 178, 191
m-raŋ high 43
s-raŋ ~ *m-raŋ* horse (145) **43**, 108, 189
rap fireplace; fireplace shelf (84) 19, **31**
(*b-*)*ras* fruit; rice 17, 123
raw = (*s-*)*raw* dry, dead, old; carcass (268) **63**
b-ray fear (450) **112**
ren equal; place in a row; line, row (346) **74**, 79, 137, 142, 143, 183
(*s-*)*rew* (K-N) burrow 68
rey rattan, cane (478) **137**, 149
b-rey buy (293) **65**, 65–6, 112, 140
ri decay, rotten; gleet (263) **62**
s-ri be, exist (264) **62**
s-rik = *śrik* louse (439) 13–14, **107**, 108, 155, 165, 170, 172, 180
s-rik ~ *s-ryak* pheasant (403) 14, **84–5**, 137, 141, 144, 172, 190
(*b-*)*rim* distribute; cast away 178
ri·m rattan, cane 107
b-riŋ See *priŋ*
s-riŋ long; elongate (433) 78, **106**
s-riŋ ~ *s-raŋ* = *śriŋ* live, alive, green, raw (404) 39, 81, **85**, 105–6, 108, 155, 170, 180
rim See *rum*
(*g-*)*rip* ~ (*s-*)*rip* grow dark; shade, shadow 113
ri·t reap, cut, scrape, shave (371) **80**
riy = *rəy* draw, mark; boundary (429) **103**, 110–11, 178
ri(*y*) dirt; odor (459) 96, **115**
roŋ cat, tiger 107
(*s-*)*row* nit (278) **64**
(*s-*)*row* pine, fir (320) 69
d-ruk six (411) 41, 45, 75, 76, 82, 83, 88, **94–5**, 114, 115, 116, 141, 146, 154, 161, 162, 171, 182
m-ru·k (K-N) steal 144
b-ru·l snake (447) 15, 43, 78, 83, **111**, 119, 137, 147
rum ~ *rim* dark, dusk, twilight (401) **84**
d-rum long for, pine (457) **114**
ruŋ = *rwaŋ* horn (85) 14, **31–2**, 75, 82, 84, 113, 142, 143, 144
d-rup = *drup* sew (456) 25–6, **114**, 115
s-rup snuff up, sip (384) **81**
rus bone (6) **16**, 75, 106, 130, 147, 155, 169
rwak rat 2, 107
rwak = *g-rwak* ant (199) **47**, 49, 74
rwaŋ See *ruŋ*
rwa-t horn 113
rwat stiff, tough (198) **47**
rwiy = (*s-*)*rwəy* slope, slant (200) **47**
rwi(*y*) = (*s-*)*rwi*(*y*) cane (plant) (201) **47**, 56
ryak = *s-ryak* day (24 hours) (203) **48**, 54, 155, 171, 190
ryak grease, oil, juice (204) **48**, 172, 189
s-ryak See *s-rik* to show
ryak layout
ryal (K-N) hail 54
(*s-*)*ryam* (K-N) sharp 53, 171, 189
ryaŋ = *źraŋ* uncle (205) **48**, 54
g-ryap stand (246) 52, **57**, 112, 155, 175, 177, 178
(*b-*)*g-ryat* See *b-r-gyat*

rya-t laugh (202) **47**, 98, 101, 159, 172, 187, 189
ryaw mix (207) **48**
g-ryum = *gryum* salt (245) **57**, 113, 177, 181
ryut grow worse; inferior (206) **48**

s-

r-sa vein, sinew; root (442) 28, **109**
sak breathe, breath, life (485) **146**, 183, 191
m-sak itch (465) **118**, 136, 144
sal clear 15
sam = *səm* breath, voice, spirit 51, 126, 183, 184
sar new, fresh 147, 172, 189
sar ~ *śar* louse 15, 53, 84, 147, 172, 189
r-saŋ lizard (70) **28**, 109
g-sat = *g-sât* kill (58) 13, **27**, 88, 110, 112–13, 126, 191
sa·w oil, fat, grease (272) **63**, 66, 118, 136, 149, 192, 193
sey fruit (57) **27**, 28, 30, 53, 65, 118
m-sin liver (234) **55**, 79, 117, 119, 144, 151, 180, 197
siŋ tree, wood (233) **55**, 79, 84, 88, 136, 142, 143, 144, 165, 180, 197
siy = *səy* die (232) 28, **55**, 61, 98, 136, 148, 151, 185, 197
m-si(y) comb (466) 101, **118**, 136
m-sow arise, awake (295) **66**, 118
soy graze (almost hit) (306) **67**
sra See *s-ra*
sram See *s-ram*
sre[ŋ] weasel, squirrel 79, 171, 183
sriŋ sister 108, 171
sru(w) aunt; father-in-law; relative 108, 171, 197
g-sum three (409) 28, 75, 81, **94**, 131, 136, 142, 143, 152, 153, 162, 169, 170, 181, 182, 186–7, 196
suŋ smell, scent (405) **85**
su·r = *swa·r* sour (42) **23**, 75, 78, 172, 190, 197
su(w) cough (423) **101**, 185
swa·r See *su·r*
sya·l See *syi·r*
(m-)syal See *(m-)syil*
syaŋ See *(t)syaŋ*
syey know (182) **46**, 54, 55, 65, 90, 149, 159, 169
(m-)s(y)il = *(m-)syil* ~ *(m-)syal* wash, bathe (493) 15, 84, **173**, 179
s(y)im = *syim* black, blue, dark (380) **81**
s(y)i·r = *syi·r* ~ *sya·l* iron (372) **80**
s(y)wiy = *sywəy* rub, scrape, shave (180) **46**

sy- = *ś-*

sya = *śa* flesh, meat, animal (181) **46**, 49, 53, 54, 90, 99–100, 106–7, 121, 123, 158, 168–9, 187, 189, 192, 197
syam = *śam* iron (228) **53**, 84, 91
syar = *śar* rise; east 28
śar See *sar*
śim sweep 170
śrak See *s-rak*
śrik See *s-rik*
śriŋ See *s-riŋ*
śu(w) grandchild 158, 169, 170
sywar = *śwar* flow; pour (241) 15, **56**

t-

ta (neg. imperative) 97
ta put, place (19) **19**, 101
ta ~ *tya-n* red 17–18, 159, 169, 188, 189, 190
s-ta knife 22
tak = *thak* (B-L) sharp 87
tak = *trak* weave (17) 14, **19**, 21, 134, 144, 145–6, 171, 183, 191
(l-)tak = *l-tak* ascend; above 52, 110, 123
tal arrow; bow 168, 169, 173, 182, 183
tan dry 190
taŋ pine, fir 69
tap fireplace (18) **19**, 21, 73
tap = *təp* ~ *dəp* fold; repeat (493) 183, **184**
ta·p capable, fit; beautiful (337) **73**
ta·r hang; impale (326) **71**
ta-s = *tâ-s* hear (415) **99**, 103
r-ta-t = *r-tas* thick (426) 16, 17, **102**, 110, 122
tay big (298) **66**, 113, 119, 160, 192, 193
tay self (284) **65**
s-tay navel; abdomen (299) 65, **66**, 106, 150
(m-)ti-s wet 16, 26, 45, 101
ti(y) water (55) 20, **26**, 30, 45, 58, 134, 135, 148, 168, 185–6, 196

(*g-*)*tśo* pour out 56, 112
(*r-*)*tśrəy* See *r-tsiy*
m-tśril See *m-ts*(*y*)*il*
tśrum See *tsum*
tsyuk = *tśuk* (K-N) hit, knock against 53
tsyuk = *tśuk* steep, adj. (353) **76**
tsyur = *tśur* wring, squeeze (188) **47**
tsywap = *tśwap* lungs (239) **56**
tsywar = *tśwar* cut, chop (240) **56**

u-

u putrefy; stale; stink (489) 147, **148**
u = (*m-*)*u* whine, howl, bark (261) **62**
um = (*m-*)*u·m* hold in the mouth; mouthful (108) **36**, 75, 84, 142, 181
up cover, v. (107) **36**
ut swaggering; noisy (109) **36**

w-

wa = (*b*)*wa* bird (99) **35**, 107, 138
wa = *wa-t* bite, chew (424) **101**, 106
wa = (*p*)*wa* man, person, husband 24, **35**, 132, 138, 174, 187
r-wa = *r-pwa* ax (441) 24, **109**, 133, 174, 187
r-wa rain (443) **109**, 167, 187
r-wa ~ *g-wa* village (444) **109**, 113–14
s-wa be in motion, go, come 105, 167, 187
s-wa tooth (437) 34, **106**, 122, 131–2, 138, 139
wal round, circular (91) 15, **32**, 168, 173, 190
d-wam bear, n. (461) 49, 104, 107, **116**, 140, 142, 143, 151, 168, 182, 189
was bee; honey 17
wat wear; clothes 24
wa·y whirl, brandish, wave (90) **32**
wiy = *wəy* (B-L) far 61
woy = (*b*)*woy* monkey (314) **68**, 107
wul = *vul* (K-N) graze (animals) 83

y-

ya night (417) **100**, 102, 138, 167, 188
g-ya itch (451) **113**
g-ya ~ *g-ra* right (hand) (98) **34**, 113, 123, 155, 168, 187
(*g-*)*yak* armpit 34, 167, 170, 189
g-yak ashamed, shy (452) 34, **113**
yaŋ = (*s-*)*brəŋ* fly, bee (492) **167**, 176, 183
r-ya·ŋ light (weight) (328) **71**, 110
ya·p fan, winnow, paddle (92) **32**, 71, 73, 112
ya·r = *ya·r* ~ *yâr* spread, extend; sail 138, 146, 167, 173, 191
yok poker; pudding-stick 14
yip See *ip*
yu (B-L) take 60
d-yuk deer (sambhur) (386) **82**, 116
(*m-*)*yuŋ* finger, toe (355) **76–7**, 77, 120
yuw = *yəw* leak, drip (430) **103**
b-yuw = *b-yəw* rat; rabbit (93) 2, **32**, 61, 69, 99–100, 111, 138, 158, 167, 192
yu(*w*) descend 101
yu(*w*) liquor (94) **32**, 167, 170
r-yu(*w*) ask, request 57
ywar (K-N) sell; buy 15, 51, 89
ywi (K-N) follow 51

z-

za child (offspring) (59) **27**, 30, 54, 90, 100, 102, 122, 135, 169, 188
zak (B-L) descend 30, 87
zik leopard (61) **27**, 30, 79
ziy = *źəy* small, minute (60) **27**
ziy = *źəy* (B-L) urine 30, 90
zlum See *s-lum*
zril worm 15, 16, 37, 171, 173
zya·w ~ *zyu*(*w*) rot, decay; digest 54

ź-

źəy See *ziy*
źraŋ See *ryaŋ*
źum (B-L) use 30

APPENDIX II

English–TB index

Note: Number references are to the series running through the text.

bird *bya* = *bya* ~ *bra* (177)
daw (B-G) (144)
wa = *(b)wa* (99)
birth, give *braŋ* (135)
bite *hap* (89)
wa = *wa-t* (424)
bitter *ka* (8)
black *nak*
s(y)im = *syim* (380)
tyaŋ (225)
block *kum* (482)
blood *s-hwiy* = *s-hywəy* (222)
bloom *ba·r* (1)
blossom *(r-)moy* (304)
blow (mouth, wind) *(s-)mut*
blue *s(y)im* = *syim* (380)
boat *(m-)liy* = *(m-)ləy* (463)
(m-)loŋ (467)
body *guŋ*
(s-)kuw = *(s)kəw*
boil, n. *pren* = *pren* ~ *bren*
boil, v. *pryo* (250)
tsyow (275)
boiled *pryo* (250)
bone *rus* (6)
bore *lwan*
born, to be *kruŋ* (383)
borrow *kroy* (312)
r-ŋya (190)
s-kiy = *s-kəy* (31)
boundary *riy* = *rəy* (429)
bow, n. *d-liy* = *d-ləy* (463)
tal
bowels *pik* (35)
brain *s-niŋ* (367)
nuk = *(s-)nuk* (483)
branch *ku·ŋ* (359)
brandish *wa·y* (90)
break *tsyat* = *tśat* (185)
be ~ *pe* (254)
breast *nuw* = *nəw* (419)
breath *hu*
sam = *səm*
sak (485)
breathe *sak* (485)
bride *mow* (297)
bring out *pro* = *pro(k)* (248)
broken *be* ~ *pe* (254)
bronze *kar*
broom *pyak* = *pywak* (174)
brother, older *ik* (112)
brother, older *puw* = *pəw* (23)
bud *bu* ~ *pu* (260)
mu·m (364)
(r-)moy (304)
buffalo *broŋ* (136)
lwa·y (208)
bug *krep* (347)
burn *bar* ~ *par* = *bwâr* ~ *pwâr* (220)
ka·ŋ (330)
ploŋ (139)
burrow *(s-)rew* (K-N)
bury *bip* ~ *pip* (376)
buy *b-rey* (293)
par
(r-)ley
ywar

c-

cage *kru·ŋ* (389)
calf of leg *bop* (30)
call *gaw* = *gaw* ~ *kaw* (14)
cane (plant) *rey* (478)
ri·m
rwi(y) = *(s-)rwi(y)* (201)
s-m(y)ik (237)
capable *ta·p* (337)
carcass *raw* = *(s-)raw* (268)
carry *ba* (26)
carry (on back or shoulders) *buw* = *bəw* (28)
carve *kut* (383)
cast away *(b-)rim*
cat *roŋ*
cattle *ŋwa* (215)
cave *dwaŋ* = *dwa·ŋ* (169)
kor (349)
pu·k = *pu·k* ~ *buk* (358)
center *la·y* (287)
certain *tyak*
change *lay* (283)
chew *wa* = *wa-t* (424)
child (offspring) *tsa*
za (59)
chin *(m-)ka* ~ *(s-)ka* (470)
choke *ha·k* (323)
chop *tsywar* = *tświar* (240)
circular *hwaŋ*
wal (91)
claw *m-(t)sin* = *m-tsyen* (74)
clean *(t)syaŋ* = *syaŋ*
clear *sal*
(t)syaŋ = *syaŋ*

close, v. *ts(y)i·p = tśi·p* (370)
clothes *wat*
clouds *(r-)muw = (r-)məw* (488)
cloudy *mu·ŋ* (362)
coerce *nyen = (s-)ńen* (193)
cold *glaŋ*
kyam (224)
cold (dry) season *pral = phral* (K-N)
cold (weather) *graŋ* (120)
comb *kwi(y)* (480)
m-si(y) (466)
come *byon* (179)
s-wa
come (out) *hwaŋ* (218)
come out *don ~ ton*
pro = pro(k) (248)
twak
compress *nip*
concave *ku[·]m*
conceal *bip ~ pip* (376)
ip = yip (114)
kway (303)
congeal, n. *kal*
connect *tsyap = tśap* (186)
contradict *ŋraŋ* (155)
convalesce *bran* (133)
convex *ku[·]m*
cook *klak = glak ~ klak* (124)
tsyow (275)
cooked *s-min* (432)
copper *griy = grəy* (39)
cork *tsuw = tsəw* (422)
cotton *b-la* (K-N)
cough *su(w)* (423)
cough up *ka·k*
count *r-tsiy = (r-)tśrəy* (76)
country *mliy = mləy* (152)
cousin *wap*
cover *klup* (479)
pun (385)
up (107)
cowlick *boy* (308)
crab *d-ka·y* (51)
crack *ak* (106)
pop (345)
crooked *guk ~ kuk*
crow, n. *ka*
crow, v. *groy* (310)
cross over *gaw* (318)
crush *nip*
cry *ŋuw = ŋəw* (79)
cry out *a·w* (273)
cubit *mu·k* (394)
cut *da·n* (22)
kut (383)
mrak = mrak ~ brak (147)
ra = ra-t (458)
ri·t (371)
tsyat = tśat (185)
tsywar = tśwar (240)
tuk (387)
cut off *lep = (s-)lep* (351)

d-

dance *ga·r* (11)
dare *hwam* (216)
dark *mu·ŋ* (362)
ŋruw = ŋrəw (156)
r-mu·k (357)
rum ~ rim (401)
s(y)im = syim (380)
tyaŋ (225)
dark, grow *(g-)rip ~ (s-)rip*
daughter-in-law *krwiy = krwəy* (244)
(m-)na
s-nam (103)
dawn *praŋ* (322)
day *niy = ŋəy* (81)
day (24 hours) *ryak = (s)ryak* (203)
dead *raw = (s-)raw* (268)
debt *kroy* (312)
decay *ri* (263)
zya·w ~ zyu(w)
decayed *tswiy = tswəy* (183)
deep *tu·k* (356)
deer (sambhur) *d-yuk* (386)
deer (barking-) *d-kiy = d-kəy* (54)
defeat *bam ~ pam* (471)
defeated, to be *bam ~ pam* (471)
defy *daw* (267)
delight *pro* (130)
demon *(m-)hla* (475)
deny *ŋraŋ* (155)
descend *yu* (w)
zak (B-L)
devaricate *ka* (469)
die *siy = səy* (232)
dig *la·y* (288)
tu = du ~ tu (258)
dig out *d-kew = d-k(h)ew* (K-N)
klaw (269)

dig up *r-ko-t = r-go-t ~ r-ko-t* (420)
digest *zya·w ~ zyu(w)*
direction *lam* (87)
dirt *kriy = krəy* (460)
ri(y) (459)
disappear *ma-t* (425)
distribute *(b-)rim*
dive *lip* (375)
divided *bra* (132)
do *mow* (280)
dog *kwiy = kwəy* (159)
door *m-ka* (468)
dove *kruw = m-krəw* (118)
draw (picture) *riy = rəy* (429)
draw (water) *ka·p* (336)
drawers *b-ni(y)* (476)
dream *maŋ = r-maŋ* (82)
dress *gwa-n ~ kwa-n* (160)
drink *am = əm* (481)
drip *yuw = yəw* (430)
drown *lip* (375)
drugs *tsiy = (r-)tsəy* (65)
dry *raw = (s-)raw* (268)
tan
dry up *kan*
kaŋ (331)
dull *r-mu·k* (357)
dumb (mute) *(m-)a* (105)
dung *s-baŋ*
dusk *rum ~ rim* (401)
dust *mu·k* (363)
dwell *na* (414)

e-

eagle *laŋ* (333)
muw = məw (257)
ear *g-na = r-na ~ g-na* (453)
earth *mliy = mləy* (152)
r-ka (97)
east *syar = śar*
easy *lway* (302)
eat *am = əm* (481)
dza (66)
edge *r-gu·ŋ* (395)
r-ka[·]m (329)
egg *di*
twiy = twəy (168)
eight *b-r-gyat = (b)g-ryat* (163)
elbow *du*
elephant *tsaŋ = tshaŋ* (B-L)
elongate *s-riŋ* (433)
emerge *twak*
encircle *hwaŋ*
enjoy *pro* (130)
enmity with, be at *daw* (267)
enough *luk* (B-L)
enter *hwaŋ* (218)
equal *ren* (346)
erect, v. *dzu[·]k* (360)
exceed *lay* (301)
excessive *hla(k)*
exchange *lay* (283)
excrement *kliy = kləy* (125)
n(y)ik = (s-)ńik ~ (s-)ńek (235)
(r-)kyak ~ (s-)kyak
exist *s-ri* (264)
extend *ya·r = ya·r ~ yâr*
extinguish *mit* (374)
eye *mik ~ myak* (402)

f-

face *mu·r* (366)
faded *ŋruw = ŋrəw* (156)
falcon *laŋ* (333)
fall, v. *kla = gla ~ kla* (123)
fan *ya·p* (92)
far *dzya·l = dźa·l* (229)
wiy = wəy (B-L)
fat, adj. *tsow* (277)
fat, n. *sa·w* (272)
tsil
father *pa = pwa* (24)
father-in-law *kuw = kəw* (255)
sru(w)
fathom (arm-spread) *la[·]m*
fear *b-ray* (450)
grok ~ krok = grâk ~ krâk; grok ~ krok (473)
kri(y) (416)
feces *e·k* (K-N)
female *pwi(y)* (171)
fence *hwaŋ*
field *low* (K-N)
fight *ran = (g-)ra·l*
fill *bliŋ ~ pliŋ* (142)
dyam ~ tyam (226)
filth *kriy = krəy* (460)
n(y)ik = (s-)ńik ~ (s-)ńek (235)
finger *(m-)yuŋ* (355)
finish *o·l* (111)

fir (*s-*)*row* (320)
taŋ
fire *bar* ~ *par* = *bwâr* ~ *pwâr* (220)
mey (290)
fireplace *rap* (84)
tap (18)
fireplace shelf *rap* (84)
fish *ŋya* (189)
fit *ta·p* (337)
five *l-ŋa* ~ *b-ŋa* (78)
flame (*s-*)*lyam*
flash *lyap* = (*s-*)*lyap* (213)
flat *lyap* (212)
pe·r (340)
flat surface *pleŋ* (138)
flea *s-liy* = *s-ləy* (440)
flee *ploŋ* (140)
flesh *sya* = *śa* (181)
flitter *lyap* = (*s-*)*lyap* (213)
flow *lwi*(*y*) (210)
sywar = *śwar* (241)
twiy = *twəy* (167)
flower *ba·r*
bwat
flute *gliŋ*
fly, n. *m-tow* = *m-thow* (K-N)
yaŋ = (*s-*)*braŋ* (492)
fly, v. *byer*
pur ~ *pir* (398)
pyam
pyaw (176)
fog (*r-*)*muw* = (*r-*)*məw* (488)
fog(gy) *r-mu·k* (357)
fold *tap* = *təp* ~ *dəp* (493)
follow *naŋ* = (*s-*)*naŋ* (334)
ywi (K-N)
foot *g-la*
kriy = *krəy* (38)
(*r-*)*kaŋ*
forest *b-liŋ* (378)
forget *b-la·p* (335)
fork *ka·k* (327)
fork (of legs) *kap* (338)
forked *bra* (132)
four *b-liy* = *b-ləy* (410)
fowl *rak*
fox *gwa*
free, v. *g-lwat* (209)
freeze *glaŋ*
fresh *sar*
frighten *grok* ~ *krok* = *grâk* ~ *krâk*; *grok* ~ *krok* (473)
frog *s-bal*
fruit (*b-*)*ras*
sey (57)
fry *r-ŋaw* (270)
full *bliŋ* ~ *pliŋ* (142)
dyam ~ *tyam* (226)
fungus *g-muw* = *g-məw* (455)

g-

gag *ha·k* (323)
gasp *haŋ*
gentle *ŋoy* (315)
get (*r-*)*ney* (249)
gills *mu·r* (366)
give *biy* = *bəy* (427)
pe(*k*) (K-N)
gleet *ri* (263)
go *byon* (179)
s-wa
go out *don* ~ *ton*
goat *ke·l* = *kye·l* ~ *kyi*[·]*l* (339)
tsit = *tshit* (B-L)
god (*m*)*hla* (475)
goitre *ba*
gold *tsyak* = *tśak* (184)
good *lyak-s* (Bod.)
may (300)
pra (129)
goose *ŋa-n*
grain *mruw* = *mrəw* (150)
grandchild *b-liy* = *b-ləy* (448)
śu(*w*)
tsa
grandfather *puw* = *pəw* (23)
grandmother *bwa* (B-L)
piy = *pəy* (36)
grass *mrak* = *mlyak* (149)
grasshopper *kaw* = *khaw* (K-N)
graze (almost hit) *soy* (306)
(animals) *wul* = *vul* (K-N)
grease *ryak* (204)
sa·w (272)
green *dzim*
kruŋ (383)
ŋow = (*s-*)*ŋow* (296)
s-riŋ ~ *s-raŋ* = *śriŋ* (404)
grind *krit* (119)
groin *kap* (338)
s-ga·l

ground *gliŋ* (128)
guard *kyoŋ* = *kyâŋ* ~ *kyoŋ* (161)
gums *r-nil* ~ *r-ni(y)* ~ *s-nil* (3)
gush *brup* ~ *prup* (151)

h-

hail, n. *ryal* (K-N)
hair (body) *mul* = (*s*-)*mul* ~ (*s*-)*mil* ~ (*r*-) *mul* (2)
hair (head) *ney* = (*r*-)*ney* (292)
(*s*-)*kra* (115)
tsam = *tsâm* ~ *sâm* (73)
half *pwak*
hammer *tow* = *tow* ~ *dow* (317)
hand *lak* = *g-lak* (86)
hang *pyan* (175)
ta·r (326)
hang down *dzywal* = *dźwal* (242)
hawk, n. *dzwan* (B-L)
laŋ (333)
muw = *məw* (257)
hawk, v. *ha·k* (323)
head (*d*-)*bu*
m-gaw ~ (*s*-)*gaw* (490)
hear *g-na* = *r-na* ~ *g-na* (453)
ta-s = *tâ-s* (415)
heart *m-luŋ* (K-N)
s-niŋ (367)
heavy *s-liy* = (*s*-)*ləy* (95)
heddles *s-nat* (436)
hide, v. *kway* (303)
pak = *pwak* (46)
high *m-raŋ*
m-to (247)
hit *tsyuk* = *tśuk*
hoe *la·y* (288)
hold in the mouth *um* = (*m*)*u·m* (108)
hole *dwaŋ* = *dwa·ŋ* (169)
kwar (350)
honey *was*
horn *kruw* = *krəw* (37)
ruŋ = *rwaŋ* (85)
rwa-t
horse *s-raŋ* ~ *m-raŋ* (145)
hot *tsa* (62)
howl *groy* (310)
u = (*m*-)*u* (261)
house *kim* = *kyim* ~ *kyum* (53)
hundred *r-gya* (164)
husband *wa* = (*p*)*wa* (100)
husks *pwa·y* (170)

i-

I *ka*
ŋa (406)
ŋay (285)
ice *kyam* (224)
ill *na* (80)
nyuŋ = (*s*-)*ńuŋ* (194)
impale *ta·r* (326)
inferior *ryut* (206)
in-law *ŋwap*
insect *buw* = *bəw* (27)
dyuŋ (B-G)
inside *tsyu·ŋ* = *tu·ŋ* (390)
interfere *daw* (267)
iron *syam* = *śam* (228)
s(*y*)*i·r* = *syi·r* ~ *sya·l* (372)
island *gliŋ* (128)
itch *g-ya* (451)
kut (383)
m-sak (465)

j-

jaw (*m*-)*ka* ~ (*s*-)*ka* (470)
jaw (molar teeth) *gam* = *gəm*
join *du-t* ~ *tu-t* (421)
tsyap = *tśap* (186)
joint *tsik* (64)
juice *ryak* (204)
tsiy = (*r*-)*tsəy* (65)

k-

kidney *m-kal* (12)
kill *g-sat* = *g sât*
kiss *dzo·p* (69)
kite *dzwan* (B-L)
laŋ (333)
knead *na·y* (286)
knee *du*
(*m*-)*ku·k*
put (7)
knife *s-ta*
knock *tuk* (387)
knock against *tsyuk* = *tśuk*
knot *du-t* ~ *tu-t* (421)
know (*m*-)*kyen* (223)
syey (182)

l-

lac *krep* (347)
laugh *m-nwi*(*y*) (191)
rya-t (202)
lead, n. *kar*

leaf *la* = (*s*-)*la* (486)
lap (321)
pak = *pwak* (40)
leak *yuw* = *yəw* (430)
lean back *ew* (K-N)
leap *ga·r* (11)
leave *gar* (15)
leech *r-pat* (45)
leech (water) (*m*-)*li·t* (396)
left (hand) *bay* = *bway* (47)
leg *bop* (30)
(*r*-)*kaŋ*
lend *kroy* (312)
length *duŋ* = *duŋ* ~ *tu·ŋ*
leopard *zik* (61)
lick (*m*-)*lyak* ~ (*s*-)*lyak* (211)
(*s*-)*lya·w*
life *sak* (485)
lift *ku*
tyak = *tək* (B)
light *hwa-t* (221)
light (weight) *r-ya·ŋ* (328)
lightning *lyap* = (*s*-)*lyap* (213)
line *ren* (346)
lineage *mruw* = *mrəw* (150)
lip *s-nes*
lips *r-ka*[·]*m* (329)
liquor *yu*(*w*) (94)
live *kruŋ* (383)
s-riŋ ~ *s-raŋ* = *śriŋ* (404)
liver *m-sin* (234)
lizard *r-saŋ* (70)
loins *s-ga·l*
long *duŋ* = *duŋ* ~ *tu·ŋ*
low (279)
s-riŋ (433)
long for *d-rum* (457)
lose *ma-t* (425)
louse *sar* ~ *śar*
s-rik = *śrik* (439)
love *m-dza* (67)
low *nem* ~ *nyam* = *ńam* (348)
lungs *tsywap* = *tśwap* (239)

m-

man (homo) *r-mi*(*y*)
man *wa* = (*p*)*wa*
many *mra* (148)
mark *riy* = *rəy* (429)
marrow *kliŋ* = (*r*-)*kliŋ* (126)
meat *sya* = *śa* (181)
meet *ŋra* (154)
middle *tsyu·ŋ* = *tu·ŋ* (390)
milk *nuw* = *nəw* (419)
mind, n. *s-niŋ* (367)
minute, adj. *ziy* = *źəy* (60)
mix *ryaw* (207)
moderate *ŋoy* (315)
moisture *hus*
mole (on skin) *r-men* (104)
monkey *mruk*
woy = (*b*)*woy* (314)
moon *s-la* ~ *g-la* = *s-gla* (144)
more *hla*(*k*)
morning *praŋ* (322)
mortar *tsum* = *tśrum* (75)
mosquito *kraŋ* (322)
mother *ma* (487)
(*m*-)*na*
mother-in-law *ni*(*y*) (316)
motion, be in *s-wa*
mouth *ak* (106)
ku(*w*) (G-B)
m-ka (468)
mu·r (366)
r-ka[·]*m* (329)
mouthful *hap* (89)
um = (*m*-)*u·m*
move *mow* (280)
much *mra* (148)
mushroom *g-muw* = *g-məw* (455)

n-

nail (finger-, toe-) *m*-(*t*)*sin* = *m-tsyen* (74)
name *rm-iŋ* (83)
s-braŋ
nauseated *on* (343)
navel *la·y* (287)
s-tay (299)
near *ney* (291)
neck *liŋ* = (*m*-)*liŋ* (96)
tuk = *twak* (393)
neck(-shaped) *ke* = (*s*-)*ke*(*k*) (251)
needle *kap* = *kəp* (52)
nephew *tu* = *tu* ~ *du* (259)
nephew/niece *b-liy* = *b-ləy* (448)
tsa
nest (*r*-)*bu* (K-N)
net, casting *kwan* = *kwan* ~ *gwan* (158)
nettle *r-ma-t* See *r-ma* (446)
new *sar*

niece/nephew *b-liy = b-ləy* (448)

tsa

night *ya* (417)

nine *d-kuw = d-kəw ~ d-gaw* (13)

nit *(s-)row* (278)

nod *n(y)it = ńit* (236)

noisy *ut* (109)

nose *s-na ~ s-na·r* (101)

o-

obtain *(r-)ney* (249)

odor *ri(y)* (459)

oil *ryak* (204)

sa·w (272)

old *raw = (s-)raw* (268)

r-ga (445)

older (brother, uncle) *maŋ*

older sister *(m-)na*

one *it*

kat

t(y)ik = (g-)tyik

open *bu ~ pu* (260)

ka (469)

open(ing) *m-ka* (468)

oppress *nyen = (s-)ńen* (193)

otter *s-ram = sram* (438)

overflow *brup ~ prup* (151)

owl *gu = gu ~ ku*

p-

paddle, v. *ya·p* (92)

paddy *may* (B-G)

pain *na* (80)

tsa (62)

paint *tsiy = (r-)tsəy* (65)

palm (of hand) *pa = pwa* (418)

panji *tsow* (276)

pant *haŋ*

pare *ku·k* (388)

lep = (s-)lep (351)

pass, v. *lay* (301)

path *pa*

peacock *doŋ = (m-)doŋ* (341)

peas *be* (253)

penis *li = li ~ (m-)ley* (262)

person *wa = (p)wa* (100)

petticoat *b-ni(y)* (476)

pheasant *s-rik ~ s-ryak* (403)

phlegm *ka·k*

pick, v. *d-kew = d-k(h)ew* (K-N)

pierce *lwan*

pig *pak = pwak* (43)

pigeon *kuw = (m-)kəw* (495)

pillow *kum* (482)

pinch *nyap = ńap* (192)

pine, n. *(s-)row* (320)

taŋ

pine, v. *d-rum* (457)

pit *dwaŋ = dwa·ŋ* (169)

kor (349)

place, v. *ta* (19)

plait *byar ~ pyar = byâr ~ pyâr* (178)

plank *pleŋ* (138)

plant, v. *dzu[·]k* (360)

plantain *ŋak = (s-)ŋak* (477)

play, v. *tsya·y = (r-)tsya·y* (289)

plug *tsuw = tsəw* (422)

plump *bwam = (s-)bwam* (172)

poison *duk ~ tuk* (472)

poisoned *duk ~ tuk* (472)

poisonous *duk ~ tuk* (472)

poker *yok*

potato *s-ra = śra* (434)

pound, v. *tuk* (387)

pour *(m-)lu(w) = (r-)lu(w) ~ (m-)lu(w)*

sywar = śwar (241)

pour out *(g-)tśo*

precipice *r-ka[·]m* (329)

press(ed) *nyen = (s-)ńen* (193)

price *puw = pəw* (41)

prick *tsow* (276)

pull *don ~ ton*

punish *nye = ńe* (252)

pure *(t)syaŋ = syaŋ*

pus *pren = pren ~ bren*

tswiy = tswəy (183)

put *ta* (19)

put into mouth *gam*

putrefy *u* (489)

q-

quarrel *ran = (g-)ra·l*

quiet *ŋoy* (315)

r-

rabbit *b-yuw = b-yəw* (93)

rain *r-wa* (443)

rat *b-yuw = b-yəw* (93)

rwak

rat, bamboo *bwiy = bwəy* (173)

rattan *rey* (478)

ri·m

ravine *grok* (122)
raw *dzim*
s-riŋ ~ *s-raŋ* = *ś-riŋ* (404)
real *tyak*
reap *ri·t* (371)
receptacle *kuk* (393)
red *kyeŋ* (162)
(*r*-)*ni*
ta ~ *tya-n*
tsyak = *tśak* (184)
refuse, n. *mu·k* (363)
related *do* (249)
relative *sru*(*w*)
relax *o·l* (111)
release *g-lwat* (209)
repay *tsap* (63)
repeat *tap* = *təp* ~ *dəp* (493)
request *r-yu*(*w*)
rest, v. *na* (414)
rice (*b*-)*ras*
moy (B-G)
rice paddy **bu*(*w*) (K-N)
ride *dzyon* = *dźon* (72)
ride (horse) *gi* (B-L)
right (hand) *g-ya* ~ *g-ra* (98)
rind *kok* = (*r*-)*kwâk*
ripe *s-min* (432)
rise *syar* = *śar*
river *klu·ŋ* (127)
road *lam* (87)
roast *ka·ŋ* (330)
r-ŋaw (270)
rock *brak* (134)
roll, v. *ki·l* (373)
roll up (*r*-)*tul* = *r-tul*
root *bul* ~ *pul*
r-sa (442)
rot *zya·w* ~ *zyu*(*w*)
rotten *ri* (263)
rough *gram*
round *s-lum* = *zlum* (143)
wal (91)
row, place in a row *ren* (346)
rub *nu·l* (365)
s(*y*)*wiy* = *sywəy* (180)
rub against *nu·l* (365)
rubbish *mu·k* (363)
rule (line) *kut* (383)
run *ploŋ* (140)
rustle *krwap* (243)

s-

sad *nyuŋ* = (*s*-)*ńuŋ* (194)
sag *dzywal* = *dźwal* (242)
sail *ya·r* = *ya·r* ~ *yâr*
salt *g-ryum* = *gryum* (245)
la
tsa (214)
sambhur *tsot* (344)
scattered *bra* (132)
scent *suŋ* (405)
scoop out *r-ko-t* = *r-go-t* ~ *r-ko-t* (420)
scorpion (*s*-)*di·k* (56)
scrape *kut* (383)
ri·t (371)
s(*y*)*wiy* = *sywəy* (180)
scratch *d-kew* = *d-k*(*h*)*ew* (K-N)
hyak (230)
kut (383)
pruk (391)
scream *groy* (310)
screech *groy* (310)
see *mraŋ* (146)
seed *mruw* = *mrəw* (150)
seize (with mouth) *gam*
self *ŋay* (285)
tay (284)
sell *par*
ywar
sesame *s-nam* (435)
set teeth on edge *krim* (379)
seven *s-nis* (5)
sew *byar* ~ *pyar* = *byâr* ~ *pyâr* (178)
d-rup = *drup* (456)
krwi(*y*) = *khrwi*(*y*) (K-N)
pa
shade (*g*-)*rip* ~ (*s*-)*rip*
shadow (*g*-)*rip* ~ (*s*-)*rip*
sharp (*s*-)*ryam* (K-N)
tak = *thak* (B-L)
shave *ri·t* (371)
s(*y*)*wiy* = *sywəy* (180)
shavings *pwa·y* (170)
shear *ku·k* (388)
shell(-fish) *kroy* (311)
shield *d-po* = *d-pho* (K-N)
shin *r-gu·ŋ* (395)
shine *hwa-t* (221)
tsyar = *tśar* (187)
shoot, v. *ga·p* (219)
shoulder *m-lyaŋ* (K-N)
shrink *twan*

shun *kway* (303)
shut *ts(y)i·p* = *tśi·p* (370)
shy *g-yak* (452)
s-rak = *śrak* (431)
sibling, younger *na·w* (271)
side *r-gu·ŋ* (395)
silver *ŋul* = *(d-)ŋul*
sinew *r-sa* (442)
single *r-kyaŋ* (34)
sink, v. *lip* (375)
nup ~ *nip* = *nu·p* ~ *ni[·]p* (400)
sip *s-rup* (384)
sister *sriŋ*
s-nam (103)
sister (of man) *dzar* (68)
sit *bam* ~ *pam* (471)
tu·ŋ = *tu·ŋ* ~ *du·ŋ* (361)
six *d-ruk* (411)
skin *s-graw* (121)
kok = *(r-)kwâk*
sky *nam*
(r-)muw = *(r-)məw* (488)
slab *pleŋ* (138)
slant *rwiy* = *(s-)rwəy* (200)
sleep *ip* = *yip* (114)
mwiy = *(r-)mwəy* ~ *(s-)mwəy* (196)
n(y)it = *ńit* (236)
sleepy *myel* (197)
slice, v. *lep* = *(s-)lep* (351)
slip *ble* (141)
slippery *ble* (141)
slope *rwiy* = *(s-)rwəy* (200)
small *ziy* = *zəy* (60)
smell *m-nam* (464)
suŋ (405)
smoke *kuw* = *kəw* (256)
snake *b-ru·l* (447)
buw = *bəw* (27)
snap at *hap* (89)
snow *kyam* (224)
snot *s-nap* (102)
snuff up *s-rup* (384)
soft *now* (274)
pryo (250)
sole (of foot) *pa* = *pwa* (418)
son-in-law *krwiy* = *krwəy* (244)
ma·k (324)
soul *(m-)hla* (475)
sour *kri(y)* (413)
krok = *k(h)rok* (K-N)
s-kyur = *s-kywar* (42)
sour *su·r* = *swa·r* (42)
span *twa* = *(m-)twa* (165)
speak *br(w)ak* ~ *(s-)br(w)aŋ*
spear *m-duŋ*
speech *ka* (9)
spindle *paŋ* = *pwaŋ* (48)
(s-)mwiy = *(s-)mwəy* (195)
spirit *sam* = *səm*
spit *(m-)tuk* ~ *(s-)tu·k* ~ *(s-)du·k*
(m-)twa ~ *(s-)twa*
spittle *m-ts(y)il* = *m-tśril* (231)
(m-)tuk ~ *(s-)tu·k* ~ *(s-)du·k*
(m-)twa ~ *(s-)twa*
twiy = *twəy* (168)
spoiled *m-hew* (K-N)
spread *ka* (469)
ya·r = *ya·r* ~ *yâr*
sprout, n. *s-m(y)ik* (237)
squeeze *nyap* = *ńap* (192)
tsyur = *tśur* (188)
squirrel *sre[ŋ]*
squirt *brup* ~ *prup* (151)
stale *u* (489)
stand *g-ryap* (246)
star *s-kar* = *s-kər* (49)
steal *m-ru·k* (K-N)
r-kuw = *r-kəw* (33)
steep, adj. *tsyuk* = *tśuk* (353)
stem *ku·ŋ* (359)
stick (pudding-) *yok*
stiff *rwat* (198)
stink *u* (489)
stone *r-luŋ* (88)
stop up *tsuw* = *tsəw* (422)
straight *bleŋ* ~ *pleŋ* (352)
dyam (227)
straighten *bleŋ* ~ *pleŋ* (352)
strangle *ik* (113)
stream, n. *lwi(y)* (210)
strength *(d-)baŋ*
stride *ga·r* (11)
strip, v. *ku·k* (388)
stump *bul* ~ *pul*
suck *dzo·p* (69)
sullen *mu·ŋ* (362)
sun *nam*
niy = *nəy* (81)
tsyar = *tśar* (187)
suppurate *twiy* = *twəy* (167)
surround *kroy* (313)
swaggering *ut* (109)

swallow, v. *mlyuw* = *mlyəw* (153)
sweat *krwiy* = *khrwəy* (B-L)
sweep *pyak* = *pywak* (174)
śim
sweet *dz(y)im* = *dźim* (71)
klum
kyuw = *khyəw* (B-L)
twi(y) (166)
swim *pyaw* (176)
swollen *bwam* = *(s-)bwam* (172)
sword *m-duŋ*

t-

tail *r-may* (282)
take *yu* (B-L)
take up *ku*
tall *low* (279)
tear, v. *mrak* = *mrak* ~ *brak* (147)
ten *gip* (16)
ts(y)i(y) = *tsyay* (404)
tend (cattle) *kyoŋ* = *kyâŋ* ~ *kyoŋ* (161)
tender *now* (274)
that *day* (21)
thick *r-ta-t* = *r-tas* (426)
tow = *tow* ~ *dow* (319)
tu·k (356)
thin *ba* (25)
lyap (212)
pe·r (340)
this *day* (21)
thorn *tsow* (276)
thou *na* (407)
thousand *s-toŋ* (32)
threaten *krim* (379)
three *g-sum* (409)
thresh *krap*
thunderbolt *gle·k* (K-N)
tickle *g-li* = *k(a)li* (265)
tie *du-t* ~ *tu-t* (421)
kik (484)
tiger *k-key* = *d-key* ~ *d-kəy* (462)
(k-)la (B-L)
roŋ
tired *bal* (29)
nyuŋ = *(s-)ŋuŋ* (194)
toad *u-prok* = *phrok* (K-N)
toast, v. *ka·ŋ* (330)
toe *(m-)yuŋ* (355)
tongue *m-lay* ~ *s-lay* (281)
(m-)lyak ~ *(s-)lyak* (211)
(s-)lyam
(s-)lya·w

tooth *s-wa* (437)
tough *rwat* (198)
trade *par*
tree *bul* ~ *pul*
ku·ŋ (359)
siŋ (233)
tube *gliŋ*
twenty *(m-)kul* (397)
twilight *rum* ~ *rim* (401)
twirl *(s-)mwiy* = *(s-)mwəy* (195)
twist *kik* (484)
ki·l (373)
na·y (286)
two *g-nis* = *g-ni-s* (4)

u-

uncle *bwaŋ*
ryaŋ = *źraŋ* (205)
uncle (maternal) *kuw* = *kəw* (255)
upper part *s-tyaŋ* = *s-təŋ* (Bod.)
urinate *ts(y)i* = *tśi* (77)
urine *ziy* = *źəy* (B-L)

v-

valley *klu·ŋ* (127)
kor (349)
valuable *puw* = *pəw* (41)
value *puw* = *pəw* (41)
vein *r-sa* (442)
very *tyak*
vessel *s-not*
village *dyal* ~ *tyal*
r-wa ~ *g-wa* (444)
voice *sam* = *səm*
vomit *(m-)tuk* ~ *(s-)tu·k* ~ *(s-)du·k*
on (343)
vulture *laŋ* (333)
vulva *dźuk*

w-

war *ran* = *(g-)ra·l*
warm *lum* (381)
wash *kruw* = *krəw* (117)
(m-)s(y)il = *(m-)syil* ~ *(m-)syal* (493)
waste *m-hew* (K-N)
water *ti(y)* (55)
twiy = *twəy* (168)
wave, v. *wa·y* (90)
wear (clothes) *bu(w)* (428)
gwa-n ~ *kwa-n* (160)
pun (385)
wat

weasel *sre[ŋ]*
weave *tak = trak* (17)
weed, v. *klaw* (269)
weeds *mu·k* (363)
weep *krap* (116)
ŋuw = ŋəw (79)
weigh *ki·n* (369)
wen *r-men* (104)
wet *hus*
(m-)ti-s
whine *u = (m-)u* (261)
whirl *wa·y* (90)
white *bok*
ŋow = (s-)ŋow (296)
plu
wife *s-nam* (103)
wind, n. *g-liy = g-ləy* (454)
winnow *krap*
ya·p (92)
withered *ŋruw = ŋrəw* (156)
woman *mow* (297)
womb *s-not*
wood *siŋ* (233)
word *ka* (9)
work *mow* (280)
worm *zril*
worse, grow *ryut* (206)
wound *r-ma* (446)
wrap *klup* (479)
pun (385)
(r-)tul = r-tul
wring *tsyur = tśur* (188)
wrinkle *twan*

y-

yak, wild *broŋ* (136)
yam *kywiy = kywəy* (238)
s-ra = śra (434)
year *niŋ = s-niŋ* (368)
yellow *ŋow = (s-)ŋow* (296)
younger (youngest) sibling *toy = doy ~ toy* (309)

APPENDIX III

Primary Tibeto-Burman sources

Abbreviations

AM	*Asia Major*
AO	*Acta Orientalia*
BEFEO	*Bulletin de l'École Française d'Extrême-Orient*
BMFEA	*Bulletin of the Museum of Far Eastern Antiquities (Östasiatiska Samlingarna)*
BSLP	*Bulletin de la Société Linguistique de Paris*
BSOS	*Bulletin of the School of Oriental Studies*
CYYY	*Academia Sinicia, Bulletin of the Institute of History and Philology*
HJAS	*Harvard Journal of Asiatic Studies*
IJAL	*International Journal of American Linguistics*
JAS	*Journal of Asian Studies*
JASB	*Journal of the Asiatic Society of Bengal*
JBRS	*Journal of the Burma Research Society*
JNChBRAS	*Journal of the North-China Branch of the Royal Asiatic Society*
JRASB	*Journal of the Royal Asiatic Society of Bengal*
MSOS	*Mitteilungen des Seminars für Orientalische Sprachen*
OLZ	*Orientalische Literaturzeitung*

POLA	*Project on Linguistic Analysis* (reports of the Phonology Laboratory of the Department of Linguistics, University of California at Berkeley)
TAK	*Toonan Azia Kenkyuu* (Southeast Asian Research), Kyoto
TP	*T'oung Pao*
WZKM	*Wiener Zeitschrift für Kunde des Morgenlandes*
ZDMG	*Zeitschrift der Deutschen Morgenländischen Gesellschaft*

Abbey, W. B. T.
1899. *Manual of the Maru Language*. Rangoon.
Anderson, J. D.
1885. *A Short List of Words of the Hill Tippera Language with their English Equivalents*. Shillong.
1896. *A Short Vocabulary of the Aka Language*. Shillong.
Baber, E. C.
1886. *Travels and Researches in the Interior of China. Suppl. Papers of the Royal Geog. Soc.* **1** (1886), 1–152.
Bacot, J.
1913. *Les Mo-So*. Leide.
Bailey, T. G.
1908. *Languages of the Northern Himalayas. Royal Asiatic Society Monographs* **12**.
1909. 'A Brief Grammar of the Kanauri Language', *ZDMG* **63**, 661–87.
1911. *Kanauri Vocabulary in Two parts. Royal Asiatic Society Monographs* **13**.
1920. *Linguistic Studies from the Himalayas. Royal Asiatic Society Monographs* **18**.
Barnard, J. T. O.
1934. *A Handbook of the Răwang Dialect of the Nung Language*. Rangoon.
Beames, J.
1870. 'On the Magar Language of Nepal', *JRAS* **4**, 178–228.
Bell, C. A.
1919. *Grammar of Colloquial Tibetan*, 2nd ed. Calcutta.
Bernot, L.
1967. *Les Cak: Contribution à l'étude ethnographique d'une population de langue Loi*. Paris: Éditions du Centre National de la Recherche Scientifique.
Bhat, D. N. Shankara.
1969. *Tankhur Naga Vocabulary*. Deccan College Postgraduate and Research Institute, Poona.
Boell, P.
1899. *Contribution à l'étude de la langue Lolo*. Paris.
Bonifacy, A. L.
1905. 'Étude sur les language parlées par les populations de la haute Rivière Claire', *BEFEO* **5**, 306–27.
1908. 'Étude sur les coutumes et la langue des Lolo et des La-qua du Haut-Tonkin', *BEFEO* **8**, 531–58.
Bonnerjea, B.
1930–1. 'Contribution to Garo Linguistics and Ethnology', *Anthropos* **30**, 509–32; 837–50; **31**, 141–57; 456–69.
Bor, N. L.
1938. 'Yano Dafla Grammar and Vocabulary', *JRASB* **4**, 217–81.
Bor, N. L. and Pawsey, C. R.
1938. 'English–Sema Vocabulary', *JRASB* **4**, 309–49.

Bridges, J. E.
1915. *Burmese Grammar*. Rangoon.
Brown, N.
1837. 'Comparison of Indo-Chinese Languages', *JASB* **6**, 1023–38.
1849. 'On the Aborigines of the Eastern Frontier' (communicated by B. H. Hodgson), *JASB* **18**, 967–75.
1850. 'Aborigines of the North East Frontier' (communicated by B. H. Hodgson), *JASB* **19**, 309–16.
1851. 'Specimens of the Naga Language of Assam', *JAOS* **2**, 157–65.
Brown, R. G.
1911. 'The Tamans of the Upper Chindwin', *Journal of the Royal Anthrop. Inst.* **41**, 305–17.
1920. 'The Kadus of Burma', *BSOS* **1**, pt. 3, 1–28.
Brown, W. B.
1895. *Outline Grammar of the Deori Chutiya Language*. Shillong.
Burling, Robbins
1959. 'Proto-Bodo', *Language* **35**, 435–53.
1966. 'The addition of final stops in the history of Maru', *Language* **42**, 581–6.
1966. 'A problem in Lahu phonology', *Artibus Asiae, Essays offered to G. H. Luce*, I, 97–101.
1967. *Proto Lolo-Burmese*, Indiana University Research Center in Anthropology, Folklore, and Linguistics, Publication **43**; appeared in the *International Journal of American Linguistics* **33**, 2, part 2. Bloomington, Indiana.
Butler, J.
1873. 'A Rough Comparative Vocabulary of some of the Dialects spoken in the "Nágá Hills" District', *JASB* **42**, Appendix, i–xxix.
1875. 'A Rough Comparative Vocabulary of two more of the Dialects spoken in the "Nágá Hills"', *JASB* **44**, 216–27.
Campbell, A.
1840. 'Note on the Limboos, and other Hill Tribes hitherto undescribed', *JASB* **9**, 595–615.
Chang, Kun
1967. 'A Comparative Study of the Southern Ch'iang[a] Dialects', *Monumenta Serica*, Vol. XXVI, 422–44.
1968. 'The Phonology of a Gyarong Dialect', *Academia Sinica: Bull. of the Inst. of Hist. and Philology*, Vol. XXXVIII, 251–75.
Chuckerbutty, R. N.
1867. *English, Bengali, and Garrow Vocabulary*. Calcutta.
Clark, E. W.
1911. *Ao–Naga Dictionary*. Calcutta.
Clerk, F. V.
1911. *A Manual of the Lawngwaw or Măru Language*. Rangoon.
Conrady, A.
1891. 'Das Newârî: Grammatik und Sprachproben', *ZDMG* **45**, 1–35.
1893. 'Ein Sanskrit–Newârî Wörterbuch, aus dem Nachlass Minayeff's herausgaben', *ZDMG* **47**, 539–73.
Csoma de Körös, A.
1834. *Essay towards a Dictionary, Tibetan and English*. Calcutta.
Das, S. C.
1902. *A Tibetan–English Dictionary*. Calcutta.
1915. *An Introduction to the Grammar of the Tibetan Language*. Darjeeling.

[a] 羌

Davies, H. R.
1909. *Yün-nan, the Link between India and the Yang-tze*, appended vocabularies. Cambridge.
D'Ollone
1912. *Langues des peuples non chinois de la Chine. Mission d'Ollone*, vol. VI. Paris.
D'Orléans, H.
1898. *Du Tonkin aux Indes*, Appendix. Paris.
Dundas, W. C. M.
1908. *An Outline Grammar of the Kachari (Dimasa) Language*. Shillong.
Edgar, J. H.
1932. 'An English–Giarung Vocabulary', *Journal of the West China Border Research Society* **5**, Supplement.
Endle, S.
1884. *Outline Grammar of the Kachári (Bara) Language*. Shillong.
Fouceaux, P. E.
1858. *Grammaire de la langue tibétaine*. Paris.
Francke, A. H.
1900. 'Sketch of Ladakhi Grammar', *JASB* **70**, pt. 1, Extra No. 2.
1909. 'Tabellen der Pronomina und Verba in den drei Sprachen Lahouls: Bunan, Manchad und Tinan', *ZDMG* **63**, 65–97.
1917. 'Vokabular der Manchadsprache', *ZDMG* **71**, 137–61.
Fraser, J. O.
1922. *Handbook of the Lisu (Yawyin) Language*. Rangoon.
Fryer, G. E.
1875. 'On the Khyeng People of the Sandoway District, Arakan', *JASB* **44**, 39–82.
Garo Mission (preface by M. C. Mason)
1905. *English–Garo Dictionary*. Shillong.
Gerard, A.
1842. 'A Vocabulary of the Kunawur Languages', *JASB* **11**, 479–551.
Grierson, G. A. (ed.).
1903–28. *Linguistic Survey of India*. Vol. **1**, pt 2: *Comparative Vocabulary*. Calcutta, 1928; Vol. **3**: *Tibeto-Burman Family*, pt 1, *Specimens of the Tibetan Dialects, the Himalayan Dialects, and the North Assam Group*. Calcutta, 1909; pt 2, *Specimens of the Bodo, Nāgā, and Kachin Groups*. Calcutta, 1903; pt 3, *Specimens of the Kuki-Chin and Burma Groups*. Calcutta, 1904.
Grünwedel, A.
1892. 'A Róng–English Glossary', *TP* **3**, 238–309.
Gurdon, P. R. T.
1904. 'The Morāns', *JASB* **73**, 36–48.
Hamilton, R. C.
1900. *An Outline Grammar of the Dafla Language*. Shillong.
Hanson, O.
1896. *A Grammar of the Kachin Language*. Rangoon.
1906. *A Dictionary of the Kachin Language*. Rangoon.
Hertz, H. R.
1911. *A Practical Handbook of the Kachin or Chingpaw Language*, 2nd ed. Rangoon (reprint, 1935).
Hesselmeyer, C. H.
1838. 'The Hill tribes of the Northern frontier of Assam', *JASB* **37**, 192–208.

Hodgson, B. H.
1847. *On the Aborigines of India; Essay the First, on the Kocch, Bódó and Dhimál Tribes.* Calcutta.
1847bis. 'On the Aborigines of the sub-Himálayas', *JASB* **16**, 1235–44.
1848. 'On the Chépáng and Kúsúnda tribes of Nepal', *JASB* **17**, 650–8.
1849. 'On the Aborigines of North-Eastern India', *JASB* **18**, 451–60.
1853. 'On the Indo-Chinese Borderers and their connexion with the Himálayans and Tibetans', *JASB* **22**, 1–25.
1853bis. 'Sifán and Hórsók Vocabularies', *JASB* **22**, 117–51.
1857–8. 'Comparative Vocabulary of the Languages of the broken Tribes of Népal', *JASB* **26**, 317–522; **27**, 393–442.
Hodson, T. C.
1906. *Thādo Grammar.* Shillong.
Houghton, B.
1892. *Essay on the Language of the Southern Chins and its Affinities.* Rangoon.
1893. 'The Kudos of Katha and their Vocabulary', *India Antıquary* **22**, 129–36.
1895. 'Kami Vocabularies', *JRAS*, 111–38.
1897. 'The Arakanese Dialect of the Burman Language', *JRAS*, 453–61.
Hughes, W. G.
1881. *The Hill Tracts of Arakan*, Appendix. Rangoon.
Hutton, J. H.
1916. *Rudimentary Grammar of the Sema Naga Language, with Vocabulary.* Shillong.
1929. 'Outline of Chang Grammar', *JASB* (n.s.), **25**, 1–101.
Hu T'an and Tai Ch'ing-sha
1964. 'Vowels with and without stricture in the Hani language', *Chung-kuo Yü-wen* **128**, pp. 76–87.
Jäschke, H. A.
1865. 'Note on the Pronunciation of the Tibetan Language', *JASB* **34**, 91–100.
1881. *A Tibetan–English Dictionary.* London (reprint, 1934).
Johnston, R. F.
1908. *From Peking to Mandalay*, Appendix A. London.
Jörgensen, H.
1928. 'Versuch eines Wörterbuches der Nevāri-Sprache', *Acta Orientalia* **6**, 26–92.
Joshi, T. R.
1909. 'A grammar and Dictionary of Kanawari', *JASB* (n.s.) **5**, Extra Number.
Judson, A.
1888. *A grammar of the Burmese Language.*
1921. *Burmese–English Dictionary*, revised and enlarged by R. C. Stevenson. Rangoon.
Kao Hua-nien
1955. 'Preliminary investigation of the Hani language of Yang-wu', *Scholarly Reports of Chung-shan University.*
1958. *A Study of the Grammar of the Yi Language*, Scientific Publishing Company, Peking.
Keith, T. J.
1873. *Dictionary of the Garo Language.*
Kerr, A. F. G.
1927. 'Two "Lawā" Vocabularies', *Journal of the Siam Society* **21**, 53–63.

Latter, T.
1846. 'A Note on some Hill Tribes on the Kuladyne River, Arracan', *JASB* **15**, 60–78.
Lefèvre-Pontalis, P.
1892. 'Notes sur quelques populations du nord de l'indo-Chine', *JA* (8th ser.) **19**, 259–69.
Lewin, T. H.
1869. *The hill Tracts of Chittagong and the Dwellers therein, with Comparative Vocabularies of the Hill Dialects*. Calcutta.
Liétard, A.
1909. 'Notes sur le dialectes Lo-lo', *BEFEO* **9**, 549–72.
1911. 'Essai de dictionnaire Lo-lo Français, dialecte A-hi', *TP* **12**, 1–37, 123–56, 316–46, 544–58.
1911 bis. 'Notions de grammaire Lo-lo, dialecte A-hi', *TP* **12**, 627–63.
1913. 'Au Yun-nan des Lo-lo p'o', *Anthropos-Bibliothek*, Vol. **1**, pt 5. Münster i.W.
Lorrain, J. H.
1907. *A Dictionary of the Abor-Miri Language*. Shillong.
Lorrain, J. H. and Savidge, F. W.
1898. *A Grammar and Dictionary of the Lushai Language*. Shillong.
Ma Hsüeh-liang
undated. *Translation and Commentary on the Lolo Sacred Book 'On Offerings of Medicines and Sacrificing of Beasts'*, Publication of the Bureau of History and Linguistics of the State Central Research Institute, Vol. 20.
1951. *A Study of the Sani Yi Dialect*, Peking.
McCabe, R. B.
1887. *Outline Grammar of the Angāmi Nāgā Language*. Calcutta.
McCulloch, W.
1859. *Account of the Valley of Munnipore and of the Hill Tribes, with a Comparative Vocabulary of the Munnipore and other Languages*. Calcutta.
Macnabb, D. J. C.
1891. *Hand-book of the Haka or Baungshe Dialect of the Chin Language*. Rangoon.
Mainwaring, G. B.
1898. *Dictionary of the Lepcha Language*, revised and completed by A. Grünwedel. Berlin.
Missionaires Catholiques du Thibet (A. Desgodins *et al.*)
1899. *Dictionnaire thibétain–latin–français*. Hongkong.
Myaing, Ba
1934. 'The Northern Hills of the Ponnagyun Township', *JBRS* **24**, 127–48.
Naylor, L. B.
1925. *A practical Handbook of the Chin Language* (*Siyin Dialect*). Rangoon.
Needham, J. F.
1886. *Outline Grammar of the Shai'yâng Miri Language*. Shillong.
1889. *Outline Grammar of the Singpho Language*. Shillong.
1897. *A Collection of a few Moshang Naga Words*. Shillong.
[no date] *A few Dîgârô* (*Târoan*), *Mîjû* (*M'jû*) *and Thibetian words* [no place].
Neighbor, R. E.
1878. *A Vocabulary in English and Mikir*. Calcutta.
Newland, A. G. E.
1897. *A Practical Hand-book of the Language of the Lais*. Rangoon.

Okell, John
1969. *A Reference Grammar of Colloquial Burmese*, 2 vols. London: Oxford University Press.
Peal, S. E.
1873. 'Vocabulary of the Banpará Nágás', *JASB* **42**, Appendix. xxx–xxxvi.
1883. 'Notes of a trip up the Dihing basin to Dapha Pani', *JASB* **52**, 7–53.
Pettigrew, W.
1912. *Manipuri (Mītei) Grammar*. Allahabad.
1918. *Tāngkhul Nāgā Grammar and Dictionary* (*Ukhrul Dialect*). Shillong.
Phayre, A. P.
1841. 'Account of Arakan', *JASB* **10**, 679–712.
Primrose, A. J.
1888. *A Manipuri Grammar, Vocabulary, and Phrase Book*. Shillong.
Read, A. F. C.
1934. *Balti Grammar*. London.
Robinson, W.
1849. 'Notes on the Languages spoken by the various tribes inhabiting the valley of Asam and its mountain confines', *JASB* **18**, 183–237, 310–49.
1851. 'Notes on the Dophlás and the peculiarities of their language', *JASB* **20**, 126–37.
1855. 'Notes on the Languages spoken by the Mi-Shmis', *JASB* **24**, 307–24.
Rock, J. F.
1937. 'Studies in Na-khi literature', *BEFEO* **37**, 1–119.
Roerich, G. de
1933. 'The Tibetan dialect of Lahul', *Journal of the Urasvati Himalayan Research Institute* **3**.
Rose, A. and Brown, J. C.
1910. 'Lisu (Yawyin) Tribes of the Burma–China Frontier', *Memoirs of the Asiatic Society of Bengal* **3**, no. 4, 249–77.
Rosthorn, A. von
1897. 'Vokabularfragmente ost-tibetischer Dialekte', *ZDMG* **51**, 524–33.
Roux, H.
1924. 'Deux tribus de la région de Phongsaly (lao septentrional)', *BEFEO* **24**, 373–500.
Rundall, F. M.
1891. *Manual of the Siyin Dialect spoken in the Northern Chin Hills*. Rangoon.
Savidge, F. W.
1908. *A Grammar and Dictionary of the Lakher Language*. Allahabad.
Schirokogoroff, S. M.
1930. 'Phonetic Notes on a Lolo Dialect and Consonant L', *Academia Sinica: Bull. of the Inst. of Hist. and Philology* **1**, 183–225.
Schmidt, I. J.
1841. *Tibetisch-Deutsches Wörterbuch*. St Petersburg.
Scott, J. G.
1900. *Gazetteer of Upper Burma and the Shan States*, Pt 1, Vol. **1**, Chap. 9. Rangoon.
Shaw, W.
1928. 'Notes on the Thadou Kukis' (edited by J. H. Hutton), *JASB* (n.s.) **24**, 1–175.

Skrefsrud, L. O.
1889. *A Short Grammar of the Mech or Boro Language*. Ebenezer, Santal Mission via Rampore Haut.
1889–90. 'Mecherne i Assam og deres Sprog', *Nordisk Tikskrift for Filologi* (n.s.) **9**, 223–36.
Soppitt, C. A.
1885. *A Short Account of the Kachcha Nâga (Empêo) Tribe in the North Cachar Hills, with an Outline Grammar, Vocabulary, and Illustrative Sentences*. Shillong.
1887. *A Short Account of the Kuki-Lushai Tribes of the North East Frontier, with an Outline Grammar of the Rangkhol-Lushai Language*. Shillong.
Stack, E.
1897. *Some Tsangla-Bhutanese Sentences*, Pt III. Shillong.
Stewart, J. A.
1936. *An Introduction to Colloquial Burmese*. Rangoon.
Stewart, R.
1855. 'Notes on Northern Cachar', *JASB* **24**, 582–701.
Stilson, L.
1866. 'Brief Notice on the Kemĭ Language spoken by a Tribe in Arrakan, Farther India', *JAOS* **8**, 213–26.
Taylor, L. F.
1922. 'The Dialects of Burmese', *JBRS* **11**, 89–97.
Telford, J. H.
1938. *Handbook of the Lahu (Muhso) Language and English–Lahu Dictionary*. Rangoon.
Tin, P. M.
1915. 'Burmese Archaic Words and Expressions', *JBRS* **5**, 59–90.
1933. 'The Dialect of Tavoy', *JBRS* **23**, 31–46.
Vial, P.
1909. *Dictionnaire français–lolo, dialecte gni*. Hongkong.
Walker, G. D.
1925. *A Dictionary of the Mikir Language*. Shillong.
Wen Yü
1950. 'An abridged Ch'iang vocabulary' (Chiu Tzu Ying dialect)', *Studia Serica* **9**: **2**, pp. 17–54.
Williamson, W. J.
1869. 'A Vocabulary of the Garo and Konch Dialects', *JASB* **38**, 14–20.
Witter, W. E.
1888. *Outline Grammar of the Lhôtâ Nâgâ Language*. Calcutta.
Wolfenden, S. N.
1936. 'Notes on the Jyârung Dialect of Eastern Tibet', *TP* **32**, 167–204.
Yüan Chia-hua.
1953. *The Folksongs and Language of the Ahi People*, Peking.
1947. 'Preliminary investigation of the Woni language of Er-shan', Publication of the Frontier Peoples' Culture Department of the Literary and Scientific Institute of Nan-k'ai State University, Vol. **4**, Tientsin.

APPENDIX IV

Author's and editor's bibliography

Benedict, Paul K.

1948. 'Tonal Systems in Southeast Asia', *JAOS* **68**, 184–91

[The following secondary sources are also cited in the text or notes.]

1939. 'Semantic Differentiation in Indo-Chinese', *HJAS* **4**, 213–29.

1940. 'Studies in Indo-Chinese Phonology', *HJAS* **5**, 101–27.

1941. 'Kinship in Southeastern Asia'. Dissertation for Ph.D. presented in Department of Anthropology, Harvard University.

1942. 'Thai, Kadai and Indonesian: a New Alignment in Southeastern Asia', *American Anthropologist*, n.s. **44**, 576–601.

1942bis. 'Tibetan and Chinese Kinship Terms', *HJAS* **6**, 313–37.

1943. 'Secondary Infixation in Lepcha', *Studies in Linguistics* **1**, no. 19.

1948bis. 'Archaic Chinese *g and *d', *HJAS* **11**, 197–206.

1966. 'Austro-Thai', *Behavior Science Notes* **1**, 227–61.

1967. 'Austro-Thai Studies: Material Culture and Kinship Terms', *Behavior Science Notes* **2**, 203–44.

1967bis. 'Austro-Thai Studies: Austro-Thai and Chinese', *Behavior Science Notes* **2**, 275–336.

1968. 'Austro-Thai and Sino-Tibetan' (mimeographed). Paper read at *First Conference on Sino-Tibetan*, Yale University, October 1968.

1969. 'The Sino-Tibetan Tonal System' (mimeographed). Paper read at Second Conference on Sino-Tibetan, Columbia University, October 1969.

1972. *Austro-Thai*. Scheduled for publication by H.R.A.F. Press (New Haven, Conn.).

Matisoff, James A.

1967. *A grammar of the Lahu Language*. University of California, Dissertation, 697 pages. University Microfilms, Ann Arbor, Order No. 67–11, 648.

1968. 'Review of Robbins Burling, *Proto Lolo-Burmese*', *Language* **44**, 4, December 1968, 879–97.

1969*a*. 'Review of Paul Lewis, *Akha–English Dictionary*', *JAS* **28**, 3, May 1969, 644–5.

1969*b*. 'Lahu and Proto-Lolo-Burmese.' Occasional papers of the Wolfenden Society on Tibeto-Burman Linguistics (No 1.), Ann Arbor, August 1969, 117–221. (Reviewed by R. B. Jones in *JAS* **30**, 1, November 1970, 230–1.)

1969*c*. 'Verb concatenation in Lahu: the syntax and semantics of "simple" juxtaposition', *Acta Linguistica Hafniensia* (Copenhagen) **12**, 1, 69–120.

1969*d*. 'Lahu bilingual humor.' *Acta Linguistica Hafniensia* **12**, 2, 171–206.

1970*a*. 'Glottal dissimilation and the Lahu high-rising tone: a tonogenetic case study', *JAOS* **90**, 1, January–March 1970 (Studies presented to Mary R. Haas on her 60th birthday), 13–44.

1970*b*. 'The tonal split in Loloish checked syllables', Occasional papers of the Wolfenden Society (No. II), Urbana. 44 pages. (Also to appear in *JAOS* in an expanded version.)

(to appear) 'Review of D. N. Shankara Bhat, *Tankhur Naga Vocabulary*', *Language* 1971.
(to appear) *The Grammar of Lahu*, University of California Publications in Linguistics (1972?).
(to appear) *Lahu–English and English–Lahu Dictionary*, University of California Publications in Linguistics (?) (1973?).